Miriam's Words

The Personal Price of a Public Life

*Selections from Letters and Writings of
Miriam Barber Judd*

Edited by Mary Lou Judd Carpenter

Praise for *Miriam's Words*

To read Miriam Judd's letters in *Miriam's Words* is to see the soul and spirit of an exceptional woman exposed. The place of a woman in the family and the world has changed dramatically in the last century. Here, Miriam, whose desires and dreams to serve her God wherever she is sent or had an opportunity to go, privately expresses both joy and anguish. Joy is expressed in words of love and satisfaction in opportunities to serve. Anguish because her opportunities to serve were thwarted and by the physical separations from her beloved husband, Walter Judd. She had the same obligations of a single mother so much of the time. Her love for Walter seemed to never waver, even though the long absences were excruciatingly painful.

Miriam's Words is a great read for women who find "they can't have it all," or are thinking of "giving up," or are just overwhelmed. It is also a good read for men – we can then understand better and maybe even learn something. I recall, not long ago, when a friend related to me a conversation she had with my wife Gretchen about my absences due to work or horse trips. Gretchen had replied, "I know what it is like to be alone." It was like a knife jabbed into me. Reading *Miriam's Words* brought that back. Public life is fascinating – service to others is rewarding – following one's dreams is exhilarating – but denying the same for the one you love most becomes the greatest regret in one's old age.

The thrill from the book is that Miriam's love, desire to both serve and lead others, and desire to use the gifts God gave her never waned. Read and meet an outstanding woman.

A note of my connection: When I was a child, I kept hearing about the China Mission and a person named Dr. Judd in conversations when Dad's four sisters visited us on the farm. It impressed me so much that when I was twelve years old in 1935, I decided that I would contribute the three-cent tithe I had saved from my twenty-five-cents allowance each month and it would go to the China Mission. Dad took me to Minneapolis so I could give it in person. I also prayed that God would not send me to China.

In 1958, when I was elected to Congress in a February special election, the Judds invited me to stay at their home in Washington, D.C. Gretchen, an accomplished artist, stayed back in Minnesota to take care of the farm and our four children, eight, six, four and two years of age.

I was present at Dr. Judd's ninetieth birthday party and for the first time heard Miriam talk. It was from her heart and her anguish and made an indelible impact on me. I wish I had read *Miriam's Words* sixty-five years ago.

> —*GOVERNOR AL QUIE – former Minnesota State Senator, Governor, and U.S. Congressman, Minneapolis, MN*

The illuminating letters that Miriam Louise Barber Judd wrote to her famous husband, Dr. Walter Judd, and others over a six-decade period bear lively eyewitness to some of the twentieth century's most significant developments. Born and raised in India of YMCA parents, educated at Mount Holyoke and Columbia Teachers College, and devoted organizer-publicist of the Student

Volunteer Movement that inspired the global volunteerism of her idealistic generation, Miriam committed her life to Christian service, human rights, and internationalism. She also sought to help her daughters become "strong useful women."

Miriam's vivid letters chronicle the Japanese invasion and Communist insurgency, which thwarted the Judd's' efforts to bring medical missions to Nationalist China's impoverished interior, the young family's relocation to Minnesota, Miriam's public denunciations of Japanese militarism, and her participation in American women's boycott of Japanese silk stockings. They also highlight her steadfast support of Walter's twenty-year Congressional crusade to contain Chinese Communism as well as her devotion to church, college, and the international YWCA, and her leadership in desegregating its Washington D.C. chapters.

Mary Lou Judd Carpenter, the book's able editor, organizes her mother's letters into chapters, each of which she prefaces with useful historical context. She also intersperses the public writings with Miriam's personal reflections, thereby revealing both assured public figure and private woman of unfulfilled aspirations. This unique resource helps us understand the women of Miriam's' generation who strove to find their own voice outside their husbands' shadows. The book will inspire a new generation of young women now moving into the forefront of twenty-first century global leadership.

—*P. RICHARD BOHR* – *Professor of History and Director of Asian Studies, College of Saint Benedict/Saint John's University, Collegeville, MN*

Mary Lou Judd Carpenter has made an invaluable contribution to Minnesota political history by collecting and publishing the voluminous correspondence and private writings of her mother.

Not only does the book, "Miriam's Words," bring her mother out of the shadow of her famous husband, former ten-term Republican Congressman and medical missionary Walter H. Judd, but it offers an intimate portrayal of a truthful and sensitive woman in a time when American women were struggling to win equal rights and recognition for their own accomplishments.

Her mother's treasure trove of letters and private papers reveal a woman in the tradition of other high profile Minnesota political wives like Muriel Humphrey, Joan Mondale, and Arvonne Fraser, who were full partners in their husbands' careers of public service.

The book is replete with fascinating scenes from the lives of the author's parents, highlighted by Dr. Judd's years as a medical missionary to China in the 1930s and in private practice in Minneapolis, and his 1942 election to Congress, where he rose to national prominence as a crusader against Chinese Communism and Japanese expansionism before World War II, and became one of the most influential members of the House on foreign policy.

Mrs. Judd's letters describing their life in China and their years in Washington, including White House dinners with Franklin and Eleanor Roosevelt, is well worth the price of the book alone.

—*AL EISELE* – *Editor-at-Large and Founding Editor of* The Hill *Newspaper, Washington, DC*

It has been a great pleasure to come to know Miriam Barber Judd. She was a splendid woman – intelligent, educated beyond the usual level for a woman of her era, courageous, progressive, committed to the value of wife and motherhood. Hers was a life of engagement and excitement, often in the center of things, particularly in the China years and in the years in Washington. And yet this busy woman yearned for some larger mission to be of service to humankind, which she found to some extent in volunteer work. Because she was a prodigious and talented writer of letters, we can know a great deal about her life and the times she lived through, and both openly and privately about her feelings, which is unusual. Her daughter has done both Miriam and us a good deed by bringing this correspondence to light, and this life to the service of history.

—MARY DUNN – President Emerita, Smith College; former Executive Director of the Schlesinger Library on The History of Women in America, Radcliffe Institute for Advanced Study, Harvard University, Cambridge, MA

For nearly a century, Miriam Barber Judd, mother of Mary Lou Judd Carpenter and her sisters, wrote countless letters and poignant journal entries, leaving a detailed account of her choices, her challenges, and her sense of faith and purpose in the midst of some of the twentieth century's most significant historical moments. Mary Lou's warm and reflective compilation of her mother's words is not only a deeply personal gift, but also a fascinating account of the changing nature of women's lives over the past several generations. Miriam's remarkable life took her to the mission fields of China and to the legislative halls of Washington D.C., where she served capably as a partner to her husband's political career. The education she received at our shared alma mater, Mount Holyoke College, remains a constant companion in the form of a probing intellect and lasting friendships. I am moved by the ways Miriam took our College's mission to heart, embodying the spirit of purposeful engagement in the world. These keenly observed entries, splendidly edited, will inspire the next generation to create lives of intentions and meaning.

—LYNN PASQUERELLA – President, Mount Holyoke College, South Hadley, MA

On these pages, readers will meet Miriam Barber Judd, a fascinating woman who was witness to – and a participant in – some of the major events of America's twentieth century. In Minneapolis, she was known for twenty years as the congressman's wife. But Miriam is much more than the cardboard cutout evoked by the label "political wife" as it was applied in her day. Her letters reveal a person of intellect, strength, leadership ability, and passion. They also indicate how such a woman quietly struggled with the confining gender roles that not only limited her options but encouraged her husband's frequent absences. Miriam became a respected leader in her church, college, and the national Young Women's Christian Association. One cannot read her spirited, heartfelt letters without wondering what greater role she might have played had she been born a half-century later.

—LORI STURDEVANT – Star Tribune Editorial Writer, Minneapolis, MN

Miriam's Words offers us the story of a woman's life that was privileged, immensely demanding because of circumstances but also because she demanded so much of herself – and filled with suffering (some of which was inevitable – the human condition!), some of which was unnecessary, much of that related to the general cultural acceptance of tightly circumscribed gender roles. The range of domestic detail – about food, clothing, child-rearing practices, social life, friends

— is astonishing in combination with all those references to broader political and social happenings in every part of her life.

The letters also open up multiple dimensions of the inner life and domestic life (not necessarily the same thing) of a woman with significant gifts for organization, improvisation, and resilience, but one who also felt – and was made to feel – that her contributions were secondary to those of her husband. The private writings interspersed with the detailed letters to her family make it clear how emotionally and intellectually complicated it must have been to keep her inner life "in order" as she wanted to do.

—MARY BEDNAROWSKI – *Professor of History of Women in Religion, retired, United Theological Seminary, New Brighton, MN*

Miriam's Words is a fascinating read. Living and working in China and not having a way to know that Japan was steadily obliterating the Chinese government and the free cities! Closer and closer but denied by official newspapers. Then after years of patiently studying the Chinese language, a sudden evacuation with three little daughters back to native but unfamiliar America. This is the story of Miriam Judd as reconstructed from her letters by Mary Lou Carpenter.

The tale is well told. The lady was clearly a lovely person, a determined mother, a devoted wife, and a true Christian. What fun after her repatriation and move to Washington, D.C. to read her new letters having metamorphosed from an inconspicuous missionary to a visible Congressional wife. These now change from concerns of obtaining proper groceries, a truthful newspaper, and news from General Chiang Kai-Shek to reports of tea with Eleanor Roosevelt and Walter's climb in national Republican politics.

It's part of the book's charm that the complex – and unhappily changing – American relationship with Chinese nationalists, Chinese communists, Japan, Taiwan, and eventually the People's Republic of China are all merely background. The internal family loyalty remains unchanged and their public policy efforts remain true to personal experiences and convictions.

This is a "must read" book. It does not make one eager to return to pre World War II China. Yet it will make the reader wish he could have known Miriam and Walter Judd.

—DONALD A.B. LINDBERG, M.D., *Bethesda, MD*

Miriam's Words

The Personal Price of a Public Life

Selections from Letters and Writings of Miriam Barber Judd

Edited by Mary Lou Judd Carpenter

ISBN: 978-0-9890489-0-3

Library of Congress Control Number: 2013903341

Brief quotes from pp. 126, 128, 130 [345 words] from THE MAGNIFICENT DEFEAT by FREDERICK BUECHNER. Copyright renewed 1994 by Frederick Buechner. Reprinted by permission of HarperCollins Publishers.

Cover Image: Vintage Journal and Quill Pen©istockphoto.com/rdegrie

Indexing by Dakota Indexing (www.dakotaindexing.com)

For more information about this book or its author or editor,
go to **www.miriamswords.com**

_____*Miriam's Legacy Publishing*

To Miriam Barber Judd

*For leaving a legacy of wisdom and truth
from her original mind,
compassionate heart,
and deep faith spirit.*

Table of Contents

Judd/Barber Family Tree

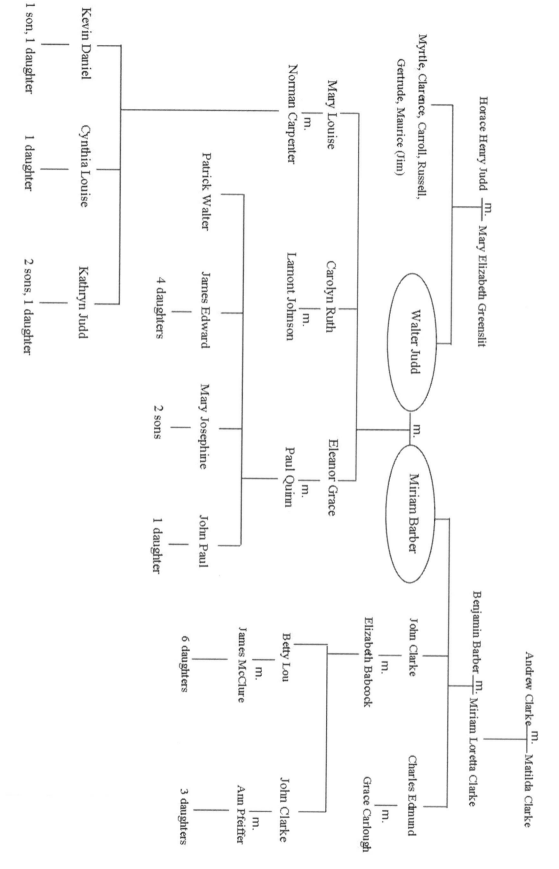

Prologue
Reflections on My Mother's Life

At age eighty-six my mother suffered a stroke and moved into assisted living in the Life Care Community where she and my father continued to live. Two years later, when Dad moved to the nursing home section, my two sisters and I began to go through their things to empty their home.

I stood alone in my mother's bedroom. She had a triple dresser with a mirror atop it. I opened the top drawer where she kept her treasured pieces of jewelry, and saw a letter tucked in the front of the drawer. The letter was in an unsealed, unstamped envelope addressed to "Moray" in her beautiful, painstaking script, as if it were ready to be mailed. Moray – I recognized the name but knew little about this man, other than that he was her former fiancé of long ago.

Why, then, was this letter sitting patiently, waiting to be mailed almost sixty years before, or even more intriguing, waiting to be found by one of us?

—Private Writing—

October 13, 1932

Moray –

Often I have wanted to write, and wouldn't let myself. Tonight I must. It has come on me so clearly, so vividly as I sat reading – the memory of our lovely hours together – and the torturous ones – and I see now what I only <u>felt</u> inexplicably before.

With you I shared, could have shared, more of beauty than with anyone I ever knew. Beauty of music, of poetry, of nature – the evening star alone in the sky over the ocean, the strange, lovely, un-earthiness of that stormy day at sea – they are always experiences set apart in my memory. And we would have grown together in our love of beauty and in our shared experiences of it. – Do you know this poem?

> *Sometimes slow moving thru unlovely days,*
> *The need to look on beauty falls on me*
> *As on the blind the anguished wish to see,*
> *As on the dumb the urge to rage or praise;*
> *Beauty of marble where the eyes may gaze*
> *Till soothed to peace by white serenity*
> *Or canvas where one mighty hand sets free*
> *Great colors that like angels blend and blaze.*

Oh there be many starved in this strange wise –
For this diviner food their days deny
Knowing beyond their vision beauty stands
With pitying eyes – with tender outstretched hands,
Eager to give to every passer-by
The loveliness that feeds a soul's demands.[1]

And when the "starved" hours come on me, the times of "need to look on beauty," I think invariably of your understanding, your deep love of beauty, your generous sharing of it. Always that will be inevitable. Parts of life that are shared that way are eternally shared. Nothing that happens afterwards can make those hours less yours and mine, less lovely. And always there will be times when in my mind I am sharing my deepest needs and experiences of beauty with you, who understand as no one else I know.

But something in me is stronger than my love of beauty. I tried to believe that it wasn't, that I could put it aside. But it wouldn't be denied. I don't know what to call it. It's sort of a "divine discontent." It might be called a supreme "love of causes" or love of humanity. It's something that will make me eternally dissatisfied with life as it is, eternally wishful to be doing something to make it different, happier. And not only in a vague general desire to be useful – but in very definite, practical immediate ways. It is not as lovely a way to travel as the way of Beauty. It leaves you always disturbed, heart sore, weary, discouraged – Oh, it's all in this poem:

Who has known heights and depths shall not again
Know peace – not as the calm heart knows
Low ivied walls; a garden close;
The old enchantment of a rose.
And though he tread the humble way of men
He shall not speak the common tongue again.

Who has known heights shall bear forever more
An incommunicable thing
That hurts his heart, as if a wing
Beat at the portal challenging;
And yet – lured by the gleam his vision wore
Who once has trodden stars seeks peace no more.[2]

And so I go the way of "creative discontent" with one who is lured by the same vision and seeks peace no more. But you will always be to me, what he cannot be, the "calm heart," and there will be times when I will come to share with you the "old enchantment of a rose" and go back refreshed to that greater, impelling thing that "hurts my heart."

Please understand this – Miriam

---

1   "Beauty" from *The Dreamers* by Theodosia Pickering Garrison, 1913.
2   "Who Has Known Heights," published in *Harper's Magazine,* December, 1922, by Mary Brent Whiteside.

I recall the moment so clearly: looking at the letter, reaching for it, as if in slow motion. Opening it, reading it. Pausing; looking at my own reflection in the mirror, seeing my mother's hopes and dreams reflected back at me in my face. I read the letter again. I was both surprised and moved.

The content and beauty of her words touched me. I stood there, reading through the letter again and again. As I did so, another woman emerged from behind the public face my mother had so carefully arranged and preserved, even for her husband and daughters – those of us closest to her. I didn't know that she had this divine discontent that preachers and therapists, lovers of causes and humanity, had. Responsible, diligent, caring, weary, discouraged – that's how we experienced her in our lives. I had never appreciated her aesthetic needs; I was more dogmatic and practical, like my father, Dr. Walter Judd – the fiery speaker, physician, and medical missionary, honored congressional representative, world citizen.

My mother, Miriam Louise Barber Judd, had never talked about Moray, the man from England to whom she was engaged for three months early in 1931. What I did know was they met onboard a ship while she was returning to the United States after teaching in India for two years. Miriam and Moray initiated an ardent romance, and they set a wedding date. I knew that Moray had come to New York the week before the wedding. But instead of marrying him, she let him go.

What stunned me was that the letter was dated just seven months after she wed my father, but it had never been mailed. I knew that she had been unhappy about moving to Washington, D.C. when I was nine, but I had not suspected that her anguish was growing earlier. Dad's intensity on a daily basis must have been trying for her. Perhaps she kept her sanity by giving voice in this unsent letter to her troubling realities, hoping to gain perspective by writing it out. I wondered in that moment: How many of her needs and preferences were set aside in the context of her continuing love and devotion to Walter, and at what price to her distinctive being? In those years, there was little permission for a woman to speak in her own voice or to disagree with her spouse.

I never did ask my mother about the letter. She was a very private person and didn't talk about her feelings. What I didn't know, and would find out as I went through the rest of her letters and discovered even more private writings, was that my parents' marriage was a match with its own private disappointments, as world events and my father's own commitments and causes often drew him away from her.

Yet I also knew that the match between my parents was one of both purpose and passion. They were deeply grounded in the Christian faith. They shared a strong desire to make the world a better place, and worked tirelessly to advance the concept that all people were equal. Their familiarity with China and their love of its people helped ease oriental immigration restrictions in this country, and perhaps helped the University of Minnesota become a center for Chinese studies and programs. Walter and Miriam were both true citizens of the world. But it was my father who became well known in the process, and my mother who often stood in his shadow.

Miriam Louise Barber was the middle child and only daughter of Christian missionaries. She was born in India in 1904 where her parents worked with the Calcutta YMCA. Repeated malaria attacks jeopardized her health and the family returned to the U.S. when she was nine, settling in Montclair, New Jersey. After her father left the YMCA in India, he spent more than twenty-five years as the personal assistant to John R. Mott, chairman of the International Missionary Council, president of the

World Alliance of the Young Men's Christian Associations (YMCA) and co-winner of the 1946 Nobel Peace Prize.

When she entered Mount Holyoke College, Miriam took to heart the college's admonition to "Be like palms in the desert, growing into uncommon women." While in college, she first met Dr. Walter Judd when he spoke at a Student Volunteer Movement (SVM) event on campus. After graduating from Mount Holyoke in the class of 1925, she worked two years in New York City as editor of the SVM magazine, *Far Horizons*. Then she went to India, her birthplace, to teach English at the Kodiakanal School for two years. She returned to the United States in 1931 to work again for the SVM while she began a master's degree at Columbia Teachers College. Dr. Walter Judd had also recently returned to the U.S. after six years as a medical missionary in southeastern China to recover from malaria. In 1931, while he again was speaking on college campuses to recruit students for the SVM and she was organizing SVM conferences, fate brought them together once more.

In 1932, she married Walter and the young couple spent two years in Rochester, Minnesota where Walter had a fellowship at the Mayo Clinic. In the fall of 1934 they moved to the interior of north China, away from mosquitoes and malaria, where Walter was Superintendent of a mission hospital in Fenchow, Shansi Province. After difficult encounters with communist bandits and Japanese militarists, my mother, my younger sister, and I fled the country in the fall of 1937, eventually moving in with Miriam's parents back in Montclair, New Jersey. Three months later my youngest sister was born. My parents were out of touch for months then, since Walter was in enemy territory and communications were non-existent.

In August 1938 Walter left Fenchow, which had been occupied by the Japanese for months, and returned to the U.S. He would spend the next two years speaking throughout the country about the risk of possible Japanese aggression against the U.S. He addressed the serious threat to the culture and freedom of the Chinese people by Japanese militarism and the civil war with the Chinese Communists. It was a trying time for Miriam. Walter was usually away, and she was left to cope with two aging parents and three daughters under the age of five. Her parents had their own ideas about childrearing, and so did Walter – when he was home.

Despite these challenges, Miriam made her own contributions. While Walter stumped the country making speeches, she regularly spoke to women's groups, working to establish a nationwide group of American women who refused to wear silk stockings, as silk was imported from Japan. The women instead wore cotton leg coverings. They adopted her motto, "American Women's Legs Can Defeat Japanese Arms!"

In 1941, discouraged by the general apathy of the public to events unfolding in Asia, Walter settled down to practice medicine in Minneapolis, though he continued to speak about the threats to world peace. After the attack on Pearl Harbor on December 7, 1941, his perspective was confirmed; he was recruited to run and was successfully elected to the U.S. House of Representatives in 1942 from the 5th Congressional District in Minnesota.

After they moved to Washington, D. C., Miriam continued to support her husband and his causes during his twenty years in the U.S. Congress. He was a noted orator and the keynote speaker at the 1960 Republican Convention, eventually receiving the Medal of Freedom from President Reagan. Miriam and Walter lived well into old age, succumbing to various illnesses and dying within four months of each other in 1994.

In an interview with the *Washington Post*, Miriam once reflected on her life. She told the reporter: "I owed something to the world for all the privileges I've had – of upbringing, of travel and education and experience. I've tried to share these things with others. But my activities have always been secondary to Walter's. I know that's not the thing to say in these days of women's lib, but our children and Walter's work came first and then I fitted in other things as I could."

"Fit them in" she did. My mother was a remarkable woman, devoted to service to humanity on a world level. She was dedicated to the YWCA, serving on the National Board of Directors as well as president of the Board for the Washington, D.C. region, the largest YWCA in the U.S. with more than 25,000 members. Under her sensitive and dynamic leadership, racial segregation was ended in the metropolitan Washington YWCA, as the two black and three white branches merged to become the National Capital Area YWCA. She strengthened the YWCA's international efforts through many years on the World Service Council.

She stayed in close contact and worked tirelessly on behalf of her alma mater, Mount Holyoke College in South Hadley, Massachusetts, the oldest women's college in the country, where two daughters and one granddaughter also graduated. A testimony nominating her as a member of the Mount Holyoke Board of Trustees in 1958 noted her "exceptional organizational and administrative ability" and "the deeply sincere convictions of her character and a great compassion born of wide human experience." She was president of the alumnae clubs in both Minneapolis and Washington, D.C., and in 1975 received the College Alumnae Medal of Honor with a citation that ended, "with respect, admiration, wonder, and gratitude."

Her deep faith was evidenced in Church activities. In 1950, she was a delegate to the Constituting Convention of the National Council of Churches. She utilized her teaching skills working in religious education at Cleveland Park Congregational Church in Washington, D.C., and also served on its Board of Trustees.

Miriam was bright, warm, and humble, a bridge builder between people. She had lived in India and China, taught both at home and abroad, and spoke regularly about her experiences to women's groups. She also wrote professionally, organized conferences, and ran large volunteer organizations. But her life and times put her more in the background, a behind-the-scenes partner to my more famous father.

It has never seemed equitable to me that men have been the makers and tellers of history. Women's voices bring another dimension to that, to help balance the scales. Fortunately, throughout her sixty-two-year marriage to Walter, Miriam recorded their experiences through correspondence between them (they were often apart due to war, evacuations, and travel for speaking or Congressional business) as well as in regular letters to her parents and family members. Walter kept Miriam's letters (sometimes two a day in the early years) in the original envelopes, creating groupings with rubber bands. In their retirement, they read them aloud with great delight in the reminiscences.

A lifetime of friendship with Mount Holyoke classmates is shown intermittently in the form of "round robin" letters. These women shared formative experiences in the 1920s and are witness to similar efforts to live out the understandings and ideals learned through their time at Mount Holyoke.

Miriam's opinions and reactions to people she encountered appear in her letters and offer glimpses into her attitudes and values. It is important to remember, however, that the bulk of these letters were written forty to eighty years ago. As such, they incorporate the worldview of that era, which could be different than current understandings. I have included these comments, even when they may be offensive or derogatory, because they represent her perception during those times. I have retained her punctuation, capitalization, colloquialisms, and occasional misspellings. For example, I have used her lowercase "n" for the word "Negro," as was common at that time. Her underlining is recorded by italics.

I have not updated the Wade-Giles Chinese names, which Miriam learned in China, to the Pinyin versions currently used. Hopefully, the map of North China in the 1930s and '40s will clarify locations where they lived or visited.

Living as a public figure requires a delicate balance – trying not to belittle or harm others while resisting the sting of words or actions that distress you. Perhaps the judgmental comments made during political campaigns, always a time of trial and suffering for Miriam, are understandable and tolerable. In the seventy years since Walter's first campaign, I see little evidence of improvement in that arena! Some of her concerns about misrepresentations in "the press" also continue today. One of my motivations for publishing this work is to show the deep human impact and cost of being in the public eye as well as the courage it takes to survive sometimes troubling remarks.

Letters to Walter begin with endearments – "Dearest," "Sweetheart." When her salutation is "Folks" or "Family," she was usually writing to one or both sets of parents (often via carbon copies) and sometimes including her brother and Walter's three living siblings. When the three daughters left home, we were often included in the carbon copies. She was especially faithful in describing her life in detail in the letters to her parents; the Barbers' early years in India made them particularly interested in her life in China as well as the public arena. Her mother took the letters out of the envelopes and filed them chronologically in manila folders. When the Barbers died in the 1950s, the boxes were moved to Miriam's home in Washington, D.C. After my sisters and I emptied our parents' home in 1993, the materials were shipped to my home in Minneapolis. Miraculously, these first-person accounts of her life and her philosophical and spiritual reflections in real time had been preserved. The boxes remained stacked in my closet for more than ten years.

Eight years ago I slowly began to organize her letters, plowing through the approximately 40-50 letters she wrote per month in the early years when she was writing both to Walter and her parents. Letters were frequently five or more pages long as she would revel in domestic details.

On Miriam's eightieth birthday, she gave my sisters and me memory books. She selected passages from 147 letters from 1934 through 1955 and edited them together for these books, then destroyed most of the originals. Inspired by her initial editing work, I now have put together a broader volume of her letters – and yet even *Miriam's Words* represents less than ten percent of her complete writings!

Each chapter begins with my summary of the material and some observations. I selected passages that seemed noteworthy and included enough information to capture the essence of Miriam's days – to show the rigors of living in a foreign land – to indicate the challenges of managing a household and parenting alone during Walter's many absences, and to tell of her strong community service. These writings show her joy in the creative possibilities of household responsibilities in China; her welcoming hospitality to many guests; her delight in people from all walks of life; and her commitment as a mother and in church and community.

Miriam's letters also are a rich vein of history: fleeing danger in China, observing world changes with wars, the creation of the United Nations. She met politicians, national and world leaders and did significant volunteer work while running a household, tending to family, and coping with the challenges of raising three daughters virtually single-handed. The letters capture the flavor of the times, and show her wry wit, pithy observations, and wise critiques, from the mundane to the magnificent. My numerous footnotes may fill in gaps and provide background to enhance understanding.

Going through her files, I also found poetry, unsent letters, and private writings that reveal her yearning, loneliness, and angst. These writings were done on scraps of paper, carefully preserved separate from her correspondence files. They reveal her early intention to reflect honestly on her life – something she set out to do in a private writing as she was beginning her first job in New York City:

– Private Writing –

"God, help me not to neglect the quiet silences of living with Thee, in the ceaseless round of activity. Guide me and show me what I must do… Be with me in times of discouragement, or forgetfulness, or disappointment, or just spiritual tiredness, and bring me back to a sense of Thee. Help me to grow in a knowledge and feeling of what I am to do in the coming year and for my life… Show me now Thy way."   *September 12, 1926*

These private writings, noted like the Prologue and throughout the book by using a different font and margins are a record of how the closeness of the early years of their marriage profoundly changed as Dad moved into the public arena. Although my parents had widely differing styles of communication, they shared a deep faith. He adored her and frequently declared she was the perfect wife for him. But it is evident in her personal reflections that she felt he did not understand her artistic sensibilities, nor recognize her sensitivities. He was direct and blunt, while she was subtle, thoughtful, lonely, and filled with longing.

Throughout her life Miriam was reticent about sharing her emotional life. But she was honest in her private writings; they reveal the depth of her struggles and suffering. They are poignant and painful; she seldom minces words about her desires and disappointments. She writes of her distress, searching for insight to help clarify her needs or Walter's limitations. Maybe seeing her reality in black-and-white provided a release for her discontent or a measure of acceptance when she couldn't find explanations in her head. Such depressing sentiments were frowned upon in those years – the stoic survivors of the Depression and two World Wars were trained to hide negative feelings. Yet she kept the written evidence in these materials and we are richer for knowing also the hidden parts – a more complete and honest portrait of a remarkable life.

Given the wealth of material Miriam has left for us (there were more than 2,000 letters all told), I am gratified that the Schlesinger Library on the History of Women in America, part of the Radcliffe Institute for Advanced Study at Harvard University, will become the permanent home for her writings. These letters and records from over seventy years will provide further value and insight into her extraordinary life and also shed light on the era in which she lived.

In this small collection, distilled from more than 500 different writings, we are able to overcome the challenge referenced by Richard Holmes, the British biographer in his book, *Footsteps*[3]:

> *…that ordinariness and that family intimacy is the very thing that the biographer – as opposed to the novelist – cannot share or recreate… The very closeness of husbands and wives precludes letters between them, and often the keeping of journals (unless one party is secretly unhappy). The private domestic world closes in on itself, and the biographer is shut out.*
> *…the re-creation of the daily, ordinary texture of an individual life – full of the mundane, trivial, funny and humdrum goings-on of a single loving relationship – in a word, the re-*

---

3   Holmes, Richard, *Footsteps: Adventures of a Romantic Biographer*, page 120. Viking Books, New York: 1985.

creation of intimacy – is almost the hardest thing in biography; and, when achieved, the most triumphant.

Miriam's Words is a first-person record in real time of one woman's experience and feelings, not a retrospective autobiography. From Miriam's words, both public and private, we can know the true and authentic woman. It's my hope that readers will share in her wisdom and perspectives, forgive her limitations, learn from her experiences, and discover hope and possibilities for living.

Mary Lou Judd Carpenter
Minneapolis, Minnesota
August 2013

1

Beginnings in New York City

1931-1932

After returning from India and ending her engagement to Moray, Miriam continued organizing Student Volunteer Movement (SVM) conferences while she studied for her master's degree at Columbia Teacher's College. What strikes me most is that like many women of the 1920s and 1930s, my mother was a fully formed, independent woman. Just five years out of college, she had already excelled in three professional positions: as an editor for the SVM Magazine, *Far Horizons*; as a teacher of English in India; and as an organizer of SVM conferences. She was regularly participating in meaningful work and discussions about the big issues of the day.

While organizing the SVM Annual Conference in Buffalo, New York, she reconnected with Walter Judd, the young missionary doctor who was to be the dashing and dynamic keynote speaker. We can assume there were a few backstage rendezvous because the couple became secretly engaged in Buffalo in September 1931, when Miriam was twenty-seven and Walter was thirty-three.

They spent the next three months apart, as Walter traveled across the U.S. to recruit college students for the SVM, and Miriam returned to her SVM post. She moved from the family home in Montclair, New Jersey to a New York City Settlement House where she led a weekly girls' group and walked on streets lined with unemployed men looking for work. She poured out her thoughts and feelings to her fiancé in her letters, sometimes two or three a day, describing her angst over the trials and suffering of people everywhere during the depression with so many people hungry and out of work. Evenings she wrote Columbia papers and hosted Settlement House "girls clubs," often returning on weekends to Montclair to support her aging parents.

The couple eventually made their engagement known; they visited Walter's parents (Horace and Mary Judd) in Rising City, Nebraska, and Miriam's parents (Loretta and Benjamin Barber) in Montclair, where they married March 13, 1932. Miriam was torn between staying behind in New York to complete her master's degree or joining Walter in Rochester, Minnesota for his fellowship at the Mayo Clinic. She chose to be with him.

The following begins in September 1931 with the letters Miriam wrote after her engagement. These letters to Walter are among her most passionate correspondence, coming as they do from her heart and emotional center. I am struck by how young, vibrant, and alive she was, every word full of energy, longing, and excitement.

~

Student Volunteer Movement Office,   *Monday, September 21, 1931*

419 Fourth Avenue, New York City

My own Walter –

What a hectic, hectic day! I managed to stop long enough at two o'clock for a glass of milk and a sandwich, but the rest of the time I've been dashing and tearing all over the place. But all day long, beneath this hectic activity, you've been singing quietly in my heart.[4] You started this morning when I first woke on the train. First thing I did was to put both arms around me and squeeze hard. It was suggestive but hardly satisfactory. Then I bounced around a bit in my high bunk just in sheer enthusiasm and joy. Finally, I started singing out loud a song called "I'm in love." Only the noisy rumbling wheels kept me from being a real nuisance to sleeping passengers. I got up (or down, rather) and dressed about 8:30, and settled down to read. You kept interfering most persistently, coming between my eyes and the book. I don't know how many times I pushed you away with dogged determination. Suddenly as I read along the most impossible things seemed to be happening to my book characters. I jerked myself up to discover that I had read a whole chapter about a woman running off from her husband and hadn't got a word of it. So I gave up reading and had a good long session with you, dear, and then when I got to the office I just relegated you to a general effervescing feeling down deep in my heart, that came bubbling up into my conscious activities every few minutes. Gosh, I never felt so funny before – but I love it. Hope I'll always feel funny. Oh, Walter, darling, I do love you so very much. It sounds cold and calculated to write it down, but I wish you could feel it in every bit of me as I do right this minute. I can't understand it, but I'm sure of it – and it is so very wonderful.

Same Monday evening

Walter darling: This time last night we were about getting to the station.[5] …Oh, my beloved, how life has changed for me, completely and joyously in such a short time. I knew it would seem unreal – remember I said so? – and it did when I came home tonight to the same house and room.[6] Somehow I felt they ought to be different, too. And Buffalo seems sort of fantastic and unreal, a dream, but a glorious one. Tomorrow when I get to the office and find your letter waiting for me I'll know again how beautifully real it is. But there's one thing I can't get around and that's the warm glow in my

---

4   Miriam and Walter became engaged the day before this letter.
5   They had said goodbye at the train station in Buffalo, New York.
6   Miriam returned to her parents' home in New Jersey.

heart. That's real, and new, and wonderful – and it's there because I know you love me, and because I love you – how much I'm beginning to see and feel.

I'm going to bed now, and before I fall asleep I'm going to live over some of our precious hours together – the fresh, eager, active hours of the morning; the beauty-revealing hours of the afternoon; the togetherness of the early evening hours; and the tiredness but confident peace of our last hours together. How many different ways and moods there are to love! I love you in all of them – and always.

In the office   *Thursday, September 24, 1931*

My sweetheart –

When I knew you were coming to Buffalo, I had no intimation in my own heart that it could mean anything at all, and I doubt if you had any definite feeling about it. But, as I told you before, I prayed that I might be ready for anything that might come – and how wonderfully God did answer that prayer! You are so very right in saying that He led us into it. Doesn't the certainty of His wanting us to love each other and work together just make our love a million times more beautiful and deep? Oh my beloved, pray God we may both be worthy of His great blessedness to us…

In Committee!   *Monday, September 28, 1931*

My darling –

What you wrote in that letter about the futility of much discussion in group meetings is finding a responsive place in my heart today. All day long I've been sitting in a co-operating committee of student secretaries of women's church boards – listening to long wearying talk – and I've wanted to shriek aloud time and time again at the superficiality and senselessness of much that goes on. We've spent hours on the correct wording of a resolution, hours squabbling over petty details, hours in non-pertinent, irrelevant discussions of non-essentials and – this is what makes me boil – missing so many chances to do something constructive and creative. We're so tied up in organizational technique and loyalty that we can't see the larger mission of service in the kingdom. I generally have a reserve of patience – but this is the first meeting of this kind I've been to since I came from India[7] and it just seems excessively annoying. There is so much splendid opportunity to work with students, and so much need, that it seems a crime to miss out on the vitality that is possible. Makes me want to be working in India again – or in China!

Then another thing that struck me between the eyes was a chance phrase that drifted across the lunch table to me from one of these women board secretaries. "What do I really know of life after all," she was saying. She went on to say that her sister, living on the campus of St. John's College in China, teaching, and helping her husband teach, and radiating the influence of a Christian home, seemed to be most ideally situated to render a real service. She seemed to consider herself a middle-aged, tired woman who hadn't found a normal woman's place in life, had had to give a secondary contribution thru church secretaryship, and had somehow missed the greater thing that she might have put into life. There was no bitterness, only a wistfulness that tore my heart. I

---

7   She had returned the previous March from two years teaching in South India.

looked around the group – all about middle aged, all wonderful women when you consider what they have done in their spheres of influence, but practically all having been denied the possibility of ministering thru a Christian home, and the joy of loving comradeship. Oh, Walter darling, God has been so wonderful to allow me the hope of serving with you, the joy of feeling that together we can do something that neither of us could do alone.

At home in Montclair, New Jersey   *Same day, late evening*

What a gorgeous moon tonight! And it's cold and clear. I wanted to walk – we'll walk and talk sometimes on cold winter nights, won't we, my love? But instead I sat in front of our open fire and listened to Mr. Chetty – an Indian who has been a professor in Madras for over thirty years… But all this talk about India, and Indians I know, made my love of India surge up strongly again. I'm afraid it will always be my first love or do you suppose I'll come to feel the same about China after I've lived there and got to really know the people and love them?

My last night at home – for tomorrow I go to the Settlement House in NYC in all that noise and dirt and crowds.

Settlement House, 237 East 104ᵗʰ Street, New York City   *Wednesday, September 30, 1931*

Walter, Beloved –

What a delirious day this has been for me with three letters from you. I am consumed with a constant wonder that you, Walter Judd, the wonderful person who has meant so much to students in this country, and to people everywhere, you who have tremendous gifts and abilities and such a rare beautiful spirit – you can find it in your heart to love *me* as you do. It just isn't explainable at all. But I feel that it is so, and I rest in that enriching certainty, and am grateful to God.

Who was it said that ideal relationships of man to man require "something sufficiently akin to be understood, something sufficiently different to provoke attention, and something great enough to command admiration." All these I find in you and oh how much more. What a complex thing complete love is, after all.

Montclair, New Jersey   *Sunday, October 4, 1931*

Sweetheart –

Dear, I love you for writing as you did. How natural to expect that there should be haunting doubts and questionings, especially since hardly eight months ago I thought I loved, and found I didn't[8]… That suffering will always be a blackness to me. But there never was any certainty in that whole relationship. There was desperate hope that I might learn to love as I was loved, that the interestingness and variety of the life might somehow make up for any emptiness in other directions, and even a dreadful semiconscious rationalization that if I were not too deeply in love with my husband I might work harder for the cause. From the very first I expressed my doubts, but they were excused for me, and I excused myself, too, on the grounds that a sudden and bad case of grippe had deprived me of any enthusiasm and was proving depressing and unsettling. But they grew until they

---

8   Moray, her ex-fiancé.

were gaunt nightmares, they haunted me every minute, I was miserable and terrified. Walter, my whole life was one long miserable doubt those days – and how I thank God that he sent courage and strength to keep me from going through with it as I almost did in my foolishness. He certainly deals with us so much more bountifully than we deserve.

So, darling I know a bit the sickening misery of uncertainty – and I know, too, that if doubts should ever come again I should have to get them out at once. I could never again try to suppress them, or try to make myself believe they didn't exist. That just isn't intelligence. But from the very first I have felt in our love a sureness that is blessed and right. You remember Pascal said, "The Heart has reasons that the Reason knows not of" – and it is true. I don't understand how or why; nor do I believe there will never be any questionings nor difficulties to face. But the fact of our love I know for the present with an unquestioning certainty, and I believe that it is, and will grow to be increasingly, a power that will conquer all problems and doubts, and will satisfy our inmost needs, because it is of God. So I say reverently and tenderly, dear, I love you.

Settlement House *Tuesday, October 6, 1931*

Walter darling –

How right you are in saying that it seems unfair for us to be apart for too long – to have no chance for immediate personal companionship between now and Christmas. Sometimes I get an acute shock when I realize what actual strangers we are. How few hours, really, we have ever been together, have had a chance to get acquainted, to find out each others pet follies and foibles. I was wondering, for instance, how it would be if I'd come in some night, as I did tonight, tired and aching, a miserable head cold coming on, feeling bedraggled after a long eight-to-ten day, not even caring whether my nose was powdered or not – imagine such a primitive state! But all days can't be lived at the same white heat as those blessed days of ours in Buffalo – and I know it'll take a lot of grace on your part to plain live through some of my blue days. You don't know how plain "ornery" I can be.

You can't possibly imagine how lonesome I am for you tonight. If you were here beside me I think I'd just put my head on your shoulder and cry – not for any special reason but 'cause I feel like it. And I don't think you'd mind. You know I love you in all days and in all moods, but tonight my love comes from your tired Miriam.

At the Office *Friday morning, October 9, 1931*

My darling –

How I wish I could write any sort of an answer to your letter which was waiting for me last night! I thrill to think that you wanted to, and could write me about the problem of your plans for the immediate future, to suggest that they were *our* plans, and yet so thoughtfully guard against their burdening me. Sweetheart, they'd never burden me… Oh, if you were only here beside me and we could together talk through the various possibilities, if you could read in my face the sureness that I speak with my lips, when I say I want you to do the thing that is best and right for you, whatever that is…

Walter, three things you know so infinitely more about – China, medicine, and Walter Judd – that the decision has to be your own without any help from me. That's not quite true, 'cause I'll be wanting so hard and praying so strong that you'll know what *is* the right decision, that it just must help. But about the practicalities I can't be much help, I fear. Just off hand, when you say that if you are ever to take the special training[9] it must be now, it seems that in your plans for the years of service out ahead, this would be most valuable. And yet I can see how you dread being away from China so long. (How would it be if I'd go out this June, study the language, teach school a couple of years, and just wait for you to get through at Rochester? At least I'd get the feel and love for China so that when we did start our lives together out there I mightn't be as great a handicap to you as otherwise! Please don't take this suggestion seriously!!) No, you'll have to weigh the factors as carefully and as impartially as you can and find out what is the right thing for you at this time. And you know I'll be happy whatever it is, if it is right.

…If I were having anything to say, as an outsider, to two people like us, I think I'd urge that they not postpone their marriage any longer than is necessary. I truly don't think this is rationalization, nor a consideration of selfish interests, but if we are to live our lives together it seems useless and unnecessary to postpone the getting started. It is inevitable that there will be adjustments for both of us to make, small but practical, and important problems that we will want to work out together, and I think both of us have waited long enough to be ready now to work together on them. I'm sure I'd say this to other people in our circumstances and of our ages, so why can't I say it to us! Oh, you know what I mean, though I have put it so poorly.

Oh, Walter darling, you do see, don't you, my spirit in all this. I want you to know what is right and to be free to do it, and I want to fit in in whatever way I can to make things easier or happier for you. I'd die if I thought I was simply another problem you had taken into your generous, sympathetic heart. You'll tell me if I'm ever that, won't you? I just want to be the accompaniment to your life's song. Yours always – Miriam

At the office   *Wednesday afternoon, October 14, 1931*

Darlingest –

Last night I thought I'd go up to Father's office first thing this morning and tell him everything. But this morning, I suddenly knew I couldn't do it. Not that Father wouldn't understand and be a sweet old dear about it, and be unspeakably happy for me, but I know he'd feel that Mother should know too – and I can't bring myself to tell her now when she's ill. I can *feel* how she'd lie in bed and worry about China being in such unsettled conditions, and think over all the tales about your ever-dangerous episodes and way of life, and her mother heart, in spite of her, would dwell on the sacrifice of giving me up so permanently and "distantly." It's not fair to bring this to her now when she is not herself. You and I have been talking about the way our mothers are used to doing everything humanly possible to make life happier for those they love, sacrificing and slaving – and how beautifully and wistfully Bess Street Aldrich's "A Lantern in Her Hand" – a story of Nebraska I've just finished that made me think of you, and especially of your mother – has brought out this idea of mothers' sacrificing so unselfishly that they make their children selfish. Here I have a chance to pay back a tiny bit of all that my mother has done for me.

---

9   Walter wanted additional training in surgery at the Mayo Clinic in Rochester, Minnesota.

Montclair, New Jersey   *Saturday night, October 17, 1931*

My dearest dear –

What do you 'spose I've done this evening? Yes, told my dear Mother and Father of the joyous radiant happiness that is my own sacred possession! Somehow I couldn't keep still any longer. When I got home today, I found Mother much better. As Father and I sat talking to her, conversation just naturally veered around to what I was going to do in the future – and I burst out with it. I think they could tell from my beaming face that there was a reality in this experience such as I couldn't even have imagined possible previously. She kept saying that she had wanted for me a happiness such as she had known through the years with Father, and that if my heart told me this was the beginning of such an experience, she was joyously satisfied with the answer to her prayers. At the end of the long evening my Father prayed such a sincere sweet prayer – for blessing for us and our life and work together, and especially for your mother in her illness. It made me feel as if we were all close together. You are the one responsible for this unutterable joyousness – you whom I love more deeply than ever tonight because I have shared you with my loved parents.

Settlement House   *Thursday night, October 22, 1931*

Darling –

Your letter from Kalamazoo wondering what students now-a-days are thinking and about the apparent futility of working with them finds me in a questioning mood too. Given an interested and willing-to-work bunch, what can they possibly do in a world like the one we're in today? I mean, just where do they dig in with any confidence of producing any constructive results?

This week I've had two rock-bottom sessions with Lee Phillips. We've been working on the negro episode for the pageant. Here was Lee, a person of rare and beautiful spirit, aching to do something for his people, training for it, and yet feeling absolutely sunk about doing anything constructive. He wants to show them a way out. Yet he just can't see one. He doesn't want to be pessimistic – in spite of the fact that Reinhold Niebuhr said last Friday at the opening of the F.O.R.[10] Conference that American students (and America in general) needed more pessimism today – not of the gloomy-despair-and-quit type, but of the kind that can recognize the criticalness of the world situation and try to do something serious about it. Lee can't see a single ray of light anywhere in the whole negro situation. People keep telling him that the negro has loved and suffered long enough and now it's time for him to do something different. But what? How can you do anything constructive when you have nothing to work with – not money, nor jobs, nor security, nor respect. Non-violence and boycotting don't do any good. Lee seems to have been overwhelmed with case after case of actual experiences to his friends and in his town to produce gloom and discouragement in anyone. He says the negro students he knows aren't going to sit passively much longer and "turn the other cheek." It gets nowhere! What can he, a potential leader among negroes, suggest as a way out? I don't know when a thing has struck home to me so vividly as the "baffledness" in his face. How helpless it made me feel – and how humble in the presence of one so entirely free from bitterness, so confidently sure that God couldn't have left the situation without a ray of hope, even if for that moment he can't find that ray.

---

10   The Fellowship of Reconciliation.

But, Walter, what *can* the public in general and the students in particular do about this mess we're in today? You talked about them being interested in China as an international problem. And I find a forum of about fifty young people in our church listening to Sunday night addresses on Russia and Internationalism. And you find hordes of students at a F.O.R. conference hearing someone speak on Gandhi and the tremendous complications of the India situation. And Ken Latourette[11] speaks out in Convention Committee and says we *must* help students to see the crisis stage the world is at, that we're much nearer to complete and final overthrow of civilization than we were in 1914. Well, after they *hear* all these things, what do they *do*? I mean, what could you and Lee and others suggest that students do so that things won't seem so futile? (And we're not going to even discuss what good it does anybody to sit at a desk and write a few letters every day, or teach Italian and Jewish girls how to cook, or study for an M.A. in English. That can be put on the pending list of things to think about – but never take any action on!)

The Settlement	*Monday night, October 26, 1931*

Sweetheart –

How I loved your tired discouraged letter of Friday. I used to think that the romantic element was all there was to this thing called love – but I know now that it's something more deep and fundamental. That what really counts is the sharing of life's joys and problems and discouragements in a spirit of love and understanding…

Tonight I went to the big Peace meeting – like so many others held in the States this week. The speeches were excellent, I thought. The negro, DuBois,[12] did as good a piece of work as any. He seemed to get down to a pretty fundamental question in the whole affair – this exploiting of smaller countries by larger ones.

The Settlement	*Wednesday morning, October 28, 1931*

Darling –

'Most time to dash for the office, but I must stop long enough to say Good-Morning. And don't you ask me in reply how I slept! At half past four I was wakened by unusual street sounds – the steady low rumble of an ordinary crowd, fairly restrained, with occasional outcries. I got up to see. Just beneath my window, two flights down, were men in two orderly lines stretching down the sidewalk, waiting for the opening of our Settlement doors to the Registry of the Unemployed Men of New York. There were over a hundred of them – I counted, as best I could, that sea of caps. A large streetlight cast funny reflections and a pale cast over this line of men – restlessly moving to and fro, calling back and forth to each other. Several were sitting on the steps – one who I thought was sitting down turned out to be a man with both legs off just below the hips – but mostly they were content just to stand there in line, waiting till nine o'clock. The pathetic part about it is they think they're going to get jobs. This registry started here in the city on Monday and our Settlement has nothing official to do with it – it was chosen as one of the centers in which to carry on. But the poor men

---

11   Ken Latourette was a Yale University Divinity School Professor of Missions and World Christianity.
12   W.E.B. DuBois was the first African American Harvard PhD and co-founder of the NAACP.

think and spread the conception that the Settlement has found jobs for them. Yesterday morning I couldn't even get out on the street because of the crowds, but had to go a back way to 105th Street. And at this time in the morning – eight – the whole block is surging and seething with men, and a low steady roar comes up to my open window, with occasionally an angry outcry for someone who has tried to sneak up in line. They tell me there are 200,000 unemployed men in N.Y. with possible jobs for 30,000 of the neediest. But a cold statistic like that becomes burningly real and vivid when you can see the men standing in line at four-thirty in the morning, to wait till nine or after in the misguided expectation of getting a job. How really this picture represents the world's suffering, but what a tiny part of the total suffering of the world it represents.

The Settlement House   *Thursday night, October 29, 1931*

Dear One –

Yesterday morning I stopped in the 23rd Street post office on my way to work, to get a stamp and put the address on your letter. As I was writing it a man stepped up to me and asked if I would write an address on an envelope for him. Without turning to look at him I took the envelope and started to write what he told me. He hadn't gone far when I knew by his accent he was from India. When I finished he thanked me politely and was about to move off when I decided to speak to him. I turned and asked him if he was a stranger. He answered that he wasn't exactly a stranger but that his handwriting was shaky and not plain enough for an envelope. Then I told him I was back recently from India, and you should have seen his face break into a broad beam of gladness. When he said he came from Calcutta I said I'd lived there as a child, and without a moment's hesitation he said with real suspicion and almost bitterness – "Was your father a Britisher?" I explained that Father was American, had been in the YMCA. Quickly he asked his name and when I said Barber he almost shouted – "I know him. He was a good friend to students in Calcutta. I know you lived at 86 College Street. I used to go often to the student meetings in the YMCA. Your Father is a very fine man, a good friend to India. Everyone in Calcutta knows Mr. Barber." We talked for over half-an-hour. He seemed disappointed that I wasn't "lecturing" on India here because he said we need people who understand, to tell the Americans that the Indians are just like them underneath – have the same hopes and sufferings. But the Americans can't get beyond the superficial differences of dress and food and customs. He feels that's one of Gandhi's greatest contributions – forcing the attention of the world to be centered on essentials and ignoring the surface differences. "We're all alike, the world over." I've heard that before…

Montclair, New Jersey   *Monday night, November 16, 1931*

Walter darling –

We actually know so little of each other and have such a small amount of common experience for our love to grow on, that I feel letters are a valuable substitute for what we both admit is a real need – time to be together. And yours are so wonderful, so full of your work, which *is* your self. Your time *is* for students now. So please know, dear, that while I love to get your letters, letter-less days will not be blue and empty for me, because I will know that it is not selfish thoughtlessness but a superabundance of self-giving that has kept you from writing…

Montclair, New Jersey   *Saturday, November 28, 1931*

My dearest –

How thrilled I've been all day long over the good news in your today's letter![13] I'm just so proud, and really thrilled, and happy.

Today I went to the Army-Notre Dame football game – my first in three years! The football itself was good, in spite of the fine, drizzly snow and the cold, and I enjoyed it. I shouldn't be surprised if I got some ribs broken in the inhumanly awful subway jams – it hurts me to breathe tonight. I always used to be crazy about football, and this may be a sign that I'm aging, but I don't think I'm going to miss the big college games so much when I get out to China! The game itself is all right, but the awful spectacles that intelligent human beings who watch, make of themselves, is sometimes depressing.

The Settlement   *Monday night, November 30, 1931*

Dearest:

How can I ever wait for these next two interminable weeks to pass! Oh heck! I'm going to try to make a vow not to refer to this matter of time until December 16. (But watch me break it!) Just like my peppy girls here at the Settlement passed an ordinance that no one should mention how cold she was yesterday when we drove out to their camp in the Bear Mountain Reservation. They are crazy about this Settlement Camp where they all go in the summertime, and have been begging all fall that I take them out there. I drove eight of them out in the camp Ford, an open "station wagon" with pews. It's a sixty-mile drive over good roads, but we struck a grey damp day and not a speck of sun. We nearly froze. We found all the wood wet and couldn't get the fire going very well. This delayed our hot dogs and our hot coffee, not to mention our thawing toes! I really think the overcast day was beautiful. The silver fog softens some of the harshness and sharp angles of bright, clear days and makes everything lovely and spider webby and quiet. The girls were a good bunch. They sang a great deal for they love good music. I gave them a talk on "Mother India" – by request – and a "sermon," a personal one, too, on some of the unharmonious attitudes I had noticed at the Settlement House among their group. They respond so quickly and warmly. I just wonder how lasting their response is. But I like them.

The Settlement   *Friday night, December 4, 1931*

My dearest –

My girls' club had another riot tonight all over the most petty and childish matters. When they get going they form gangs, hurl bitter and profane invectives, pile up hatred, anger, retaliation, taunts, sullenness, ad nauseum. I'm wondering whether a Settlement like this does any permanent good in the long run toward changing lives and building a better world. Or is it simply a convenient and agreeable spot for people to put in spare time. These girls have all known splendid young workers here at the Settlement and as counselors at Camp. Oughtn't they to have caught something from

---

13   Walter was accepted for a fellowship at the Mayo Clinic in Rochester, Minnesota.

these fine spirits to make their lives more lovely and gracious? I hate to see such ugly spots in the characters of girls who are individually so loveable and who have real potentialities. What good can I do in my few hours with them? Maybe I can't help them.

Montclair, New Jersey   *Sunday night, December 13, 1931*

My dearest –

Can't be long now – only a few centuries. Gosh, I hope I don't see you first in the front lobby. I sang all the way in on the train this morning. Father thought I was crazy. Guess I am! Do you want an insane wife? Might at least be a good "case study."

The Settlement   *Saturday morning, February 6, 1932*

My darlingest dear –

I'm so exuberant and danc-y and joyous and aching and contented – if you can be all those things at the same time! …I can't seem to get away from my flippancy down to the serious consideration you need. Last night Frances F. tried to get me to guarantee that you would be present and speak to a N.Y.C. medical symposium on March 12. I insisted I was not making dates for you. (Except one important one!) I am sorry, Madam, the doctor is out. I do not know when he expects to be back. Yes, I'll deliver your message. Well, I don't mind a bit being office secretary for you, dearest. Probably I'd be better at answering phones than at cooking or housekeeping. At least I've had more experience there!! (Miriam! Will you kindly cut out the fooling and get down to business. Do you realize that I have to let thousands of people know what I'm planning to do? Sorry, Walter, dear, but when I'm not in the serious mood there just isn't much use trying to make me come to decisions.)

…I had rather thought you wanted to turn down *all* speeches in the interests of study and work on your indices before April first. (Well, I can't say that putting in a wedding in March helps my study much, Miriam!) Speaking *very selfishly* now, I feel that student generations will come and go and you can't fill anyway all the demands for speaking that you get. But we'll be married only once, and I wish for ourselves, and especially for Mother, that it could be done unhurriedly, without too breathless a pressure of activities before or after.

The Settlement   *Tuesday night, February 9, 1932*

Sweetheart –

Last night I had the most awful dream – a nightmare that woke me in the middle of the night and has been shadowing me all day. I was about to be married to Fred M. when suddenly it burst on me that I didn't want to marry Fred, that fine as he was I didn't love him, that I wanted to marry Walter. I remember telling myself sternly that I had had my chance with Walter and I had given it up, and that I couldn't go back to him now, change my mind again as I had changed it so radically last spring. Then came the most awful sinking feeling, the despairing realization that I loved you better than anything in the world – and was doomed to a life with someone else. All the vivid ache and terror and misery that I went through last spring before I told Moray came back – too really – in my dream. I woke myself saying out loud "Walter, I love you! Walter, I love you!" and I waited for you to answer and you didn't speak. Then in a moment came the blessed realization that it was only a dream, that I could marry you still and that you do love me even if you didn't answer. You can't guess what a wonderful relief it was! But the suffering in the dream was so real that it has sort of stayed with me today. How impatiently I'm waiting for the day to come when you can answer me when I call your name in my sleep!

Montclair, New Jersey   *Friday morning, February 12, 1932*

Sweetheart –

About the wedding – I'm so glad you approve of the Sunday thirteenth date[14], and I think we'll have it around four so we can get away by six and drive somewhere not too far for the night. (The after-the-wedding plans can wait till you're here.) Now *before* the wedding: I've been heroically self-restrained about saying I wanted you here for fear you might definitely want to get in some of those speeches. But, please please know that we want you with us in Montclair as much time as you don't actually *need* for speeches. And this isn't wholly selfish either. After all, as Father says, I'm going to be married to you a long time (but not nearly long enough!) but he and Mother won't get a great deal of time to be with you or know you, and they do covet all your extra minutes. And they are right, I think, to want to know you well, for it will be a delight to them, and so much easier for them after I am gone to have a really *acquainted* feeling with you as I write them what we are doing together, and how we are thinking about things.

Montclair, New Jersey   *Saturday morning, February 13, 1932*

Dearest –

It did me tons of good to have you rave as you did about the attitudes and outlook of people like our editor friend P. I've often felt riled up tremendously about things that are done in the name of the church or religion or missions, and sputtered a bit, only to be admonished to calm down, not to be so critical, not to overlook all the good that is being done in the name of the church or religion, or missions. Then I'd sort of go off by myself and decide I hadn't the right kind of mind or sufficient Christian grace or something to put up with the "demands" of the Christian enterprise. I see where I was wrong now, but to a certain extent I enjoyed my "prodigal" years in India because I was associating with people, who, regardless of what other faults they had, weren't hypocrites, or insincere in pretending to stand for a cause or an ideal that they *just weren't* standing for. Perhaps many of them weren't standing for anything worthwhile, but at least they didn't claim to be doing so. They were what they were. Well, I'm glad things like what P. did bother you too. At least we can be bothered together.

Montclair, New Jersey   *Monday afternoon, February 15, 1932*

Sweetheart –

It's been hard for me to write since getting your special yesterday and your air mail today in which you are so torn and suffering for China.[15] There's nothing I can write to you about China –

---

14   Walter had approved Sunday, March 13, 1932, for their wedding.
15   In early 1932, there had been news that the Japanese had just captured Manchuria.

except my understanding and sympathy. It seems almost sacrilege, almost flippant to write of my plannings and doings in the face of such tragedy. I've struggled bewilderedly with wondering about what was the thing to do, to say, in this particular situation. But just now a tiny ray of light broke as I lay on my bed trying to figure it out. It isn't much, but it gives me something to work on. It's this: I can't do anything right this minute about China. I can't make any of our officials act, even if I knew what action would be right. I can't influence the League[16] to get down to business. I can't do a solitary thing that will make immediate changes in the situation. Oh, I can read about what's going on, try to be intelligent about it and to further intelligent thinking, sympathize and pray and suffer with the people who are suffering. But in the meantime the routine of everyday life must be maintained. People everywhere are going to eat and sleep and love and live and die, as usual, and human need and human suffering are going to continue. Well if I can't do anything about China, perhaps I can do some small thing where I am, to relieve distress. I can't establish World Peace but perhaps I can establish peace between a father and son or peace in the heart of a troubled boy. I can't influence leaders on world matters but I can talk tomorrow afternoon to a group of women in New York about India's women and their needs and suffering and perhaps stimulate a deeper understanding and love for humanity. Oh, do you see what I'm saying, darling? I don't want to be callous or disinterested in these world tragedies. What I want to be sure is that my deep concern for a far-away suffering isn't blinding me to opportunities for service that are mine to deal with. So I can go along and live the daily routine, not less sensitive to suffering, I hope, but more sensitive, through the far-away suffering, to what I can do here. This isn't much of a letter, but it has helped me to write it. Please understand.

Montclair, New Jersey   *Sunday morning, February 21, 1932*

Sweetheart –

How sweet these days of preparation are being! I wonder if you have any idea, sweetheart, of all that a girl thinks about as she gets ready to leave her own home and family and friends and surroundings – everything that is familiar and precious to her – to start in a strange new life with one whom she knows very little. Some of the thoughts are bound to be sobering, some a little sad, for breaking of ties is always saddening. Some are questioning, wondering, about the experiences out ahead, some are eagerly anticipatory. But through them all, my darling, runs a strain of confidence and trust in the One with whom my life is to be shared – you, my Beloved. And with it comes a sureness that this is right, is God's plan, that he has willed it so that together we can serve his world. In it all is no fear, nor doubt, nor uncertainty but a deep inner peace and joy.[17]

Wedding day

16   The League of Nations was formed after WWI to ensure world peace.

17   The wedding took place Sunday, March 13, 1932, at the Barber home in Montclair, New Jersey.

The Inn at Buck Hill Falls, Pennsylvania   *Wednesday afternoon, March 16, 1932*

Dearest Family –

We are about to leave this beautiful spot,[18] but we can't go on without each of us writing to our dear families. Every day since we got here we've meant to send along a little note, but the hours have been so full of precious nothings that we've been selfish about writing. But if we haven't written, we've talked of you thousands of times – of all your dear sweetness in making our wedding day and our wedding so perfect and lovely. It was simple and sweet and unpretentious and unrushed just the way we wanted it. So many details you planned with all your loving thoughtfulness so it would be a day of beauty for us. It was a day we will never forget.

Buck Hill Falls, Pennsylvania   *Thursday, March 17, 1932*

Dear Gertrude –[19]

It was so thoughtful of you to call up on Sunday.[20] We had been missing you – especially Friday when Walter and I did errands in New York on the day that had been saved to show you sights, and

On their honeymoon

in the evening went with my brother and his wife to the theater – a party we had planned for you. Then next best to you being right there was having you call. It meant so much.

The wedding we had at my home, in front of our fireplace at one end of the longish sitting room. It was banked with palms and ferns, and had flowers and burning candles on the mantelpiece. There were about thirty-five there for the ceremony. My sister-in-law[21] sang two songs at four-thirty, and then as Walter and the ministers came in from the dining room, I came downstairs with father. My family stood behind us during the ceremony, and when it was over we stood there by the banked fireplace to greet our friends. I wore a blue crepe afternoon dress – powder blue with shoes to match – and had the loveliest bouquet of pink roses and lilies of the valley, tied with pink. We stayed and visited while the supper was being served, then got off at six o'clock in Father's car for a nice auto trip through Pennsylvania and on to Washington, till next Monday. Walter gave me a platinum pendant with a lovely diamond. We picked it out on Friday in NY, and I adore its simplicity. Well, we're having a perfect time and we're just awfully happy. I don't need to tell you how dear Walter is – but I can tell you we both love you and talk about you every day.

---

18   Miriam and Walter were honeymooning here.
19   Gertrude was Walter's sister who was living in Evansville, Indiana.
20   Gertrude was unable to attend Miriam and Walter's wedding, so she called them on the day – an expensive rarity!
21   Elizabeth Barber, wife of Miriam's brother, Clarke Barber. Elizabeth grew up next door to the Barbers in Montclair; she, Miriam, and Clarke were all close childhood and college friends.

2

Years in Rochester, MN and China Preparations

1932 - 1934

It's often been said that opposites attract, and I think this was true of my parents. Miriam was from a humble, service-oriented family. Her parents, Loretta Clarke and Benjamin Barber, were scholarship graduates of Northwestern University just before the turn of the twentieth century. Their patterns of family living were influenced by their initial twelve years working in British India where Miriam was born, as YMCA leaders, and were impacted by a combination of formal British diplomacy and commitment to a social welfare organization.

Walter grew up in a town of 500 on the prairie in Nebraska, where his father ran the lumberyard and his mother taught school. He was Midwestern through and through and retained an earthy sensibility throughout his life. His experiences growing up near farmland combined with his medical training made him comfortable discussing anything from childbirth to menstrual cramps – often to the dismay of his wife and daughters. (Yet we were more knowledgeable than most young ladies of our era, thanks to him.)

Walter was direct and blunt. Miriam was gentle, warm, and perceptive. After living in Minnesota, I believe she grew to appreciate the straightforwardness and Midwestern sensibilities of its people. After their wedding, they visited the Judds in Rising City, Nebraska and then continued on to Rochester, Minnesota for Walter's Mayo Clinic surgery fellowship. He turned his full attention to medical work, and Miriam to setting up a household, immersing herself in the minutia, and then describing it in flowery detail in letters home to her parents. There are fully twenty-two pages of one letter packed with charming and painstaking descriptions, including snapshots and careful drawings of the apartment-furniture arrangements.

These early letters are less exciting than her China or Washington, D.C. reports but are important for understanding Miriam's intentions when the roles for women were usually limited to domestic efforts. Almost all of the Mayo Clinic Fellows were male and few women worked.

I imagine it was an adjustment for her to be at home and not be engaged in meaningful work. Miriam quickly realized that some of the doctors' wives were more interested in playing bridge – a thoroughly useless game, in her opinion – and had no interest in helping the needy. So she did the only thing she knew how to do: she got involved with the YWCA and started a current events club for some doctors' wives, and gave speeches, primarily about her experiences in India.

From the start, Walter was prominent among the other medical fellows, given his unusual background of living and doctoring in rural China for six years, as well as his perspective on international relations. Decades ahead of his time, Walter thought the western way of medicine was only part of the story; he was invited to give a lecture to the Mayo Clinic staff on Chinese medicine, complete with his acupuncture charts.

During this period, the private writings of Miriam began to surface. In them we see her quiet commitment to self-improvement and her belief that she could read, study, and set intentions to improve herself. In college, she started a loose-leaf notebook of collected poems and comments that meant something to her. She kept the notebook her whole life. She even took a self-inflicted Roth memory course to help in remembering names. And during two summers she returned to live in her parents' home in New Jersey, while finishing her Master's Degree from the Teacher's College at Columbia University in New York City.

The date on the letter that Miriam wrote to Moray, her former fiancé (see Prologue), is seven months after she and Walter were married. I wonder if she was beginning to realize that Walter's world was broader than she anticipated, leaving her alone for many hours. However, I think she was still picturing working side-by-side with her husband in China. The letter speaks of her desire to choose the life of service and sacrifice over the life of closeness and beauty she would have had with Moray. She and Walter truly sought to follow the model and teachings of Jesus.

Despite Walter's frequent absences, their relationship was warm and loving when he was home, and after a year she became pregnant with me. She wanted to be a mother and thought it was a high calling. I was born January 1, 1934, and she immersed herself in my care with some tentativeness and great love, supported by her parents who visited.

During the couple's last four months in Rochester, Miriam was firmly focused on preparations to relocate to China. Issues related to life in Rochester faded in importance as her eyes were turned toward the young family's next adventure. Already acquainted with the pleasures and perils of living abroad after her experiences in India, Miriam was able to plan for the needs the family would have in a remote area of China – an assignment that was expected to be lifelong.

She looked forward with a sense of excitement and her strong faith in God's guidance. She believed that "from those to whom much has been given, much is expected." Miriam felt called to serve, to help others – it was the purpose she had inherited from her parents, and the activity that gave her the greatest sense of joy and meaning. And China held the promise of it all.

Rising City, Nebraska   *Wednesday, March 30, 1932*

Mother dearest –

We're packed up for our start for Rochester, MN. Mrs. Judd is fairly well, but in bed all the time. She has adored seeing our things. Last night some friends of Walter's had us out to dinner. After dinner we were *serenaded* by the town orchestra and band, arranged so as not to disturb Mrs. Judd at her home. Then these band players with their wives, husbands, children et al. came in to this farm house, thirty or more of them, were introduced and we sat around and visited and sang. They are folks who have known Walter for years and they love him. Homey, good-hearted, hard working, honest farmer families, mostly, with a refreshing genuineness and simplicity. Conversation was largely about the crops and the stock and neighbor friends. I loved the wholesome naturalness of it all. Walter had worked for many of them there as hired boy, plowing, haying, etc. It was a lovely town reception of warmth and sincerity and I adored it.

Rochester, Minnesota   *Wednesday night, April 6, 1932*

Mother dearest –

Every single day I've put off sending you "just a note," hoping I'd find time for a real letter with all the Rochester news. But I guess I'll have to give up that hope for the present and send this off to tell you I'm well and oh so happy! With trunks & boxes & piles of books in the center of the sitting room floor, unpacked clothes and bags under the bed in the bedroom, crates of unpacked and unwashed and un-excelsiored dishes in the kitchen and confusion everywhere, I can't sit down to letter writing. I know you understand and are patient these first days, but I know too how eager you are to hear. Everything came through without a scratch, thanks largely to your supervision. The 4 boxes arrived Monday. Then stuff today & the big box. Also the picture proofs. Thank you ever and ever for "all 4 sings."

We have the apartment that Walter told about in Montclair. It belongs to people who go to their cottage on the lake near here for six months each year. Everything is beautifully furnished and kept and we are thrilled to be in such a lovely spot. We got into it on Saturday afternoon, worked that day but none on Sunday. Monday I started in cooking three meals a day, Walter started at the clinic and we keep settling and unpacking as we can. It will take time but it's all such fun.

People are lovely to me. I've met some fine wives already and I like them. I love the cooking and the marketing and being a housewife and most of all I love being Mrs. Judd. Walter is just too dear and loving for words. We talk of you all every day and *miss* you. More later.

Rochester, Minnesota   *Thursday, April 21, 1932*

Mother, dear –

I haven't told you how the social life for the doctors' wives is organized here. There's the "Magazine Club" to which everyone automatically belongs, called that because originally wives used to get together occasionally and read a magazine article. They have luncheons during the season – all activities stop in April. And it was to the last of these that I went that first Monday. This Club is subdivided into the Dramatic Club, which reads plays aloud, the Reading Club, which reviews current books, the Music Club, which studies composers, the Glee Club, and one other I think. These meet every two weeks for their activities and for tea drinking and you can belong or not as you choose.

Our alarm goes off at seven in the morning… Walter's off by ten to eight and then I "housekeep." Dishes, carpet sweep, dusting, mopping, bed-making, bathroom cleaning everyday. Tuesday at ten is my time to wash and I'm learning all the wrinkles. A darling young girl lives across the hall, been married nine months. She's told me a lot about where to buy things; we go marketing together every day; she showed me many tricks about washing and ironing; we borrow back and forth and are most congenial… I've learned how to soak the clothes, use water softener, clorox for whitening, what soap makes best suds, how to make starch, et al. The washing is very easy, takes only an hour and a half for all our things. I hang them outside on a reel so they get white and smell fresh. The ironing I do Wednesday and Thursday mornings. It takes me long to do. Is that 'cause I'm slow or is good ironing always a long process? Should it take me twenty minutes for one of Walter's shirts? And twenty minutes for a big sheet?

Friday mornings I vacuum the rugs and clean thoroughly the bedroom and sitting room – moving all furniture and knickknacks, vacuuming the upholstered furniture, etc. Saturdays I clean the icebox, stove, scrub the kitchen floor (linoleum) and the bathroom floor (tiled) and finish up putting the house in order for Sunday… I get out every day, at least for a trip downtown.

Walter finds his work keenly interesting. Cases are generally obscure or complicated in some way or they never would come here… He enjoys the beauty of the place, the medical atmosphere, the splendid equipment after great limitations in China, and the mental stimulus of these keen-minded men. He's very happy at the Clinic and at home too! We're a radiating pair.

Rochester, Minnesota   *Tuesday, April 26, 1932*

Mother dear –

We had a grand weekend! Walter had been asked to speak at a YM-YW student conference. Took a 1:30 bus Saturday noon for Minneapolis; got there at 5; were driven thirty miles out to a lovely Y camp on Lake Independence, where 160 students from Minn. and nearby Wisconsin were weekending… Sunday morning I was invited into the Interracial Relations Seminar group while Walter led the International group. I helped a bit to make situations concrete by examples and illustrations from some of my negro and Indian friends. Present in the group was Mr. Thaddeus, dental student at Univ. of Minn., an Indian, former YM secretary for fifteen years in India. He is keen, attractive, modest, thoughtful, fine. And then *we* won't let him swim in Lake Michigan, "even after I assured the police officer," he told us, "that my color was fast and wouldn't come off." Ha! We must exclude Asiatics from our superior country! And Jesus was an Asiatic, hence excludable also! That's the trouble, of course. We have excluded Jesus.

Rochester, Minnesota   *Monday, May 23, 1932*

Mother dear –

My "diary" for this past week would be a full one if you could read it. Besides the daily cooking, cleaning, washing, ironing of the regular schedule it would look like this:

Monday: Ladies Aid Luncheon with the "Young Married Women's" group of our Church. Met some fine younger women and sewed on diapers for the charity visiting nurse in Rochester and enjoyed a good luncheon and meeting… Paid off a coupla calls.[22] Evening, went to Mrs. Alvarez's home which was empty and played the piano for a long time. Walter went along and read.

Tuesday: Tea party at Mrs. Alvarez's. About twenty of the young wives there and we sat and sewed or knitted and gossiped and got fat on a most *delicious* tea. Her garden is lovely, and she gave us all lilacs and lilies of the valley to take home.

Wednesday: The last missionary meeting of the year, held in the *beautiful* home of Mrs. Balfour, Dr. Mayo's daughter and wife of a famous surgeon. The talk was on Egypt given by Mrs. Terry, charming German lady who has lived most of her life among Russians… Wed. night had Dr. Wu to dinner, a Chinese Fellow here… Walter had a *grand* time talking Mandarin, showing him many Chinese things. I had a grand time cooking steak, eggplant, strawberry shortcake.

Friday: The Babcocks[23] came and it was a great moment…

Saturday: They were off by 9:30 a.m. It was such fun to have them here. Late afternoon we drove up to Minneapolis with a Dr. McKinley and his wife who had come down to get us. We drove right into a glorious sunset, through beautiful green fields and past more and gorgeous-er lilacs than I've ever seen. We went to Northfield, saw Carleton campus & St. Olaf,[24] had dinner there and on with a grand full moon. They have a lovely home & it was a real treat to be with them overnight. Sunday Walter spoke twice at a Presbyterian Church, in the morning at the Church service, at five to the young people. We came back on the bus, got home at eleven.

Monday: Today, tea at Mrs. Terry's with eight other doctors' wives… Afterwards I went to call on Mrs. E. Starr Judd, wife of the world's most famous and skilled surgeon. She had called on me last week when I was out and I was tremendously impressed for she never calls on the Fellows' wives. It's 'cause we're both descended (by marriage) from Thomas Judd, Farmington, Conn., 1638. She was cordial and gracious and unpretentious and I had a very nice call – and departed forgetting to leave our cards. What a desperate faux pas!

Rochester, Minnesota   *Wednesday June 15, 1932*

Mother dear –

Last night we had the girls who work down at the Clinic with Walter – four of them: a nurse, a stenographer, a reception desk and appointment girl, and a records and histories girl. They're so interested to know we are missionaries!! All their old prejudicial stereotypes about missionaries have to be revised. Walter had the time of his life putting on his Chinese clothes, showing them embroideries and paintings… I had whole tomatoes stuffed with shrimp salad, stuffed eggs, potato chips, and a hot buttered roll on a plate. For dessert, brownies and strawberry mousse that I made all myself – and it's so unbelievably easy with a Frigidaire.

---

22   At that time, when a new person arrived in a community, the practice was that neighbors would stop by for a welcome call. Those calls were often reciprocated. People would often leave a calling card so that names could be remembered.

23   Miriam's neighbors from Montclair, New Jersey and parents of her sister-in-law, Elizabeth Babcock Barber.

24   Carleton and St. Olaf are two colleges in Northfield, Minnesota.

Montclair, New Jersey   *Friday night, July 29, 1932*

Sweetheart –

Here I am all wound up like a child's toy all waiting to be started off. I wish it were time for the exam right now for I feel as if I could write volumes on any subject.[25] The real value in preparing for this exam is that it has opened up whole realms of thought and experience and personality that I never before knew existed and has sort of enticed me into a new and different interest in reading and seeing life through the eyes of some of these great men…

I've got two awfully good (?) papers all prepared in my mind – outlines, points, development, illustrations and all. One is on character development in nineteenth century novel and the other on the influence of Ibsen in modern drama. Now all I have to do tomorrow, when I see the list of subjects from which we chose one to write an essay on, is to use a certain amount of ingenuity and wrangle one of these two papers around till it fits logically some phase or some corollary of one of the required subjects.[26]

Rochester, Minnesota   *Saturday, a.m., September 10, 1932*

Dear Mother –

This is the great news! – We bought a piano…a darling little apartment-size, practically new for $100. It has good tone and action and I'm so pleased. We may have to stop eating and live in the park when Walter's annual insurance is due in December!…

One of my new ventures started this week. I'm to be advisor to the Junior College YW… The Junior College is practically only a continued High School – no campus, no college spirit or life – and the poorer girls attend who can't go away to the University. Many come in from neighboring small towns or farms, board in town, and are scared and lonesome away from home. YW is their only "club" activity. I've got to work on programs for their meetings. It will be fun, I think!

Rochester, Minnesota   *Friday morning, September 30, 1932*

Mother dear –

Our trip to Nebraska was a very precious time to us and all the Judds.[27] …Mrs. Judd has lost weight, looks white and thin, but was better, they said, since all the family started coming home. We children talked long and late. It was an insight into Walter's life and characteristics to hear reminiscences of their younger days… Sunday was Walter's birthday, and Tuesday Gertrude's. So we had the birthday dinner Monday noon. Mother Judd came to the table in her wrapper. There we were around the table – the first time in years and undoubtedly the last time, and it proved almost too much for the family. Though they don't generally have grace at the table, Mrs. Judd asked Walter to say it for this special occasion. He tried, and broke down, and the rest did, too, and when the meal was being passed round and an unnaturally brisk conversation was going on to cover up the emotions, the crowd

---

25   Miriam returned to her parent's home for six weeks to attend a summer session at Columbia Teacher's College.

26   She passed her comprehensive exam, and returned to Rochester and Walter at the end of the summer session.

27   They visited Walter's parents and three living siblings who also came home to Rising City.

surreptitiously blew noses. Oh, you can't describe a warm living moving emotion in paper and ink – but the feeling that was there holding them all together was beautiful and very revealing to me.

Rochester, Minnesota   *Monday evening, November 21, 1932*

Mother dear – and everybody –

We had a perfectly grand weekend…drove up to Minneapolis. Made the 90 miles in 100 minutes. The game was a corker and we didn't freeze. [28] We went to dinner with an old empress dowager. She had invited ex-Gov. (of Minn.) Bernquist and wife to meet the famed Walter and since Old Berny and his Republican party had just been defeated for Congress, guess what we talked about! Right!!

Sunday a.m. Walter spoke at the Thank Offering service at a Congregational Church. In the evening a union Cong. young people's meeting produced over 500 and we had to shake hands with many of them. The drive home with some friends was cozy and enjoyable. Thus endeth — !

Fate has practically compelled me to have a small tea tomorrow. In Minneapolis yesterday a lady gave us a perfectly swell huge angel food cake, which I iced today with a thick mocha frosting, and last Thursday when Walter spoke at our Church they gave me afterwards a huge bouquet of yellow chrysanthemums. My house is beautifully clean, floors all oiled, everything spick and span. Don't you think those combined factors indicate a tea? I've asked eight of the wives to come and sew. Almost all have Christmas sewing now – or at least sox to darn. Many are knitting mittens for the Community Center…

The local YM has closed up for lack of support, no more activities and the whole thing has ceased operating. The Clinic has, for the first time, had to charge for ministers, rabbis, priests, etc. who were served free previously. If anyone tells you the depression is over laugh at them.

– Private Writing –

November 25, 1932

"Religion can be made to produce definite observable results in improvement of human living." H. N. Wieman.

Let me try to prove this by daily study with a forced regularity if necessary. But let each day's study be spontaneous & natural and fitting the needs & moods of that time – sincere worship.

I must get to know and love individuals.   *November 26, 1932*

Shut your mouth.   *December 2, 1932*

Rochester, Minnesota   *Friday night, December 2, 1932*

Mother dear –

The sad bit – the catastrophe of which you may have read in the papers. Last Saturday afternoon at two the power plant, a fairly new million dollar affair that furnishes heat and light for the Clinic,

---

28   Miriam and Walter indulged in a University of Minnesota football game.

practically all the hospitals and some of the hotels, blew up. There was a huge bang, then from our apartment window only three blocks away we could see all the smoke, steam, dust, and debris spurt up into the air alongside the tall chimney of brick that is always a landmark. We grabbed our coats and dashed down, and what a sad sight it was. Every window in the place was smashed, and the glass had rained all over the streets and nearby buildings. The steel window frames were all collapsed, bits of machinery had blown thru the brick walls, torn & twisted metal was lying all around in queer masses, a whole row of stone cornicing and bricks had been torn up and fallen all over the street, and the bricks around the chimney base were loosened so they feared it would go any minute. Police, ambulances, fire hose and wagons to extinguish the blazing interior, town officials, & many of the Clinic doctors were there in a twinkling, not to mention the curious throng. All hospital electricity was off until those buildings got connected with the town plant. The cause, it was later discovered, was that three careless workmen, who thought themselves smart enough to beat the regulations, tapped a huge gas main that brings the natural gas all the way from Oklahoma to Minnesota, without first turning off the gas. Two of these men, well-known citizens of the town and faithful members of the Presbyterian church, and both with three to five small children died in hospital shortly.

But the saddest part is this: I wrote you that the State Hi-Y was meeting here and Walter spoke at their banquet on the night before and was to speak at their 3:30 meeting Saturday. At 2:15 the whole group of 150 was to have been taken on a tour thru the clinic & power plant. The explosion was at two!!! But three out-of-town boys were exploring by themselves and were in the power plant. One, a fine boy excellent in football, was killed instantly and the other two are in the hospital. Tonight we went to see them. Their mothers are both here and were so pleased to have us come. One boy with a fractured jaw is doing fairly well and has raved to his mother about Walter's Friday night speech. The other hasn't regained consciousness yet. He talks about Walter in his delirium – he has a badly fractured skull. Isn't that pathetic – these fine young boys giving up their Thanksgiving and then have to suffer for someone else's carelessness. It has been a sobering affair.

Rochester, Minnesota   *Wednesday December 21, 1932*

Merry Christmas to all of you –

Wherever you're gathered for the Christmas celebration, you'll know we are with you in spirit. I'd better tell you how we'll celebrate this week. It really started last night with a lovely buffet dinner at the home of the head of the Urological Service. About twenty-five doctors, wives, and assistants there and their beautiful home looked lovely. We did jigsaw puzzles afterwards and had a most riotous evening.

Tomorrow night is the Clinic Party, a large affair for everyone. Friday I'm to help at the Health Center where they're assembling baskets of Christmas dinners for the six hundred destitute families. Friday night Walter and I will take our own private basket to the family assigned us personally. Usually they have only eighty families to care for and this year six hundred, so I've been calling up some of my friends among the Fellows' wives trying to get some interest. Most of them claim they can't afford it and I know eight hundred a year isn't a very big salary to share on, but they could all do it easily if they had the interest!

—Private Writing—

Rochester, Minnesota   *December 31, 1932*

New Year's Resolutions –

1. *To better organize myself, learn how to conserve, extend and best use my energy, which seems so pitifully limited, to get rid of a feeling of futility & discouragement with the results of my efforts.*

2. *To think differently of the problems of action & attitudes in connection with & relation to:*
   > *YW group*
   > *the circle who might be, or need close friends*
   > *the clubs and contacts in general*
   > *my possible speeches*

3. *Some definite daily plan for: hours of sleep; memory culture; "reading with a purpose"; music & practice*

Rochester, Minnesota   *Sunday, January 9, 1933*

Mother dear –

We started on another round of Sundays away from home that stretches now clear up into April. But this one wasn't too long or far. Walter spoke in the Congregational Church in Austin, fifty miles from here. At the parsonage we had a chance to meet and talk to five most interesting men from Waterloo, Iowa. They are working there to organize the unemployed, being themselves jobless, yet men of real brains and ability. They take to the farmers whose produce is spoiling because they can't afford to pay men to harvest it, groups of unemployed to shuck corn, dig potatoes, pick cabbages, etc. They are paid in these foods. They help some man cut his lumber and get paid in wood. A man who can't pay taxes on his empty building gives it to them for a headquarters – for buildings used for charity are exempted from taxes – and here they dispense food, clothing (old stuff), fuel to members of their group who buy it with scrip. This scrip they issue has no monetary value but is based on hours of work. Then they buy with it, say, ten hours worth of pork or sauerkraut. One of the chief values of this scrip is what remarkable things it does to a man's self-respect. To have some "money" in your pocket again that you have earned and that is able to produce food, etc. makes a formerly completely disheartened man hold his head up again. This group is anti-religious… Yet they're doing some excellent things in actually rehabilitating the unemployed, *not dispensing charity…*

I'm glad to have the dolls.[29] The High School girls were thrilled with them when I spoke to their YW club last Thursday. About fifty girls were there and all seemed so interested. I cut an easily spared yard of cloth off my long sari and made a tight blouse using the inch-wide gold border at the selvages to trim the sleeves and neck. Then at the meeting I dressed Miss Booth, the girls'

---

29   Miriam's mother had sent several dolls from Miriam's India years.

work secretary, for she is dark and has long hair and is a good type, and it's easier to explain on someone else than on yourself… This week I'm to speak at the Episcopal Church Missionary meeting. I'll take the dolls again. I'll talk there, as I did last week, about the kind of village education I saw in Asinsol.[30]

The Curtis Hotel, Minneapolis, Minnesota   *Monday, January 16, 1933*

Mother dear –

Here I am in Minneapolis lending moral support to Walter while he struggles through his six two-hour exams in clinical subjects: medicine, surgery, obstetrics, etc. The weather was warm enough – fifty degrees above today to consider driving up in a rumble seat, so we came up this afternoon with the Butschs. Janet and I are going to roam the city streets and go to the theater. Tonight we had a swell dinner (for fifty cents!) in this lovely hotel dining room…

Walter's big speech was Thursday night – the scientific honorary society. He spoke on the development of Chinese medicine and showed some valuable old (fourteenth Century) charts of Chinese ideas of anatomy, etc. that he had been given as a present in China. These charts, five feet long, are wearing badly so I spent some time pasting them, with wall-paperers' paste, on muslin to preserve them and did a pretty good job, if I do say so! Everyone was enthusiastic over the lecture. A Fellow rarely gets a chance to talk before Sigma Xi, so we feel pretty proud.

Rochester, Minnesota   *Saturday, January 28, 1933*

Mother dear –

I find myself a weekend widow, but I have so many things planned that I don't think I'll have time to get lonesome. We got an emergency call from people in Winona whom we'd had to turn down on a previous engaged Sunday. So I'll get an 8:30 train tomorrow morning, and do my first pulpit speaking, but to a very small group. It will be on India.

At the YW dinner Monday night I was elected to the Board, so now my troubles begin!

I was right about the Board cutting us off after April 1[31]. We each have enough accumulated dividends on our life insurance to pay our 1934 bill of life insurance. Walter makes about $200 (estimate) on speeches not connected with churches, which he is entitled to keep. We have a little bit ahead, and if we continue to live on just about $100 we can probably break even. If we need to we'll borrow. We're not starving yet, and we're terribly terribly happy.

---

30   Asinsol was a town in India Miriam visited when teaching in south India.

31   The American Board of Commissioners for Foreign Missions (ABCFM), chartered by Williams College graduates in 1810, sponsored hundreds of missionaries, including Walter in China. When home in Montclair, on October 19, 1932, Miriam received her commission from the ABCFM at its 123rd annual meeting: "This testifies that Miriam Barber Judd is appointed a Missionary of the Gospel of our Lord Jesus Christ in the North China Mission under the rules and regulations of the Board, and is entitled to all the rights and privileges attached to that office." The commission was signed by Rockwell Harmon Potter, President of the Board.

Rochester, Minnesota   *Wednesday, February 1, 1933*

Mother dearest –

Today was music club and we had a treat: two doctors' wives played a Beethoven sonata for violin and piano, and it was exquisite. The pianist talked first about Beethoven and his music and explained this sonata and its main themes so it was easy to listen to intelligently… I've decided to take lessons from her, an hour a week. I'm going to use that twenty-five dollars you sent me for Christmas and it will last till I leave in June, for she charges only $1.50 an hour. You see, I've been practicing anyway and I felt I might as well have some guidance and direction while it is available and while I have time, and store it up for the "famine" days in China. So you and Father are giving me my piano and my music lessons – as you have given me all the music I know. What a lovely immeasurable and permanent gift that is from you two whom I love so much.

Rochester, Minnesota   *Sunday, March 5, 1933*

Mother darling –

Imagine having a Sunday at home! Our first in two months! It's such bliss we don't know how to act. We slept all morning – lazy children! And the only reason we're home this weekend is not because invitations are giving out – I write ten to fifteen letters for him each week on matters about his speaking engagements – but because he's on call at the Clinic this weekend and can't be away. And next Sunday we refused all invitations – just because! Two successive Sundays at home! That's anniversary celebration enough for me!

We have plenty of money in the bank – some $400 – but there's no telling how long banks will be closed. We happen to have about $15 cash to go on but they say our bank is perfectly sound so we aren't concerned about being high and dry permanently. How are you getting on?[32]

Poor Walter has been so upset by the terrible editorials in our paper here on China, displaying the deepest ignorance of the factors involved, lack of appreciation of what is going on and our part in it, and the general selfish materialistic attitude toward it all. It isn't only because he loves China so that he feels it so strongly but because of what it's doing to us, and to European nations who stupidly won't stand firm against Japan's marauding.

Rochester, Minnesota   *Wednesday a.m., March 8, 1933*

Mother dear –

Our ten dollars cash is still holding out, for I had a supply of canned goods. Banks reopen tomorrow, I hear… Last night to the Nurses' Reading Club I reviewed *The Good Earth*.[33] I gave a bit of background of Pearl Buck and some comments on the criticism of the book, and then read for an

---

32   This was the height of the Great Depression. Banks frequently closed their doors to customers to preserve what little cash they had on hand.

33   A novel about rural China by American writer Pearl Buck, 1932 Pulitzer Prize and 1938 Nobel Prize for Literature winner.

hour, sticking to those parts that would help them to get an idea of woman's place in Chinese culture. I commented on various customs, and I enjoyed tremendously doing it.

Rochester, Minnesota   *Monday, March 13, 1933*

Mother dear –

We knew this would be too busy a day for us to celebrate properly and anyway we kinda liked the idea of celebrating on Sunday. Really, we started on Saturday with my lovely crocus plant that arrived with a precious card, and also a lovely rose for me to wear on Sunday. I cooked a special dinner for Saturday night so we wouldn't have so much cooking on Sunday. We had a roast chicken – my first – and it was yummy. Candied sweets, boiled onions, dressing, a tomato & cucumber salad – our first this year for fresh tomatoes have been too expensive for our pocketbook – still are except for wedding anniversaries! – hot biscuits (I'm good at them now) and Walter's favorite strawberry shortcake for dessert, with fresh strawberries as another luxury. Sunday we went to church and Walter says it was the first time he'd heard anyone but himself speak for months…

In the afternoon we enjoyed Cadman, Fosdick, and the radio, not to speak of our reading and each other.[34] And we got out our precious wedding ceremony book and read the service through together and looked over our signatures of guests and lived it all again. How radiant a spirit you were to start me off on my great adventure. I hope I can be like you in your lovely unselfish life.

Rochester, Minnesota   *Monday, March 27, 1933*

Mother dear –

Thursday I sewed at the church in the morning and at noon made my initial burst into a men's club. It was my Kiwanis luncheon and I must admit I *was* scared for I have never spoken in front of Walter, for one thing, and I wanted to do well, and then the Kiwanians are used to good speakers because they can draw on the Clinic transients and I didn't want to give them a lot of slop. So I'd worked quite hard on it and managed not to forget any major item in my 40 min. talk, and Walter said it was O.K., but I'm just plain glad it's over.

You asked about my old letters. I see no chance of my ever being famous enough for anyone to want to publish them with my life, and I'm not sure that as literary masterpieces they're great enough to be used as examples. There might be a few India descriptive ones…of the Poorubari village I wrote about in March 1929 and perhaps some of my north India trip ones. Perhaps I could look them over when I come home.

Rochester, Minnesota   *Tuesday, April 11, 1933*

Mother dear –

Today seven of us "brides" (!) got together and over a cup of tea exchanged recipes with much profit and pleasure. We checked up on all household matters, management and expense, and I discovered my $25 per month for food is a bit higher than most of the others' pay. I thought I was

---

34   Dr. S. Parkes Cadman and Harry Emerson Fosdick were both preachers on the radio at the time.

being very economical and I can't see where I could cut down unless we *never* have our occasional steak and mushrooms or chicken. We use the cheap vegetables almost entirely – cabbage, carrots, parsnips, etc. Well, I'll try harder for each month our expenses seem to run higher than we anticipated – generally under $125.

Rochester, Minnesota   *Sunday, April 16, 1933*

Mother dear –

Your letter came last night and it meant a lot to me. I was thinking after Walter went at 7:30 to the hospital that my life so far has been unusually free from burdens and sorrow. Death and suffering and burdens will come and I just hope that I will have strength and courage and faith for them when they are my lot. I hope I can face trials with half the faith and persevering sweetness and courage and wisdom that you've shown, my Mother dear – I was touched by the little cross you painted for your Mother. Does it ever give you any regrets that you weren't able to keep up your painting?

Rochester, Minnesota   *Friday afternoon, April 28, 1933*

Mother dear –

I've been to two lunches and six teas in the last two weeks. But the YW activities have taken the most time. All year long I've been hoping we could send a delegation to the annual YM-YW spring Conference not far from Minneapolis. Tomorrow morning at 5:30, thirteen of us start off to drive to it. That sounds simple enough but what hours of work have gone into it: talking to the advisor of the YM to get the boys interested; working out a YM-YW pre-conference banquet to get up pep – never before have the YM and YW had *anything* to do with each other so cooperation wasn't easy; we had to earn and raise money to pay delegates' expenses. Last night we had a delegation meeting with some education, suggestions, and discussions to help them orient themselves in the group. I know they'll be lost for they aren't as mature as high school kids in Montclair. However, I hope it will jar some of them loose.

One of the most exciting events for us was buying a car. For months we've talked of it, because Walter's speeches consume so much unnecessary time when we have to rely on bus schedules. So when the Minneapolis Women's Club sent him a $50 extra check in addition to the original $75, we started looking at secondhand cars. After five weeks of looking we finally got a 1930 Chevy Coop without rumble seat. It cost us only $150 so we think we did very well.

Rochester, Minnesota   *Saturday p.m., September 2, 1933*

Mother darling –

Had a good train trip[35] and my Walter waiting for me at the station. You remember the very thing I said he thought he'd never do – buy me a nightgown? He did it – for my birthday – a heavy French

---

35   Miriam was returning from Montclair after completing her master's degree from Teacher's College at Columbia University.

crepe peach with lace and a sash, bias cut to fit. That was a true gift of love when he hates so to buy ladies' underwear – the old sweet.

Must run – I feel fine – everyone is thrilled and surprised at my news.[36]

Rochester, Minnesota   *Thursday, September 14, 1933*

Dear Pater – [37] Happy birthday to ye –

I wish you could have been here last night to see a thrilling thing – medical science progressing and history being made right under our eyes. Dr. Rosenow spoke at Staff Meeting to a packed room. He was back that morning from St. Louis where he had been doing five days work of his own on sleeping sickness… Dr. Rosenow is likely the outstanding bacteriologist in the country… a missionary type of individual, sincere, enthusiastic, terribly devoted to his work in medicine as a humane study, not to bring glory on himself… He *can't* be hard boiled, cold, objectively disinterested as the medical men often 'pose to be… For this, many medics sneer at him, and for the fact that he has been able to produce results no one has so far been able to duplicate… Naturally he got no invitation to go to St. Louis to work on the epidemic. A doctor got him a private invitation to come down and take a look. So he sneaks in, as it were, by a side door, though all the officials knew he was there. He had no kick to find with the "filterable virus" theory they were all working on, but felt that a "streptococci" theory would show up the cause more readily. So he went at it from that angle, midst jeering and nasty non-cooperation in one hospital though he was allowed free access to patients in the Catholic hospital… His eyes filled with tears and his voice broke as he described the symptoms of the wretched patients – they're human beings to him, not an experiment – and went on to explain about the cultures he made from patients in different stages, from exposed members of families, and from people who had no contact with sleeping sickness patients. Some of the cultures he sent to his lab here in Rochester… The lab assistants here, not knowing which cultures were which, for they were merely numbered for identification, got the same results with their rabbits as he was getting in St. Louis, showing that his theory was right, although it still remains to be worked out.

When he was sure of his discovery he rushed back here to report under the auspices of the Clinic so they get the permanent credit… That huge room sat still as death as he made his report in an almost breaking voice. Then he brought out on the stage six of his rabbits still living but in different stages of the disease, with the symptoms he had been describing very marked. Everyone rushed up front to view them as the meeting broke up… He also said the lady doctor, whose "discovery of the cause of sleeping sickness" was heralded in the press this week or last told him herself that that wasn't so, that again the newspapers had jumped the gun for something sensational, that she had just found one tiny step in the whole problem. And Dr. Charlie[38] piped up with a true remark – "Well, Rosenow, those two-hundred doctors before whom you demonstrated your rabbits and findings before you left St. Louis will be terribly busy now trying to think up ways to crucify you rather than trying to think up ways of furthering and using your discovery!" Isn't it too bad that medical science, as so much of living today, has to be dominated by jealousy and personal interest rather than by the service-to-

---

36   Miriam had shared the exciting news of her pregnancy.
37   The Latin word for father, which was how Miriam addressed her dad.
38   Dr. Charlie Mayo founded the Mayo Clinic in 1889 with his brother, Dr. Will Mayo.

mankind motive. I'll never forget that meeting, the intense atmosphere of expectancy, the feeling of the marvelous power of man's mind working toward God's purposes.

Rochester, Minnesota   *Sunday, September 24, 1933*

Mother dear –

I spoke at two missionary meetings this week – the first our Congregational meeting at one of the doctor homes. Mrs. Alvarez asked me to tell why I was going into missionary work myself. Well, that is a harder thing to do than a general talk on India for it calls for an expression of some of your deepest convictions and ideals. I spent a lot of time on it. Another afternoon we had our organization meeting of our private study club. We certainly have a varied group – one Jewess, several Catholics, Universalists, varied Protestant groups. We have three good Socialists in the gang so we ought to be able to paint Rochester red or at least a faint pink.

Rochester, Minnesota   *Wednesday p.m., October 18, 1933*

Mother dear –

Walter wanted to see all he could at the Fair.[39] …We went into the Oriental bazaars and were so disappointed and disheartened with what we saw. Catering to an American public with not much money to spend, not much knowledge of oriental art, not much interest beyond a curiosity in something odd, their wares were of the cheapest kinds, inartistically displayed, often unattractive. Too bad that they have learned our commercialism to such an extent that they could not even exhibit some of the lovely work they do. That must have made Indians and Chinese humiliated with its ordinariness and unloveliness when they know what beautiful things their people can produce. In one place a Chinese girl was painting freehand scenes on "handmade Chinese embroidered linen" that I'm sure came from Woolworths.

A coarse American girl was blabbing out that she was one of China's greatest artists imported especially for the fair, and would paint people's names in Chinese characters on a hankie. The painting cheap and inartistic. I stopped to talk to the girl, told her I lived in China, found that she *didn't*, but was born & brought up in some Chinatown in this country.[40] She wore ill-fitting American clothes and was a smart-alecky sort of person – even said she didn't believe I'd ever been to China! And that's what's representing China to America! But we (America) taught it to them (Orient) – anything to make money, regardless of its truth or beauty. At places supposed Mohammedan girls with thinnest chiffon veils on and nothing much else above their waists – and the Mohammedan women being so terribly particular about the exposure of the feminine person! That gets money from our American public so we should worry about any erroneous impression it may give about Mohammedans!! Oh, we were wearied and disgusted with this cheap, sordid part, especially when it could have been made educational and lovely, but not so profitable!

---

39   Miriam and Walter had driven to Rising City, Nebraska, for a vacation and returned through Chicago to see the 1933 World's Fair. The theme was "A Century of Progress."
40   In early 1931 on her boat trip home from two years of teaching in India, Miriam had spent a short time in China.

Sunday morning I went to the University of Chicago chapel – a magnificent sermon – a magnificent organ… The whole service was so quiet and dignified, so impressive and inspiring.

Rochester, Minnesota   *Monday p.m., October 30, 1933*

Mother dear –

I'm on the Girls Work Committee of the YW Board. I resolved to buck some of the inertia and stupidity that goes on. So when the Chairman phoned me about *three* hours before the meeting last week and asked me to lead devotions, I protested at the lateness of the request because of the lack of time to plan. She answered that devotions aren't very important, make them short, read any old scripture, say a prayer – to which I replied that was probably why much of our work was so ineffective – we rushed into God's presence without any preparation, bowed to Him as we dashed on with *our* plans. She didn't get the point at all! And I led the devotions since I really did have the time to prepare. Afterwards I was blowing off and found we were all of one mind. So I was elected to go back to Chairman with suggestions from us all as to a *good constructive inspirational* program. I did, but she just has *no* idea what the YW is all about – the building of character into girls in the community. I'm out for a year of fighting, if necessary. They may be glad to see me leave next year, but I'll bet they know there's some people think the YW job is more than a superficial Committee meeting fosterer.

Rochester, Minnesota   *Sunday night, December 3, 1933*

Mother dear –

I was talking to Walter and he's so enthusiastic about the baby, talks sweetly about it, often wants to listen with his stethoscope to the tiny heartbeats because he says it's not fair for me to have the baby all to myself these months. The little fellow is a lively one and kicks quite lustily and rolls around in great fashion. We're both so anxious to *see* him. Maybe just four weeks from today he'll be here.[41]

Rochester, Minnesota   *Thursday night, January 25, 1934*

Mother dear –

Everywhere are evidences of your visit here, from the slop jar in the bathroom, to darned stockings, to the begonia, new curtains, the rubber sink drainer in the kitchen, contributions you made to our lives – the strength and courage and happiness and cheer and support and suggestions and burdens carried – an endless number of things you *are* and you *gave* to us those happy weeks together and no thank-yous will ever be able to say what we feel.

And now for the only news we have that seems of any importance – just a few nothings about your granddaughter. She is a precious lamb, changing so every day, and getting dearer and dearer. I'm beginning to really enjoy her a bit now. I was too awed and nervous at first to have much abandon with her but it's coming and I can see that in a week or so I'll feel completely at home with her. She is following things with her wide blue eyes, using her hands a lot, stretching much more actively. She still is colic-y, but that's to be expected, but she's good at night, and I don't have any difficulty

---

41   "The little fellow," daughter Mary Louise, was born on January 1, 1934. The Barbers came to Rochester to assist.

with her or mind staying those nights alone. Walter continues to simply spoil her. He's just nuts over her… My ever-deepening love to you, now that I'm a mother too.

Rochester, Minnesota   *Wednesday, March 21, 1934*

Mother dear –

Dr. Fairchild wrote that the North China people were definitely counting on our returning…and the Board has budgeted our travel & salary for this year[42]… We'll sail in September early, finishing the fellowship the end of June, staying during July for him to do observing he wants to do, vacationing August in Nebraska.

Rochester, Minnesota   *Thursday March 22, 1934*

Mother dear –

I've been working on the everlasting clothes problem. I've had my blue suit cleaned, stretched and pressed and the hem let down. Then I got a perky blue and white plaid washable blouse that looks darling with it – 98 cents. The cute grey straw hat that I got in Omaha and always loved I'm having reblocked and a new trimming of some sort put on, so that will be a nice outfit, and suitable for fall and shipboard traveling. This week the College Women's Club had a day as salesgirls at Massey's and got part of the profits for their work. I got two cute wash dresses that will do for warm weather travel. One was $3.95, the other $2.95.

Rochester, Minnesota   *Tuesday night, March 27, 1934*

Mother dear –

You asked about Mary Lou… Her major difficulty is her pylorus spasm. That still kicks up trouble about once a week, like this afternoon when she lay on the big bed and in twenty minutes vomited up huge amounts of milk and tomato juice, in spurts or fountains. We are keeping her on atropine for that tends to relax the spasm. She will outgrow this but it may be months. But she is such a good baby in spite of her difficulties, laughing and playing between vomits. Of course, she takes a lot of cleaning up at times like this… She's beginning to discover her hands and examines them carefully, though most of the time we keep her arms in cardboard rollers so she can't get her hands into her mouth. We want that habit stopped before she gets to dirty China…

Well, I guess we're full-fledged missionaries now for we've received our first missionary barrel. The ladies of Union Congregational Church collected old baby clothes and sent us a box. The things were clean – but that's the most I could say for them. A wash wool bathrobe, faded and with the satin binding all frazzled and worn out; a grey (once white) pair of knit leggings all out of shape and with such heavy darns that you couldn't find the original material, etc. They were trying to be thoughtful and I'm sure have a real feeling of self-satisfaction at having made their contribution to missions. I hope sometime some of these folks will discover what missions *really* is. If we can help them do this, I'll forgive them their first missionary barrel mistake.

---

42   Dr. Fairchild was the China Secretary of the ABCFM, overseeing all the China mission stations.

Rochester, Minnesota   *Wednesday afternoon, April 4, 1934*

Mother dear –

Mary Lou has had a long train trip and a visit away from home… Mrs. Judd had another attack last week… We would never forgive ourselves if she went on without seeing her only grandchild… So we went. Mr. Judd met us, and you should have seen his face beam as he saw the baby. It was a study!! We parked her on the floor of his big car, in her bassinet, and went back to the station to get breakfast. Mr. Judd had eaten but we urged him to come in and visit with us, as the baby would be all right – she never fusses or needs any attention, it seems. But he just guessed he'd stay and watch the *car*!! That tickled us a lot… And was Mrs. Judd glad to see the baby! She was not strong enough to hold her but she could watch her. We had such a short time there that we just stayed quietly at home. Everything went so well and things were comparatively easy to manage on Pullmans and trains and visiting that I feel so much more easy about the thought of heading for China when the time comes.

Rochester, Minnesota   *Sunday, May 13, 1934*

Mother Dear—[43]

My days seem to have become increasingly dominated by "much thought for my body and none for my soul" – the necessary details force themselves on one to the exclusion of all else, and I am "anxious and troubled with much serving." I don't want the deep intellectual and spiritual needs of my living to go unnurtured because my husband must be fed, my baby must be cared for, my

house must be clean. So as I have been working on this idea, I have found things that have helped me to rise above many of the petty annoyances, and necessary routine.

There is nothing more I can send you on Mother's Day than my devoted love, which you have *every* day, and a few of the best moments of my living returned to you, where all my best has come from. And in the sharing of these thoughts of others with you, and in all this year you will be closer to me than ever before, because I am knowing now a little of your sacrificing and deep love for me, as I join you in the great gift of Motherhood.

Rochester, Minnesota   *Monday afternoon, May 28, 1934*

Mother dear –

Since your wire this morning with the word that you will be here next week, things begin to seem final after these weeks of waiting and indecision. The cable has come from China assigning us to Fenchow (pronounced Funjo)…which has a larger, better-equipped hospital, only one of the five in North China with x-ray. Walter will

Miriam with Mary Lou

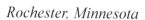

43   To celebrate Mother's Day, Miriam prepared a book of poems and excerpts for her mother. Selections included *Methods of Private Religious Living* by H. N. Wieman, *The Old Sailor* by A. A. Milne, *A Kitchen Prayer: A Poem* by John Greenleaf Whittier, and the scripture passage about Mary and Martha. This is the introduction she wrote.

be able to do better professional work there. It also has the school where Carleton sends students to teach each year.

Can Father bring home from the office plain business-size envelopes, plain *thin* typewriting paper, a package of blue or black carbon paper, up to fifty sheets or so? I thought he might have these he could buy from his own office stock, and cheaper than I could do here. We could well take 500 envelopes and 500 sheets of paper, the latter of *thin* weight, because (a) letters home from China cost 25 cents Chinese and excess postage quickly mounts up and I am apt to write a lot, and (b) I will likely want to make carbons often to send to Walter's family, or close friends.

Rochester, Minnesota   *Wednesday noon, July 4, 1934*

Mother dear –

Oh, it was so nice having you here. But I hope you weren't too exhausted with all the heavy work you both did for us – the packing and the sewing. I felt badly afterwards, Mother, to think that I let you keep at the sewing so continually… Friday afternoon we all three got vaccinated and Mary Lou and I got our second typhoid shots.

Rochester, Minnesota   *Wednesday afternoon, July 11, 1934*

Mother dear –

Saturday night we had a lovely time. The Clinic entertained the doctors & wives of the County Medical Association at a buffet dinner & hobby show. Various doctors exhibited some of their hobbies – painting, photography, woodcarving, old coins, books, stamps, etc. Walter had some of his Chinese artwork & his clothes there and received many favorable comments on those lovely paintings on silk – the Four Seasons.

Mr. Judd phoned today that he & Mrs. Judd & Olive[44] will start early tomorrow for Rochester and be here by supper. Walter does so want his mother to go thru the Clinic. She hasn't been a bit well recently & he fears this may hasten the end. We are anxious.

Rochester, Minnesota   *Monday afternoon, July 16, 1934*

Mother dear –

The days since the Judds arrived have been rather full ones… She has been in bed in our room, and sleeping a good bit of the time. I have visited with her only ten minutes & Walter not much more. Olive does everything for her – bed baths, enemas, fixes her food, which has to be done with care for she can eat no sugar…

Friday they took Mrs. Judd to the Clinic (using wheelchair everywhere)… Saturday they did the blood tests and later she went down to be seen by a group of doctors all together. They all think she has cancer of the uterus (she had a cancerous breast removed twenty years ago) and want to make a test to find out. But this requires hospitalization and some anesthetic and she fears to go ahead with

---

44   Olive Doty was the Judds' live-in housekeeper in Rising City.

it… They have only once before been away, always living in their tiny town, and things here are strange, and the unknown holds so many fears, and she determinably wants to die at home… Mr. & Mrs. Judd want to go home. I say nothing but try to keep the works running quietly & smoothly while all the problems get discussed. And darling Mary Lou is our lifesaver. She comes into the tense situation with her joyous trustfulness and happy innocence and relieves the strain again and again, lying on Grandma Judd's bed and relaxing the fears and worries there.

Rochester, Minnesota   *Friday p.m., July 20, 1934*[45]

Walter just phoned to say they had finished the small operation on Mrs. Judd & discovered no cancer so everyone is much relieved! Things have been most tense all week.

Rochester, Minnesota   *Monday evening, July 23, 1934*

Mother dear –

Mrs. Judd is getting on well… I must admit I get tired to death of the eternal arguing about every heartbeat and every degree on the thermometer. It *has* been unbearably hot & sticky. Mr. Judd & Olive do fuss. I feel remarkably well & not too tired.

Walter, Olive, & I went to the Cities today to finish the shopping. Got several sizes of shoes for Mary Lou and some for Walter; got wool shirts & sleeping suits for Mary Lou for next winter, and a few toys; arranged about inner spring crib mattress, bathinette & walker; got lots of toiletries at a cut-rate drug store; some clothes for Walter. Now our shopping is *all* finished.

Saturday about 5 Walter and I took Mary Lou out to the Mussey cottage for the picnic they had for their Mayo Clinic section. After supper Walter & I went canoeing and going along the shore at dusk a lovely big bass jumped & landed *in* the canoe. Walter brained it & we proudly went home with a one-pound fourteen-inch bass, with no line & bait & no license!! Did we get razzed. A true fish story.

Rochester, Minnesota   *Thursday July 26, 1934*

Dear Mother –

Judds left 2:45 a.m. on Wednesday to drive before it was too hot. Friday – today has been cool & lovely. China Hall packed *all* our dishes & silver, and kitchen crockery, lampshades and lamps, trays, knickknacks, clock, etc. – Walter finished books & magazines while I worked in the bedroom & linen closets. Opie will keep the piano for us till we get to China & decide if we want it or not. Everything is going much more easily than I anticipated…

A lovely couple, Dr. & Mrs. McKelvy went thru here last week on way to Peking to teach obstetrics in P.U.M.C.[46] They're Canadians, just leaving John Hopkins. She is charming, has lots to her – is to have a baby in October. I had her up here to visit while Walter visited hospitals with him. Hope to enjoy them in Peking next winter, especially since we will both have babies.

---

45   This was a postcard Miriam sent to her parents.
46   Peking Union Medical College.

Rochester, Minnesota   *Wednesday p.m., August 1, 1934*

Dear Folks –

Settled into Costellos's[47] until Sat. night when we will take night train for Omaha. Got seventeen pieces of freight & five trunks out of the apartment at six p.m. last night, which will be shipped, & moved fourteen pieces of hand luggage after supper. I had a permanent this afternoon. Tomorrow will pay bills & close up business while Walter finishes at the Clinic. Must take Mary Lou to the Clinic once more too. Can't think straight to write, will send a good letter from Rising City.

Rochester, Minnesota   *Saturday a.m., August 4, 1934*

We are finding *many* last things to do which keep us busy every minute. Had our passport pictures done yesterday – not too bad. Everyone keeps phoning, dropping in, asking us out for meals – seven meals out this week! – bringing farewell gifts which we are having to squeeze into duffle bag as trunks are full & stored at station. Off tonight – farewell Rochester!!

Rising City, Nebraska   *Wednesday, August 8, 1934*

Mother dear –

What a crowd to see us off at the station Sat. eve. I felt very badly at leaving for we have loved it there and people have been so nice to us...

Rising City, Nebraska   *Thursday, August 9, 1934*

Mother Dear –

The baptism service was lovely. The Church in Omaha doesn't have services in August but the Assistant Pastor called a number of our friends, and seventy-five showed up on Sunday morning. The service was simple and brief. Many folks to greet afterwards... Mr. Judd got there in time for the ceremony, which was a real satisfaction to us to have at least one grandparent there.

Rising City, Nebraska   *Monday, August 13 , 1934*

Darling –

I was so happy to find your little love note this morning.[48] It was like a good-morning kiss – only not quite so intimate! The first night you were gone I had quite a bit of heartburn & regurgitation and I figured that was a pretty speedy reaction!! But the second night I had cramps enough to nullify the former!!!

Miriam and Walter with Mary Lou

---

47   Friends of Miriam and Walter with whom the family was staying.

48   Walter returned to Rochester to complete work he missed when his parents were visiting.

Our little cuteness entertained right royally yesterday afternoon. She laughed & played on the floor and sang and got up on her hands & knees often, trying to crawl. Gosh, it's funny how a tiny bit of life can be so infinitely important – and dear—isn't it, my darling.

Rising City, Nebraska   *Wednesday, August 15, 1934*

Mother dear –

We're having the magazines *Time, Christian Century, World Tomorrow*, and Walter's medical magazines sent to China. Yes, we'd like to have the *Atlantic & Readers Digest* after you've read them. Send them to Walter (American Board Hospital, Fenchow, Shansi). Our joint salary is to be $1100 with rent free. They will pay my tuition at the language school but no other expenses… Been trying to get caught up on letters. Have written over twenty-five. My address is just Union Language School, Peiping.

Rising City, Nebraska   *Tuesday, August 21, 1934*

Mother dear –

I had meant to write a lot but have had to stop to type letters for Walter and it's late now. We leave here Friday night. Glad you understand & love me so well I can just write scraps & you know I still love you very very much.

Just out of Salt Lake City, Utah[49]   *Sunday, 11 a.m., August 26, 1934*

Mother dear –

We had a 5 o'clock supper and then fed Mary Lou at the Judds on Friday and off we went. Walter was quite broken up as was Mr. Judd when we parted. He sat in back & held Mary Lou all the way to the train and talked to her & loved her to bits.

San Francisco, California   *Thursday September 6, 1934*

Dear Family all –

It was fun to hear all your voices last night and it sounded so natural – but when it was over it gave me a sort of weak and funny feeling to realize I had been talking clear across the country to our own house. I could see you all gathering after the heartless operator had called our lightening three minutes, talking about how well you could hear and what you forgot to say. We talked here too. Uncle Alma told me he attended in 1915 in an armory in New York City the opening of the cross-continent phone lines and said it cost $27 to phone across… He says they'll soon have phone lines to China…

Now we're aboard and everything's fine – good cabin – boat leaving now – All my love –[50]

---

49   The family traveled by train from Nebraska to Los Angeles, visiting there with Walter's three siblings, and Miriam's aunt and two uncles.

50   Miriam, Walter, and Mary Lou sailed on the S.S. President Hoover on Friday, September 7, 1934, from San Francisco.

S.S. President Hoover   *Monday, September 10, 1934*

Dear Folks –

Here it is a nice bright sunny Monday morning – And now it's Tuesday – Just as I started to write, Walter came along and said that everyone was swimming on the top deck and I just couldn't resist. And was it a grand swim – a fairly good-sized pool for second class.

The train trip from Pasadena was uneventful.[51] It gave me a funny feeling to be standing on the platform and see the uncles and aunts moving out of sight and realize that I wouldn't see them for a long seven years. Fortunately, the Small Thing needed my attention so I didn't long have time to stay with my thoughts…

The boat sailed on the dot, with the usual streamers and waving and cheering, and the lovely San Francisco line slowly receding in the distance… Then the breeze came up much too briskly, and the waves danced much too high and before we were out of sight of land, Walter was in bed, as were most of the passengers, and I followed him very soon. All in all, the first night was bad, the baby didn't like her tiny baggy bed and we were glad when morning came and the weather was calm and lovely and warm. Since then everything has been grand.

The next day we got things organized and found that all was going to be easier than we had expected. Our cabin has a long panhandle alley off the main room that led down to the porthole, most convenient for putting our two wardrobe trunks and stringing up the clothesline. We have running hot water in the room, and it's boiling all the time, so the diapers get rinsed out as soon as they're taken off and hung up to dry. The little dresses, shirts, and nighties get washed out in Lux in the hand basin each morning, and our traveling iron is useful for ironing small things, with the bottom of a drawer for an ironing board. We have two beds and two upper bunks.

The baby makes her home and playpen and bed in one of the beds. They got us a wide smooth board and it makes a perfect fourth side for her bed. She can see over it but can't climb it. So she plays there quite safely when we're off at meals, crawling back and forth, or lying with her little bottom up against the wall and banging her heels on the woodwork, or swinging the beads which hang from the upper bunk and which swing themselves with the motion of the boat, or squeaking her pussy, or just dropping off to sleep when she gets tired…

Miriam and Walter on the ship

---

51   The family had taken the train from Pasadena to San Francisco to meet the ship.

We set up our little sterno traveling stove and manage her food most easily. While I was bathing her in the hand basin, Walter sterilized the bottles and nipples without much difficulty.

We had lovely letters and packages to open when the boat sailed, for many friends had remembered us. We go off happily, feeling that dear friends and family are loving us.

Aboard S.S. President Hoover   *Thursday, September 20, 1934*

Dear Folks –

Here we are a day out of Japan and our good luck has changed. We woke up to a rolling, heavy sea and a gentle rain – and we find walking is dangerous, eating a risk. Walter is reading on the bed – a purely precautionary measure!! Mary Lou is happily asleep.

Leaving Honolulu was a romantic sort of dream-like experience. Everyone was covered with the heavy-scented flower leis. The Army Band was playing on the dock and as the boat moved slowly away and the mass of colored paper streamers, thrown from the boat to friends on the dock, started to break and blow away, they played the lovely Aloha Oe. Then they started to throw the leis into the water, and as we got farther out, the shining coppery Hawaiian boys jumped or dove from the top deck of the boat, their slim bodies flashing gracefully through the air and being lost in the foaming water far below us. We passed close by the newest and largest of Uncle Sam's battleships and then on out of the harbor, watching a tropical sunset at sea, which was painting all the clouds and sky far around with gorgeous quick-changing tints of varying shades. Then slowly it faded and a tiny moon came out, and we could look back to the dark mound on the horizon, covered with myriads of twinkling fireflies that was Honolulu.

The days since have been lovely ones. This institution of putting the clocks back forty minutes every night is one I'm highly in favor of making an international custom. I like starting to bed at ten and getting there at nine-thirty.

Aboard S.S. Hokurei Maru   *Thursday noon, September 27, 1934*

Dear Folks –

By this time tomorrow we should be on land. These boats can't go up the river to Tientsin till there is more water in the river, so we have to land at Tanku on the coast and take the train. We feel as if we're on the last lap of our journey.

Losing our baggage has had a distinct advantage; [52] Walter had saved much writing to do on this boat; now everything is in his briefcase, so he hasn't been able to write a bit. I had hoped to type many letters, too, but none of my paraphernalia is here – Even my knitting is absent, so my hands have even rested.

This crossing has been well planned so that we've been on the open sea at nights and along the

---

52   Some of the family's baggage was lost during the boat transfer in Japan.

coasts and islands during the day. Every day we've been in sight of land; the first two days along Japan's coast and Inland sea, simply filled with islands; the next along the coast of Korea, with more islands; today along the China coast. The sea's been like glass, the days nice warm fall weather, the nights full of moonlight on the water and lighthouses on rocky points. We've been completely lazy, doing nothing, not dressing up – lying on deck watching green islands of all shapes and sizes rise out of the water in the distance, steal slowly toward us, and then recede as slowly, vanishing into the horizon.

I must tell you another good joke on us. We had no tickets to ride this boat and no money to get any. Well, Walter asked what the fare was, went ashore at Moji the first day and cashed his last small traveler's check into enough yen to cover the charge. Back on the boat, after we were several hours out from shore he went to the purser to pay and discovered that they had told him the price of *one* ticket. So again he didn't have enough money!! They didn't like this irregularity much either, so he passed the hat among the passengers & collected enough to get us to China. He borrowed from the Tientsin missionary who can easily be reimbursed by our North China treasurer who lives in Tientsin – Mr. Grimes. He is our business agent out here, manages our freight, our orders, our money, etc. This has certainly been a funny bundle of mix-ups, only none of them has seemed to upset us very much. I'm learning to take everything very calmly! …

We're all well and happy and rested and eager to get going. And privately, I'll tell you & Dad that I'm awful terrible glad I'm Mrs. Walter H. Judd. My very bestest love to you both.

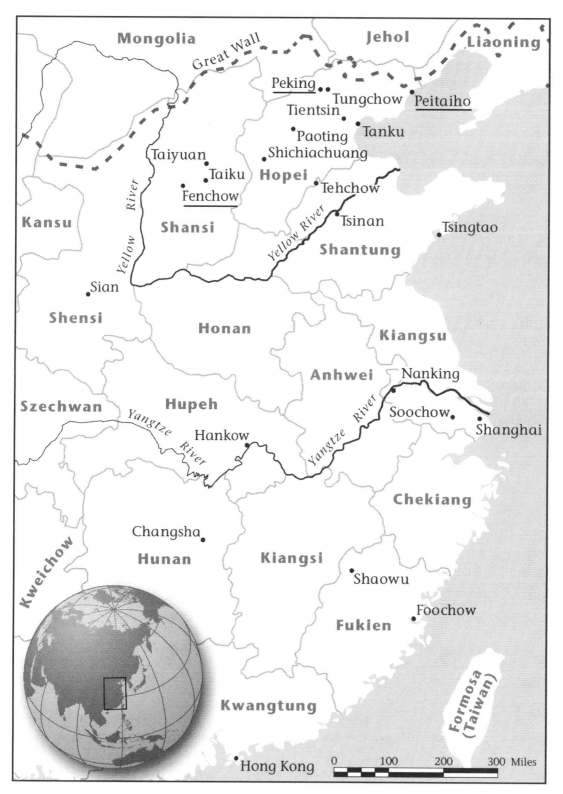

Map of China during the time period the Judds lived there.
Map by the University of Minnesota Cartography Lab.

Historical Background for 1930s China and Shansi Province

Courtesy of P. Richard Bohr, Professor of Asian History and Director of Asian Studies,
College of Saint Benedict/Saint John's University

What Miriam saw in Fenchow and throughout Shansi Province was the convergence of cataclysmic historical forces, including a protracted civil war between Nationalists and Communists as well as Japan's intensifying occupation of China. After Japan surrendered in 1945, the Communists, promising a more populist solution to China's problems, defeated the Nationalists. (The Judds strongly advocated for US support of the Nationalists.)

The China Setting

By 1850, America began paying attention to China, which was increasingly plagued by poverty, famine, and civil unrest following the collapse of its old imperial order and the incursions of European and Japanese powers. Missionaries went there in hopes of helping with huge needs including education and medicine. Medical missionaries went there at the forefront of this effort. By 1900, China had become the most popular of all American mission fields.

Americans strongly supported the efforts of Dr. Sun Yat-sen, a Christian convert trained in Western medicine, to transform China along U.S. lines. In 1912, Sun and his revolutionary supporters replaced two millennia of dynastic rule with the "Republic of China," based on Sun's American-inspired "Three People's Principles" of nationalism, democracy, and government services. He formed the Nationalist Party (KMT) to implement a U.S.-style government based on separation of powers. In 1921, Mao Zedong founded the Chinese Communist Party (CCP) to eradicate poverty, illiteracy, and inequality through rural revolution, ostensibly in the spirit of Sun's vision and with some Soviet inspiration.

Sun hired Generalissimo Chiang Kai-shek to create a Nationalist army to force China's warlords to unify under the KMT. In 1925, Sun Yat-sen died of cancer. Two years later, Chiang began driving urban Communists into rural areas like Shansi. By 1928, he had achieved China's nominal unity and established the nation's capital at Nanking.

Since 1912, Shansi had been governed by General Yen Hsi-shan, the "Model Warlord" who adopted Western science and technology and promoted women's education, abolition of foot-binding, and eradication of opium. He also supported Madame Chiang's leadership of the New Life Movement, a campaign initiated in 1934 to reform individual Chinese through Confucian "propriety, justice, honesty and self-respect" as a counter to Communist revolution. Madame Chiang, a Methodist, infused Christian idealism into the New Life Movement.

By 1936, Shansi was locked in a vice grip. From the east, Japan's troops advanced into north China from their puppet state in Manchuria. From the west came the Communists, guerilla fighters who promoted land reform among the impoverished peasants. Yen's troops were not strong enough to battle both enemies at the same time, and he requested that Nationalist troops be dispatched from Nanking. Japan formally invaded the whole of China in July 1937, precipitating Miriam's evacuation as described in chapter five, and prompting her public condemnation of Japanese imperialism and her campaign to urge American women to boycott Japanese silk stockings.

Chiang's Nationalists and Mao's Communists combined forces against the Japanese and were victorious – following which their civil war resumed. After four years, the Nationalists were unable to turn back the Communist tide. Mao proclaimed the "People's Republic of China" on October 1, 1949, and Chiang and thousands of Nationalists retreated to the island of Taiwan and proclaimed the "Republic of China" on Taiwan.

If the U.S. had been more willing to support the Nationalists, might the outcome have been different? America was facing an isolationist streak at home, was preoccupied with war and reconstruction in Europe, and had little interest and limited expertise in the Orient. Because Americans are gradualists by nature, few of them supported Mao but felt uncertain about Chiang's leadership. The Judd's perspective was that Chiang's difficulties were not unlike those in the U.S. after our Civil War – exhaustion, confusion, and a good bit of corruption. They generally rejected Communist totalitarianism and subjugation by force, vastly preferring the Nationalists as the lesser of two evils. The rest of the story is history.

—Prepared by P. Richard Bohr and Mary Lou Judd Carpenter

3

Peiping Experience

1934 – 1935

Miriam at the Great Wall

Walter and Miriam arrived in China on September 28, 1934 after three weeks on board ships, and then traveled five hours by train to reach Peking. Walter spent ten days helping Miriam and Mary Lou move into a student dorm/hostel and get somewhat acclimated with a native "Amah" to care for Mary Lou. Since Walter had spent a year in Nanking in 1925 learning the Chinese language, Miriam would spend seven months in Peking doing the same. Walter left for his hospital in Fenchow, which was thirty-three hours by train further inland in Shansi Province. They would not see each other for three months.

Miriam settled into dorm life and classroom studies at the College of Chinese Studies. It was a stimulating time for her. Naturally gregarious and curious, she made friends easily with her fellow students, and with the many people who came through the college on their way into China. Her thirty-nine fellow students came from all over the world, ranging from some sanctimonious missionaries to transferred military people, physicians like her husband, and reporters covering the news of this remote country.

In addition to caring for Mary Lou, Miriam visited places of significance, met Madame Chiang Kai-shek, and taught American cooking to Chinese women from the Peking YWCA. She participated in the Double 10 Club, comprised of ten Chinese working to learn English meeting with ten Americans trying to learn Chinese. I was mostly taken care of by my Amah, who spoke only Chinese and helped us both learn the language.

My father had a tough time at the mission, as he found the hospital in disarray. He had to fire some people, including a Chinese doctor, at the same time as he was trying to fit into the community. Miriam wrote him supportive letters as she continued her language studies, especially after he received a wire that his own mother had died back in Nebraska. Sadly, his mother's letters to him kept coming after she had died, given the slow pace of mail.

Walter remained at the hospital alone for seven months, only coming once for two weeks to join his little family for Christmas in the dorm. Finally, in May, he came to take us on the long voyage to the

Mission Station in Fenchow, which was to be our new and permanent home. There was a tremendous volume of luggage, including rugs, Victrola records, and provisions, such as cloth for the garments Mother would sew for me as I grew.

Peking   *Saturday, October 2, 1934*

Mother dear –

Our Japan boat got to Tanku Bar 2 a.m. Friday last, waited until 5 for the tide to take it over the bar and into the river, docked at 6 a.m. Then swarms of coolies were on board, & moneychangers & officials & a man with a note for us from the Mission in Tientsin & instructions to care for us. He managed our luggage thru customs, paid coolies, weighed & checked it at the station, bought our tickets etc. – a Chinese man. Mary Lou had her cereal and then slept blissfully thru the terrible noise of the cranes unloading with their rumbling motors, coolies calling, talking loudly, moving up & down corridors. I stayed in the cabin with her & read till noon when we had our lunch & went ashore to the nearby railroad station to get our train to Peking… It was a rainy grey day, we went thru waterlogged countryside and little villages disconcertingly filthy with mud and massed hundreds of heaped-up mounds that are graves; in the train, our second-class car was full of soldiers and common people, no other whites, and babies cried; the waiter constantly walked up & down the aisle with hot tea or food, or Chinese books & magazines, or hot towels; the spittoons, which are mere holes in the center of the aisle every few feet, were used frequently – altogether, I was glad when our five hr. trip was over.

At Peking we were met in a car by our North China ABCFM General Secretary[53] and in a few minutes were in our rooms in the Language School. And then started Mary Lou's four-day siege. She'd had too much travel and the attention & handling that goes with it; too many new places & people & ever-shifting scenes. She started in the minute we put her in her nice wooden crib, and cried practically four days straight. Always before she would play happily for hours when left alone. Now, not only did she not want to be left alone but she wanted to be held, holding up her little arms to be picked up & displaying terrible temper when we failed to do what she wanted. She cried herself to sleep in a few minutes the first night, slept all night; started crying in the morning right after her six o'clock bottle – we stuck it out for half an hour – then gave in and held her. We gave the Amah strict instructions *not* to pick her up except to change, feed, or bathe her. Then we hardened our hearts to the great & continuous bellows of rage… Sunday she cried most of the time she was awake. Monday I went off to school, Walter supervised the Amah, still Mary Lou cried – tho' weaker & less frequently. Tuesday we could tell she was pretty near broken, tho' she wouldn't give up & kept on at intervals. Wednesday morning she woke up with a smile and a great burst of enthusiasm and activity in her play – the first since we landed (Friday) – and we knew it was all over. Since then she's been her old sweet heartbreaker self, flashing smiles constantly, playing alone in her pen happily for hours, sleeping well & eating well, & even suddenly producing two new upper teeth… We are so glad we stuck it out when we did – mutually reinforcing each other's weakening backbones – for now I know she will be all right & I have no qualms about Walter leaving.

---

53   Earle Ballou was the American Board of Commissioners for Foreign Missions (ABCFM) North China General Secretary.

Our five bags from Japan landed here this morning – but the trunk that went on to Shanghai has not yet showed up. Walter will leave for Fenchow tomorrow night, Sunday, probably.

Peking   *Monday, October 8, 1934*

Walter – My darling –

Today has been as busy a day as those you spent here. I've missed you and I've thought of you constantly, but I haven't had the blues or the "all gone" feeling. In fact I've been strongly "sustained" and kept happy (perhaps because so busy) and enthusiastic. Mary Lou has been a darling, trying to make up to me for the loss of you – and what a comfort she is! I put her to bed tonight – she got the giggles as I was undressing her and we had a great old romp on the bed… I took her down to the sitting room with me after tea when Miss Chien, the YW General Secretary, came to see me. She wanted me to take the English class,[54] which I gracefully refused, but probably got myself in for a cooking class. I'm embarrassed at the tho't of trying to teach Chinese ladies foreign cooking… What they want really is to appear smart in serving foreign dishes when they entertain, and I guess I can fuss with them over those as well as anyone. I'd like the contact with the Chinese women.

Peking   *Saturday, October 13, 1934*

Walter – My Darling –

We've had the gorgeous-est day at the Summer Palace! The Mayor of Peking sent his secretary personally with us, Mr. Chen. First off, he took us to the Princess's great Audience Room. This is plainly marked on the outside – not open to the public – and none of the ladies had ever been inside… It was thrilling to see the seal broken by a soldier at the command of Mr. Chen. And it was more thrilling to be inside where all sorts of ambassadors and diplomats had been received… There were two gorgeous cloisonné vases about five feet or more tall, and some lovely old bronzes. All the furnishings were exquisite – carved seats, brocades, and silks that were scrumptious, two huge peacock feather fans, glorious porcelains, and "knickknacks" of all sorts. We ate our picnic lunch in the boathouse beside the lake, all arranged for us with chairs and tables. Then on we trekked in the afternoon to see the Empress's living quarters including her huge bed, the Princess's rooms, the rooms where the Emperor was imprisoned by his mother, the courts of the ladies-in-waiting and the chief eunuch; climbed up all the steps to the temple of the ten thousand Buddhas, came down the steep hill thru some lovely rock gardens and caves; saw the bronze pagoda that was not destroyed as were all the other buildings in 1866 when the place was burned; saw the lovely bridges, the bronze cow, the jade fountains in the distance, the marble boat – but this must sound just like a stock market report!

What I enjoyed most was the beautiful walk around back of the hill, visiting the ruins of the former palace, the delightful sheltered little paths and pavilions and waterfalls and streams and tea rooms and fish ponds that make up the "estate" where the Dowager loved to wander & which most tourists don't bother with. To me it was more lovely in its natural beauty and glorious views of the hills and scenery than the front of the hill where all the gorgeous splendor is. Someday can we just wander out there all day – with a book, maybe, and a picnic lunch? I can't think of anything I'd enjoy more.

---

54   Miss Chien wanted Miriam to teach the YWCA English class.

Last night I went to a meeting of the Double Ten Club at Hoovers.[55] The Hoovers started it in 1931 to strengthen international friendships, establish student contacts, and practice language speaking. All foreigners must speak Chinese; all Chinese, English. They have short talks, corrections by the language critics, games, refreshments, and it's generally an informal group. I think it will be interesting to be in – meets every other Saturday eve and I enjoyed it last night.

Peking   *Wednesday, October 15, 1934*

Dear Folks –

This is a grand place to live. Not just Peking, which is the most interesting city in the world, I'm sure, but the Language School. Everything is most modern, with home-style buildings, plumbing, heating, and furnishings. There's rather an extensive grounds, enclosed inside a high wall, as is everything in China, and opening onto a narrow muddy alley just wide enough for a car to traverse, and looking in general like the back door to someone's barnyard. But inside are beautiful grounds, lovely gardens with the fall flowers growing in profusion, grassy lawns with wicker chairs arranged for leisure. There are two main dormitories, one for most of the students and the other for "people with babies" and for tourists or travelers of whom we have a continually changing stream, for this is a most reasonable place to stay in China. We all dine together and the dining and sitting rooms are lovely. Upstairs we have two large rooms connecting, with a small kitchenette next door and the bathroom just down the hall, and loads of closet and storage space… I have a grand Amah for the baby – her name is Ma Ni Ni, which I believe means Grandmother Elephant (the elephant for my India background, I suppose). She has taken care of Language School children before so she has excellent sense about the tremendous necessity of sterilizing everything, which is such an inviolable law in this germy land. To get a clean Amah is like finding a precious jewel. She and Mary Lou love each other to pieces. She does the baby's daily wash and all my personal things and irons, mends, darns, sews for me…

And what about the language study? Well, I still love it; I'm learning so fast that the terribly discouraged stage hasn't arrived. There is a very small school this year – under forty, I believe. Twenty or so are beginners, scattered among the English, Scotch, Canadians, Irish, Danish, Swedish, Americans, and one New Zealander. The first week we just listened from 8:45 to noon, with a recess, and from 2 to 4. Every half hour a new Chinese gentleman in his graceful brocade gown would enter, we would rise and bow respectfully to our teacher as he returned the bow; then we would listen to him repeat the words we knew and say sentences using just the vocabulary we were familiar with, and occasionally adding a new word, the meaning of which was made clear with actions, gestures, facial expressions. They really are the most marvelous actors and it's quite thrilling to enter class each day and wonder what new words will be added to our vocabulary and how they will be introduced, for not a single word of English is ever spoken. It's just like attending a theater daily…

The second week we were allowed to try out saying the sixty or so words we had listened to all the week before. We said sentences after the teacher, and were given sheets with the written characters for all these words, which we had to learn to recognize and read, but not write. So here I am at the beginning to the third week actually able to read a lot of inspiring sentences like "I have no pen; I will not write." "Who is speaking?" It does get a bit monotonous at times… At least I got

---

55   The Hoovers were YMCA leaders.

about ten inches knitted on my green boucle skirt! Now we have two general classes a day where we all meet together to learn the new words and for review. Then we work in groups of four, changing every half hour to a new teacher, or else with a private teacher who drills on individual pronunciation difficulties. Besides this, we have three-hour lectures on China: history, geography, background, culture, religion, literature, art, and the rest. These are in English, given by various authorities on the difference lines and are most interesting. I want you to get the idea that I'm enjoying it all tremendously…

Sunday is hardly a day of rest for me, for the Amah has that day off, till four in the afternoon, and I have a chance to get reacquainted with Mary Lou and also to learn just how much time it does take to bathe her, cook for her, feed her, change her, pick up her toys, take her out for a bit of an airing. Church is at 5:30 in the afternoon here, a nice little Union American church with about a hundred in the congregation usually…

We have been entertained to death. We ate dinner out every night Walter was here, except the first two when we were getting settled. One of the first nights there was a big mission supper at the Mission Compound for Brewer Eddy, with Sherwood Eddy.[56] Ate a Sunday dinner with Egbert Hayes, now student secretary at P.U.M.C.[57] They had a house full of Chinese guests, some fine Christian people, progressive & active, some in YW and YMs, others doctors… Went to a big "5-7 reception" of YM folks at the Dwight Edwards & met many friends, new and old. I went to the College Women's Club Fall luncheon. Over 100 women there & more than half are M.A.s, PhDs, M.D.s or Phi Betas! They had a clever skit, & announced the year's program, which sounds most interesting so I joined that – meetings once a month – and one does have to have some outside interests for relaxation after the strenuous concentration of Language Study. I dream a jumble of Chinese sounds & a muddle of Chinese characters & a hodgepodge of Chinese teachers these days.

– Private Writing –

October 16, 1934

    We – missionaries especially – say we're looking for God to open doors of opportunity. Sometimes we're opening our own doors & asking God to follow us in. We say we're doing God's work. Sometimes we're just doing our own work & hoping for God's O.K. Then when he comes right out & asks us to do a definite thing, suggests something he wants done, we say – "But, Lord" – it seems inadvisable, or too difficult, or absurd, or impossible, or against convention or the "rule of the mission" or too out of the way; or else it would necessitate leaving the work you're now doing, neglecting what is perhaps a useful contribution that you enjoy, that you've been at a long time (rut?). We don't stop to think that Ananias, a disciple, sent to hunt up Saul, of whose reputation he knew, said "But Lord –" (Acts 9:13-17). Fear he would be killed – Peter had a "But, Lord –" in his heart which God had to remove (Acts 10:28).

    But God can see farther than we can. "He is working his purpose out" and he will never ask us to do what we cannot, nor require of us things for which he does not give us the strength and ability – Acts 22:19-21

---

56   Brewer and Sherwood Eddy were brothers working with the YMCA in Asia and the ABCFM.

57   Peking Union Medical College.

Peking   *Sunday night, October 21, 1934*

My darling –

Your letter today, written last Monday made vivid what I'd already been feeling – the hospital situation is anything but straight sailing, or a bed of roses, and you'll have lots of messy work to do before you can go ahead to make your largest contribution. I'm sorry that it has to be so, and it more than ever makes me wish we could be with you. For tho' there's nothing we could do about it, still perhaps it would help to have someone to come home to and talk things out to, as you perhaps can't to the other Fenchow-ites. And perhaps it would help to have a tiny girl's inspiring smile and sweet innocent spirit to relieve the tensions of the strenuous days. So tonight you rest yourself a little bit with me, and I rub your forehead, and press the little tired hollows above your eyes, and stroke your strong, loved face, and kiss your temple, and whisper a little nothing-at-all in your ear, and leave so many things unsaid – that's my love for you, my husband.

Peking   *Monday p.m., October 22, 1934*

Darling –

Although I want you all the time, last night I *needed* to reach out and touch you. I woke in the middle of the night from the most ghastly dream of a baby's death – our baby evidently, but not Mary Lou – the horrible details were so vivid that the thing has stuck in my mind. It was all because she had been worse yesterday. Her temperature was up to 102.4. It's an intestinal upset, I feel sure. Tonight I promise not to have bad dreams.

Peking   *Sunday, October 28, 1934*

Dear Folks –

Yesterday was a Big Day for me, for I met Madam Chiang Kai-shek! Out at Yenching University they were having reunion luncheons for all the people hereabouts who went to Smith, Vassar, Bryn Mawr, Wellesley, Radcliffe, and Holyoke. I went out on the noon bus, rattled round over the narrow and deep-rutted streets full of fish, flesh, and fowl, studying my fifty Chinese character cards the whole way. Madame Chiang had been asked to come, being a Wellesley College graduate in 1917… She is a charming person to meet. Slight, or perhaps slender is a better word; she speaks English without any accent and in a lovely toned voice. She was wearing a black cut velvet Chinese gown with dark red flower pattern in it, earrings dangling to her shoulders, her hair in a knot low in the back of her neck, not bobbed as so many Chinese women have, and she looked much younger than her college graduation date would make her…

We had a real Chinese meal, with its characteristic bowl after bowl and course after course of deliciously cooked things. (Not to eat a little bit of everything would be most discourteous.) Luncheon being finished, the college group adjourned to sit in front of an open fire and talk informally with Madam Chiang, after each of us had been presented. There were about thirty in the group so we did have a feeling of intimacy. Then the questions started Madam Chiang talking about the New Life Movement and about the trip she and her husband are just completing through the northwest to see the work that is being done.

When people say to her, "Think of China's glorious past, her magnificent culture," she says she always remonstrates, because the glories of the past were for a limited number of people, and she is more interested in considering China's distressing present, particularly the state of the common people. There's no use trying to get back China's glorious past, for it wouldn't meet her present needs, but there is much of good in the past that can help her build in the present. The New Life Movement is founded on the four ancient principles: *courtesy*, a more than superficial politeness, something that comes from a deep-seated consideration of others; *social consciousness* (at least that is what we would call it and as near as I can put into a word what she was trying to explain); *honesty*, an important principle in a government that has so often been ruled by corrupt officials (sounds a bit familiar doesn't it?); and *modesty*, or unconcern about social position, as she put it.

This New Life Movement has been working in the frontier Provinces, trying to rehabilitate and reclaim rural districts formerly overrun by Reds.[58] They go about the villages trying to meet the need of each particular locality, whether it be supplying of money and supplies on easy payment terms for rebuilding of deserted villages and destroyed homes (the Cooperatives loan money at about 10%, a great improvement over the 40% to 60% generally charged), or the supplying of able-bodied young men to help plow and plant in districts where all the young men have been driven out leaving only the aged, or supplying assistance with the harvesting, organizing adult education and village industries, starting leader-training courses of three to six months where one outstanding man from each village may be trained to meet the particular needs of his own village – a better system than training outside leaders and sending them into localities with whose customs and families and needs they are not familiar, helping to eradicate the opium growing from those Provinces where it is excessively used, starting special clinics for medical needs of particular localities, such as trachoma, in the places where it is so universal, etc., conducting public health and sanitation work everywhere, and so on.

The work of the "Rural Economic Council" and of the "Five Provinces Educational Council" is carried on largely by young enthusiastic college graduates who are motivated by a desire to serve China. When asked about qualifications necessary to go into such work, as many women there were interested in connecting up college graduates of their acquaintance with such a valuable piece of work, Madam Chiang over and over reiterated that it was essential to have strong health – the living conditions are difficult and unsanitary – to have common sense, a characteristic she claims is too often lacking in college graduates!—and to have more than a general diffused idea of service, but a real passion for sacrificial living. This is tremendously important, for in China particularly the scholars of the past have not been imbued with any idea of the true purpose of an education being to better serve one's fellow men, and too often they have not been interested in taking on hard positions with little pay. The college trained men and women who are now doing this work for New China are getting about $30 (max.) a month for their living and personal expenses, and some of them could have had better paying jobs with big concerns. Madam Chiang said that when this Movement was started people told her the time was ripe for its foundation but that they could never get the personnel who were willing and qualified to undertake such a huge task, whose hardships I haven't taken time to write much of here, though she made them vivid to us, for she has been visiting these frontier places and seeing the work firsthand. But she said that the response to the call for workers had been

---

58   Chinese Communists bands.

most gratifying, for there had been more than they could possibly use at the beginning showing perhaps that the young intellectuals of China are eager to build up their own country and ready to live lives of utter sacrifice in their concern for their people.

Some one asked if these young people were Christian and she replied that most of them were, and that was quite logical for it took a person who knew and was trying to follow Christ's principles to know the meaning of sacrificial living as it was demanded of them. She paid the highest tribute to the missionaries whom she had met in these interior places where it sometimes takes five or six weeks to get a letter to Peking, and where contact with the outer world is so remote. She said it was not so much the physical privations that impressed her as the strain of carrying on unfalteringly in loneliness and often under discouraging conditions… She read a most interesting letter she had just received from George Shepherd, Walter's friend, who was just a day or two's journey from him the years he was in Shaowu[59] and with whom he often toured in the villages, the two of them doing medical-evangelistic work. Mr. Shepherd is now working as one of the secretaries of this Movement, and he drew a succession of vivid paragraphs – pictures from his own recent experiences showing how the work was slowly but surely bringing changes into the lives of the people and the villages.

I never could tell you all of what was said during the afternoon, nor give you the real picture of that gracious person talking so enthusiastically about the work she and her husband are so concerned with. It was interesting to me to think that here were the leaders of the government concerning themselves with the conditions of the common people in China, such a departure from the China of the past; and that these leaders were Christians.

Now if you don't mind descending from the sublime to the ridiculous, I'll tell you about the cooking class for Chinese ladies that I got roped in on here, under the auspices of the YWCA. When Miss Chien, the General Secretary, came to see me about teaching it, I asked her a number of things which she wasn't able to answer (she's new in Peking herself) but she said she'd find out – what economic background the women came from, how much money was available for materials, what they'd cooked in their class last year, and what sort of things they wanted to cook this year, what utensils were available, and what things were purchasable in Peking. The next thing I knew I had word that the class would start on Thursday of that same week at 4:30, and would I send her at once the recipe for whatever we were going to make the first time and a list of necessary materials. I was stunned. To all my definite questions she answered vaguely, if enthusiastically, "everything will be all right. I'm sure you're a good cook. We can get anything you want, *anything*." …I got good advice from some of the American ladies here, and armed with this started off for Miss Chien's Chinese home where the class was to be held.

I had thought it best to start with something easy, something that all could have a hand in, something that required no stove…that had variable ingredients in case Peking couldn't produce the materials I was used to at home. So I planned fancy sandwiches for teas and had sent along a modest list of supplies, of which Miss Chien had "forgotten" to get at least half. With a smile large enough to cover my sinking heart and my quaking knees I set to and with the use of chopsticks, bowls, knife, and hot water – the *only* utensils available in this tiny, dark, not-too-immaculate Chinese kitchen – managed to stir up some enthusiasm! Of the seven members one spoke enough English to translate. She is

---

59   Walter was practicing medicine from 1926 to 1930 in Shaowu, a region in northwestern Fukien Province, in southeast China.

older, a YW Board member, has a lot of sense, and I think will help me greatly. The others are younger married "ladies of leisure," apparently fairly well off. We conducted this first class with the ladies having their heavy coats on and their pocketbooks held tightly under arms while they sliced bread and tomatoes, cleaned celery, mixed mayonnaise, and what not. No telling what they thought of me with my coat off, sleeves rolled up, big apron on.

Miriam teaching Chinese women American cooking

In spite of the handicaps we managed to turn out a delicious and good-looking sandwich loaf, and a large plate of assorted fancy sandwiches, and they seemed pleased at the results. One of the ladies was a bride of two weeks and when her husband came to take her home, as we were eating our tea and sandwiches, she proudly showed him our handiwork, pointing to the sandwiches that she herself had made in flower petals, stars, hearts, etc., and with much decoration! I had just that day learned the Chinese words for teacher and pupil, so I told them that I was the pupil, they were the teachers, for I didn't know how to do things in China. I really did learn a lot – good training for my later housekeeping days! Miss Chien evidently learned a lot, too, for as I'd give each person a job to do, in my best English-Chinese-cum-gestures, they'd evidently asked Miss Chien for implements that were not available. Just as I was leaving, she asked if I'd help her get some cooking utensils before next time, "for the YW ought to own some!"

Peking   *Tuesday p.m., November 6, 1934*

Darling –

The little girl is much better today – no temperature all day – but she had a few little tummy pains last night… So we're keeping her on milk again today… It certainly is heavenly music in my ears to hear her laugh and sing and talk again!

Mrs. R ate lunch at our table today and embarrassed me horribly by going on & on about what a martyr I am to be here studying, etc. Maybe if I took up a collection from all the people who think me a martyr, I'd have enough to come down to Fenchow for Thanksgiving. Oh no! I forgot! I can't! That's when I'm going to write my Christmas cards and letters!

You never wrote how your hard maternity case and your first GSW[60] came out. Are they both living? …Why don't you make a rule people can't get shot out of office hours? This letter tonight is useless but I know you can read in it all the things that aren't written –

---

60   Gunshot wound.

Peking   *Friday p.m., November 9, 1934*

Darlingest –

…I was interested to hear that the Japs were using some of their "returned Boxer indemnity" money to build a center for Chinese culture here in Peking. They hope to buy up old & rare books, objects of art, etc., and "preserve them for the Chinese!" This three-story building now being constructed has a well-built basement floor, and the roof is being put on in reinforced cement – why, can you guess!!

Peking   *Sunday, November 18, 1934*

Dear Folks –

I wish you might have been present at our Armistice Day sermon in our Union Church. Professor Nash[61] gave the most powerful talk I've heard in a long while. It was no idle sentimentality about the value of peace on earth, or pious sentiments about wishing that wars may cease. It was realistic in its pessimistic analysis of the present state of the world, and infinitely optimistic as to the possibility of creating a warless world if we're willing to pay the price of really being Christians – but it was made vivid that most of us today are not truly Christ's followers or wars could never be. He reminded me a bit of Reinhold Niebuhr in his epigrammatic and forceful way of saying things. It's when I hear things like this that move me that I miss Walter most, for we so rely on the sharing of experiences like this and of discussing and enlarging on them afterwards.

Peking   *Thursday p.m., November 22, 1934*

My husband! –

Isn't this a glorious moon! Last night was an absolutely perfect one and all evening long I just ached for you till it hurt. Will these weeks ever pass? Will I ever be able to have that delicious contented glow that comes when you snuggle up warm behind, put your arm over and hold me till we both drift together to sleep? Darling I need you so badly that I'm being a crybaby for a minute – but please don't lose any sleep over my recorded misery. I'll go on being busy and happy and studying hard and missing you like h--- just as I have done all these weeks – and soon it will be over. But gosh, doesn't it hurt to love.

Peking   *Saturday, November 24, 1934*

Dear Family All –

This week the College Women's Club presented two plays, followed by dancing at the Peking Hotel, to raise scholarship money for Yenching and Ginling[62] girls. I went with Dick Irwin, the boy who came to teach at the "Oberlin in Shansi" School (Congregational) in Taiku… Every once in a while the electric plant in Peking goes fluey and it would happen this evening that all lights went off when I was getting into the unfamiliar green evening dress. However, the moon was full and China moons are bright as day, as India moons are. So with blinds up I could see enough to not put toothpaste on my face in place of cream. Lights were off for two hours, so the candlelight dinner was lovely.

---

61   Professor Vernon Nash was an imminent Quaker thinker and proponent of world government.
62   Two local universities.

Peking   *Sunday, November 25, 1934*

Dearest –

Here's a lovely Sunday again, with our little girl playing happily on the floor beside me as I write, crawling around to investigate all the rugs, furniture, toys etc.

Darling, I'm getting terribly bothered about writing characters. It seems they want us to be able to write the first hundred by the end of the term. I feel it's all I can do to keep up with the memory work and reading the new characters and lesson sheets, an hour a night study. On top of this to learn to write characters, with their Romanization, tones, radicals with their numbers is a chore that comes very hard for me. No one has ever explained character writing to us or told us about the requirements or given us any help. It took me an hour to learn the first ten…

Friday I had quite a visit with Mr. Ballou in his office. I like him, tho' I never feel I know just where I'm at with him. He wanted to know all about Fenchow – how much am I supposed to know or tell about things there? Or is mission work everybody's business? Or does he know all about everything anyhow? He seems tickled to a toothpick with the firing job you did, says it's been needing doing for a long time and no one there could do it, says the Chinese General Secretary came back & reported good things of your job and said that Dr. W.[63] never could have done that "because he was too much like a Chinese!!" But they all seem to expect a whale of a lot of "crossy work at the dirt roads" and are holding their breaths till you start getting the kickbacks and the knifing and the underhanded meanness from the opposition. He gives you six months to get into a mess of trouble. He kept harping on this theme so I finally asked if he were preparing me to be a widow. He also mentioned how unsettled all the hospital personnel (of foreign doctors) is as far as to where they will work after this year. I feel sorta walking on eggs like about this whole missionary business. Come up'n see me some time. We could have more than a talk.

Peking   *Sunday, December 2, 1934*

Mother darling –

I've been putting in a lot of time studying, for exams come next week. But I have had time to barge around too. Monday night I went to ladies night at the Men's Brotherhood of the Union Church here… Over 200 ate a delicious Chinese meal, then listened to Dr. Hu Shih, the leading Chinese philosopher, head of National University in Peking, a well-known leader of thought. He talked most interestingly on "Is China Making Progress?" – talking of how much China had to do in a negative way, how much she had to destroy or eliminate before she could truly be great. A forum followed. It is so interesting to meet with such a live and cosmopolitan group – Chinese, English, American et al. – people doing things…

The Thursday Thanksgiving Church Service was lovely – a sermon by our Mr. Ballou and such reminders of our splendid American heritage as to make my throat quite lumpy. I don't think ever at home I was touched with such a feeling for all that is fine and strong and right in the history of our country and its makers, and hated worse to think of the black spots in its reputation and present actions.

---

63   The previous hospital superintendent.

Peking   *Wednesday, p.m., December 5, 1934*

Darlingest –

For two days I've deliberately kept from writing you, for I was afraid my letter wouldn't sound very stoic. I guess there's not much use trying to disguise the fact that I want you plain bad. You can't get here any too soon for me! Life is much too short and far spent now, for us to go on living so tentatively. It's plain not right for you to be missing all of Mary Lou's inspiration and loveliness… Perhaps I'm a little tired, and worried about the exams – but you keep crowding in between me and my memory work, your face slides in between me and the characters, your presence comes in and steals away my concentration. I love you, my darling, and this is one of the times when I can't make anything else matter. (Snap out of it, Miriam, and get some cold facts recorded!) I'm going off to bed. I love you.

– Private Writing –

Friday, December 7

I found today one answer for that secret dread I have always had of "going stale" in a small or isolated mission station – "In the wilderness shall water break out, and streams in the desert, and the glowing sand shall become a pool, and the thirsty ground springs of water. In the habitation of dragons (CHINA!) shall be grass with reeds and rushes… And a man shall be as a hiding place from the wind, and a covert from the tempest; as rivers of water in a dry place, as the shadow of a great rock in a weary land." (Isaiah 35:6, 7; 32:2) – What a promise! And what a challenge!

Peking   *Sunday, December 9, 1934*

Mother dear –

I wish you could see Mary Lou playing around on the floor here as I write. She has on funny little dark blue overalls with red edgings that the Amah made for her. She bought the material herself. They just don't appreciate our love of pale pinks & blues and whites. But she felt very proud of her purchases, and this navy won't show the dirt so quickly after Mary Lou spends a day dusting the floors, so I'm saying nothing…

Thursday & Friday we have three exams – I can read all our 350 characters and write the 100, though I'm not absolutely certain of all of this. But 'cause Walter was so good in Chinese (as in everything!) I'd love to do well in these exams – matter of pride! He's been writing me not to overwork studying, as he realizes that the baby takes no little time & effort so doesn't expect me to do brilliantly – which is all the more reason why I'd like to surprise him!

Yesterday our Double Ten Club had its Christmas party. Each took a ten-cent gift. We folks from the Language School gave three scenes from the Bethlehem Story, which the Chinese seem to have enjoyed. Very few of them are Christians. On Friday afternoon we students had given our school party for the Chinese teachers, their wives and children – forty-one teachers and 135 children. We had a program in the auditorium – stunts, acting out of Chinese proverbs etc., music.

Last Sunday after church I went home with Dick Irwin to the Chinese home where he stays. The family are highly educated people… We had a Chinese supper – then sat in front of the fire and talked long on many subjects… One of her sons is engaged to an American girl & Dick is interested in a Chinese girl so the subject of mixed marriages got some attention.

I love getting your letters Mother dear. They bring you so close – How I love you for all the strength you continually give me – not take out of me – I love you for lots else!

Peking   *Wednesday, December 12, 1934*

Darling –

Your sweet understanding letter with the advice about exams was waiting when I came from my written and oral exam. It fitted the occasion exactly. It's funny how much you know about me without my telling you! The written exam was a cinch – and stupid, too, as far as testing our knowledge of Chinese language usage, I tho't. We were each given eight minutes for oral exam – most took ten, some fifteen. When I walked into Mr. Hayes's exam room, he said "I think I can finish you off in about three minutes" – which I took to mean not that I knew so little that I could say it all in three minutes (which I might have tho't if I were less conceited!) but that he tho't I knew my stuff generally and wasn't going to bother with me. Tonight I saw him at the big binge and he said "Good exam today, Mrs. Judd." …

Hope the time will come when I don't have to go out evenings with a substitute for my husband and don't have to go to bed alone at night. Your lonesome and love-wanting – Miriam

Peking   *Friday, December 28, 1934*

Dear Family All –

Our first Christmas in China has come and gone, and what a happy time it was for us, as we hope it was for all of you. Walter came along, getting here Christmas Eve about eight o'clock, and with a steadily improving throat which is almost its normal self now.[64]

Christmas morning was a happily confused time for us three. Mary Lou wasn't sure that she was going to approve of this strange man that had suddenly appeared in her domain so she kept a safe distance, eyeing Walter seriously. He ignored her at first – watching her out of the corner of his eye all the time! Mary Lou was terribly intrigued with the tissue paper as it came off the parcels. It makes such lovely sounds when crinkled and tears in tiny pieces. What fun we had opening up the boxes, thumbing through the books, watching the gleam in Mary Lou's eyes as she made a grab for the cloth dolly that squeaks, the small box of blocks, the cloth picture book, and abandoned them all very quickly again for her beloved tissue paper and string.

Our victrola played Christmas chimes and sang Christmas carols and soon our breakfast appeared on trays, a concession to Walter's bad throat. So if you'd looked in on us at about ten o'clock on Christmas morning, as several of our friends did, you'd have found our Christmas-wreathed rooms

---

64   Snow and a bout of strep throat had delayed his departure.

a happy jumble of torn tissues paper strips, strings and ribbons, scattered toys, books and gifts, breakfast trays empty – and all presided over by three bathrobed figures, one particularly important in inverse proportion to her size! Soon she decided that Walter was not going to chew an ear off so became more friendly but they didn't get too close that day till Walter's throat should be improved. Now she has quite accepted him into her circle, allows him to play ball, ride her in her kiddie car, and hold her occasionally if she's too tired to want to play.

They had a nice Christmas dinner here at the school for the dozen or so students who hadn't gone visiting for Christmas and the twenty-odd transients who make this their headquarters in Peking. Next evening our mission had their big Christmas party, with the American Boarders from Yenching University in to Peiping for a turkey dinner at which forty of us sat down. It was a real *family* party, with carol singing and Christmas readings afterwards and we had an interesting time visiting with friends and co-workers that we don't often get to see. Today Walter has gone to Tientsin for a day for errands, shopping for Fenchow, business for the hospital. Last night we had a huge batch of mail, and what fun we had reading the family letters together, and the many cards with messages from friends who were thinking of us. That's one of the things we miss most in being separated – the reading together of letters from home.

Peking   *Friday, December 28, 1934*

Mother dear –

We are in the midst of a joyous time, being together again. Walter is simply reveling in Mary Lou, content to sit and devour her with his eyes for hours on end. Yesterday he said she was the best thing that had happened to him in thirty-six years. I don't know where that leaves *me*, but I'm not terribly worried! …

I must answer some of your questions. The Amah speaks a few English words but mostly talks to Mary Lou in Chinese, and she and I always talk in Chinese. She sleeps here at the school, in the servants' quarters but when I am out evenings, sits in my room knitting till I get back. Goes home Saturday p.m. till Sunday 4 p.m. Gets paid $16 a month plus $6 to the school for her board.

For our own plans, they are still indefinite. *Entre nous*, Walter and I are not finding the Language School as helpful as we had expected. He thinks the work here much inferior to that in his Nanking school. We have talked to a number of authorities on the subject of language study since he came, including Dr. Pettus[65] and perhaps there will be a few changes for the good this coming term. Partly the fault is not with the school but with the unbelievably dumb bunch of students this year – the stupidest Dr. Pettus has ever had by far, he says. We feel that one more term here will be enough for me. After that I'm sure I can go much faster and better studying alone, with the good teacher they have in Fenchow. So it's likely that when this next term ends, the middle of March, I shan't stay on here but move into Fenchow, perhaps living with the "single ladies" in their big house for a bit, so I won't have to do housekeeping but can study hard. The Reynolds go on furlough early in June & we are to have their house…

---

65   Dr. Pettus was the director of the College of Chinese Studies.

Before Walter arrived, I went on a big binge with the Hoovers. They were having a dinner party for a girl who was to be married. After the dinner we all went down to the famous Peiping Hotel to the annual Rotary Charity Ball, a big affair where all the elite of Peiping were assembled, including most of the missionary community and many Chinese – practically all the members of my cooking class in their beautiful Chinese gowns. Lyman Hoover bought lottery tickets for us & to my embarrassment, I was the only one in our group of eight to draw a prize – two lovely hand-tinted framed photos of famous Peiping scenes. I didn't like the whole evening too well. It was too ambitious and expensive to fit into my ideas of what missionaries are here to help China do, and I'm afraid even the tho't that the money was going for charity didn't sooth me much.

Peking   *Tuesday, January 8, 1935*

Mother dear –

Walter left last night, having been here exactly two weeks! I never saw him so reluctant to leave before – Mary Lou is just too strong a magnet. We didn't do many outside things. He was perfectly happy to stay here & play with our young scamp, and play the victrola. He didn't write a single letter while he was here nor read any.

Peking   *Tuesday, January 15, 1935*

Mother dear –

Now to answer a few questions. You mentioned that no opium is grown in Shansi, etc. This Province has what has been called the model governor, but he, Yen, has degenerated greatly and the Province is not nearly as high as it was. There is much opium smoking and Yen himself controls the opium trade & makes money off it. But it has the reputation of being the *one* Province in China where banditry is absolutely repressed…

Chiang Kai-shek is the military head of China, which amounts to his ruling China tho' he is not technically the President. He is always spoken of as China's number-one man… About P.U.M.C., there were 300 or so M.D.s on the staff & probably under 100 are foreigners…

Wen-li is the classical language of China in which all the great classics & books of wisdom are written and differing considerably from the spoken and written language of today – tho' the *characters* are all the same, constructions & idioms & expressions are different.

Peking   *Friday p.m., January 18, 1935*

Darlingest –

I thrill like a blushing schoolgirl every time your letters come, my husband – lover. It's a deep, moving tide of joy and love that wells up inside at the thought of what we mean to each other. You are an old sweet to write for me to get the silver tea tray set. Of course I won't get it. But I don't want you to think it's because I have any ECM[66] feelings or false heroics about being a *poor*

---

66   Early Christian Martyr.

missionary. It isn't. It's that I don't want it. That's true. As I look back over my life there have been few things that I've wanted – I'm talking about buyable things now. Oh, there were lots of things I liked, enjoyed seeing because of their intrinsic beauty or loveliness, and I may even have said "I'd like to have that"… I've always realized that there were many things not within reach of people like me and no useless wishing would make them so. Having them and many more were no guarantee of happiness. Besides, I have so much not-buyable to make me happy that *things* don't seem to worry me. I do remember vividly once something I wanted, and I could even have had that, if I hadn't been scared to speak of it to Mother – thinking it would be selfish and wrong to ask for more clothes out of our small income. It was when I was "growing up" – just starting high school and my clothes didn't seem to be like the other girls' and I felt conspicuous and out-of-style in them, and yet I knew they were good, durable, wearable things and I shouldn't complain. I was shy and self-conscious and longed for attention from the boys – even then! – and thought my queer clothes branded me forever as *different*.

I suffered more those coupla years than any other time I can remember. For one thing a child can't stand, at the self-conscious stage, is to be *different* from the others. I hope I may be sensitive enough and close enough to our children when the time comes to save them from any *needless* suffering of this kind. Not that I think they can always be bought everything they want, but there are ways and ways of meeting problems and I hope I'll be able to devise some… If we are going to try to live more simply and nearer the Chinese, there's no use starting with piling up *things*. So you may always hear me say I love perfume, and silver tea services, and a new Ford 8, and all sorts of thises and thats, that I could use, but I don't truly want. But a silver tea set is in the realm of the "admired but unwanted" still. When I really want something I will come and talk it over with you, and for the rest, you may expect to hear me chatter away senselessly about something "I'd just love to have" and would never buy if I had the money.

Peking   *Friday, February 1, 1935*

Mother dear –

Beginning today noon, we have holiday till next Wednesday for China New Year & this breathing space comes most appropriately for my needs. But China New Year is also the basis of my difficulties. My Amah, as near as I could discover, wanted to go off somewhere for four weeks at this New Year time – they all like to get back to their ancestral home if they can. Since there had been a number of places where she was sadly falling down I decided to let her go permanently. But good Amahs are *impossible* to secure here and are passed on from friend to friend. I hadn't realized this nor appreciated how lucky we were to have Mrs. Pettus bring us this good Amah our first day here – for she has been lovely with Mary Lou. I spent *hours* calling up my friends to help me – and a phone call here is a day's work, with only Chinese-speaking operators and no American efficiency, and Chinese-speaking servants answering the calls. I nearly got frantic… Anyhow, I have an Amah now and I hope she's going to work out all right. I have had to stay closer home to keep my eye on everything. I don't want her to slip up on sterilizing bottles and food jars, and on the cooking – and this is all new to her…

This China New Year for celebrating just backs our Christmas festivities right off the map. The shops are lavishly decorated with red paper cutouts and paper hangings, gorgeous colored lanterns; everything is colorful and festive; the streets are thronged; everyone is in a gay mood and expects double pay for rickshaw fare or any other duty; and no serious work can be done for days before and after *the* day, which comes next Monday.

Miriam and Mary Lou in Peking

Peking   *Wednesday, February 6, 1935*

Darling –

I'm back from one of the nicest and most stimulating evenings I've had in a long time. It was a supper meeting of the Mother's Club, held at the church. Betty Price & John Hayes, two members of the "Born in China" club gave an entertaining as well as intelligent "conversation" or dialogue on the subject of children raised in China. Betty had written to folks now in China who had been children here for their reactions & had received frank & interesting replies…on such conflicts as "conforming vs. individualism;" having *no* country, since in China you are a foreigner, in U.S. an alien; varying sets of values; the home as a center for teaching the best of Chinese culture & friendship or creating a "little America," etc. Such problems as inferiority & superiority as applied to children raised here, the servant problem, schools, emotional & social stability, health, family separations, etc. all came in for good discussion. Betty's going to make a further study, writing to those in U.S. who *didn't* return to China, after being raised here, to get their slant.

– Private Writing –

February 11, 1935

"Ultimately our choice lies between a world within ourselves and a world outside; the crux of character is in that decision." And now I go to live in places in China where the "world outside" as I have heretofore known it, is largely taken away. Will I find the world within myself an ever satisfying and ever enlarging one? Or will my life still be longing for and dependent on the world outside? God knows my prayer. He will answer it.

Peking   *Tuesday p.m., February 19, 1935*

Darling –

Today in the "lecture period" Betty Price & John Hayes did again their "conversation" on bringing up children in China. Such things as gaining a false sense of importance because of the position we seem to have in this country, the problems that arise from conflicting values, conflicting loyalties, the whole question of our strategic position as interpreter of two cultures to each other – these I think would be of extreme value to all our group as missionaries to think thru. But at lunch, as usual, the discussion ranged round the stupid waste of our time. I tried to point out that it had touched some deep points on the life of the foreigner in China. C. said he tho't it was bad policy to anticipate difficulties and think out problems beforehand, that when the time came God would give us strength for whatever we faced. I am always disgusted with them… They haven't the faintest idea about China and its culture and hopes and strivings and aspirations and peoples. They're living in their own tiny world from which, when the time comes, they will emerge regularly to preach the gospel at stated times & then retire again to their narrow box. I've felt like screeching at them all day – and instead I just spilled over to you, my safety valve.

Darling, is it a dream that I was once married to you and we used to live together? It seems to me I have *always* been separated from you. Let's not ever do it again, my beloved – never, never. I need to be beside you… Good night, my husband. Tonight I shall cry a little.

Peking   *Monday, March 4, 1935*

Mother dear –

There is a doctor at Fenchow who is giving much trouble now – being careless professionally, exposing all the children's ward to measles with his own sick child, and many of them contracted it; allowing a Bible School teacher's child to die thru neglecting to take serious care of it; not taking precautions with diphtheria cases, etc. – and feeling Walter is picking on him when he insists on higher medical standards. The man has real ability & skill when he hasn't a peeve on and Walter has been doing everything to avoid an open break with him, which would destroy his "face." For with Walter already having fired thirty-eight hospital employees, he'll get a bad reputation for firing people if he has to discharge this doctor. With a debt of $8,000 and this staff insubordination problem, Walter is finding his hands full.

Peking   *Friday, March 15, 1935*

Mother dear –

On Saturday we had a gorgeous trip to the Great Wall. The Language School put up picnic lunches and these we ate on the train before we reached our destination. We bargained for donkeys. The picturesque donkey boys guided our ponies along the narrow stony footpath about a mile, to the steps that led up the monstrous wall. There we left the donkeys and walked along on top of the wall, climbing up the mountain for over a mile. It was a grand sunny day, with a strong breeze blowing – strong enough to take my tam off over the mountains, to be chased half an hour by a donkey boy and eventually bro't back to me, all for ten cents. But the feeling that the Wall gives you just can't be described. You stand there on one of the very high points, look up and down valleys and mountains for miles around, just barely can see one tiny village and no inhabitants and no civilization, and yet there remains this solid stern wall, winding gracefully around the curves of the rises and valleys, built at what cost no one knows, and by what methods one can only guess, standing thru the centuries as a sentinel guarding this ancient people. There is something solemn and humbling about entering into this experience. You *can't* feel self-important or restless or small in the face of this enormity, and of such endless and eternal expression of nature in the mountains for miles around. I felt as if I had grown noticeably, and pettiness, smallness had left me, and the gale that was blowing up there on top of the world blew away much of the unimportant details that clutter our lives and left a sense of some of the deep and abiding values. I shall not forget this…

Miriam at the Great Wall

Letters have come again from Mother Judd who seems better now tho' for two weeks she was so bad she can't remember much of what happened. Gertrude writes that she is slipping fast, and everyone wonders how her heart ever stands even these attacks…

You almost make me jealous describing the lovely Sunday radio music. How I miss it! But the victrola is a great comfort. And last Sunday I went to a "tea concert" at the Peking hotel given by their orchestra – mostly Russians, and some nice solo singing as well…

No, I think there's no reason to avoid the subject of war with Japan in any correspondence. I don't think any of our letters are watched. But we don't hear much interesting or stimulating conversation here. The students are mostly dead from the neck up.

Peking   *Monday, March 25, 1935*

Mother dear –

School is going extremely well now that I'm about to leave! I'm studying in the mornings only, doing the regular class work except for the last hour in the morning when I have a private tutor and learn the "household words" – cooking and sewing terms, furniture, bedding, washing, marketing and all. They've given me the best teacher in the school for this class, so I'm having a *grand* time. I'm also making up the character writing I didn't do last term…

I'm busy buying supplies for Fenchow. I spent the whole afternoon in an excellent Chinese cloth shop, getting samples of bath toweling, curtain materials, cotton and prints, wool materials for winter dresses, silks, muslins for sheeting. I also got myself materials for making two single bed comforters for my guest room. (Perhaps you think that in such an out-of-the-way place we won't have much use for a guest room, but not so. Mrs. Reynolds said theirs was hardly empty all year. You see, travelers in China come through for all sorts of reasons and there are no hotels so we must be prepared to take in those we don't know. It seems a lot of Peiping folks come down in the winter for a short vacation and many of the men for hunting.)

I've been ordering food for the months ahead. It was a real job to guess how much we'd eat in what length of time, not knowing how many meal guests we'll have. Some things I've bought foreign brands, as coffee, spices, extracts, cans of vegetables, salmon, corned beef, tuna, etc. Some things I've got by bulk, yet sent from U.S.: dried fruits, soap chips, macaroni, dried peas & limas & lentils and navy beans, cocoa. Other things I've got Chinese: starch, soap, toilet paper, oatmeal, corn meal, sugar, cleansers, toilet disinfectants, etc. Some things I've got both Chinese and foreign to compare qualities. Butter comes in pound tins from Australia at $1.00. Also got mops & floor polish and such things as clothes rope, clothespins, oil lanterns, mothballs, etc. These things, fortunately, can be secured in one Chinese provision store where I have been getting things all year so the shopkeeper and I are acquainted. Thereafter, I'll write to order what I need. He'll pack & send by freight, allowing about a month to get to Fenchow. I'm laying in a supply of German knitting yarns; hunting up Singer sewing machine needles (I'm to use Mrs. Reynold's machine); ink by the quart; having fountain pens repaired; getting tennis balls, a ping pong set, blackboard & chalk… Are you interested in all this cataloguing?

I'm trying to do a bit of sightseeing here in Peking. One afternoon I went with a crowd from the School to visit a few of the Mohammedan mosques and see their most interesting centers… Another day I went with a group of nurses to see the "Bean milk station" run by the Methodists in a poor section of the city. They have two nurses and a part-time woman doctor to care for the daily clinics. They give out free bean milk to mothers of children that need it. They have some classes in homemaking & care of children – all extremely simple but valuable – and classes for children who couldn't otherwise go to school. It's a splendid project down among the poorest of the poor. After that we went all over the Sleeper Davis Hospital and then thru the Men's hospital that specializes on eye work. It's good to begin to get an idea how hospitals are run in China so I'll have some basis of comparison when I get to Fenchow.

Another evening I went to the Chinese theater. We went by full moon, a ¾ hr. rickshaw ride in the Chinese part of the city, to see one of the famous actors play. We've been having some interesting lectures in school on the Chinese drama, even had an actor come to "make up" for us, a complicated and meticulously important procedure in their system. The acting was splendid and the costumes worth going a long way to see. The din of the "orchestra" perpetually deafening one with its banging still bothers me. But I drank tea & munched melon seeds continuously, used the hot towels thrown to one from the head "ushers" at various parts of the theater with never-erring aim, and enjoyed trying to see how much Chinese I knew.

Peking   *Sunday a.m., April 7, 1935*

My Husband –

Last night after 1:30 I was wakened by a knocking and when I discovered it was a telegram I was so dopey from waking out of a sound sleep, it took me several moments to grasp the fact that the cable was from Rising City, and that your Mother was gone. What a blessed release for her.

After that I couldn't sleep. I wanted to be near you when you got the word, so that I could share in your thoughts as you look back over her life…the things she has done and been, so that we could reach out and touch each other in the night as we thought of Death and what parting from one's nearest means. For a while I held Mary Lou on my shoulder as she slept – she, a part of you whom I wanted to be near, and a part of your Mother who is gone…

It seemed so strange – your Mother's March 11 letter lay here on my desk – I had been reading it in the evening and thinking of her and of all your family. Then *your* Tuesday night letter told of your being so dead tired and going to bed early. Perhaps you were feeling her last tiredness, and suffering with her. Would she have got your special letter to her? I've been thinking almost constantly ever since of the events in Rising City, and particularly of your father. His years with her have been so long and so unbroken; his loneliness will be intense.

Nothing else seems very important to write. Mary Lou is no better today. Couldn't even keep milk down yesterday. I'll get Dr. Todd after breakfast.[67] I am especially with you these days.

Peking   *Saturday night, April 13, 1935*

My Darling –

It has seemed sort of a Divine Mockery that we have to be apart now and any attempt to see it otherwise has seemed like thin Pollyannaism. But tonight as you've been here with me while I wrote, it has somehow "come right." For I seem to realize afresh that even though the physical presence of a loved one can comfort in a particular way, it is the absolute understanding and trust of our deep love that bears us up and gives us rest – and that is a constant whether we are together or not. Somehow God, too, feels closer tonight than I have felt Him in a long time, as if he were saying reassuringly, "Can't you trust *me* to give Walter the comfort and the relaxation you are aching so to give?" Of course I can trust Him for this, Darling. So tonight I feel that we are all together – closely, in a realness that *is* real – God and your Mother and You and I – yes, and my Mother too. And feeling this I am ready to come to you, or to wait for you – whichever is best – without any restlessness.

Peking   *Sunday a.m., April 21, 1935*

My Beloved –

It's Easter Sunday morning! …Two years ago we had planned to go to church together in Rochester

---

67   Dr. Todd was a missionary doctor staying at the College and she cared for Mary Lou.

and instead you worked with two sick little boys to give them back their health. And tho' we did not worship *together in church* that day, as we will not today, our worship would have been less than right if we had purchased our "togetherness" at the price of sacrificing our duty or the clear path of what was right for us to do. So as we worship *apart* today we will be close to each other and to God because our lives are right… If we loved less we could never stand to be apart so long – there would be too much chance for misunderstandings, too much need for continual evident manifestations of our love. – Not but what I could stand a few manifestations! But I don't *need* them to know that I belong completely and only to you forever.

Poor little Mary Lou can't understand what's going on. Barbara L. (age sixteen) is trying to pass her Scout tests, one of which requires caring for a child for twenty-four hours. She came over yesterday at 2:30 & had a grand time outside playing with Mary Lou on seesaw & swing etc. But when bedtime came Mary Lou couldn't understand why her friend didn't go home, as usual… Barbara was a bit fearful lest something should be done wrong, lest the baby cry, etc., and our little tyrant sensed this and protested against the stranger washing her hands & face. I stayed out of the affair to give Barbara every chance, and because Mary Lou must learn; but she eventually got to screaming hysterically, so I had to send Barbara away & calm the tempest. She came back to spend the night here & we had a good talk on the handling of such occasions. This morning Mary Lou & Barbara had a grand time during the bath – I stayed away – but she shrieked again for a familiar hand at dressing time and the louder she yelled the scareder got Barbara, so again I had to intervene, finish the dressing & breakfast. Now they're out playing happily and at noon when she comes in for chicken soup & nap I'll be off at church, so the hope is that Mary Lou, not seeing her Mummie, will submit cheerfully to Barbara's tender ministrations. I'll be home soon after 12 so can patch up anything necessary.

Peking   *Wednesday a.m., April 24, 1935*

My Sweetheart –

It doesn't look as if any substitute doctor were in sight, from anything I know about it. That keeps you there indefinitely. Shall I come to you now, Darling, or shall I wait till you come for us? I want to wait for some reasons:

1. The joy of going to Fenchow as a united family, with *you* to carry our little girl in your arms.

2. The help you could give me here, advising about certain purchases, helping with crating or packing certain large unwieldy things.

3. The hope that if you did come in a month or six weeks or two months we could then still have our little vacation – honeymoon trip, or at least a few restful days together in the Western Hills.

4. The chance of finishing up the household course (and some more general work).

So Darling, if it's right that these considerations tip the balance, I shall be honestly content to stay tho' I shan't be any the less lonesome for you. But my mind & heart are quite at rest now.

Peking   *Friday a.m., April 26, 1935*

My dearest –

Yesterday afternoon Mrs. Bingham and I got a car & went to see the Hill Murray School for the blind, outside the City West gate. The driver supposedly knew where we were to go, but…he stopped in the middle of nowhere. It seemed he was lost. We started asking farmers along the way and they all had original ideas as to the road to take, and finally we met some rickshaw men who said they'd take us there as the car couldn't pass on the narrow road. We knew they were crazy because lots of people drive there so we insisted the car go on. The rickshaw men thereupon directed us to the wrong road, a short cut, and we soon discovered the car *couldn't* go! We were driving in a ditch, two wheels up on the side, the extra driver out walking along holding the car from tipping over. Eventually, we got out & just then met a blind man heading for the school so we attached ourselves to him & sent the car back to find the right road & get to the school. We felt funny tramping across dusty but cultivated fields in the middle of space, but we found the Blind School quite worth the trip when we reached it. They do excellent weaving, making of wicker furniture, making wood toys for children etc. I got an engine for Mary Lou (and Walter!).

Peking   *Wednesday, May 1, 1935*

Mother dear –

Tonight has come a telegram saying Walter will be here on Friday night to get us, and we'll be leaving for Shansi on Saturday night. And this is Wednesday! This means that he has asked Leonard[68] to come over from Taiku to take the afternoon outpatient clinics and tend to any emergencies over Friday, Saturday, & Sunday while he is away.

I've got two days to do a tremendous amount of packing, paying bills, last things which I have been waiting to do with Walter and must now do before he comes. Unfortunately, we're to go into Burton's house (they're on holiday) so I'll have to be concerned with running servants, etc. Meantime, you can be thinking of our great joy in being at last *in Fenchow together*. My, how good it is to have a deeply understanding Mother, whom you feel follows you in every move.

Fenchow   *Friday, May 11, 1935*

Mother dear –

Walter landed in Peiping on Friday at supper time, two days after his telegram saying he was coming. I had worked incessantly, had all the trunks packed, most of the errands done, but still a lot of "finishing up" things…and the next day was a mad scramble! All morning we shopped, using a car for speed; railroad for reservations, bank, drugs, hospital supplies, watch repaired, food for

---

68   Dr. Leonard Wilbur was the superintendent of the Taiku Hospital.

Mary Lou on the train. When Walter decided we had enough money to get a couple of rugs, I knew which place to take him to. We got two lovely ones, both 9 x 12.

In the afternoon we had Victor Hayward and Dick Irwin helping us mail boxes, run out to buy the two extra trunks needed, do errands, and by six when we put Mary Lou to bed everything was *in* somewhere. Walter got reckless and got a first-class sleeper for me and he sat up all night in the second class car next door. Our train left at 11:45 p.m. and we had a car to take our bags and us to the train. Boxes and trunks had gone in the afternoon – and rug rolls. Mary Lou we took in her nightie, inside her steamer rug with zipper and she didn't fuss in the least bit and was soon fast asleep again down at the foot of my "bunk."

The next morning we got to Shihchiachuang about 8:30 and we disembarked and took rickety rickshaws over the dusty cobbled stones to the Salvation Army workers' home… The Chinese preacher in charge was there and he took us into his clean home. They got us tea and cakes and I got out our sterno stove, cooked Mary Lou's cream of wheat. (I bought a cheap Chinese thermos for boiled water, used your good one for her fresh milk, bought a convenient lunch basket with places to carry those two thermos bottles as well as fruit, etc.) We boiled up the dishes and wandered leisurely back to the station to get our next train, shortly after 11 a.m. We had a comfortable second-class compartment to ourselves with a table between two benches on which they served us a delicious steak dinner, and on which I cooked Mary Lou's rice and egg and warmed her vegetables. She slept but mostly she had to be up and looking out the window. The scenery was lovely, climbing mountains all day, going thru the famous coal regions, seeing the terraced hills cultivated to the last inch, seeing the caves used for dwellings, watching donkey and camel caravans carrying coal and provisions along the footpaths. At 7:30 p.m. we landed in Taiyuan. It wasn't long till we were in the Meyers home and Mary Lou was washed and in a clean bed and fast asleep. The Meyers are the Disciples mission, but he's loaned to the YM now and everyone puts up with them going thru Taiyuan. I slept soundly that night too!!

The next day we left about 8:30 in the comfortable Fenchow hospital car. When we drove up to the hospital gate at noon all the nurses were out to welcome us with firecrackers in the proverbial manner. Inside the residence compound were all the foreigners waiting. Mary Lou was the center of it all gracious and friendly through the whole proceeding. But her letdown has come since, and she's cried tempestuously when I was out of her sight… Now she's getting acquainted with her new Amah, the servants, this huge house, and is much happier. We're *so* happy at last to be here together. Walter's pride in Mary Lou is limitless, and our family is reunited joyously.

4

Life in Fenchow and the First Evacuation
1935 - 1936

At the beginning of their tenure in Fenchow, Miriam accompanied Walter to the hospital, saw him deliver a baby, and tried her hand at nursing two premature infants. Whatever idealistic thought she might have held about the two of them working together, side by side, soon faded in the face of the reality of the situation. Her duties at home were new and difficult as she struggled to adapt to the somewhat primitive living conditions and the challenge of managing servants – a necessity given the lack of running water or electricity except between the hours of six p.m. and ten p.m.

The pattern that would hold for the rest of their lives became firmly established in those months of finally being together in China: Walter's responsibilities came first, before the family. Increasingly, his duties kept him at the hospital for long hours and he often was late for dinner.

Miriam settled in to the role that was left to her: that of traditional housewife, mother, and volunteer. I'm sure she missed the intellectual stimulation she had had in Peking, Rochester, and New York City. She continued the study of Chinese every morning with a tutor. Her gifts as a hostess were well utilized as she entertained frequent houseguests and visitors – from the governor of the Province to hunters to college students. She enjoyed the other ten women (and four or five men) of the mission staff and families in addition to teaching music to nurses at the hospital and playing a wheezy old pipe organ for worship services.

Her private writings continued as she pondered what greater plan God had in mind for her. I felt sadness as I read these musings, so full of self-sacrifice to her husband's more essential and demanding work, and of her longing for intellectual stimulation and work that made a difference for others. Additional strain came from the movement of Communist soldiers in next-door Shensi Province under Mao tse-tung. They were in a civil war with the Kuomingtang Nationalist Party under Chiang Kai-shek for control of areas of North China. Also of deep concern were efforts of Japan's military to enlarge their territory beyond Manchuria, which they had seized in 1931.

Carolyn Ruth Judd was born February 26, 1936, just as the nearby Yellow River froze, creating a route for Communist bandits to cross the river and move toward our city. Thirty hours after giving birth, Miriam and her newborn were carried from the hospital on a stretcher for evacuation to the ABCFM Mission station in Taiku, sixty miles away – a four-hour drive. In her letter home, Miriam put her usual positive spin on what was clearly a difficult situation.

The next morning Walter returned to Fenchow after Miriam and Carolyn were settled into the Taiku hospital; the Amah and I were housed with other evacuees. In Fenchow, Walter spent sleepless nights operating on wounded soldiers. Everything was uncertain; communications were so rudimentary that it was difficult to know who was doing what to whom. When reports surfaced that more than 3,000 Communists had been killed in nearby battles Walter decided to send Miriam and his daughters into safer territory. As he could not leave the hospital, he turned to Carl Huber – a Carleton College student teaching in the Mission – for help moving his wife, Mary Lou (at age twenty-seven months), and Carolyn (one month old) to far-away Peking. The trip was harrowing with two train changes, sick children, and jammed train cars of refugees and troops. To prevent her parents from worrying, she tended to minimize these happenings in her letters to them.

$\sim$

Fenchow   *Wednesday, May 22, 1935*

Dear Family –

Mary Lou now quite approves of the old, slow-moving (because bound-footed) lady with the completely un-understandable local dialect that takes care of her. Neither of them can understand each other, and I can't understand either of them, so none of us get in each other's way! In the yard she has a sand pile and loads of old tin cans which are her great joy; a wooden slide which she can't climb up herself. There are two little girls for her to play with[69]…

We've been here two weeks and I don't seem to have accomplished much but I've kept busy. I've attended my first Chinese church service and my first Chinese women's meeting in the church, where children from a month up attend with their parents, run around the church, play, laugh or cry, tend to their needs, are nursed, go to sleep on the benches, all while the service goes calmly and unmindfully on. It doesn't seem to bother either the speaker or the audience.

This week came the graduating exercises at the Nurses' Training School. I played the processional and recessional on a stop organ the likes of which I had never seen, and what a fearful and wonderful sound I produced. The speakers, honored officials, and the three graduating nurses all marched in as the friends, relatives, patients, interested members of the church community, foreigners, etc. all rose. Then followed such items as singing the School song, the China Nurses' Association song, the reading of the Florence Nightingale pledge, advice and counsel to the graduates from Walter and an excellent address by the Chinese preacher from Taiku, our station fifty miles away, who has just

---

69   Mary (age three) and Alice (a few months younger than Mary Lou) were daughters of Mike (the hospital business manager) and Esther Burton. Miriam and Esther shared "mothering" together.

returned from several years study in Oberlin. Everything was done in Chinese, so I had good practice listening. Most of it I didn't get… Tonight Walter and I are having the three graduates and Miss Noreen, the Nursing Superintendent to dinner and tomorrow is a big alumni dinner at the hospital with loads of great Chinese food. So the festivities go, even in this far interior station.

We've been busy, too, entertaining the celebrities. Governor Yen Hsi-shan of Shansi has a chief, General Yang, something like Military Governor of the Province. Yang has been here at the hospital for observation and treatment, as has his number-two wife. He had Walter and Miss Noreen to a feast before I arrived, and the first day I was here he came to call and pay his respects. I had to find out which would be considered the most honorable chair in our living room and insist that he sit there, and that his private secretary take the second place, and on down to our unworthy selves, and also see that his attendants, who stayed on the porch and couldn't come in, were served tea and cakes as well as ourselves. It was my first taste of the real ceremony of old China, with the much bowing, the polite refusing and insisting that goes with each action, the polite questions about my age and my children and the conventional remark about how well I spoke Chinese! Then ceremony required that we should give a "feast" for him, so we asked him to dinner with his wife and two flunkeys. That was fun. He himself is a cultured man, and kept asking questions about everything in our foreign house; the salt and pepper shakers, the frog to hold the flowers of the centerpiece, whether our house had an upstairs or not, etc. It was graciously done and with a sincere interest so didn't seem over curious or rude. The food interested them, too, for we served our own kind. After chicken soup came parsley potatoes with salmon loaf that I had made myself and they asked about what kind of fish it was and were intrigued to hear that it had come from America in a tin. Then we had "chicken pillau" – rice heaped up on the center of a platter with pieces of chicken all round the edge, and a generous sprinkling of fried onions, raisins, and peanuts, served with chicken gravy. They seemed to take heartily to this. But Mrs. Yang just played with her food. She hasn't had much contact with foreigners and was a bit scared of our food… The two attendants who had all this time been holding their hats, wraps, canes on the front porch, had been offered food by our servants but had refused, happily, for I hadn't ordered enough for extras. Walter says General Yang is by all odds the most cultured and gentlemanly of any military man he has ever had anything to do with, and I thought he was fine. He wore an ordinary Chinese gown.

The next night we practically repeated the feast, this time entertaining another General of lesser rank who was visiting here from Taiyuan, the Provincial capitol, and who had formerly entertained Walter when he was a patient here. With him we invited his eighty-two-year-old father, and the old boy was as alert as they come, interested in everything, ate practically everything majoring on the delicious hot rolls our servant makes, dominated the conversation, as is his due, so that his son, the "ruler over many," sat quiet and left the conversation to his respected father. One thing struck me funny – the idea of entertaining in two languages where Walter could remark to me in English in a perfectly conversational tone: "I'll wring that boy's neck if he doesn't keep the glasses filled." I wore my new Chinese gown, all gold and red. The collars, stiff and high on ladies' gowns to be fashionable, remind me of the whalebones our mothers used to wear in high collars when they were in college. As long as it's correct in style, I won't mind how stiff I have to hold my neck!

I seem to have gotten myself in for teaching music to some of the nurses. I'm taking eight pupils in two classes of four each, for there's more stimulus and competition in class lessons than in individual ones, and I can correct their mistakes in general and save their faces from embarrassing individual comments, as well as save myself considerable time this way.

I suppose you'd like to know what I think Fenchow is like. You have a fairly good idea from having read Pearl Buck. This is farm country for we are in the Fen River valley where crops are raisable. The greatest impression is one of dust. Everywhere is thick finely powdered yellow dust, and if it's on the ground outside, you can imagine that it is all over our floors in footprints and all over our rooms whenever the wind blows. Our floors get dusted twice a day and they're always dustless for the thirty seconds right afterwards. Rain is needed badly now. If it doesn't come in another week the crops will be burned up. Our own flower and vegetable gardens and the grass and bushes round our houses get watered everyday with water carried from the wells on the compound. We have fresh lettuce daily from our garden, small amounts of asparagus, radishes, and peas just starting. We certainly are reaping where others have sowed.

This compound is as extensive as many a college campus. On it are the kindergarten, the primary school, a men's and a women's Bible school, which seem to teach Bible and everything else under the sun, a coed middle school, and the nurses' training school and hospital, besides five large residences for foreigners. These residences are in the middle with students constantly coming and going through the grounds. The gardens behind the houses are generally walled off for the small children to play in without disturbance. The grounds have been beautifully planted with evergreen hedges, thousands of rose bushes, lilacs, trees. Our houses, we all agree, are huger and more unwieldy than we would have built but otherwise comfortable.

Fenchow   *Saturday p.m., June 1, 1935*

Mother dear –

Today it was my turn to have the weekly "afternoon coffee" – a 4:30 gathering of the foreigners for sociability. The cook made a layer cake – he's a swell cook! – and I made ice tea and added a few tablespoons of lemon powder and juice from a precious can of pineapple. Seemed to be a good drink, after the boy had turned it in the ice cream freezer to get it cold – we have no ice boxes, only cold cellars for our food, and "dirty" ice for ice cream! I'm going to make several gallons of root beer from the extract and homemade yeast, to have as our "treat" drinks this summer.

A number of the tuberculosis patients have been moved out to the Valley, as they call the place eight miles from here, named Yu Tao Ho, where there are a cluster of summer cottages. Walter has to go out twice a week to see them and I went with him one afternoon. We rattled along over bumpy roads in the old Ford, part of the time traveling on the dry river bed because the road had been washed out in last fall's rainy season and not yet repaired. This Valley is definitely cooler. A stream comes rushing down from higher hills farther on, and in the rainy season becomes a real torrent. On either side of this riverbed stand old mills no longer used except by the foreigners who have turned them into delightful summer cottages by building on a screened big verandah here or there, whitewashing the insides, cutting in extra windows to make them lighter, setting up the huge mill stones on a stump of tree indoors to make a rustic round table, etc. Some folks have built cottages. There must be twelve or fifteen all scattered two miles up and down the banks of this riverbed. It is a quiet, cool, restful place – one tennis court, no swimming, "church" in someone's home or in one of the groves – primitive and near to nature but a real oasis in a desert… I made rounds with him at the Men's & Women's Mills where the twenty or so tuberculosis patients were; then we hiked up the Valley, jumped across the stream on stepping stones and had a lovely time. We brought in a few luscious ripe strawberries…

Emma, the nurse, had gone to Peiping for Council. She left in the hospital twin girl babies, three pounds each, two weeks old, children of the YM Secretary here, a Chinese. Walter decided to put them on the same lactic acid formula Mary Lou had with the rather expensive Carnation milk, to see if he could save their lives. With Emma not here to supervise, and Walter too busy to take time out to oversee things, I got the job. I hunted up Mary Lou's bottles. The local bottles can't be boiled, and the nipples are much too big, so they were glad to see our foreign implements. I took the nurse in charge to the kitchen, showed her about boiling everything, made up a batch of formula with her – finding all sorts of ways of adapting Chinese stoves, utensils, chopsticks, etc. to my uses. While we waited for the stuff to cool I saw my first delivery case, a fine boy. It was one of the most thrilling things I have ever seen to watch a baby arrive into the world and see Walter manage the whole thing so nonchalantly. Then back to the nursery to watch the twins take the newly prepared milk. Only with much coaxing did their tiny mouths manage to suck down an ounce, but we hope that this formula is going to suit them. Such a tiny handful of baby each was as I picked her up to bubble her after feeding – an operation the nurses had been neglecting. They aren't as big as many dolls I've seen little girls play with. I do hope they can be saved.

My weekly duties have included studying two hours with my teacher daily, teaching my eight piano pupils, drilling daily the three Matthews children on singing "Trees" for tomorrow's church service, which I'm to lead and have spent some time on preparing (I mean our "foreign service"), taking Mary Lou on a daily walk around the compound, being shown by Mary McClure her women's Bible Training School and newly developed wool work: weaving, spinning, hooking rugs etc., doing quite a bit of typing for Walter on behind correspondence, overseeing work on the Reynolds house. It is to be lovely when done. We plan to stay at Burton's through the summer.

Mary Lou feels grown up today. She wore a pink hair-ribbon tying back the lock of hair that's always falling in her eyes. As soon as she got it on she went to the long glass to look at herself and then kissed herself repeatedly in the mirror. She isn't very vain! She's crazy about dogs, isn't quite as friendly with people, but I'll admit they do fuss over her.

It's good to have your letters – makes me feel as if I'd dropped in that living room – *home* to my loveliest memories. A big batch of love from your little girl and her little girl – two M.L.s.

Fenchow   *Monday, June 17, 1935*

Mother dear –

Walter's been unusually busy at the hospital. He's had lots of emergency and peculiar or obscure cases. He's been working hard with those tiny twins…but one by one everything went wrong. They got a bad diarrhea and too weak to nurse the bottle so he had to tube feed them, & also give them liquids under the skin. One day a nurse got hold of the wrong bottle and poured what she thought was medicine down one twinnie. It turned out to be a strong acid and the tiny thing died. Walter redoubled his efforts on the other one for he wanted to prove it could be saved, for the nurses had said from the start there was no use working with it and so hadn't been trying. Esther Burton who has loads of milk and is weaning her year old Alice sent milk to the twin and it was improving nicely when it got infected with erysipelas from a patient on the men's ward (thru nurses being careless) and soon died. While Emma Noreen was in Peiping he discovered a great deal of laxity, carelessness, inefficiency etc. among the nurses. So that has required patience and delicate handling and stern insistence on better work…

Walter was trying to get the unpaid bills from patients paid, without much success, till he found out accidentally that the fine Christian (?) Chinese who has long collected bills for the hospital had a private system of graft and squeeze that he was trying to work, while outwardly seeming to be Walter's best friend and most loyal cooperator. Things like that are more discouraging and wearing than any amount of hard work on patients, or even death among patients, which are to be expected – except those through carelessness!

Walter admits that he is tired and would like a vacation. This week arrives Dr. Tuan, an older doctor who is considered excellent. July 1 come the two young interns, both Fenchow boys who have been helped thru medical school by friends here. And next week arrive two medical students from PUMC to work and observe without pay for the summer. So Walter won't have to be on duty twenty-four hours a day.

The American-Oriental bank in Shanghai failed several weeks ago. *All* our savings were in it. We lost $900, including Mary Lou's educational fund. Lots of mission money was in it, as well as personal accounts. (We have money in Nebraska banks but I don't know how much – a little.)

Fenchow   *Saturday, July 6, 1935*

Mother dear –

Esther came in from the Valley on Wednesday to wash her sheets & towels. Afterwards she took me down into town – my first *real* expedition outside our vast mission grounds – and we had fun poking around. I was surprised that you can buy quite a good deal here – flashlight batteries, snaps & buttons, and not too bad cotton, prints, rayons, & silks. We poked round some old curios shops, where people who needed cash had brought their precious possessions to sell and there were odd & interesting valuables and invaluables displayed. Bought some heavy vases that are easily wired to make attractive table lamps – tho' shades aren't available here unless you make silk ones yourself. It's interesting to see the life on the main street – the buying and selling of a few coppers' worth of vegetables, or a hunk of pork, lard, bean sauce in a broken beer bottle, colored coarse sewing thread in skeins, not spools, horribly smelling Chinese cosmetics & toilet articles, cheap earthenware bowls & cups & teapots stacked ceiling high in varying sizes – all the sights and sounds and smells of a busy town in the interior. You must see it sometime.

In the afternoon Esther and I made up some apricot jam, which came out quite well. When she was ready to go back to the Valley, she insisted Mary Lou and I come along with her for a change and rest. I took the Amah and a few clothes and off we went. We were there three nights. And what nights! Sleeping on a broad screened-in verandah right alongside a rushing stream that gurgled all night long, cool enough to use blankets, stars close around and all the loveliness of the out of doors. No meals to plan, no Chinese to study, nothing to do but lie in the lounge chairs or big couch swing, read, knit, or talk lazily. It was a lovely rest.

Fenchow   *Monday, July 15, 1935*

Mother dear –

I don't know what to write about the Japanese or Chinese situation, which you often mention and of whose mention in the New York papers we are glad to have the clippings. Walter's comment: It seems to be nothing new, nothing more than the Japanese have been gradually doing the last four years – slowly inching down on China's territory, using or creating one pretext or excuse after another, then lying low till that incident blows over and they can start another. The Chinese characteristically withdraw, arbitrate, negotiate, make every effort to give the Japs *no* excuse for a big fight, tho' the Japs seem to be trying their darndest to provoke a real fight, with the demands. The process goes on with the occasional flare-ups that fan the flame.

As far as we're personally concerned, there's no slightest danger and we see few signs of the conflict. The last bunch of Fenchow foreigners who went up to Peiping were delayed on their train about eight hours because they had to wait on sidings for Chinese troop trains to pass – where the troops were being moved to, I don't know. When the Japs were menacing Peiping recently, loads of Jap soldiers were seen marching in the streets, Jap planes flew overhead daily. Finally the city put on a nine o'clock curfew, closed up everything & wouldn't let people on the street without a permit, hoping to avoid any unpleasant incident with the often drunk Jap soldiers. This ban is off now. They talk of building an airfield here in Fenchow, one of a series of Chinese fields from the coast west so they can quickly control these Provinces, and airplanes have been seen over Fenchow, an unusual sight. I understand the missions in North China received communications from *Japan* last year asking them to list all their mission property and institutions in North China, with valuations, so that "in case of any future hostilities they could offer us adequate protection!!" But these things are all sort of incidental that people mention in passing to show that the Japs are gradually working at their plan, but no one has serious or immediate ideas that our work's going to be closed up soon.

Well, I've been holding off several weeks telling you about our planning for "Little Brother," expecting to get over the worst of the first bad weeks before writing you. But so far there have been no such scenes as I made in Rochester those weeks in May and June when you and Dad were there to sympathize with me. And if it's a Little Sister, we won't mind. We're quite proud of our first effort in Little Sisters! We're both happy as can be at the prospects.

Fenchow   *Saturday, July 20, 1935*

Mother dear –

Waiting again for Walter to come home from taking x-rays… His tummy seems to have been knocked out by something he ate so he took a day off. Having Walter home gave me time to talk with him about the Japanese situation. He says the trouble now is the silver policy of the U.S., which has drained China of money and made it impossible for China to launch any sort of defensive against Japan. China needing money is practically forced to borrow it from Japan, so that Japan is slowly getting economic control here. It's a matter of common knowledge that the North China newspapers – about 100 of them – each has a Japanese "advisor" on the staff, so we get what news it suits the Japanese to have us get. Walter says individual Japanese are fast moving into North China cities to gradually get control of the business, newspapers, banking etc. So they keep working steadily, if inch-by-inch, at their project of taking over North China and the rest of the world sits by and won't believe it or can't see it. However, we are in no danger ourselves. This is not Pollyannaism. It is the *truth*!!

Fenchow   *Monday, August 5, 1935*

Mother dear –

Walter and I went out to the Valley around 4 p.m. expecting to hear Owen Lattimore's[70] lecture on Mongolia to the summer crowd out there – almost seventy, I think. The facts that their time seems to have crept up half an hour ahead of ours, and that we were delayed meant that we got in at the tail end of the talk – worse luck! But there followed questions on various subjects which were interesting to hear answered, and Walter was tickled to find his views and Owen's coinciding on the Jap-China situation. Owen feels that the Japs must inevitably come in and take over China's northern Provinces, now that they've gone so far on that regime, unless something drastic and forcible stands up and stops them. After the talk and the meeting with the crowd there, the Lattimores insisted that we go home to dinner with them.

It was a grand dinner – good food and scintillating conversation. Their guest Mr. McDonald was there, the Peking correspondent for the *London Times*, a man of wide and interesting experience. The three men nearly forgot to eat, so busy were they in sharing information and answering questions about the particular parts of China each knew best. It was thrilling to sit and hear the history and romance of this great country and its present leaders unfolding before your eyes from the mouths of eyewitnesses. They were interested to hear what Walter had to say of Communism in Fukien[71] from firsthand knowledge, and Owen discussed Communism in these northern Provinces that border on Mongolia, etc. They discussed the governors & military heads of the various Provinces whom they knew personally, and their attitudes toward the present Japanese affairs; the opium traffic; state of the national government etc. and all with personal incidents to make their points. Walter had a lot to say from his visit to Taiyuan last week and his several talks with the various officials – he failed to see Governor Yen but feels he is making progress with his head secretary toward a gift for the hospital. They say 100 Japanese have moved into Taiyuan since the recent Japanese flare-up in Hopei Province in June – and no one knows why they have come or what they are doing there – they're just

---

70   Owen Lattimore was an American author and scholar, raised in China, editor of *Pacific Affairs* journal, considered a communist sympathizer by some whose indictment for perjury was overturned in 1955.

71   Fukien was the southeastern Province where Walter practiced medicine from 1926 to 1931.

there, that's all!! It was impossible not to feel that you were where history was making [sic] as you listened to those three men. Walter enjoyed it tremendously, for the thousand details of the hospital are constantly absorbing his attention & he gets little occasion to rub minds with such like-minded folks, a process he loves and misses.

Fenchow   *Sunday, August 11, 1935*

Dear Family –

Heavy rains last week have played havoc with all the motor roads. The Fen River not far from here has overflowed and backed up in the fields with the result that lakes have collected here and there, roads are underwater in some places, some bridges are out. Yesterday afternoon, Walter and I rented bicycles at fifteen cents a day (men's bikes – they don't know what a ladies' bike is out here!) and rode out into the country three miles or so to see one of these lakes. It was a body of water of vast proportions, covering many fields through which the tall stalks sometimes poked up their heads. The water was several feet higher than the road on the right side, and all the farmers with fields on the left side of the road were hard at work building up banks to keep the lake where it was. The wind was blowing little ripples in the water and it looked as if any one of these might gently slide over the mud dykes and send the lake down onto the still-growing crops on the left of the road. In one place the water had slowly been seeping through the porous soil, had made its way under the road, and just as we got to this point had burst through on the left. Then with great shouts for help to all the hundreds of men lining the roads, they jammed long poles down in the mud, put down pieces of woven matting over the hole and had half a dozen men standing down in the water holding the matting tight over the hole till they could cut grass and weeds and even the crops to bring and patch the hole. There without any organization or management, with the primitive methods used in the early days, and simply by the use of sheer numbers of China's manpower, they got that leak stopped and that disaster averted in little more than five minutes. It was a great sight!

Buses have not gone through to Taiyuan for over a week now, mails have been irregular, sent around by a different route and brought here by runner from a town some miles away. A bunch of people from the Valley have been trying to arrange some way to get to their respective cities, have considered rickshaws, oxcarts, buses, private cars when available, and roads leading in any direction. A bunch started off in rickshaws yesterday, but not till after they had argued all morning with unwilling pullers. They had all been up since five at the Valley; hoping to get an early start, had come to Fenchow and by noon had developed headaches, weariness, and much irateness over the chances of getting away. It was funny how one by one they gave up arguing and appeared at our door, the only foreign house now open in Fenchow, begging lunch and a place to rest. One by one I put them to sleep in the few beds and couches we have available… Every fifteen minutes or so I went into the kitchen and told the cook "One more guest for lunch." It didn't bother him any as it was Monday and he was doing the wash, so about a quarter to twelve I got perturbed myself, went into the kitchen and put the cabbage and squash on to boil (he had the pork roasting in the oven and the rice cooking) and made a deep apple pudding. Our other boy was running around frantically sending telegrams for the distracted people, doing errands of one kind or another trying to collect the belongings of the would-be-travelers scattered from bus station to rickshaw station to hospital and back. We finally collected eight persons for our two-man lunch and most of the folks finally got off in the afternoon. Now we're awaiting reports of their being carried thru the floods. So it goes.

Fenchow   *Monday, August 26, 1935*

Dear Family –

We've been living in our new house for a whole week and what a joy it was to get into it, our first home in China really, our first *house* anywhere. Practically everything in the house had to be washed – windows, woodwork, floors, furniture. Then we started unpacking, airing and beating rugs, moving the furniture that had been huddled onto an upstairs and a downstairs porch all summer. After that to unpack dishes and kitchen things, wash them all and the shelves on which they were to go, carry upstairs the baskets of linen, clothes, furnishings…

All the rooms are comfortably large. Each bedroom has a convenient washstand in its large closet and the large family bathroom is almost the most agreeable room in the house – much more acceptable than I had ever tho't one could be without running water or plumbing.

Fenchow   *Saturday, September 7, 1935*

Mother dear –

I get up at 6 with Mary Lou, usually find her dry, she…then plays and sings and talks happily in her crib until the Nai-Nai[72] comes at 7:30. I go to sleep again and we generally don't get up till after 8 – sometimes 8:30 – as that is one time of the day Walter *does* sleep. With my teacher arriving at 9 and time to supervise the housework, it's lunchtime before I turn around. Afternoons I rest 2-4 and then walk with Mary Lou, go to see the school goats milked or the newborn baby calves – or to see Esther & the children & soon it's bath & suppertime. It turns out Esther is pregnant too – baby due the middle of April. So we will keep each other company.

It's two weeks ago that Walter's soldiers started coming in and kept on coming for four days. The first day arrived a captain and a colonel, and after that some of the not-too-badly wounded ones, leaving the worst ones for the last. They had come by litter six days from across the Yellow River in Shensi where they had been sent to fight the Communists that are thick in the northern part of that Province.[73] Being Shansi troops, they came here for hospitalization, commandeering men at each village to carry the litters the three miles or so to the next village. Altogether they took in just under fifty, and you can imagine how that crowded the hospital that was already running fairly full. They admitted that they had been utterly routed by whoever they were fighting, but because this defeat was such a disgrace, or because the common soldiers didn't know and the officers wouldn't tell, no one could find out where the fighting had taken place or exactly who they have been opposing, and whether or not it was the Communists that defeated them, or some other squabbling group. But regardless of who shot them, they were well shot, and the next days were crowded ones for Walter, taking x-rays of the wounds, extracting gunshot, operating, resetting of broken bones etc. Several days he didn't get home for lunch at all, or stop to eat at the hospital except a cocoa malt or a piece of pie that I'd send over, and often it was 10 or 11 before he'd stop for supper. In the midst of this extra work came the added responsibility of having to close up the tuberculosis hospitals out at the Valley and move all the patients in.

---

72   Another Chinese word for Amah.
73   Shansi and Shensi were two different but adjacent Provinces.

Last week arrived the Carleton boy and girl [Carl Huber and Beatrice Brown] who have come to teach English in the school here – and it fell to our lot to take in the boy for a week. Since Carl speaks no Chinese, I had to more or less help him with various adjustments.

One day Walter did get bighearted and take time off and that was on my birthday. Esther had asked all the inhabitants to a buffet out at the Valley. It was a swell supper – with birthday cakes.

Last Sunday we went out to the Valley for dinner with the Binghams and Lattimores, a sort of farewell, for they left this week to return to Peiping. They had some interesting guests staying with them – the German, Bruno Lasker, of fame for his work in social surveys in various parts of the world, slums, housing problems, real estate; and Dr. and Mrs. Witfogel, he a German, she a Ukrainian Jew, not able to return to Germany, champion of the depressed classes, and he a supposed leading authority on Chinese economic history though this is the first time he has been to China and he's only been here two months now: all three of them parlor Reds, or if not Red, as Owen says, at least a bright pinko! Add Owen Lattimore with his intimate knowledge of Mongolia, Tibet, Turkistan, and his witty dry remarks, and Dr. Bingham with his researches in Chinese history and his decidedly not-Communistic background, and Walter who generally has an idea or two, and you can guess what kind of conversation ensued on that cool porch that afternoon. It sparkled, and there was enough disagreement of opinion to keep the arguments lively. The past and future of the world in general and China in particular came in for a good bit of rearranging, and even so everyone parted friends! It was a most enjoyable and interesting afternoon and quite a change for Walter from his daily diet of wounded soldiers.

The Witfogels are interested to see all aspects of China so came to Fenchow to see the mission work, and life in the city. I went with them to the huge match factory, Fenchow's one industrial plant – a foreign factory run by the Chinese. I can't say much for the conditions of work: no safety devices, moving parts not covered, boys from twelve up, ten-hour shifts, and the phosphorous rooms hard on the health. They say the Chinese hate to work there because of the deadening routine and will go only as a last resort – almost 500 employed, no women.

Fenchow   *Monday, October 7, 1935*

Mother dear –

We had a happy weekend with Victor Hayward from Taiyuan visiting us. Walter had to do emergencies at the hospital after supper so Victor and I visited till after one. We discussed much about our theories of mission work, cooperating with older and more conservative members of our missions, the Christian attitude toward the everlasting servant problem, how you go about speaking to people who obviously need help on personal problems (foreigners and associates, not Chinese) without seeming too brusque and hurting them, and yet being fearlessly constructive – He does my thinking and my spiritual life a lot of good. Sunday morning Victor and I went to Church. After dinner we all drove out to the Valley and had a good walk up the river bed, thru some of the ripe fields of millet, climbed some of the cliffs on our side of the valley and got a grand view of the mountains around, purple and blue-black in their brilliant sun and shadow, and of the Fen River plain and Fenchow in the distance; investigated an old temple set back in a tiny village, containing images as horrible as any I'd ever seen in India. Mary Lou adores the car trip to the Valley and climbing around when she gets there, and Walter even more enjoys Mary Lou enjoying it – even to carrying her part of the way when tiny feet get too tired. In the evening we had a lovely church service for our foreign group here at our house – a blazing wood fire, orange candles, big bowl of autumn-colored snapdragons, special music, Walter presiding and Victor giving the meditation on the spirit of adventure – Abraham went out not knowing whither he went. It was informal but worshipful. It is nice to get a voice from the outside world occasionally, for the twelve of us here get to know each others' ideas pretty well.

Esther and I entertained the regular Tuesday Women's meeting of the Church at a social gathering in Esther's lovely garden. Nearly forty women came and many children. We had a short devotional service, then served tea, cupcakes, with apples for the children. We gave them stuffed animals to make for the church bazaar before Christmas – elephants, camels, and dogs…cut out of gay-colored ginghams or flowered prints, stuffed with sawdust after they were sewed. They worked diligently, even the old half-blind grandmothers, though the *idea* of a sewing meeting or working for the *church*, not themselves, was a bit novel to them. We got a lot of cute-as-the-dickens toys, which ought to sell well, and the women enjoyed sewing & chattering.

Fenchow Mission community
Miriam, left front sitting on step; Walter standing right back row

Fenchow   *Monday, October 14, 1935*

Mother dear –

Walter got a sudden urge to get out his horn, which he found intact among his Foochow[74] things when they arrived, and he and I played a bit together. I wish he could find time to practice each day for he is good, only out of practice, and he would find this ability useable in the meetings and gatherings where we are always asked to take a part – sing or perform. Besides he enjoys it and it is a relaxation to him…

Governor Yen decided to send his wife and married son who is an incurable epileptic down here for physical examination by Walter. All the Chinese are thrilled to death at the "honor" that this brings us – for Governor Yen has just plain passed by the English Baptist hospital in Taiyuan for ours here. Walter does feel pleased that the medical standards here have improved enough to command the confidence of Governor Yen. But he sees a lot of disadvantages too: the ordinary routine of the hospital practically at a standstill while everyone rushes to bow and scrape before the High and Mighty; the inevitable feasting and entertaining, and Walter will have to attend all functions, thus neglecting his work, which he hates to do; the expense and trouble involved in preparing a suitable place in the hospital grounds to house such distinguished guests: Mrs. Yen, her son and wife, three chauffeurs, two cooks, two women attendants, two personal bodyguards, two men servants, her own nurse, and the secretary in charge of arrangements! Sixteen in all. The Chinese with their deep sense of conventions, ceremonies, and the correct ways to entertain are deeply involved in preparations and poor Walter is generally disgusted at the way they will drop all ordinary responsibilities for the care of the sick to make a big noise over "The Great."

Fenchow   *Thursday, November 14, 1935*

Mother dear –

Seven Christmas boxes got started off to America last week. We can buy nothing here of the kind of gifts that are available in Peiping. However, they do have a "fair" here in the fall, where the various vendors set up their stalls in the court of an old unused temple. They have the most fascinating assortment of things that they have picked up around the interior from families whose circumstances are so reduced that they have to sell the old Mandarin gowns. The embroidery on these things is perfectly beautiful, especially on the full skirts the scholars used to wear. You have to keep wandering and looking through the things and bargaining for anything you want. It's more fun than going to a movie to spend an afternoon down there…

Each foreign house here has a servant's quarters attached to it where the servants live, but *not* their families, except that our woman has her old mother and her daughter with her. They cook their own food on little stoves in their quarters, or sometimes on our kitchen stove. They eat from ten to eleven in the morning, and have off from two to four in the afternoon. Not the Amah. She is off twelve to two, when Mary Lou is sleeping, and eats her breakfast before she comes at 7:30 in the morning. If we are ever out evenings, she sits in the house.

---

74   The capital city of the Fukien Province was Foochow, where Walter left personal belongings in 1931 upon returning to the U.S.

Our guests don't pay unless they stay some time, or unless they are strangers whom we are putting up for their convenience. They always leave a tip for the servants, which I divide with them at the end of the month, so they keep happy doing the extra work of guests.

Yesterday I gave my talk at the women's meeting on India. It certainly was funny to try to think up ideas that would be simple enough for those women to grasp, and second to get ideas simple enough for my poor Chinese to express. The little children first, and then the women insisted on leaving their seats and crowding up around the speaker's table and picking up and examining all the things I had there and asking questions in the middle of the talk, but I'm learning to talk right on thru squalling babies and playing children and talking mothers.

Fenchow   *Sunday, December 1, 1935*

Dear Folks –

We are back safe and sound from our Taiku trip.[75] We don't celebrate Thanksgiving on Thursday as it breaks into the work of the week. Friday morning one group went and after lunch the rest of us started. Walter drove. A few miles out of Fenchow we came to the place where water remains standing in the fields. The road is still "out" for several miles, but we struck off into the country over cart road, through several villages. I wish you could have seen the ruts, the mud, the narrow "one-way-traffic" paths where we couldn't pass the carts we'd meet, the ditches too close on either side for comfort, the huge holes in the road that no one would take the time to fill up. We bounced and jostled and crept along till we finally found ourselves back on the main road, at the end of an hour having made eight miles. Mary Lou adored it, thought each bump was made for her personal enjoyment, exclaimed over each one and laughed at Walter driving. In fact, she kept the rest of us cheerful when we might have been inclined to cuss! We got to Taiku at dusk and from then on we dashed madly from one place to another…

After inspecting the hospital, on Saturday, at ten-thirty we had a lovely Thanksgiving service in one of the houses, with special music, the reading of the President's proclamation, and a good talk. There were thirty or so of us Americans so it seemed like a real church service…

Walter and I went over to the other compound for lunch…where the Oberlin Shansi Memorial School is, supported by Oberlin in memory of the missionaries martyred during the Boxer uprising. It is probably the finest school in the Province, with almost a thousand boys, and around fifty girls. The campus and buildings are lovely enough to compete with any American campus. There is a beautiful graveyard where are buried the Chinese Christians and the American Board missionaries from Taiku and Fenchow who were massacred in 1900.[76] Dr. H.H. K'ung was for a long time the principal of this school; he's now China's Minister of Finance. He and his wife, one of the three famous Soong sisters, wives of Sun Yat-sen, Chiang Kai-shek, and K'ung have done much for the school. Each student entering the upper middle school has to take three hours work a week in the Industrial Department the first year, the same in the Agricultural Department the second year, and

---

75   The ABCFM stations at Fenchow and Taiku celebrated Thanksgiving together, alternating locations each year.
76   The Taiyuan Massacre was part of the Boxer Rebellion. On July 9, 1900, nearly fifty Christian missionaries and their children were killed.

another three hours of advanced work his last year in either of these departments. This is a splendid idea, I think, for it teaches the boys to be able to do something practical, work with their hands, instead of having only the classical traditional education when they leave school, and this is an important step for China's future…

For the Thanksgiving dinner party at the Moyers' home, twenty-eight of us sat down at one long table, nicely decorated, and proceeded to devour three turkeys, sent in from Tientsin as well as all the usual fixings. Everyone ate too much and was thoroughly uncomfortable in evening clothes that get worn about once a year out in the sticks and hence seem unnatural. I was glad I had a good excuse not to wear evening dress and am large enough so what I eat doesn't make any noticeable difference anyway! There are compensations in having babies!! …

The next morning we got an early start for the drive home. When we came to the detour we let Walter take the car round it empty and the rest of us walked a mile or so on a footpath that went along the flooded fields on either side, and took an old flat-bottomed boat that some Chinese poled across a hundred yards of lake to the footpath on the other side. Mary Lou enjoyed this.

Fenchow   *Monday, December 16, 1935*

Dear Folks –

This has been an unusually busy week at the hospital, three night calls. Then an epidemic of flu got into the school. They had to open up another ward at the hospital and take in about twenty-five students and made one of the dormitory rooms into another isolation ward. The girls' dormitory also has sick folks, and these all have to be seen twice a day. Some of the nurses are sick, and the last ten days they have been giving the National Board Exams for the nurses… One of the nurses had to be expelled for cheating in exams and that took a lot of discussing and arguing and pleading… Governor Yen's son and wife came back. Like many others of the official class, they have a false sense of their own importance and feel everyone should jump to attention. Walter does not "jump" and it gripes both them and the Chinese at the hospital. They went off suddenly in a huff the last time. When Walter sent the reports to Taiyuan he said the examination was not completed, and when Governor Yen got back from Nanking he laid his son out and sent him back. The boy is nineteen and the wife seventeen, and they have two children.

This week started an influx of hunters from Peking – Captain Bales of the American Marine Department. He stayed overnight with us. I wish you could have seen the outfit that set off the next morning. Two donkeys to carry the cooking paraphernalia, cot and sleeping outfit, food, ammunition; two mules for Bales and his cook to ride; donkey boys, the head hunter and a few extra interested folks who hoped they might make fifty cents a day beating up the wild pig. He will go into the hills twenty miles, stay ten days, nights in some Chinese home that the head hunter will take him to, have his own cook prepare his food and rough it – and I hope he isn't freezing to death. We almost are here in a heated house. After he left came another party for whom Walter had been arranging a bus, hunters, donkeys and donkey boys, food supplies. These two men only stopped here for lunch and to pick up their guide…

Sunday we went to a huge feast given by the grandfather of one of the nurses who is finishing at the hospital. Her father is a General off in Shensi with the Shansi troops now subduing the Communists. The family has money, but the girl herself is sweet and democratic and unspoiled and popular with everyone, as if she didn't have a cent. He is a good friend of Walter's, on the Hospital Board of Managers. The old ancestral home is here, and the remarkable old grandfather gave the feast for his granddaughter. She's the best nurse at the hospital. I was amazed at the details of our home dinner last spring that the Old Man remembered. He is "of the gentility."

Fenchow   *Thursday, December 25, 1935*

Mother dear –

Christmas has come and gone and it was one grand time. But before I tell you about the occasion itself, I must say a bit about the week that preceded it! First the cook, who'd had an infected thumb for two months, submitted to Walter's taking the nail off, and this put him out of commission for a day or two. Mary Lou's cold started to develop broncho-pneumonial proportions and I spent time trying to keep her happy in her restlessness and fever – putting on daily mustard plasters followed by antiphlogistine, and trying to get lots of liquids down her. The Amah couldn't do much with her – she's too polite! We were thankful that some of the Christmas packages were here and we could open and get her out a new plaything every few days. Altogether she was in bed a week.

The cook, gradually getting better from the terrifically sore thumb, developed a real flu and we sent him to the hospital and got a substitute. That means quite a bit of explaining and showing, for no matter how well a man can cook, he doesn't know how you like things cooked and served or where you keep supplies and utensils, etc. The cook came the same day Captain Bales got back from his hunting trip, and we managed to have a perfectly rotten dinner that night, but I guess Bales was so glad to get back into a warm house and a bath that he didn't care. He had nearly frozen, but had had good luck. He gave us one of the deer and we have been feasting on venison ever since. It's more delicious meat than I would have supposed. Several people dropped in to hear of the hunting trip, and our meager supply of cookies was soon exhausted. I hurriedly made toasted cheese sandwiches and suddenly realized I'd used up all the bread we had in the house. Fortunately our neighbors are used to borrowing. But when the dessert was brought in, the new cook, finding neither cookies or cake to serve had dug out two old and dry cupcakes that should long since have been discarded. Walter and I had to laugh out loud at that though we had managed to keep straight faces when the soup was served in shallow sauce dishes! But Captain Bales is a fat, jolly, good-natured sort of person and he didn't mind a few irregularities in our household. He left and we could turn the radiators off in the guest room.

All week long there were things to keep us extra busy: A feast for the Chinese General Secretary of our North China Mission who was visiting here from Peking; rehearsing Christmas music with the nurses; getting off the China Christmas cards; getting out the Christmas decorations – the red wreaths with the electric candles in them had to be rewired to be used on our electric plant here, but were much admired when hung and worth all the trouble they took.

On Christmas Sunday we had our monthly meeting of the Music Club and then at 5:30 Christmas

Vespers at our house. We sat in rows facing the glowing fire, and the four pairs of red candles on the mantelpiece and on the piano and the red wreaths with the electric candles in the windows and no other lights anywhere. We had a simple service.

We can get all the mistletoe we want in the Valley just for the picking of it off the trees, so we had that to decorate with, on our mantelpieces or windows, or bunches tied with big red bows and hung over doorways. We had sent out a man to the hills to get Christmas trees and he came back with the trees all right, but with all the lower branches lopped off because they were easier to load on his donkey that way! All that was left was a bit of fuzz on the top of a pole! Well, that was enough for us, anyway, for we had planned to have a small tree for our small family. We planted a little four-foot tree in a flowerpot, set it up on our bridge table and decorated it with the precious things we had brought from home. Christmas morning we got Mary Lou out of bed and dressed. You should have seen her big eyes as she saw the glistening tree and the various toys! She made a dash for the Mickey Mouse for that was familiar to her; she had already played with it in bed several days. She was bewildered, but took one thing at a time, dashed around to show it to the servants who stood watching, put it in a big chair and went back for more. Then she gave out the things for the servants and a package or two for Daddy and Mummy, something for the Amah's little girl who was enjoying the fun. All during breakfast she ate automatically not realizing what was going in her mouth, with a far-away look in her eyes. She looked right through us without seeing us, evidently trying to figure out what this celebration was all about.

At nine we had the "Station Christmas Tree" at the Matthews. We had each drawn a name and prepared a gift for one person. Walter did have to go to the hospital and I had things to do in preparation for the dinner. Chinese friends at the hospital and elsewhere kept sending us cards and gifts and I had to think of the right things to say for each even when the gifts were a pair of hideous coral-colored glass vases with white glass posies all over them. One of the wealthier "grateful patients" sent a tray full of "Chao Tzes," a delicious dish the Chinese eat – small "pancakes" filled with chopped meat and vegetables and squeezed together at the edges. These are steamed and eaten hot, so we had a Chinese lunch.

In the afternoon started the process of collecting things we needed to set and serve our table, and the food prepared at the various houses. We borrowed two long tables to seat sixteen and chairs enough. Bea and I decorated the table and had the most fun doing it. Her mother had sent out a dime store funny gift for each person, with a silly poem attached. She'd never seen any of these people, but from Bea's descriptions in letters she had guessed at them, and done very well. These gifts were wrapped and piled in the center of the table, inside a two-foot house I had made out of a corrugated packing box. It had red shiny paper pasted all over the sides and the chimney, cellophane windows, and white cotton snow on the slanting roof. We had some tiny pretend Christmas trees and tiny candles in candlesticks for lampposts at the two doors. I'm interested to find how many things we can go without or make in a community where nothing can be bought.

When all the guests had arrived a little after seven we opened the folding doors between sitting room and dining room and went into a room blazing with red candles – on the table, sideboard, mantelpiece, and one tiny one at each place. We had one boy from each house helping with the serving – the servants always get a big kick out of an "affair" like this and cover themselves with glory. At the end we distributed the joke gifts, reading the poetry aloud. After dinner we sang Christmas carols and sat and talked, and soon the day was over – and a very happy one it had been too. All of you helped to make it happy with your remembrances.

Fenchow   *Sunday, January 5, 1936*

Mother dear –

We've been miserable here this week. Walter has the worst sinuses he's had in years with a splitting headache day and night and extra things at the hospital such as several deaths necessitating some autopsies, one night all night at the hospital, and difficult operations.

Last Sunday he got to our evening church service by 8:30 and we had supper afterwards. Monday he got to the station meeting by 8:30, at which I was elected Chairman of this station for the New Year – not much responsibility except to preside at meetings. Tuesday night he got thru supper at nine and we then joined the progressive New Year's Eve party. Wednesday we were to go to Esther's for noon New Year dinner. But Walter had emergencies all day and missed the delicious food and the fun. By the next day I had caught the bug from him. Then poor little Mary Lou got the bug. But we're all much better now – Walter sang while shaving today.

—Private Writing—

January 23, 1936

"Ye have not chosen me, but I have chosen you." How true! How little likely that I should have chosen China, or Walter, even. Yet here I am, and I cannot help but feel that it is in line with some plan that I can't see the workings of, that I haven't made myself. If that is so, surely there is a place for me here and work for me to do.

I have been impatient. I have not stopped to consider the thirty years of training and preparation Jesus had for the few short years of his ministry. These are my years of training and preparation. Am I being prepared? In the language? In my knowledge of China's background and my understanding of her people and her problems? In my general reading and understanding of world problems today? In my sacred obligation of training up children? In the infinitely hard task of adjusting to the peculiar life in interior stations? Most important of all in my growth in the experience of God, "ultimately our choice lies between a world within ourselves and a world outside," what of the world within myself?

And perhaps I have not seen the place at which I can make a great contribution by giving up rather than by clinging to. Walter has a great work to do and a great ability and passion for doing it. Help me to be willing, God, to give him up completely to his work and to find ways in which our deep love may be nourished and fed in the little in-between-times, through the homely little sacraments of common life. Perhaps my contribution in China is to be made through helping and smoothing and easing his life in the great work he is doing. And then I shall surely find the mental and spiritual and social satisfactions I crave in other places.

"Our fervor and profiting should increase daily," Thomas à Kempis[77] says. If this were being true of me, wouldn't my fears soon leave instead of tending to increase? He has chosen me – what room is there left for fear? Daily cultivating of the "world within" will help to drive them out. What if I could attain that "sense of something thrusting through life that makes for power?"

You have chosen me, God. Sustain me. Help me to grow.

Fenchow   *Monday, January 27, 1936*

Mother dear –

The China New Year's day is over and it wasn't nearly as hot and noisy as Peiping last year. I let one servant go to his village the day before New Year's and return the afternoon of the next day. The cook was with us till noon New Year's, then was off till the next day. I let the Amah have a half day off on New Year's too. We gave the servants presents of money and people sent us gifts, fruit, and canned goods, etc. The hospital is down to the fewest patients it's had since Walter came – around fifty. That's given Walter extra time to write up back histories, get caught up on hundreds of details, get correspondence up-to-date, and work on the business of collecting outstanding bills. Our chauffer's wife had a baby the day before New Year's. It was one year old, according to their reckoning when it was born, and the next day turned two, since all children age one year on the Chinese New Year's. So now it's ostensibly as old as Mary Lou.

As for me, I'm feeling fine, and have lots of energy. I have an idea I'm bigger than last time but I don't seem to have gained too much. Esther and I waddle around together taking our little girls for walks frequently and enjoying each other's society immensely or sit and knit and drink milk.

Fenchow   *Monday, February 3, 1936*

Mother dear –

I'm to take my first-year language exam this week and the 400 written characters seem to be impossible to remember. If I were using them daily in writing as I learn them, they would become second nature; but as it is, they're pretty nearly a pure feat of memory. Some are logical and some make no more sense than the way we spell "bough" and are as consistent as we are when we spell "bough" and "cough" alike and pronounce them as we do. So I've been putting three or four hours a day on them and it's concentrating, confining work…

Yesterday Walter and I were walking down to the post office to get a package – and we decided to take Mary Lou. This is the first time Mary Lou has walked outside the compound. You should have seen the sight. Children were playing everywhere in the narrow dusty streets and as soon as they saw this little white-face mite trudging independently along by herself – she refused to hold our hands!

---

77   Thomas á Kempis was a medieval Catholic theologian.

– they'd leave their play to run along beside her, laugh at her, make comments, try to play with her. We soon had a train of seventeen children from four to twelve in ages, *all boys*, all completely surrounding Mary Lou as she walked behind us. And did she love it, though! She laughed at them, scuffed her feet to kick up the thick clouds of dust, ran to look in open gates to courtyards inside, started climbing on stones to jump off, which amused them so that she did it all the more, fell down in the road, which produced roars of delight so she went on falling down on purpose. They stayed with us all the way to the post office and back, and Walter and I were nearly convulsed at the expressions of supreme satisfaction on Mary Lou's face and at her antics. I know that it isn't good to let her be such a center of attention. She is getting spoiled by thinking she runs the show. When Walter is home to see her so little, it is hard for him not to want to play with her or watch her or talk to her every time he has a chance, so I fear she begins to think she is a pretty important person. It will be good for her to have to share attention with a tiny baby.

Last night as we sat around talking after our Sunday worship service, we got onto the subject of Japan's inroads on North China. I was interested to hear the whole group agree that there isn't anything we can write home. We're too close to it to know what *is* going on. Your papers can publish stuff that never could get into our papers here. When we read the Christmas week clippings Father sent, there were front-page headlines on the Japan doings, which naturally must give you all the impression that things are serious. But our life goes on normally. We know that Japan is quietly and persistently edging her way into North China, that she already considers her control of the first two Provinces an accomplished fact, and that the other of the northern Provinces must inevitably follow – but this plan of hers was clear long ago, when she started in Manchuria. It was just a question of time for her doing it.

Incidentally, one of the clippings sent – the one on Yen's land socialization plan and anti-Communist propaganda – was sent to New York by special cable by a correspondent named Fischer in Peking who was my partner at the Rotary Club charity ball last winter. He seemed to have the dope pretty straight on Yen's ideas. A group of teachers from the school here, as well as from all schools in the Province, had to go to Taiyuan for ten days in January to sit under Yen and his advisors for daily lectures on these schemes. On their return the school had an hour a day in general assembly where the ideas were explained to the students. This went on for two weeks. Our servants, too, between certain ages, were supposed to attend classes for a week under the local magistrate on this same business of Yen's, but exemptions seemed easy to arrange in the servant class of people for none of ours went…

A new general has been transferred to Fenchow in charge of this district. He was in to see Walter yesterday to make arrangements about having his wounded soldiers cared for in the hospital. He thinks there may be trouble with the Communists in the next district west of here, for they are coming nearer to forage for food, and if the river keeps frozen they can cross easily at this particular point, where it is impossible north or south of here. He reported that recently two divisions had been completely wiped out in Shensi by the Communists and when Walter expressed surprise at not having read of this in the Chinese papers, he said quietly that that sort of news doesn't get into the papers. So again, it is hard for us to know what's what. But poor Governor Yen is having his hands full trying to cope with Communists on the west and the approaching Japanese from the east.

Meanwhile our lives go on quietly and uninterruptedly and as far as we know, life is all peaceful everywhere! You write us if you get a different impression!

Fenchow   *Saturday, February 15, 1936*

Mother dear –

We've moved Mary Lou out of the room adjoining our bedroom and put her in the room at the back of the house. I was afraid she might raise objections to leaving "her" room, so we went at the thing gradually, moving all her furniture first but letting her continue to sleep in her former room. She gradually got the idea that all her things were in another room and began going there to play. Then one late afternoon when the baby basket was all finished, I asked her to help make up the bed for the baby while the Amah was making up her bed for a big girl in the back room. She was thrilled, helping to pat the pillow and fix its dainty pink cover, smooth the embroidered sheets and the pink wool blankets saying, "Don't want the baby to be cold!" When we got it all done, we put it in her former room for the tiny baby to use, and she went to bed proudly in her new room, feeling big and independent.

I've had to institute a new system of checking on the cook and what goes on in the kitchen. I was too trusting and naïve in the beginning. I found our sugar and flour and other things disappearing much too fast. I always hate to check up on such petty dishonesties. But Walter has been trying to get me to see it from the point of view of the cook, to whom it doesn't seem dishonest to get off with a little each day of the apparently inexhaustible supplies we have. He has good qualities, he is pleasant and cheerful and cooperative, and he never makes the least complaint about the hours we have to wait for Walter for meals, so I've decided we can't look for perfection and am now dealing with him the way Walter says the Chinese really admire your dealing with them. I keep absolutely everything locked in our food storeroom and every day dole out enough sugar for the stewed fruit, enough flour for gravy, enough kerosene for the lamps, etc. I've reduced the use of some staples about half, which is quite a saving. I suppose that he makes up for this cut in his "squeeze" – probably by buying poorer quality or smaller quantity of meats, vegetables, and fruits on the street than he accounts to me for. We discovered our coal was walking out the back door *with the ashes*. Since he sees that I mean business and am checking on everything I give out, he is doing better himself. I keep a pad and pencil in the storeroom and write down what things I give out when, so I don't have to rely on my poor memory. He was never accused directly and openly of taking our things. It was suggested delicately that we were using up too much sugar, flour, bacon, etc. and then locking up the foods and having him have to ask me for whatever he needed told the rest of the story, and he understands, and I know he understands, and he knows I know he understands – and we're all perfectly happy!! Great system.

Taiku Hospital   *Monday, March 2, 1936*

Dear Family –

I haven't the faintest idea what Walter told you about our little Caroline in his notes written the day she arrived.[78] I don't think he could have described her very much, for you can't tell how a wee person

---

78   Carolyn Ruth Judd was born on February 26, 1936. Miriam's original letter had Carolyn spelled as Caroline.

looks the first five minutes, and since then he's been too busy to take a good look at her… She's the best little baby in the world making no slightest objections to all the excitement she's been subjected to, doing everything just as she should and gaining nicely. I'd forgotten how cuddly and precious and tiny a new baby could be – and I'm so happy to be learning again on our darling little Carolyn.

But Carolyn had to share front-page honors for the week with other exciting events. We'd known the Communists were coming nearer, leaving Shensi for lack of food and supplies. On the 24th there was rumor that they were getting close and the Chinese, as always, got panicky and started to pack up and move off – going almost anywhere just to be going. We foreigners at a station meeting Sunday night decided to sit tight till something more definite was known. Things seemed quieter in the countryside the first of the week, but we didn't want to wait indefinitely for the baby's arrival, which is why Walter started me "taking things" Monday night. I was glad I found this ordeal so much easier than Mary Lou's coming, and was feeling very fine. On Friday, the third day, I could tell there was much tension in the air from scraps of things I heard the nurses saying and the distractedness of anyone who dropped in to see me. I had no chance to ask Walter what was what – he was busy seeing the local magistrate, General in charge of troops in Fenchow, other officials, meeting the Chinese members of our station committee, and discussing with the foreigners.

At 4:30 p.m. he popped into my room in the hospital and said – "We're going to Taiku. What do you want me to get from the house?" In the next two hours he and Emma and the Amah packed clothes and bedding for Mary Lou, for Carolyn, collected clothes for me, packed up the Amah and her little ten-year-old girl, fed Mary Lou and dressed her warmly, made a truly comfortable bed for me in the car where I could stretch out fully, swathed me in warm sweaters, stockings, bathrobe, carried me out in a stretcher, loaded up and we were off – the Burton's car leading and Esther taking care of our not-yet three-day-old Carolyn. How I wished I could have gone home and packed the things I wanted and gone off like an ordinary mortal instead of being so useless. All I could do was to lie still & wonder what dresses they would pull out for me – wondering if they packed any shoes, if they've brought the things I'll need for Carolyn when I leave the hospital, if Mary Lou has all the clothes she needs – and just lie helpless. But since no one knows whether we're here for two weeks, or out of Fenchow for six months, or for good, I probably couldn't have packed with any more intelligence. And fortunately, the day before I went to the hospital, I had taken Walter all around the bedrooms upstairs showing him what was in which closets, which trunks, which dressers, in case he might have to pack suddenly.

That was a strange night drive to Taiku, over the same bumpy road I described in my letter about Thanksgiving. But I was *really* completely comfortable – no exaggeration for home consumption – and could lie and watch the stars, or look up into the faces of Chinese men who came with lanterns to peer into the car as we stopped often to put water into our frozen radiator. Mary Lou lay down beside me after a bit and we sang together and talked until she fell asleep. The Amah was too carsick to hold her. And at 10 o'clock we drove into the Taiku hospital compound and I was soon in a nice room there, with little Carolyn in the nursery next door with three Chinese babies. Walter had done everything to make the trip easy for me, had driven very carefully, and I honestly didn't suffer one bit from it, tho' I'll admit to being tired!

Esther has set up housekeeping here in a house that was empty because folks were on furlough. Her servants and provisions came over by cart after we got here. Mary Lou is staying with them, and I will go there with Carolyn when I leave the hospital. Walter took the car and drove right back to Fenchow the next morning. All his doctors have left and many nurses so he is extra busy with all the wounded soldiers coming in. Our house is closed up, tho' a servant is sleeping there, and our coal has gone to the Matthews who had decided not to leave yet but wait and see what develops. Their coal had given out and it's impossible to get it in the city now.

One reason why we were particularly anxious not to be involved in any trouble in Fenchow was that if any harm should come to foreigners from the Chinese Communists or lawless elements, Japan would have an excellent excuse to rush in to "quiet things down, maintain order, protect the foreigners, etc." – and U.S.A. and the world would doubtless unitedly approve her actions, and thus solidly back and support her taking over of more North China property. We don't want to help Japan with any more excuses for her actions. Then, too, the local military men had all sent their families away to safety and said they would feel better defending the city if women and children and non-mobile elements were removed. It was only fair to them that we leave.

The Taiku car goes back and forth to Fenchow daily, bringing Chinese who want to get away etc. and carrying our messages. The passenger and mail buses are all commandeered by the military and it's impossible to get carts and drivers that are willing to risk heading out on the road with passengers. Just now the car has returned from Fenchow with a note from Walter saying things are quieter, the government has finally got excited and sent many troops…

You're not to be worried about us. Remember that if anything drastic had happened and we'd all had to move to Peiping you would have news of it by cable. No news is good news. I'm really getting on well and everyone is so good to me. Meantime, remember that Communists have been operating in China for years now and will likely go on – and so will we!!

Taiku   *Tuesday, March 10, 1936*

Dear Family –

This has been one of the longest weeks I've ever spent. Things are better now and life is beginning to get more normal, as I get used to the little lady, almost two weeks old now, and used to the routine with her, and used to being without Walter, and used to living the life of a refugee, and used to the rumors and reports that come constantly about Communist activities in our region.

The week was long because I had nothing to do but lie in bed at the hospital and think. People were awfully nice about dropping in to visit, but I don't know the folks here well. I had no concern for little Carolyn other than to play cow at regular intervals when she was brought in to me. Now I have her all to myself and she keeps the day much too full for me to have extra time to think. We left the hospital on Sunday and came to the house where the Burtons are living tentatively. And she has been a model baby. Sleeps continually, has to be awakened for each feeding, hasn't cried a total of an hour since we arrived and in general is behaving as tho' she knew that there was plenty else for us to have on our minds besides a fussy baby, so she'd behave. I'm feeding her at three-hour intervals (four hours at night) and manage to sleep a good bit of the intervening time. It is nice to have Esther to do all the housekeeping and the Amah to take care of Mary Lou as well as doing the baby's wash, and my meals sent upstairs to me. Mary Lou and the two little Burton girls have to come in continually to take a peep into the basket to see the tiny baby, which they cannot understand very well. Mostly she plays outdoors all day. So you can see that our domestic situation is quite posh for refugees!!

Another reason why last week was so long was because of the constant uncertainty and the constant changing in the rumors we got. Hardly an hour went by, but someone would drop in to my room at the hospital and say that an evacuating missionary from hither or yon had just arrived with the report that our town was surrounded, or besieged or being fought over, or that he had seen seven trainloads of National troops being moved into the Province, or that three new generals had been sent by Chiang K'ai Shek from Nanking to help out, or that no mail had gone to Fenchow for a week, or that the mail was going over by runners some of whom had been shot, that Chinese families of many of our Fenchow Church people had arrived in Taiku with the report that the situation there was bad, or was much improved, that food was scarce, and food all gone, that shops had reopened and confidence was being restored, that new provincial troops from Taiyuan were pouring in with tons of ammunition to defend the city and on and on. No use telling you all the rumors and reports, but I will list a few of the facts that seem to be definite.

Because Walter is getting the wounded soldiers in the hospital he is on good terms with the military folk, and is a good friend of the General in charge of defending Fenchow, so reports he has are apt to be as accurate as any. The Communist fighting did get up to within a few miles of the city tho' no one ever decided how many Communists are in this band that has crossed the Yellow River. Whenever the Communists fight they seem to win; partly they get the common villagers and drive them in front of their own men to be shot down first, and the defending soldiers refuse to fire at many of their own countrymen and their own villagers. Partly, too, the Chinese soldiers are terrified of the Communists and refuse to fight because these Shansi troops are no good. But Shantung and Nationalist troops are coming in to help with the defense as well as bombing planes from Nanking, so things look hopeful for a drive that will send the Communists off in some other direction or back into the mountains, their favorite haunt. It seems they are making for Taiyuan if possible, but if they should be badly routed down our way will give up this plan and go on off up North into Mongolia.

As for Fenchow itself, the city is well defended now, the walls recently repaired, more than 500 troops within the city and lots of ammunition, the Headquarters of the Provincial Bandit Suppression Bureau moved to the city under a very able Chinese General – the one we entertained at dinner about the first week we were in Fenchow, last May – and no one thinks that the Communists will be so foolish as to try to take the city itself. The city could easily hold out for a three-months siege. But there is danger outside the city and on the roads, from the small groups of Communists found in the villages and particularly from lawless elements in the country normally held by law and order in the Province, but now running rampant because everything is confused and disorganized. The general consensus of opinion is that it may be months if not years before Shansi will be really peaceful again.

What about the work inside Fenchow? Well, it's had of necessity to close down, except the efforts of individual evangelists among the Chinese, who are finding things they can keep doing, and except the hospital. This is a terrible blow to the Chinese Christians, and they are saying that the "Church is finished in Shansi," and are discouraged and disheartened. For this reason, Walter is determined to keep the hospital open and running as normally as possible. It is the only organization the church is maintaining now, and he wants it to be a tower of strength to those Chinese who are so upset. So he and Emma are going about the regular routine as if nothing had happened, mainly in order to maintain the morale among the staff. One of the Chinese doctors was faithful and remained. Only two nurses fled so that side is well cared for. The business department is in a bad way. Walter has been working nights on the books as late as 3:30 and 4 a.m. trying to bring order out of chaos, for he will not have his regular daytime medical routine broken into. The consul telegraphed for Americans to get out to a place of greater safety so Harold Mathews sent his family out to the coast. But Harold is remaining in Fenchow to work. Mary McClure and Louise Meebold are remaining to carry on what work they can among the poor disorganized women, and to help out in the hospital wherever possible.

And of our immediate future? That is all guess, too, for we just live from day to day. If things should begin to get nervous over here, Walter would want us in Peiping, and I'd pack up our few belongings and the two little girlies and get on the train here taking the Amah and stay at the American Board compound there for the time being. I am afraid it will be a long time before we can settle down as a family again in Fenchow, if ever. We have nothing with us except a limited supply of clothing, the silver, and a few of our documents. Altho' possessions are the least of our concern in times like these, still we do have a certain attachment to our own things, our wedding gifts, the things we have used and enjoyed, our books, and particularly Walter's medical books. But Walter's last note said that if things remain quiet he would try to get over this weekend to see us. Perhaps he remembers it is about our fourth wedding anniversary. And perhaps he feels as I do that we can plan things a great deal better if we discuss them together. For after the minute he came into the hospital room and announced, "We're leaving for Taiku," I had no more than five minutes conversation with him and we didn't make plans in that time…

Please be sure that none of the stuff I write in these letters about the Communists gets into the papers. I would hate to be responsible for adding to the vast sum of unconfirmed reports about China's condition that constantly appear in the U.S.A. papers. If you want to make general statements about the greatly disturbed conditions due to the Communist advance that's O.K. Things are much more encouraging now than I thought they'd be last week. There is truly little personal danger as long as Fenchow is well protected, and we are here right on the railroad.

I am not going to be writing many letters these days to friends, partly because I need to conserve my energy for Carolyn and for the vicissitudes of these days. It does seem rather tragic that this should happen just when Walter's intensive and concentrated work of a year-and-a-half was beginning to show such good results and we were beginning to get caught up on our back work and letters read. It will be a long time till Walter gets things back to normal. No telling what will happen to the finances of the hospital, for the ordinary middle class Chinese from surrounding places will surely not come to Fenchow Hospital in these disturbed times, and they were the backbone of its support. I hope the military will pay its bills. Time will tell.

Addendum to Mother –

How much I have thought of you these last days. I knew you were thinking constantly of us all here – and that has helped as much as anything to sustain me. Your February 2 letter Walter sent over from Fenchow to me the day after we left there. Do you remember how you ended it? "You are so safe in His loving care. I feel so sure of it." When you wrote that you couldn't know what a message of courage that would be to me through difficult days. It has helped me so much to have the knowledge of your strong faith that "all things do work together for good." And your often repeated verse "As thy days, so shall thy strength be" has borne me up in a real way. You are very near and very dear to me, my Mother… I didn't want to rave too much in the general letter but Carolyn is an *adorable* little girl. How I love her, and how her warm little body against mine comforts me these days.

Taiku   *Thursday, March 19, 1936*

Dear Folks –

Walter has been over for his proposed visit looking quite chipper, except that he was tired. He arrived Saturday night and left after breakfast Monday. I'll jot down the main items of political and military news as I can remember them.

Some days ago the Communists tapped the telephone wires and discovered the plans for an attack on themselves so were ready and waiting at the place, and overwhelmed their attackers. The provincial troops discovered this, so worked a fake telephone message off on them some days later, saying they heard the Communists had left a certain spot so they were going on from there to other places. The Communists rushed to this supposedly deserted place, a gully in the mountains some fifteen miles outside Fenchow, and all day long Fenchowites could hear the fighting in one of the worst battles and worst defeats the Communists have been known to have in their years of fighting. They generally avoid an open combat whenever they can. But this day, the field guns boomed all day, airplanes kept flying over Fenchow on their way to and from Taiyuan and bombed the fighters, and altogether 3,000 Communists were reported killed in this, their First Route Army. They have four armies and no one seems to be able to discover where the other three are. But this was a crushing defeat to their best one. Many provincial troops were killed too, but at least they did fight, and so often previously they have run. The Communists pulled a stunt during this fighting, I hear. They disguised some of their own men as common villagers and got up right close to the Provincial troops without being fired on, and then pulled guns on them! They say a thousand wounded soldiers have been taken into Fenchow. The military has a temporary hospital there with a "staff" of over two hundred, and lots of the soldiers are lying on the floors of temples. The worse cases and those needing x-rays are taken to our hospital, and Walter is called out to see some of those in other places. About fifty wounded soldiers are in our hospital and as many ordinary cases so they are busy. Some of the wounded Communist troops have also been brought in and Walter talked to them, but they are troops who fought the Communists last year and were captured and then found it healthier to stay and fight in the Communist army than to protest – so they are not Communists by conviction!

After this big defeat, the rest of the Communists withdrew into the mountains. They probably know that the Government means business and is out after them from all angles, and it seems likely they will go off elsewhere, but this again is a prediction that no one can be sure of. The discouraging thing is that many of the Communists in small bands of four to forty go into the villages and towns and propagandize among the people or live quietly there until they can get recruits or a foothold and stir up the people to a later uprising.

However, things within the city of Fenchow itself are peaceful. Buses started running regularly again; business is going on with only ordinary precautions. They were even considering seeing if they could get enough of the Ming I students to return to reopen the school when suddenly in popped a General who is going to direct activities from Fenchow, and as he and his retinue couldn't find a suitable place to camp in the already full city, they took over some of the school dormitories. I guess the school won't try to get going this spring. Perhaps some of the lower schools will reopen… There has been an order to shoot anyone seen on the streets after eight at night, so Walter has had to stay at the hospital nights, going home in the morning to wash up and have breakfast and see that our household things are all fine. One of our servants is working in the hospital in these busy days and the other is watching our house, keeping a little heat in two of the rooms. In the evenings all the remainder of the foreigners – four single ladies and Harold Matthews and Walter – have supper together and talk over news of the day…

I've been out to two luncheons and a dinner this week, so you can see I have entered the gay life! The weather remains cold, with snow one day each week recently. Spring ought to have come and we're all hoping it will arrive soon. Walter packed up our things and sent over to us in case we should have to stay here for some time, or go on to Peiping, and these I've been opening up and getting into use. So there's plenty to do every day, even though we are just "refugees."

The night before I went to the hospital, while I was taking castor oil and quinine and various things to hurry Carolyn along, Walter wrote out an article for the *Shanghai Times*, of which he is the "Shansi correspondent" (gets the paper free and hasn't written a thing in it this year!) about the Communist situation which was threatening then, and I typed it. It got a front page in the *Times* and an editorial comment and has been copied in various other papers. I send along a copy. It isn't up-to-date now for lots has happened since then but it helps you know what's what.

American Board Compound, Peiping   *Tuesday, March 24, 1936*

Dear Walter –

There's no use being Pollyanna and pretending our trip to Peiping was a pleasant jaunt, though we're here safely. Carl was a prize, doing anything and everything quietly and cheerfully and quickly, even to washing out Carolyn's soiled diapers and mopping up Mary Lou's vomited dinner – and that takes some devotion when the children aren't your own![79] Your wire to leave came at seven Thursday evening. So we packed till midnight, finished up the next morning including all the arranging with anxious servants who kept worrying us to death, and left as quietly as we could. Took the 11:30 train on Friday, with a second-class compartment for the Burtons and Judds and twenty-one pieces

---

79   Carl Huber was a Carleton student teaching in the Mission School in Fenchow. When Walter was unable to leave the hospital, Carl was charged with moving Miriam, Carolyn, and Mary Lou to a safer place.

of hand luggage besides all the checked. The little girls had eaten before leaving home and we ate sandwiches on the train and Carolyn ate on schedule. My maidenly modesty is completely gone now and I nurse her when and where! In Taiyuan we went to Meyers. I had Mary Lou lie down an hour with me though we didn't sleep. Went to send you a wire at the telegraph office with Carl and discovered the communications were cut. Got some fruit for the train, dried out some wet diapers, got everyone fed and went to the train in the English Baptist mission car. Mike Burton and Carl had gone to watch baggage.[80] Had a second-class compartment again, with Esther up on one side, Mary Lou and Mary together up on the other, Mike and Alice –down on one side, me on the other, and the tiny baby on the table in the center in her basket – *and* the twenty-one pieces of baggage strewn hither and yon. Not very crowded!! Carl insisted on riding third class. It was stifling hot so that we were all uncomfortable and with the little girls waking scared at the strangeness or wanting to use the pot at various times and Carolyn crying occasionally when we stopped and having to be nursed several times, besides all the noise and confusion outside – so guess how much we slept.

Fleeing the China turmoil. Mary Lou (front in snowsuit) and Miriam (sitting on suitcase) with Carolyn.

When we got to Yutze we were so glad we had gone on the earlier train and got settled at Taiyuan. For after we left Taiku came the word for the foreigners to move on, as Communists were near, and then Taiku was in an uproar. Many were on the train without reservations or space and had to sit in the aisles with small children. At Shihchiachuang the next morning we met the China Inland Mission's Mr. Thompson. He's a corker, funny as anything but knows how to get things done. He took hold and managed old ladies, babies, baggage, and rickshaw men for us, sending the old ladies to the hotel with much of the baggage and us to the Salvation Army. It was a relief to get into a house with stoves and hot water and be able to wash up the dirty kiddies and ourselves and eat a good breakfast and tend to Carolyn's needs. Back to the 11:30 train, which was crowded, so that we had to sit in the dining car all day.

Mary Lou was crazy about trains from the start, continually kept asking to go on another whenever we were ashore, loved looking out the window at toot-toots in the station. But by lunch time she was terribly tired with all the strangeness and rushing about, ate lightly of the rice and boiled eggs and bananas we gave her, and refused to lie down and sleep. She got unbearably fussy, and I tried to make her be quiet and had finally succeeded in getting her to sleep after heroic efforts when the train stopped at a station and she popped up. Well, I had to tend to Carolyn then, so Esther took her and held her in her arms and after a little struggle and crying she gave in and dropped dead asleep and slept two hours, through all sorts of noises, and through more than a half hour wait at Paotingfu.

---

80   Mike and Esther Burton and their two young daughters were part of the group.

As always, the last bit of the trip was the worst. Everyone tired and dirty and terribly hot, and the fruit and baggage and books and toys being strewn pretty well over the car. Mary Lou was cross when she woke up, and evidently sick for all her lunch came up. Fortunately we had just moved Carolyn's bed to another seat so we could use the table to eat on, or we would have had her to clean up too. Carolyn slept nicely which was a help, for Mary Lou needed constant attention. By the time we pulled into Peiping after eight, she was too tired and fussy for words, a bit scared at the lights of the big city in the darkness, not interested in seeing any more new faces. And there were thousands of Chinese folks all anxious to be helpful to the poor *flees* and practically all of them insisted on carrying Mary Lou. She screamed with terror and clung to me, and I had to beg them to leave her alone, and then they insisted on carrying Carolyn and I again tried to be firm and still polite in asking them please to leave me alone, but finally one of them literally tore Carolyn from my arms and I didn't see her again for ten minutes, during which time as they hurried on ahead of slow-moving Mary Lou, the baby was probably passed from one to another. She was screaming bloody murder when I got her back and continued to do so for an hour, which is the first time I've heard Carolyn go at it like that. Carl stuck by; after he had loaded baggage on a platform truck he came and carried Mary Lou, which she permitted her old friend to do. We were soon in a taxi with Mrs. Shaw and the necessary diaper bag and one suitcase, and after we reached the Shaws' it wasn't ten minutes before Mary Lou was asleep, dirty as she was, without washing or eating. I got Carolyn quieted down by giving her a warm bath, for she was covered with prickly heat from the terribly hot car. After I got Carolyn fed I dropped into a hot bath and bed myself, without eating – at 10 p.m.

Now we're gradually trying to forget that trip. Poor Mary Lou was hardest hit. There have been so many new experiences and strange faces in these last weeks that she's stood about all she can and seems terrified of everyone, just clings to me, wants to kiss me and hold my hand all the time, refuses to have anyone dress her or feed her or play with her or touch her and is rude to everyone who tries to be nice to her, cries easily and frequently. I don't blame the poor little girlie. I feel a bit that way myself. But it is difficult when her waking up and eating hours come when I have to be tending to Carolyn, and when she will let no one keep her out of all the things there are to be investigated in a strange place. Everyone is eager to do what they can, but for now it is my job alone, I feel. I'm trying to get as much rest as I can between times so Carolyn will have a bit more to eat. I got a temporary Amah yesterday. I still have to be at hand to give the food – I'm determined not to have Mary Lou's good eating habits spoiled.

We have decided to go out to Tungchow to live.[81] The people out there invited a number of the refugees. We are to live in the Hunter annex, three rooms up and downstairs and board with the Hunters at $2 a day for me, less for Mary Lou. I think this will be nice, for we will have a bit of independence and privacy without having to run our own house…

The Ballous have asked that we come with them to Peitaiho, and I can't think of anyone I'd rather be with.[82] I'll accept, for Peiping is too hot to keep the little girlies in. Incidentally, they said there would be room for you!!

---

81 Tungchow, also called Tungshien, was a few miles east of Peking with a large ABCFM station.

82 Peitaiho was a town on the Pacific Ocean where some missionaries and Peking Americans had summer cottages.

Addendum to the families: I am sending on this copy of my letter to Walter as there is neither time nor energy for anything else. The Communists are an unpredictable element, as you can see by the suddenness of our move to Peiping. They are getting nearer to Taiyuan and wanting to cut railroad communications to Peiping, so we came while we could. Two letters have got thru somehow from Walter in Fenchow so that's encouraging even tho' the phone and telegraph connections are cut. Walter is quite safe inside Fenchow and will naturally make no attempt to leave there just now. Our days are difficult but not dangerous.

Peiping   *Monday, March 30, 1936*

Dear Families –

Tomorrow we make our last move – at least for a while. I wrote Walter that I envied his father and mother living for forty-six years in the same place! I think things are going to be happy for us to live out in Tunghsien this spring. This place is a suburb of Peiping so I can get into the city occasionally. There will be small children for Mary Lou to play with on that big compound, so she should be happy.

The Communists seem to have left Fenchow behind, and have gone on to Taiyuan, which seems to be in some danger now. Walter writes that all is quiet in the city with the gates opened some days and some days not. They are extremely busy in the hospital: he had three babies in one day, plus a Caesarian; typhus was breaking out among the wounded soldiers. I think Walter is arranging to be away from his children while they're small and have to be up at night!

5

Last China Years

1936-1937

On porch of Fenchow home

The little family, sans Walter, found refuge fifteen miles outside Peking in Tunchow (also called Tunghsien) at another ABCFM mission location staying with the Hunter family. Finally, Walter was able to get away for a week to help relocate the family to the Pacific Ocean shore town of Peitaiho, where they moved into the large summer home with the Ballou family. Walter returned to his hospital and we remained at the coast for the summer.

In some ways it was an idyllic time. The area was populated with gracious homes and cottages for missionaries and Americans escaping the summer heat in Peking. Despite the tranquil surface, however, the threat of Japanese aggression lurked, with Japanese troops painting large white Xs with unknown meaning on the beach rocks at regular intervals. When Miriam sprained her ankle, Walter came back to help and actually took one of the few extended vacations of his entire life, staying for six weeks.

More private writings of Miriam's emerge from this time. She adored Walter and it presented her with a terrible dilemma: she loved him deeply, yet felt alone, sad, and unable to effect his priorities. The religious and cultural teachings of the time reinforced that the man was the head of the household and the woman's role was to support him and fit in "around the edges." Her writings reveal that she was doing her best to fit into that role, and yet it was like fitting a square peg into a round hole.

In September, the young family returned to Fenchow after the Communists had been pushed out, and they settled back into life there, where they remained for an entire year. Later that fall, Miriam pondered about the great divide she felt between herself and the Chinese people, comparing her own family's home and many possessions with the meager housing and limited possessions of a fine Chinese doctor and his young family nearby. While everyone was always courteous, Miriam felt that many Chinese were private, not outgoing and gregarious like most Americans. Miriam was no doubt realizing that her expectation that she would be a co-missionary with Walter to improve the life and welfare of the Chinese was not reasonable. "If I'm going to be honest and realistic, I'll have to admit that our home, in itself, is making no contribution to China," she wrote privately.

In April 1937, Miriam and Walter embarked on a month-long trip to several cities throughout China, leaving the Amah and the girls at the Tungchow mission station outside of Peking where they had been the previous spring. Miriam was ecstatic; it was an exciting time for her, since she had wanted to see other parts of China. The couple visited other hospitals within the North China mission. Their last stop was Shanghai for a major medical conference. Miriam met interesting people, some from Walter's prior work in southeast China, and some cohorts of the Nationalist leaders. The movements of the Communists and Japanese were a constant concern everywhere.

After the family's return to Fenchow, they spent much of the summer of 1937 in the nearby Valley where it was cooler and Miriam could rest during the unsettled weeks of her new pregnancy. A Japanese coup in Peking increased the uncertainty and anxiety of a Japanese takeover of all of North China, and by September, communications were again cut off. Miriam and Walter were concerned over what to do. While Walter did not feel he could leave his hospital post, he worried for the safety of his young family. On September 20, 1937, when Miriam was four months pregnant, the family left Fenchow.

It was to be yet another arduous journey, south to Hankow. There were wounded soldiers on the train. I have a vague memory of the train stopping in the middle of the night as the Japanese were running bombing raids on trains. I also have a hazy sense of being underground in a bomb shelter. After a week in Hankow, Walter put his family on a flight to Hong Kong, and he returned to Fenchow. It was traumatic to split up the family. We stayed in Hong Kong with a friend of Miriam's, as it took a month to book passage on a ship to the U.S.

This was the end of Miriam's life in China – at age thirty-seven, after just three years there, instead of the lifetime she had imagined – although she did not know it at the time. Throughout all her adventures and misadventures, she managed everything well. She was loyal, organized, energetic, creative, and courageous, and what she did, she excelled at. But she never talked about the lonely, difficult parts, whose memories lived on in her heart.

Walter returned to keep the Mission's hospital open, eventually under Japanese occupation. Miriam soldiered on alone, arriving back in the U.S. on November 3, 1937 with her small children. She traveled by train to Montclair, New Jersey, moved into her parent's home and waited.

Tungchow, Peiping East   *Monday, April 6, 1936*

Dear Families –

Our beginning down here was not auspicious. The first day they had the worst dust storm they've had in years. Mary Lou's cold was a good one. Carolyn's stuffed-up nose didn't like the dust, nor did it help my cold any, so all in all we were a rather sad lot. But there's a fine doctor here[83] and he came down twice a day to see us and besides prescribing for us helped with all sorts of arrangements that

---

83   Dr. Hugh Robinson. The Judd and Robinson families remained close, even after returning to the U.S.

weren't quite in the medical line. Now the colds are improved, spring has suddenly broken, and all of us liking our surroundings very much.

This is the largest of the American Board Compounds in North China. They have a big boys' school on it, and a girls' school too. For American children they have sixth grade through high school here, about sixty pupils. The hospital is down at the other end of the compound. There are six families stationed here, Americans I mean, and a number of single ladies, teachers, nurse, etc. so there is more variety in the foreign community than we had in Fenchow. Almost everyone has had to "refugee" at some time during their China career.

Mr. Hunter does agricultural work. Just now he is hatching chicks in his cellar trying to improve the Chinese poultry by selling cocks and his good foreign eggs to Chinese hatcheries. In the winter he has a ten-week school for farmers and has a lot of projects going. The Hunters are such nice people that it is grand being in their Annex. Carolyn has gained splendidly during these trying days. Mary Lou adores her and there seems to be no jealousy so all's happy.

From a recent letter of Walter's I will copy out a section, much against my will – but I'm always obedient to my husband, so here goes. "A letter from Mrs. Meyers said 'A week ago today the Burtons, Mrs. Judd, Carl, and others were here and took the night train. Mrs. Judd was the best sport. Here she was with a baby three weeks old, tried to telephone or telegraph her husband only to find the wires cut, and starting off to Peiping not knowing where she could stay. When she could get no message through that afternoon to her husband she came back and played the piano for quite a while in spite of being dreadfully disappointed.'

"I was so proud when I read that paragraph – and humble. Who am I to have *you* as my partner. I appreciate fully that it takes lots more courage and control for you to play the 100% sport all these weeks as you have, than it would say, for me or someone else with a much less sensitive nature than you have. All the more honor and respect for you. I admire *steadiness* under fire about as much as anything I know, and you have it. You never have let me down once, my Comrade, in the four years we have had together. I hope to be able never to let you down in the forty years I trust we still have ahead of us. You don't realize how heartening it is hour by hour to know you understand what I am trying to do and are for me to the limit, no matter what the cost to you is being. I only wish I could be more help to you.

"I ought to copy the above and send to your family. Please send the whole thing to them. Perhaps it won't hurt them to know what I think of you as well as what Mrs. Meyers does. And I have a notion I know you even better than she does – yes, in a few respects, even better than your family does. They built their lives and hopes into you in *faith*; I have seen the results thereof in the actual hours of testing."

Isn't that sweet of Walter to write and to want you to hear it too? I must admit I wasn't liking it much any of the time. But I knew he was feeling terribly about our having to go out without his help. I'm awful glad he stayed where he was, where his job needed him.

Tunghsien   *Monday, April 20, 1936*

Dear Families –

Just a month ago today we pulled out of Taiku, bag and baggage and babies! Now we are settled into a quiet, simple, domestic routine. Harold Matthews came from Fenchow to Peiping last weekend and brought with him our lovely Fenchow Amah. And were we ever glad to see her. It was almost like seeing one of the family again. We're much happier now… She is so responsible – I mean dependable. She'll go to the beach with us.

Mother dear – It has helped me more than you'll ever know to have your letters of courage and faith, with the strong note of sureness that we would be strengthened and cared for. (It seems so strange to have two little girls – ME, Miriam Barber being the mother of two little girls!! I feel too young to be a mother, and even sometimes I want my own Mummie pretty bad.)

Tunghsien   *Monday, May 4, 1936*

Dear Families –

I'm to lead chapel for the American School – their regular six o'clock chapel service before supper. Dr. Rugh talked to them yesterday about being a Christian, and I think I'll add the single thought that *it's not easy* – that is, it involves suffering and sacrifice and ridicule, etc. I think that's a most important idea to be grasped by young people these days when the general tendency is to get something for nothing, not to want to take the slow difficult way, to the really worthwhile achievements in life.

Tunghsien   *Tuesday, May 26, 1936*

Dear Families –

I had fun yesterday with Olga Robinson, wife of the doctor here. We went over into the city – for you see this lovely compound with its several schools is outside the wall, so you don't get to see much of the life of the Chinese people. But I wanted to see it, for it has been an important city in China's history, and continues to be now as the seat of the East Hopei Autonomous Government.[84]

We were mostly interested in the place where Yin had established his headquarters. He had been made supervisor of the demilitarized area with offices here, and because of a Japanese wife, and evidently very genuine sympathy with what the Japanese are trying to do in North China, declared this "Autonomous Government," which is quite under the thumb of Japan, managed by Yin. Last week 150 new Japanese soldiers were landed out here amid protests from Nanking. We saw three drug shops and dispensaries, and Olga says they are all heroin shops. This new administration of Yin's has taken over all the Chinese schools, run them under their own jurisdiction with *free* tuition,

---

84   After military action by the Imperial Japanese Army brought northeastern China under Japanese control, this area of Hopei Province was declared a demilitarized zone. In November 1935, the Chinese administrator Yin Ju-Keng declared it "autonomous," and it became a puppet state of the Empire of Japan.

board, and room. And guess what sort of propaganda they are getting into the pupils! Well, draw your own conclusions as to Japanese aims in north China.

He has taken over a large, old Confucian temple and its adjoining courts and buildings, has renovated it completely, painting up the temple proper in a brilliant red outside and furnished with red lacquer and red satin inside. We walked boldly in the front gate, disregarding a rather incongruous polite "hello" from the soldiers guarding, getting all the guards excited as to what might be our business there, tho' we kept assuring them we only wanted to see the redecorated temple inside the first courtyard. We could see the reception room set with tea table, saw "secretaries" rushing around with documents and official-looking letters, loved the brilliant red and the contrast of the big old gnarled trees that grew up in the courtyard… We went outside, past the loads of good-looking cars sitting around at the front gate, around to the back where is the famous old pagoda connected to the temple. It is a beautiful structure, towering up thirteen stories, six sided in shape, and with twenty bronze bells on each of the six sides of each of the thirteen stories, which makes more than fifteen hundred bells in all, if my arithmetic is correct. You can imagine how lovely the sound is as the breeze gently rings the bells.

As we came out from the pagoda grounds we saw two men, obviously "gentlemen officials" of the Yin administration arguing roughly with some poor old Chinese people in the midst of a lot of debris of wood and household goods. We waited till the gentlemen went on, for we wanted to see if our guess about the situation was correct, and it was. The old woman told us that she and another old lady had lived there till twenty days ago when Yin's men came along and pulled down her house, told her they wanted this land to beautify the grounds around Yin's establishment, gave her twenty dollars. She couldn't get land and erect a house for twenty dollars, and had no where to go, so had just thrown a bit of cloth over a horizontal pole to make a shelter hardly big enough for a dog, and she and her friend had been sleeping under this ever since, cooking out in the open. Today the men had come back again to order them off the place. Do the common people love the officials!!!

The people connected with this Yin outfit seem to be the old-style Chinese, without modern education and the new outlook, so it seems like a definite regression to the China of twenty or thirty years ago. And it being a stronghold for Japanese activities, you can imagine how popular it is with the Chinese and with the foreign group who have to live alongside it and watch the situation develop.

Tunghsien   *Monday, June 1, 1936*

Dear Mother –

We've been watching the Japanese soldiers arrive in Tunghsien this week – several special train loads of them last Saturday, 650 men with horses and machine guns. You will have read about all the protests about this increasing in the Japanese garrisons, but I don't see that the protests are doing much good. We all wonder what this is leading to, and there seems to be a general feeling that there will be some big trouble with these neighbors, perhaps even this month.

Since our recent experience of having to leave Shansi, I have developed an altogether new outlook on the main troubles China is constantly facing, and the way they involve the missionaries. I begin to feel as if I'd been initiated into the "Brotherhood." Everyone asks about our Shansi troubles, then goes on to tell about similar trials they went through some time. One after another incident has come to my attention in these weeks, about people having to leave Tientsin, or Shantung, or even Tungchow when the Japanese bombed it in 1930. And although these experiences are not what we would have chosen, still they have been gone through by the missionaries with courage and faith, and looking back on them afterwards, they feel that they have been valuable in their own growth of character. I read yesterday in the new *Reader's Digest*, "Things that happen, however painful they are at the time, do not matter very much for long. Only how we behave to them matters." So I feel that our life in China is to continue to have uncertainties and difficulties of one kind or another but they won't be the things that really matter, as much as how we meet them.

3 Lighthouse Point, Peitaiho Beach, Hopei Province   *Tuesday, June 16, 1936*

Mother dear –

Here we are a happy united family in one of the most lovely of all the summer cottages around here, right on the rocks a few feet from the ocean…

Walter got to Tungchow at 7:30 p.m. Wednesday, and when I saw the train pull in and his head out the window, I could hardly believe it, for it had been so long and so hard a time since we had been together. The following days continued hot and hotter. I finished packing and Walter slept a lot – he was tired and quite thin. Saturday we started on the exciting train ride that Mary Lou had looked forward to! Our second-class compartment on the thru train to Mukden was a lovely one – new, clean, electric fan, etc. We left the train about seven a.m. at a junction and took a small shuttle train about twenty minutes across to the Beach Station. And from there about half an hour by rickshaw brought us to the Ballou house. It was an easy trip, with an Amah, a Daddy, congenial companions, comfortable arrangements, shorter hours and all in good health – such a contrast to that nightmare of a trip to Peiping.

The family at the Peitaiho Beach

The Ballou house has a lovely location. It's built on rocks with the water down a rocky incline a few feet in front of the house… The PUMC and official folks have more pretentious houses. This is of stone with a wide verandah and wicker porch chairs and lounge chairs inviting. My idea is to sit and watch the sea keep rolling up on the beach, pretending I'm on shipboard. At night the lights about twenty miles away across the bay twinkle…

Peitaiho is spread up and down along the coast here for several miles, with groups of houses at various places. There are different beaches for bathing in the various little bays – one just off to the west of the Ballou house, which Mary Lou and the Amah can run down to in a minute and enjoy the sand, and the water when she gets used to this cool, moist atmosphere. Most of the missionary folks we know – Presbyterians, Methodists, & Congregationalists – live at East Cliff, twenty minutes walk from here. This place (Lighthouse Point) is much quieter, just a few houses. We have a downstairs bedroom and dressing room large enough for Mary Lou's bed, and the porch outside our room. The Ballous all sleep upstairs – they won't be coming till July 6. On the porch are a swing for Mary Lou and a couch swing, so there is much to play with and enjoy.

Today we took rickshaws over to East Cliff to see where the Matthews, Robinsons, Hunters, Todds, et al, live. Mary Lou was delighted to see Johnnie & Phyllis again. I am going to send her over to play with them often because I keep thinking of our going back to Fenchow where she has no one. We went to the Meeting House where they hold church and the other entertainments and meetings. They run a library, and it seems to be the center of many activities.

Peitaiho Beach   *Monday, June 22, 1936*

Mother Dear –

Walter left Thursday night, back to the hottest weather they've had in Peiping in twenty-five years. Hope its cooler back in Fenchow now as he gets back to work… Mary Lou is crazy about the water, splashes in fearlessly. Spends hours on the sand picking up shells, digging, carrying water in her pails… Rickshaw fare to East Cliff, where most is going on, is 50 cents return trip. So I've bought a bicycle for $25, had them fix a seat on the back for Mary Lou and hope to save money.

Peitaiho Beach   *Tuesday, July 7, 1936*

Dear Families –

Fourth of July had a lot of celebrating here but we went only to the baseball games. First the fathers played the sons and then the married ladies played the single ladies. These latter couldn't get enough together for a team so brought in a lot of high school girls. We managed to run up a score of 18 to 4 against them in the three innings we got played before most of the married ladies' team had to go home to nurse small babies!! None of us had played in years and didn't even know the present-day rules so we took a lot of coaching from the sidelines, not to mention a good deal of razzing. I played third base, and managed to bring in three or four runs. Mary Lou played with her friends Phyllis and Johnnie over in the fields, and when it was over I hauled her up on the frame on the back of my bike and off we rode home. She certainly does love the bicycle rides, hangs on splendidly to the little handlebar that's been made for her, sings like a bird as we go zooming down the hills.

As it grew dark they had lovely fireworks out over the water and I sat on our porch and enjoyed them from an easy chair. Soon a gorgeous red full moon rose right out of the sea, and was better than any of the fireworks to watch.

I just got a Peiping language teacher and we're conversing for an hour a day, trying to increase my poor vocabulary and improve my bad pronunciation acquired in Shansi.

– Private Writing –

Summer, 1936

<u>*What do I want of God?*</u>

Elimination of growing fears

> *of death*
> *of life in Fenchow*
>> *lack of social contacts*
>> *lack of vital work to do (language)*
>> *lack of Walter*

To make Walter an understanding Companion as well as the strong man and a tender lover he already is.

To help me to grow in spiritual grace and depth –

Walter completely selfish in his unselfishness and his devotion and his desire to serve.

> *—hospital is all he knows*

> *—he does all the talking*

> *—inconsiderate of others' time and plans and arrangements, subconsciously inferring their service is less important than his. "His motives are fine!"*

I've felt that because he works harder than any man I ever knew, because of my terrible inferiority to him in every way; because he has more dirty breaks than anyone I ever saw, because he is the strongest, finest man I ever knew, because he never criticizes me, because I love him so desperately, I have no right to criticize him. I think this is not so. I think that my love for him demands that I "speak" out what's in my heart, and his love for me will make him understand.

His motives are fine yet isn't he sometimes an "occasion for stumbling?"

Peitaiho Beach   *Tuesday, July 21, 1936*
Dear Folks –

We haven't had new babies or Communist invasions or anything exciting to write about for several months, so I sprained my ankle in order to get a good story for this letter home. So I've had a nice sightseeing trip to Tongshan (a city about three hours from here on the railroad where the British have a large hospital to care for the miners in their Kalan Mining works). I had to get up at 4:30 to get Carolyn fed and myself dressed, hopping on one foot, breakfasted, and forty-five minutes by rickshaw to the station. One of the girls I knew in Peiping went with me, carrying the lunch, thermos bottle, raincoats, etc; buying the tickets; getting rickshaws by special permission through the gates onto station platforms – for we had to change trains once; offering me a strong right arm while I used a cane in the other and hopped – gracefully I'm sure! – on and off trains.

The Tongshan Hospital is a beauty. They made me two beautiful x-rays. But they couldn't discover any fracture – only a badly sprained ankle with a lot of bruising. Dr. M. put on a special kind of mercurial dressing to relieve the swelling before he strapped it up. The trip back was a bit cooler for the long-needed rains had broken. At the junction where we had to change trains, we met a Methodist missionary doctor who had heard Walter speak in America, and to show his appreciation (I guess) he just picked me up and carried me up the long ramp, over the tracks, and down onto the other platform where our train waited. That's some appreciation, I'd say. So now I'm learning how to amble about on a pair of crutches. I've had to give up swimming – darn it!

Last Friday night they had a grand entertainment put on by various of the missionaries. It was going home from that that I hurt the ankle – fell off my bike when I stopped too suddenly to avoid hitting the special-delivery postman who suddenly loomed up out of the dark. Others took my bike home and I got a rickshaw and went to the doctor's house to see what they advise. They said to soak it in hot and cold water that night and then bandage it the next day, which is rather hard for every teacup of our water is counted these days when there isn't any to spare.[85] We have continued to wash Carolyn's diapers, but nothing else.

Peitaiho Beach   *Wednesday, July 29, 1936*

Dear Families –

Well, the sprained ankle has brought its reward, if you can call Walter a "reward." When he heard about the accident, he decided it wasn't fair to ask other people to chase after Mary Lou or to do the extra work on Carolyn. And for once luck was with him. Dr. Wen had turned up the day before my letter arrived, ready to work till the end of August. So Walter turned over his eighty-five cases, spent twenty minutes in the house collecting his belongings, and made a record trip to Peitaiho, getting here in less than forty-eight hours.

Since he's been here, I've been going around in a rickshaw, he riding my bike. We've been to a series of lectures on Chinese Culture and the Christian Religion. There are teas and dinner invitations, as well as various meetings and gatherings. And as soon as a good movie shows up we're going to bust ourselves and go see it. I haven't been to one for over fifteen months.

---

85   The region was experiencing a severe drought.

Peitaiho Beach   *Thursday, July 30, 1936*

Mother dear –

How wonderful it is to have Walter with us. We are *really* having a vacation, practically our first since we've been married. Walter is doing domestic things, which I can't manage with my bum ankle. Can you get this picture: Walter and me sitting in long wicker chairs with plenty of pillows on a verandah looking out across endless expanse of sea with tall mountains to the left, no other houses or people near, a cool sea breeze blowing; a beautiful baby lying in her basket kicking her heels, on the verandah rail; a curly-headed ray of sunshine running here & there on the porch with her toys, coming often to us to offer a kiss or show us some trifle of great importance – nothing to do but rest and love our growing girlies and relax in the beauty of nature and human nature. Do you wonder we're happy?

Peitaiho Beach   *Monday, August 10, 1936*

Dear Families –

Last week we had a Holyoke alumnae tea. There were twelve of us and we discussed having a man as next president of the college. There is some strong and bitter feeling about this, you may have heard. People feel it is too bad if women's education in America is not turning out any women able to take the presidency of a college.

One morning last week a small Japanese flat boat appeared in our "front yard." It was motor driven, and was flying the Japanese imperial flag. It came at half-speed along our rocky shoreline, sounding for depth with a long bamboo pole. They anchored on our sandy swimming beach and an officer, correctly attired in white gloves and attended by two guards with rifles, stepped into a boat and were rowed ashore. Workmen floated ashore poles and ladders, carried them up the slope about a hundred yards back of our house, spent the day erecting a tall tower on the top of which they floated a white and red barred flag. No one knows the significance of this flag, though we have seen any number of them stuck in the ground around these parts, but none on such a tower. The tower is erected on privately owned foreign property, not Chinese property, and the property owners are going to have a meeting to decide on what action to take – likely will protest through the American embassy. The Japanese have spread whitewash on the rocks along the shore disfiguring the landscape, and a few weeks ago they set…depth bombs offshore of the East Cliff houses. There are a lot of theories as to what all this activity signifies, but no one seems to have definite information. The smuggling activities however are no myth. They continue right in the open. So we're seeing history taking place right before our eyes, I suppose.

Your July 10th letter has made me do a lot of thinking. Sometimes I know people think Walter is harsh and ruthless, but he is only so with evils he sees must be rooted out – never with people. He has helped me tremendously along this line for I tended to be too emotional in my thinking of people, not objective enough. Jesus was quite violent in his denunciation of certain *evils*, but no one ever *loved people* more truly. Walter's old illustration holds here: Doctors often have to cut into people and give them intense pain, not because they don't love them or want to inflict hurt, but because they *do* love them and want to cut out the part that is creating trouble.

Peitaiho Beach   *Tuesday, August 25, 1936*

Dear Family –

One more week here and our happy summer is over – eleven weeks of play and friends in this glorious spot – and Walter's had six restful weeks total too. He and I have had a chance to talk long hours – and it has been most relaxing and re-creating – a thing we've never had time for since we've been married – or engaged even!

Mrs. Matthews will be going back to Fenchow with her Charlotte. I had looked with a bit of dread on the idea of returning to Fenchow and having no married lady there, no children for Mary Lou to play with, and Walter so ceaselessly busy in the hospital. I find now that I am able to look ahead with considerable equanimity and even with some eagerness to what may come. I don't think it will be an easy year and I'm not asking it to be that – only that I may have a strength and serenity of heart in meeting the problems. Walter himself has given me quite a bit of reassurance. He spoke about seeing clearly that he must find some way to have more time away from the hospital – for his own study & reading, for his relaxation, and for his growing family. He means to plan things that way this year if it is at all possible, but we will have to wait and see how things work out. Our talking about things together has brought me a new confidence as I go back to a place I haven't learned yet to really love, nor its people.

En route to Taiyuan   *Tuesday, September 8, 1936*

Mother, dear –

We hated to leave Peitaiho for our days there were lovely. The last night Walter and I went to the movies to see *David Copperfield* – it was a moonlight night so bright and beautiful we wanted to walk. But I wasn't sure enuf of my ankle so we took the bike. It was such a happy evening to remember the summer by.

Peiping found us too busy. Besides buying rugs, we did all sorts of little errands and seeing people. I had to order the provisions sent in for the winter and found certain things like coffee, canned fruits & vegetables, syrups, canned meats, cocoa malt they couldn't ship to us in Shansi. They've evidently bought these things from the Japanese who've smuggled them in without paying the duty. In Peiping they can sell smuggled goods, as the Japanese are so largely controlling things there. But when they ship them into Shansi, they have to pass customs inspection at two places – for the Chinese are trying hard to stamp out the shipping of smuggled goods along these two railroads we use to go to Shansi. All goods must be accompanied by receipts for customs duties paid. They say they are getting another shipment direct from U.S. soon & can then supply us & there is nothing we will suffer for lack of in the meantime.

We left Peiping last night at midnight. Carolyn rode in her bassinette on a lower berth with me in a ladies' compartment – two Chinese ladies & two little kids in with us – and Mary Lou slept in a lower with Walter in a men's compartment. We left that train at 8 a.m., went to a hotel where we got cleaned up, had breakfast, rested, got on this train 11:30 and will be in Taiyuan tonight at 7:30. We'll stay overnight with Meyers and go down tomorrow to Fenchow. And will we ever be excited to be home again after all this Oddyssean adventure of over six months.

Fenchow   *Wednesday, September 16, 1936*

Dear Mother and Dad –

As I anticipated life is rushed. I haven't kept house for so long that I've sort of got my hand out of things, and I've never kept house with two children. The servants have got lazy and careless. It is a hard comedown after the excellent servants the Hunters and Ballous had. Then our good Amah is sick in the hospital. As I expected, a few things are spoiled – some jellies & canned goods; some cereals are moldy. Walter did a good job at putting things away and he and the Amah got essential woolens put away secure from moths – only a few minor things got eaten.

Now my work is cut out for several weeks ahead: canning & jelly making, sorting, repacking & rearranging summer and winter clothes; checking inventories; catching up on all the sewing, mending, repairing; all the details of running a large house complicated by one tiny girl who demands food and attention every so often, and one larger girl who loves to help but mostly hinders when she tries to assist. We'll go along slowly with things – and it's all a life I love.

Fenchow   *Friday, September 18, 1936*

Dear Friends-in-need –[86]

In the Board's publicity we often see pictures and write-ups of what the missionary is doing for the people of the country he serves. What he does for other missionaries isn't mentioned, yet it may be nearly as time-consuming, and perhaps even more appreciated, than his "regular work." At least there are two of us who are more grateful than we can say for the countless kindnesses shown us by members of our missionary family. The Communist-confusion-complicated-by-Carolyn disconcerted us less than it might have done because at every turn there were those who graciously and generously helped to make things easier – offering bed and board, assisting with travel trials, chasing children – or changing them! – running errands, inoculating and doctoring, lending of accessories and incidentals, and giving – even of advice! For all these we are grateful.

And even more do we want to express appreciation for the intangible gifts that can't be tabulated – the way you took our family in and made its problems and burdens and interests your own. You not only gave comfort and happiness to three of the family, but also peace of mind to the remaining member through his knowing that such was the case. What fine friendships and enriching experiences we have had during these months because of you all! For such things as these that we treasure away in our hearts we cannot say an adequate thank you.

Fenchow   *Sunday, September 27, 1936*

Dear Folks –

I have started in school teaching – one class in English at the middle school. There are thirty-five young hopefuls in the class, eleven of them girls and they probably think I'm as dumb about learning their names as I think they are about being able to say anything in English. They sit like bumps on a log and refuse to show any signs of intelligence.

---

86   This letter was sent to ten families who had helped the Judd family during the six-month evacuation.

Fenchow   *Monday, October 5, 1936*

Dear Family –

Dr. Ch'ung is staying with us for a week to speak at the meetings in celebration of our fiftieth anniversary.[87] They followed right after the two-week Institute for Evangelists. Many guests have come for these meetings, one of the Chinese pastors walking a *nine*-day's journey to get here. There are about eight foreigners parceled among us. We're having guests for meals for we want to visit with those who are here. Carl shot a wild goose and we ate it today. It was delicious.

I've not been to many of the meetings as they're all in Chinese and I can get little of what goes on. Partly it's because this Shansi dialect is so terrible to understand, and partly it's because I haven't had enough of the semi-formal Chinese vocabulary and style of speaking that are naturally used in public addresses. It discourages me. But the teacher should get here the end of this week and then I'll get down to study again.

There was a musical evening for those attending the Institute, and tomorrow night there will be another for those attending the Anniversary Celebration. I worked up a piano selection for each, accompanied a Chinese man who sang rottenly. A group of us foreigners are going to sing and we rehearsed here last evening. There's always something.

I'm enjoying my English class and am glad I took it. I like getting to know the youngsters and working out lessons for them – it's a different experience from teaching American kids.

Fenchow   *Saturday, October 24, 1936*

Mother, dear –

The weather keeps warm enuf for us to go without coats and I'm glad. One day this week I made a picnic for Mary Lou and me and Mrs. Matthews and Charlotte (aged ten). We went to an old temple about a mile outside the city. Last year it was quite deserted, but it has been taken over and used for kitchens to cook food for the laborers on the nearby barracks. Nanking is making Fenchow one of its military centers in Shansi, since it was convinced this spring that old man Yen can't handle things in this Province any more. They're making 300 rooms above ground and 200 below the surface. With the railway coming in here now and this a military center, interior Fenchow is due for some changes.

Yesterday afternoon we took the car and the children and Carl and drove out ten miles or so to the place where they shoot ducks & geese – Carl and Walter got two ducks and three geese between them in an hour. You've never seen so many in one spot in your life – the sky just black with them as they fly up. Mary Lou and I threw stones in the water and played around the car watching Carolyn. Can you smell our goose roasting right now? Come and have some!

---

87   Dr. Ch'ung was the head of the China ABCFM Board, which was celebrating the fiftieth anniversary of Fenchow being an ABCFM mission station.

Fenchow *Monday, November 2, 1936*

Dear Dad & Mother –

Last Tuesday we had some of our Chinese friends to dinner…the middle school Principal and Dr. Wen (the older Taiku doctor loaned to Fenchow for six months) and Mr. & Mrs. Wang, the principal of the Bible School, and the pastor and his wife. They are fine people and we enjoyed them. They came at seven and the ladies immediately asked where the children were and couldn't believe that they were in bed and asleep. Even in families of education it seems the children in the home stay up till the last dog's hung. Our conversation was all in Chinese. The ladies speak no English and the men not enough to converse, tho' they can read readily. We had tomato juice first – they all like this – with deviled eggs and sardines on toast. Chinese feasts always open with eight cold dishes, on the table when you sit down, at which you pick till the hot dishes arrive – such things as smoked eggs, slivered cold meats or chicken, cabbage slaw or other cold vegetable salads, pieces of fruit. So my hors d'oeuvre was quite in line with their customs. Then duck soup and for the main course a meat loaf, because it is easy to eat with a fork and they don't like to wield our knives. I have individual ring moulds and in them I had baked puree spinach with white sauce and egg. Creamed lotus root was our other vegetable, with potatoes, and it's delicious. According to custom, dinner was a drawn-out process with much conversation and fun – they are clever folks – and ten minutes after dinner was finished and we had adjourned to the living room, they all left – also according to custom. I enjoyed it a lot and hope they did too. Mr. Wang of the bible school is a rare soul. He is head of the Hospital Board of Managers and has been a great help to Walter for he is absolutely fearless and honest, a trait often sacrificed among the Chinese for surface politeness.

I'm working hard to get the *Fenchow* to the printer. I'm editor again. This time it's to be a fiftieth anniversary number. This, with the school class, Chinese study, choir rehearsals, and just plain housekeeping and loving a family, keeps the days – and nights – busy.

Fenchow *Monday, November 9, 1936*

Dear Mother –

Wednesday night at the compound dinner we talked about the election. We were excited to hear who had won, but the general feeling was that Landon would get it, since the Literary Digest poll put him far ahead, and they have been right so often on straw votes. Of our group here most had never voted for President – so you see what we give up being missionaries. We planned to go over to the school to listen to the English news broadcast from Nanking at nine o'clock, but Nanking time turned out to be ahead of Fenchow's so the broadcast was over. We went back at ten for the Chinese news broadcast. This was difficult to understand. Meantime the lights had gone off and we were sitting in the dark – just a candle – in the cold library. The count was not complete but Roosevelt was leading. I'm glad it went that way. I think it would have been difficult, if not dangerous, to make a change at this stage of the game. Roosevelt's not perfect and he's made mistakes, as anyone would have, but I think his New Deal deserves a little more time to be worked on.

Fenchow   *Monday, November 30 1936*

Dear Families –

The tumult and shouting have died, and the captains and kings have departed leaving a rather limp Fenchow station behind. There were twenty-one people came from Taiku for the Thanksgiving celebrations, and we were a group of only nine to entertain them. We had the Thanksgiving worship service at 10:30. Immediately afterwards, the car started taking loads out to the Valley for a picnic. Some went hiking up the Valley. Others had ridden their bicycles out and found it quite enough exercise to ride them back again. At the "Thanksgiving dinner" at the Ladies' House at eight o'clock, twenty-three of us sat at one long table. The Taiku group had got up a clever takeoff on grand opera, which they presented, and then we sat around and sang songs. The party broke up, but the young folks, with the Judds for chaperones, adjourned to the Carleton boys' house for a little dancing.

Fenchow   *Friday, December 4, 1936*

Mother dear, & Dad, also dear –

I get less efficient every day. I can't get done the things I plan, at least not in entirety… The Fenchows have arrived and there are hundreds of those to address; I have to give another talk on India to the women's meeting next week – in Chinese; Pat Wu's here for a month, which means extra time to meal planning; Walter's discouraged with certain aspects of the hospital management and has a baby revolt on his hands because of reforms he is trying to institute, which cut across the liberty of certain staff members; station coffee is at our house tomorrow so I must go to bake some date nut bars; I wish I could see you at Christmas. You two are my only sacrifice in this missionary life.

– Private Writing –

Late 1936

> *So far, I don't like the Chinese people very much, and don't know them very well. Perhaps the latter is the reason for the former. Perhaps I don't like them because they are hard to know. I have felt a definite disappointment in my relations with them, but not a discouragement, for you notice I wrote "so far." I had counted on having genuine friends among the Chinese and letting our relationships speak out things that could not be put into words or lectured about. But I have no friends. Oh, I know, I've been busy. Had a baby, studied the language, set up housekeeping and tried to get used to Chinese ways and servants, etc. But none of this would prevent one making friends. The language has been a barrier, for though I know enough to keep house and indulge in superficial conversation, the abstract words, the ones dealing with one's inner joys and sorrows and problems, I haven't got. Sometimes I want to blame the Chinese. They are not friendly. Oh, superficially, yes. Always courteous but aloof, evasive. You never know where you are with them. They will not tell you what they think, or what you want to know, but only what would flatter you, or sound nice. I fancy this is not so true of Chinese at the coast. But we are in the interior. Life here is pretty conservative.*

> *Furthermore, the people of this particular region are known all over China for being unusually clannish. Walter had said so much while we were*

in America about the Chinese as friends that I actually felt deceived when I got here. But he himself admits that these people are not in the slightest like those in the south among whom he lived before. He has not made real friends here either, but at least he has the knowledge and warmth of friends elsewhere in China to keep his attitudes balanced.

Another difficult element is that previous foreigners have not left an easy road for those of us who have come after. Some of the earlier men came in the days when money for missions was running freely in America. They dispensed it lavishly, foolishly, taking on many employees who never worked but only drew a salary, passing out money at every request, impoverishing the spirit and morale of the decent Chinese, building up concepts of themselves as "benevolent despots" with limitless resources, flattering to their egos but earning in the end no real, fundamental friendship with the people. We cannot carry on this regime. It is hard to get things onto an honest-labor-honest-pay basis. The hospital nearly had to close because of heavy debts and Walter has worked for two years harder than any human being should work to get the debts cleared off. It meant cutting budgets, doing without all but the barest essentials, firing the hangers-on. The Chinese can't understand but that he is making money personally out of the reductions. It is so disheartening. There seems to be no loyalty to the institution, or to what the hospital is trying to do for the sick and poor of Shansi. Instead, petty bickerings over what each can get for himself.

I am over-conscious of our too-large house. Perhaps I cannot make friends because the women are too awed by these "lords of wealth" as we must seem to them. I don't blame them. A doctor's family here, with a graduate nurse wife, educated fine people, two little girls just the ages of our two – three small rooms, sufficient bedding and clothing for warmth, enough to eat and two dishes apiece to eat out of – all you need – a toy for each child, no extras to store in trunks, keep the moths out of, keep dusted, to make their rooms look fancy or cluttered – and they are happy in their work and children. Their happiness doesn't consist in possessions. What a natural barrier I have built between her and me by having three servants, a huge house, hundreds of books, toys, piano, victrola. Does she want her children to play with mine and learn discontent with simple things? No wonder she doesn't come see me or bring her child to play with Mary Lou. Nor could I ever give her anything – toys, clothes, new or cast-offs, for it would widen the barrier, put our friendship on a "money" or "things" or "giving" basis.

But on the other hand, I have my children to think of. They are to be brought up for an American society. They are already deprived of many advantages that American children ordinarily have, by living in China. Am I to further curtail their educational and cultural and social opportunities by depriving them of books, toys, music? What kind of an adjustment can I make between the things I want to do for them and things I'd like to do for the Chinese friends? Perhaps there is no balance. Perhaps it is choice. I hate to give up my idealism as to what a Christian home may mean in influence in a Chinese community, but if I'm going to be honest and realistic, I'll have to admit that our home, in itself, is making no contribution to China. Perhaps I can render some service through my English teaching at the school. But that is quite disassociated from my home. I as a teacher go to their classroom, wearing my Chinese gown to cover up my curious Western dresses that would otherwise detract from the attention to the lesson.

Fenchow   *Friday, December 18, 1936*

Dear Families –

The text of my message for this letter is (a) life is hectic at present, but (b) relief is ahead. First of all, the electric light plant has been on the bum for about a month now. The hospital electrician kept optimistically thinking he could get it running while we asked hopefully every day: Electricity or kerosene tonight? Finally he had to admit he was whipped and with much loss of face give up and let the thing be sent to Tientsin for repair, a matter of four weeks. We had to hunt up or buy extra lamps, keep broken chimneys replaced, wicks trimmed and tanks filled. In the evenings we sit and work where the reading lamp is more convenient for all concerned, rather than off in the study.

Then too we've had to sit where it was warm. The furnace has been on the bum too. The new servant we took on in October not only knows nothing about furnaces, but also hasn't the sense to listen to instructions from those who do. The thing was leaking steam badly and had to have water put into it every day. Walter has spent hours trying to get the thing to work. The hospital electrician put a little time over here, too, after he stopped working on the light plant, and now we have a warm house. Then the Christmas preparations have taken extra minutes.

As for the political situation, I'll say nothing. Things look gloomy. Chinese papers are censored, you likely have as much news as we have if not more, and everyone is trying to guess what this latest move may mean, or may lead to.[88]

Fenchow   *Sunday, January 3, 1937*

Dearest Mother –

The grandest thing that happened on Christmas Day was the news that came just before the 7:30 Christmas musical at the church.[89] There'd hardly been a minute in those twelve or thirteen days Chiang Kai-shek had been in captivity that we hadn't talked of the horrible outlook for China if he were killed, or not soon released. It was *the* one topic of conversation everywhere. Here at last China begins to show real signs of national unity after years of struggle and suffering and if Chiang were gone the years of struggle would start all over again, for no other person at present in public life is able to hold the loyalty of China as Chiang does. I do hope you've gotten all the reports – for they show Chiang to be utterly fearless in acting for the good of *China*, not his own ends or safety as has so continuously been the case with Chinese officials. We had to go to the church for the musical. Walter went up and told the news to the presiding chairman who announced it with appropriate

---

88   Chiang Kai-shek had been kidnapped in Sian on December 12, 1936 – known as the Sian Incident.
89   Chiang Kai-shek had been released.

remarks and it was a great sight to see the joy and relief break over the faces of that group. There was much firecrackering around the compound and the following night a big student lantern parade to celebrate. So Christmas was a day of unusual rejoicing here.

Three days after Christmas I gave my English class their semester exam and school closed for the six-week winter holiday. I got quite a thrill from seeing about 125 students all in one room writing exams for two hours that afternoon. My students were the only ones in the group using pen and ink and writing script. All the rest had their brushes and their ink slabs and were making the most beautiful characters in their exam books. The last question on my exam was to write a letter to a friend, giving them free scope for their composition. Practically every one of the boys wrote something about Chiang Kai-shek's release, or about planning to be a soldier after finishing school and fighting the Japanese who are now invading their beloved country. The national feeling certainly is running high these days.

Fenchow   *Friday, February 5, 1937*

Dear Mother –

Five days till New Year's – and the atmosphere is charged with excitement. On the day itself we'll have the cook prepare special Chinese food for our noon meal with enough extra so our servants can eat, too, the same as we have – a gift to them along with a dollar apiece. Invitations have come in to feasts with our friends, and grateful patients have started sending "the Doctor" gifts –baskets of fruit, which are a luxury to us. Tomorrow afternoon when we go to "coffee" at Louise Meebold's, we'll go through the streets of the city and see the decorations on the shops and the people in gala mood thronging the shopping streets – like our Christmas shopping crowds. I say we'll go thru the city streets, because Louise has moved two miles away to the East suburb where there is a group of strong Christians living, with their own church, and she felt she wanted to live nearer the people. I'll take Mary Lou along on the donkey for the outing – she gets so circumscribed by the narrow limits of our compound here that she doesn't see anything of Chinese life. Whenever we take her out she is a curiosity. People crowd and stare and want to touch her lovely white skin or pick her up and she doesn't like it any more than we.

Fenchow   *Wednesday, February 17, 1937*

Dear Family –

Yesterday a group of six of us walked around the city wall. It was a lovely early spring day, and we had a good view of Chinese life – children playing in the courts in which you could look down from the wall, soldiers drilling and going through the beautiful but difficult rhythmic sword dancing and boxing exercises, people thronging in the streets in gay attire and holiday mood. Last night I had the foreigners here for dinner – ten of us at a long table. We seemed to be in a light and festive mood – so played charades and other games… Nanking has decreed that China celebrate the foreign New Year, and the trains and post offices have to continue business as usual during the time of the China festivities, but can't remake 4,000,000 people with a heritage of 4,000 years by a decree from the government, so John Chinaman continues to celebrate the biggest festival of the year in his own fashion.

Nanking   *Sunday, March 28, 1937*

A travelogue of our trip, Monday, March 15–Thursday, April 15 –

Preparations – Mary Lou filled suitcases with toys, dumped them out the next day, then did it again. I aired and brushed and put away winter clothes; arranged for a load of fertilizer to be sent out to the Valley where the caretaker of the Pettus's Mill, which we have rented for the summer ($150) will have our garden started before we get back; arranged for flower and vegetable seeds for our Fenchow garden; arranged "spring housecleaning" to be done by the cook; and we were off in the car, baggage piled high, for the noon train at the station in Fenchow.

To Tungchow – Not a bad trip at all! The train goes at twelve to fifteen miles an hour because the line is newly put down part of the way, so the sixty miles trip took us four hours. In Taiku we went to the Oberlin kids' house, had our dinner, and were off to the station. A two-hour ride brought us to the Taiyuan-to-Shihchiachwang line where we had to wait on a cold platform in the dark with two sleepy babies – but only half an hour. We had steamer rugs so bundled up the cherubs and sat on our baggage. By ten p.m. we were on the next train, and luckily were given a compartment together. Eventually we all slept, and comfortably. Shortly after seven, we got off at Shihchiachwang, the terminus of this line, and waited four hours in the French hotel. We were able to get cleaned up, wash diapers, have breakfast. Walter went off with Dr. Tuan, who is head of the big railway hospital there, to examine a difficult case – no vacation for him!

The train for Peiping was not crowded. We established the two cherubs with blankets and pillows opposite each other (day coach) and they slept for two hours. When they awoke the late lunch was much appreciated. First the alcohol bottle and cotton to wipe off hands. Then hot rice and eggs from the train diner to piece out our sandwiches, fruit, and individual gelatins from home. Then a *long* afternoon while we entertained the two ladies, told Mary Lou stories, looked at books, let Carolyn chew on Walter's watch and Phi Bete key, had more sandwiches, fruit and eggs for supper, and finally at 8:30 p.m. reached Peiping. There we got a car and drove out to Tungchow in an hour. The trip was a dream, compared with the nightmare one I had last year at the same time, but without Amah or husband, and with anxiety and weariness overpowering me. The next days were taken up with visiting in Tungchow, two trips to Peiping to arrange about train reservations, to arrange for money, always a problem in China where different localities have their own kinds not useable elsewhere.

To Tientsen – Sunday noon (March 21) we fed our little girlies their lunch, kissed them goodbye and we were off. *Loads* of Japanese riding the Peiping-Tientsin train, including many soldiers… Reached Tientsin at six, taken at once to a big Chinese feast… Then to the Chandler home where we visited until 11:30, train time.

To Tehchow – At 7:30 a.m. we arrived, were met by the hospital car and taken outside the city to the mission compound. We stayed with the Gilberts. He was student Y secretary in Yale 1925 and Walter knew him then. Lois is a dear and we had fun comparing notes on our common problems. How I wish she and I could be in the same station. She had a lovely ladies lunch. After a rest I was taken to tea and had a thorough tour and inspection of the hospital. Walter was eager to get ideas for a few changes on ours so I investigated with him. In the evening a compound supper and later a visit with the Gilberts alone before bed.

To Tsinan – The ride to Tsinan was three hours and we found ourselves in Shantung's capitol. It was originally built by Germans who had large control in the Province. It's a nice town, and outside one of its walls nestled at the foot of lovely mountains is Cheeloo University or Shantung Christian College, its foreign name. The campus is large and beautiful. There must be thirty or more foreigners on the staff of the University – Theological Seminary, Medical School. They are British & Americans of many denominations. We stayed with the Phil Prices – he's now superintendent of the hospital. They have about thirty doctors, interns, residents and only forty more beds than we have with our four doctors. Besides they have no administrative or financial or mechanical details to bother with so their efforts can be concentrated on medical work…

Octavia Price had a swell dinner party for us one evening, and a tea for Chinese friends another day. To this came Alice Yao and her husband, a second-year medical student.[90] Talk about Shaowu and Shaowu dialect flowed freely, as you can guess. The evening we left Tsinan these Yaos gave a feast for us at a restaurant before our train went. I don't know which did Walter more good: visiting with the Yaos again or talking hospital matters with his good doctor friends. Anyhow, it was a *very* happy and full two days there.

Mrs. S spent one morning showing me thru the most unique and fascinating Institute. Chinese come there to look at the models & exhibits showing what happens to the people who smoke opium, what is the difference between homes kept clean & screened and sanitary and those not, and scores of such like. Lots of models on the course of the Yellow River, the reforestation work & the way it lessens the danger of floods, modern model factories, etc.

To Nanking – We left for Nanking at 9 p.m. and landed the next day around 4 in the afternoon. It has been fun to watch the scenery change en route, to see rice fields appear and the bamboo tree and mulberry trees, cultivated over acres & acres for the silk worm. The Grand Canal kept playing hide-and-seek with us in the distance, with its picturesque junk sails on the horizon, and countless smaller canals and waterways laced thru the land. This country is certainly wet compared with our dry Shansi, and fields are green, but I miss the hills. I'm reading *Gone with the Wind* and knitting a next-winter dress for Mary Lou, so the time went fast. It's such fun traveling with Walter, too, for he is so observing of significant details.

We stayed with the Riggs family who were in Shaowu with Walter and now teach in the University. We got dressed up to go to the American Embassy at Ambassador Johnston's swell new home. Nanking was Walter's first home in China and there are still *many* folks there whom he knew in Language School days, so we kept running into friends at every turn. Sunday afternoon before church Mrs. Riggs gave a tea for many Chinese from Shaowu who are working in Nanking – business, nurses, government, etc. – and there was more "foreign" dialect… All for now – Love to you two dears from a happy honeymooning couple.

---

90   Alice Yao was a young nurse with Walter in Shaowu in the late 1920s, who likely saved his life during a malaria episode.

Mother dear –

I'm going to try to finish up the story of our trip. If you get a chance, do see the latest copy of the *Missionary Herald* for an article about Madame Chiang Kai-shek and the George Shepherds. The Shepherds were a day or so away from Shaowu all the time Walter was there, and he was very fond of them. Mrs. Shepherd is a doctor and a fine woman. Walter used to walk over the hills for a day and meet George for a day's visit once in a while during those years when he was so alone, and they have much in common. George is now one of Madame Chiang's righthand men in the New Life Movement so they are living in Nanking. They were delighted to have a chance to visit with Walter. George is close to the Chiangs and had a lot of dope on government affairs. Walter was pleased to hear many of the things George had to say about the famous leaders, for in China you hear all sorts of rumors and guesses as to their sincerity, their aims, and their attitudes. George himself has to be most judicious about his job and remain "undercover" as it were – for the New Life Movement is supposed to be an entirely Chinese affair, a turning away from some of the too-foreign influences back to the best of what was in China's past. But it had started to become a political machine with people working in it for what they could get out of it in position and money. Madame became greatly concerned, and eventually asked George to come to Nanking to sort of see, in an undercover way, that a different class of leaders got in and that it took a different trend – one of service and up building for China, really a Christian ideal in the last analysis. Many of the things George told us were not for the public, but he was eager to share with Walter, whom he trusts highly, because his own position is so strategic that he feels he needs advice and help in some of his important decisions.

The Shepherds took us all thru the New Life Movement headquarters, took us out to the beautiful Sun Yat-sen[91] memorial outside the city, a building on a level with the Lincoln Memorial in Washington for its beauty, simplicity, and impressiveness; drove us thru new parks and playgrounds and athletic fields; showed us the Chiang home and the school for sons of the martyrs of the 1911 Revolution. The Generalissimo and Madame were down in Hangchow where he is resting and receiving treatment and physiotherapy for a broken vertebra, a fact not generally known for it has not appeared in any of the China papers. The papers have said that he was "resting up" after his ordeal in Sian, and some people have intimated that he is taking a "political rest" because he is scared after what happened to him in Sian, or else scared because he must have "sold out" to Chang Hsu Liang in order to obtain his release. But that's all bosh! He has a severe back injury, received in Sian when he was being let down (or climbing up?) a wall and the guard who was assisting him and holding onto him from above was shot dead, dropping the Generalissimo. That's how near he came to death himself!! George himself was present when the x-rays were taken and saw the plates. The Chinese Superintendent of the Nanking University Hospital is off for a month as the Generalissimo's private physician, and has flown back to Nanking a couple of times to get physiotherapy apparatus from the hospital for treatments.

The Shepherds say that the diary the Generalissimo kept while in captivity is remarkable. It has been translated into English and is to be (or is being?) published by the *New York Times* and the money from the sale of the rights to the *Times* is going to help the families of guards and associates of

---

91   Sun Yat-sen was the first President and founding father of the Republic of China in 1912 and Premier in the 1920s.

Chiangs killed in the Sian affair. He had 200 copies privately printed and gave them out at a dinner after he got out of captivity, but called them all in when he sold the rights to the *Times*. But George has a copy and says it is most unusual.

Easter morning we went to the University students service and in the afternoon to the foreign service. That evening we went to the American Embassy to dinner. It's nice every once in a while to see "how the other half lives." Course after course moved along in ease, and melted in your mouth, while the table conversation scintillated.

We left Nanking early Monday morning and were in Soochow in time for lunch. It seemed so good to be with a younger bunch again, more of our own generation, for we are quite the babies in Fenchow, and practically the youngest in our whole North China Mission. That is a thing of grave concern and discussion: the fact that we are not getting new young people in our mission. Walter led chapel for the hospital staff the second day we were there.

Shanghai made us almost feel we were back in New York. Tall buildings, bright lights at night, many large shops and theaters, both of which I made good use of! We went to the opening reception of the Medical Conference.[92] Another night we went to a dinner party with the Dr. Humes and went on afterwards to hear Mischa Elman play, and perhaps you don't think that was a real treat after no music and no radio in Fenchow.

I spent lots of time shopping but didn't buy much, for shops are spread far apart and distances are great. I looked up several girls I knew and we went to lunches or teas, and my three and a half days there flew by altogether too fast. Saturday Walter put me on the train for Peiping while he stayed another five days for the medical meetings.

Fenchow   *Wednesday, April 21, 1937*

Mother dear –

My trip alone from Shanghai to Peiping and Tungchow was easy. At Tehchow Lois Gilbert got on the train to go to Tientsin with me. I can see that she is to help me a lot. Just to know that someone like myself is living in an isolated place like my own, with no *good* friends and no playmates for children and dealing with the servant problem and the other peculiar problems that life in China presents – all that helps no end. We had two nights and a day together in Tientsin before I went on. We are going to use the same book for our devotions these next few months so we'll have something to guide our thinking in the same direction and serve as a basis for our exchange of letters.

I must admit that as I got nearer and nearer my little girls I got more and more anxious to see them. I went first to the Robinsons to see Carolyn. She didn't know me, as I had expected she wouldn't. I went in and out of the room where she was playing for the next hour, unpacking suitcases and chattering to Olga and calling a hello to Carolyn every once in a while. I think she knew from the start that I looked vaguely familiar and after a while decided I belonged, for when

---

92   The conference was for the China Medical Association.

I picked her up she gave me the loveliest smile and cuddled her head down on my shoulder, so we were both completely happy.

Well, Mary Lou made up in warmth anything that might have been lacking in Carolyn's reception. Maude Hunter said she'd been fine while we were away but that doesn't mean she & Phyllis hadn't got into mischief – like pasting all the 25-cent stamps on the study wall, etc.! The next four days I had to go into Peiping a couple of times for the dentist and for my final shopping: getting lamp shades made to fit our lamps, getting dresses & suits cleaned, watches & clocks repaired, shoes made for the children, groceries ordered, and what not.

Walter landed in Tungchow four days after I did, and then we had one final binge – into Peiping on Saturday night to see a good movie and spend the night. On Monday I organized lunches and we started off about 4:30. I hated to pull out of Tungchow. It has many lovely people and is a beautiful compound, and I miss the folks there, as Mary Lou does her playmates.

Now for *Council News*. About thirty altogether in the group, two thirds Chinese. (We feel very proud of our *joint* work.) It started two days after we got home, lasted a week, *all* the meetings being in Chinese. We had Earle and Thelma Ballou with us and I had such fun fixing up the guest room for them – new curtains, twin beds we borrowed from Matthews.

First, various reports for a day. Then breaking up into the small sections: educational, medical, evangelistic – to discuss specific recommendations and problems; then back to the main group for passing votes. Many were details of the mechanics of our work.

One question that had some discussion was about the status of our Tungchow schools. Since that is the center of the Yin Ju Keng so-called "autonomous" government, there have been many difficult problems raised by "officials." They want their flag flown over the school. The school has compromised and flies *no flag*! They want their seal on the graduates' diplomas instead of Nanking's ministry of education; and they want the right to inspect at any time and authorize changes, *especially in the civics courses*! This leaves the poor school authorities wondering whether to appeal to Nanking, to close up or what. If they should appeal, an "incident" would be precipitated which everyone is anxious to avoid. If they should close up, the "autonomous" government would take possession of the buildings and establish their own school. So all is not simple these days. They have a splendid Chinese principal, a

Bike ride on a rural road

tactful and keen-minded person, and he is dealing well with the situation, but no one knows just yet what the outcome will be.

Council closed Thursday night with a quiet, worshipful communion service. Friday morning the delegates left. Friday afternoon was the nurses' commencement exercises at the hospital for which I had to furnish a hundred cookies and a freezer of ice cream, and some organ playing, and Walter had to furnish a speech. Eleven nurses graduated, four of them men. Walter's back now on full schedule at the hospital since the council closed – much too full, for one of the doctors is away with a sick father. He had a baby at 5:30 yesterday a.m. and another one early today to start out a day of fourteen operations. I've had no meals with him today nor seen him since early morning and it's now long after 10. So I guess we pay now for the glorious vacation we had!

Fenchow   *Monday, June 21, 1937*

Dear Families –

Yen Hsi-shan has been ill.[93] He is not popular anymore, and almost everyone would be glad to see him die, and then let Nanking come in and take charge and do things right. He's evidently been secretly shipping gold to Japan hoping to get away and spend the last of his life there in peace, for some of it was intercepted by one of the Nanking generals, a vast amount. The other day came a phone call from Taiyuan asking the hospital to send two Chinese nurses to care for him. The papers carried the word that three doctors had arrived the previous day to consult about him, one from Tientsin, and a Chinese and a German from Peiping. He sent a swell car for the nurses and off they went. As is usually the case with high officials, none of the doctors is willing to take responsibility and say what is wrong or what to prescribe. Each passes the buck to the other so the poor man is getting worse treatment than an ordinary farmer would get at any hospital. No one knows what is wrong, except that he has had amoebic dysentery, but everyone hopes it is his last illness!

The Valley (Yutaho)   *Saturday, July 10, 1937*

Mother dear –

We had a grand Fourth of July picnic on Saturday the third, with twenty-four present. Walter couldn't come. Afterwards we had firecrackers & singing & much fun. We have a gang of our missionaries, three from Tungchow, two from Peiping, one from Tehchow, a number from Taiku so we are quite a center. Sunday Walter was due to come out during the p.m. but sent word he was "having a baby." By 10 he hadn't shown up so I tho't he wouldn't come, locked up, & started to bed when he appeared. The car had tipped over an embankment. The workers on the road had been instructed to repair with stone and instead used loose earth, which after the heavy rains of two days didn't hold when Walter suddenly jerked over onto the shoulder to avoid a bicycle rider. The car nosed down the embankment and eased over gently and none of the four occupants were hurt. Plate glass windows were broken & lots of oil leaked out. Road workers just picked up the car and

---

93   Yen Hsi-shan was the governor of Shansi Province.

put it back on the road, after the passengers had crawled out the windows. When they got the oil fixed all was O.K.

Monday I let the cook go into Fenchow for two days to can apricots, make jam, can beets of which we have a *lot* in our garden, and I turned cook. It's easy to pick fresh peas and beans and lettuce and radishes in the garden and soon have a good meal. Monday evening I sprained my ankle – not the one I sprained last year and not as badly but it swelled and pained enough to have to be soaked and bound up. Then Tuesday I went bad with what seems to have been a strep throat. This one laid me out fairly flat. It had extra special complications that added to its severity. You see, we've ordered another baby to be delivered about on Carolyn's second birthday, and whereas I've been feeling fairly chipper up till now, the strep infection seems to have put the kibosh on my eating. I had three *bad* days. Food, water, medicines – nothing would stay where it was put, so I got weak and ached and pained besides. Walter's been grand. He's been out every single night after his full hard day's work in town, has given me fluids in the vein and injections for my strep throat. Today feel much better, tho' I'm taking no chances. I'm so glad I have such reliable servants this summer. That helps no end. People have been nice about coming to take Mary Lou away to play & the Amah can manage Carolyn.

Yutaho   *Tuesday, August 3, 1937*

Dear Families –

Walter's so-called vacation started the first of August. Today he was here, though he worked most of the day writing up some of the several hundred histories he is behind at the hospital. Still, as he says, it is a vacation not to be at the hospital and to have a chance to watch the children play and to eat meals with his family, to play the victrola, and visit with the various friends that keep dropping in. He keeps on serving as extra chauffeur when there's need for both cars being driven back and forth to town. Travel now is uncertain and people are not sure how to plan their return trips to their own stations. One reason has been the heavy rains. Walter and I spent one night moving our bed on the porch around every half hour or so to see if we could find a place where it would not leak on our faces at least, and at last spread newspapers over our heads and let it leak. The roads are terrible. There is a washout on the Taiyuan road. The railroad didn't run one day for the roadbed was too bad but now goes again.

No use trying to write about what's going on around us. The day we have been expecting has come, and this time it looks like a sure enough fight.[94] We hear damage has been done in our Tientsin and Tungchow compounds. We are not allowed by the government to buy kerosene – keeping it for the army and fighting – and we have been using a five-gallon tin each month in our house and the hospital one a day. We seem to be cut off from Peiping, no letters coming and there is no telling when we can expect freight shipment of food supplies, for the trains are used to transport troops and their supplies. No one advises moving toward Peiping at this time.

---

94   The Japanese troops had captured Peiping in late July.

Yutaho   *Tuesday, August 10, 1937*

Dear Dad –

This is going to be a special letter to you just because you're having a birthday… It continues to be hard to write any news. Our private life goes on calmly and happily, the children well and enjoying a few little friends. Walter has to go to Fenchow about every second day. Our lives are governed by uncertainty and concern and distress at all the reports that come thru. The new Oberlin & Carleton young teachers were supposed to have landed in Shanghai two weeks ago but not a line or wire from them and it is puzzling to wonder where they are and why held up as trains to Shanghai are available via Hankow. Schools open next week here and poor Taiku is short four English teachers.

The people from Peiping are perplexed as to how and when to start home. Direct train route is closed but there are a number of round-about possibilities involving changing lines, and going by bus or donkey across various distances. Most of our group here travels third, which means no sleepers, hard benches, often no food on the trains. Every day groups gather to discuss possibilities and any recent news or new developments, and we all have but one topic of conversation, and only one answer to all our wonderings: "Who knows? Who knows?"

Taiyuan seems to be in a panic. No schools are to open there this fall, they say. They have dug air raid cellars and are having air raid drills, closing the city gates a good bit of the time, not burning streetlights at night, etc. Shops and places of business are all closing up and people are moving out in great crowds. They say three thousand have already landed in Fenchow. This is because Taiyuan is the next provincial capitol in line after Hopei Province.

Yutaho   *Tuesday, August 31, 1937*

Dear Mother –

Here we are at the end of August, at the end of the summer, and I hope shortly at the end of this excessive rain. We're running short of coal and our cooking supplies. We're getting things packed up and will move whenever we get a sunny day.

The money problem is acute for checques can't get cashed when all communications with Peiping and Tientsin are cut off. Walter has been helping as many people as he can with his influence with a local banker in Fenchow, but all such checques cashed are over Walter's signature so he is left holding the sack in case we can't send them to the coast for collection within a few months. Furthermore, money to pay hospital salaries, for the schools, and evangelistic work in Fenchow and for the use of the missionaries personally can't come in from our Treasurer in Tientsin so things are a bit acute.

We've received no newspaper for about three weeks. A friend in Taiyuan has an excellent radio and he listens regularly. Then he types brief abstracts…and mails to us every few days. In this way we have been able to keep up with the bad fighting in Shanghai and all the evacuation, cholera in Hong Kong, and earthquake in Manila whence the British and Americans respectively were evacuated, etc. What we get is bad enough to make us heavy hearted.

Fenchow   *Tuesday, September 14, 1937*

Dear Families –

I started this week again teaching one class in English at the middle school – the same class of girls I had last spring. The enrollment of the school has increased more than a hundred, with so many schools in the Peiping area, etc. not opening this fall. Also we have extra nurses in the training school, who have come from the Tehchow Hospital, which I understand has closed its nursing school (all the foreigners have evacuated Tehchow). So you see people seem to think Shansi is a safe place to be, at least for the present.

But will it continue to be so indefinitely? Within the last ten days we've received three communications from the American consulate – recommending that women and children, and where possible men, too, who are in fighting areas, or threatened areas, leave for safer places in China, with the idea of going on as soon as convenient to Manila or America. Last night's wire reported U.S. transports ready at a certain place to take evacuees to Manila.

Walter and I are terribly perplexed as to what is the right thing to do with our family. Needless to say, we don't want to leave here for another long period of separation from Walter unless it is going to be dangerous or disagreeable to keep the children here. But if eventually I must go with the children, we'd rather have me leave now, when travel is possible, when the weather is not cold, when we have this opportunity of going on U.S. transports, and particularly before I get to the place where travel will be difficult and unadvisable.

We want to move soon – within the next few weeks – if we're going to move at all. So always after our discussions we come back to the same uncertainties, the same perplexities: Let's wait a day or two and see. This indecision is devastating, for I cannot get settled down to my fall's work: teaching, studying, & sewing etc. I also can't get started on the long-neglected letter writing for I never can be sure what to say.

These days we are learning how to do without many things or substitute what can be had in Fenchow. Our food supplies are holding out fairly well, except cereals, which are gone. So we are using locally ground wheat, millet, soft rice, bran, and doing well on it. The good cook is putting up as much fruit as we have jars for – peaches. If we run out of butter the children can eat jams and jellies on their bread. We're having a pair of shoes made here in Fenchow for Mary Lou to try. A good tailor from Taiyuan has moved his shop here and is fixing maternity clothes for me, a warm bathrobe for Mary Lou. So we are living well within our city and its resources.

As I have been writing this letter, another wire has come from the consulate that the U.S. transport has been cancelled, so that solves our immediate problem. If we go later, we will figure some other way of getting off. Our future is too uncertain, and all our inclinations and desires are *against* leaving here. I keep remembering again and again how you wrote so comfortingly at the time of the Communists, and quoted "As thy days so shall thy strength be." Please believe that we are in *no* danger whatsoever now, that we are not suffering for lack of anything, that we are all well – I'm fine – and happy in our own home with our two little rays of sunshine, and are only sad for the suffering and sorrow in war-torn China, and in the other places of the world.

Hong Kong   *Friday, October 1, 1937*

Darling –

Our air trip was just O.K.[95] People moved to let us have the two adjacent chairs near the front – not in the smoking cabin. We ate our lunch, looked at maps, and soon found ourselves in Changsha where we stayed ten minutes. From there on we flew high, though we had been flying low before. The plane was on time, Grace & Kenneth Keen were there with their swank blonde car and we had a cool drive across the ferry to the island, out the eight miles to their home. Soon had the children bathed, fed, and in bed… Mary Lou in a single bed close to mine & under one mosquito net.

The place here is palatial – immense rooms, the sea down below as at the Ballou's only further down, lovely grounds, flowers – six servants! It all depresses me – living on such a scale for two persons. But needless to say, we are very comfortable. It's beastly hot. The first night Mary Lou was sick, vomited her supper all over the bed. I think it was nothing but excitement of the trip, tiredness, and the heat. I'll keep close watch on her. Carolyn is O.K… Wonder where you are, and how – I'm *so* anxious to hear. No one here knows there's a war! All yours, forever.

Hong Kong   *October 3, 1937*

My dearest –

Yesterday afternoon came your airmail letter from Hankow and it seemed somehow like a breath out of the past, for you are so far away. The news about Shansi in last night's papers means that things will be in worse disorder than ever, and the hospital will need you… No further word about sailings. I'll call tomorrow and see. An airmail letter written Thursday a.m. in Hankow says Mr. M. B. Hansen is bringing my luggage as the railroad people refused to ship it.

Mary Lou is her own Comanche Indian self. Poor Carolyn's upper trunk, neck, and scalp are thick with prickly heat and it is itchy and irritating. Mary Lou has a spot or two. Sleeping under mosquito nets keeps it hot and they are drenched. Carolyn is difficult to manage…

Went to a movie with Keens. A lovely song "Be Still My Heart" made me cry, a thing I *never* do in movies. It was too real – for my lover, too, has gone away and my heart cries for him. But darling, as you said in your last letter, it is *right* – and that feeling is buoying me up daily so that my mind has been at rest. For ourselves all is simple ahead. But *you* are to have weeks of tremendously difficult living. Mary Lou has beseeched me several times very earnestly to take her back to Fenchow to see her Dad – "because I like him berry much" – bless her heart!

Hong Kong   *Wednesday, October 6, 1937*

Dearest Mother & Dad –

Do you know anyone – YM Secretary or friends – in Seattle who might help me? And do you know names of hotels or places to stay? … You might send letters to me at American Express or direct to the boat… Would you ask Wynn Fairfield to send me to the boat in Seattle a statement certifying

---

95   The family left Fenchow on September 20, traveling south by train to Hankow. After almost a week there, under Japanese air bombardment, Miriam and the girls took a plane to Hong Kong, and Walter returned to Fenchow.

I am a missionary of the ABCFM etc., that I can use to get the reduced railroad clergy rates. Next, do you know if DL&W Railroad from Chicago to Hoboken goes via Detroit, as I should love to see Jerry & Evelyn. This is not too important. But I tho't DL&W might be easiest to come on & to check baggage on, right into Hoboken or Newark. (I have one small trunk, six bags.)

Hong Kong   *Thursday, October 7, 1937*

Darling –

Keens are out so we have the run of this palatial residence. I bathed the girls in one of the six tiled bathrooms, fed them upstairs, tucked them in mosquito nets, changed to a long flowing negligee of Grace's – being worn constantly for dinners here to protect legs and ankles against mosquitoes – majestically swept down the broad polished stairs, was served a solemn dinner, correct & complete as "what will missy drink?" while two white-coated figures hovered about. Somewhere in China there's a war & people are suffering!!! This life is awful – but now I'll have a quiet evening to visit with you. The weather remains sweltering. The promised typhoon missed Hong Kong tho' there were gales and storms…

Baggage arrived Monday. Left the trunk in town & have the bags here. I am thankful to have it. Went Tuesday. a.m. to see if there were any faint chance of sailing on the *Wilson* but there wasn't. Went Wednesday and found word just in from Shanghai that the *Hoover* was completely booked. Seattle sailings are just as crowded…but there had been a cancellation on the *Jefferson*, which they offered me. It can't sail before October 13. I was in a quandary; didn't *at all* want to go to Seattle where I know no one, where we may strike bad weather and cold. This is an emergency situation not a pleasure trip; your relatives and mine would have to understand our passing them up under these circumstances.[96] Now that I'm started, I want to get on. So I decided on the inconvenience of Seattle as against the delay of L.A.

Oh yes! I'm forgetting to say that your "Arrived" telegram came on Tuesday. I was so relieved to know you were back in Fenchow. Newspaper reports of Shansi fighting, evacuating of Taiyuan, Yen fleeing, moving capitol to Linfun, etc., all made me feel travel might be greatly delayed & difficult, if not impossible. But you are back after two weeks and finding tons to do…

Will carry travelers checques for I know no one to endorse my checques in Seattle to allow me to draw cash. The American Express has written their man to meet me in Seattle & manage baggage, train arrangements, etc. American Express here has been exceedingly helpful, patient with little girls who dip hands in inkwells while I'm occupied, etc. I've been there almost every day. Tomorrow or Saturday will go for my tickets, settle up. Children have to pay half fare each.

Hong Kong   *October 14, 1937*

My darling –

I must have a short note for you tonight – my last before leaving China, for – how long? Today came your first letter from home, October 4. Oh, it was good to have this Fenchow letter to carry with me.

---

96   The family had hoped to visit relatives in Los Angeles as they did on their trip out to China.

I still have a stunned feeling about going to America – as if I might wake up & find it not true. The whole thing seems so unreal that I can't grasp it. But I won't let myself start on that now.

Mary Lou is all pepped up about the boat trip, tho' she says frequently "Let's go back to Fenchow." She wielded the scissors on Carolyn's hair, which was beginning to look quite girlish, & now we have a rather moth-eaten effect. It's not too short, but patchy! Don't worry about us; we'll be O.K. and in good hands. We aren't going "home," for that is where *you* are, always. Oh my Beloved, God keep you strong and courageous. Good-bye – good-bye.

P.S. Friday, October 15, 1937 – Boat postponed again today till 6 a.m. tomorrow.

Today begins the long distances of separation when it will take two months at shortest to get a reply to any question. I'll send letters direct to you unless I hear from you to send them via Hong Kong. I feel terribly *final* in this letter – sort of like the end of the world. Will I ever see China again – or you, my dearest heart?

On board the S.S. President Jefferson   *Tuesday, October 19, 1937*

My dearest –

We got on board all by ourselves perfectly O.K., but I must say I was surprised at Kenneth letting us go off the way we did…without finding out the taxi fare, knowing we had to go to the tailors to get my three necessary dresses, and I had to stop to buy fruit, disembark at the ferry, get myself, children, packages, & coolie with the handbags across the ferry, into rickshaws, along that awful wharf and aboard. The wharves were terrible, cranes loading baggage and coolies carrying loads and noise and danger. The rickshaw couldn't get near to the ship, so I had to disembark & carry Carolyn and coats & fruit and tell Mary Lou to hang on to my skirt. Then along came two plain-looking English women who had been to see a friend off, and they good-heartedly took in the situation, one took Mary Lou by the hand & her "suitcase," the other all my bundles and went with us right up the wobbly steep gangplank and to the pursers' office. They certainly were friendly & helpful – the "common folk" – not "gentlemen!"…

Sailed before I could get the children dressed and on deck to see things. At 7:30 breakfasted – by mistake! – in first-class dining room. By 11 we hit a storm, which everyone assures us, is unusual in its severity and has delayed us more than a day into Kobe, Japan. It's been as bad as anything I ever want to see. I've been terribly sick. I'd sorta vomit between putting on each sock & shoe for them, hurry them up on deck, stopping at every ladies' room en route to make a contribution. Children's meals were served an hour before ours and I'd order for them, get them started, then the terrible heat in the dining room & and smell of food would send me running. By the time I was thru feeding them & had them in bed, I couldn't face returning for my own meal. I'd just stagger up on deck to my chair. Really it was ghastly, and the poor youngsters suffered – not sick themselves, but my disposition was terrible and they couldn't understand why I'd have to lie down in the midst of dressing them.

Then came news that we all had to have cholera injections before the boat would be allowed into Kobe and Yokohama… I went to see the doctor about it. When I was getting us jabbed I told him of my *terrible* seasickness. He gave me a couple of pills and whatever they were good for, at least I slept that night. Today I'm O.K., only occasional uncomfortable feelings but three days of it was plenty. Now for the good news. Who do you suppose is on this boat? A good part of the women & children of Foochow. Altogether over thirty children and Mary Lou & Carolyn are happy playing on deck all day. Betty Thelin I knew in high school. The day I was sickest she felt O.K., took the children to the dining room to feed them, had sandwiches & apples sent to me on deck. Stewardess bathed the children one evening. Bellboys have been helpful about carrying Carolyn up & down stairs. Almost everyone has been more or less sick, even some of the children. All in the group are grand about helping each other out. The girls have been eating lightly but I don't force them – I envy them eating at all. I get a tremendous kick out of Carolyn. She is much more friendly, enjoying the trip loads, talking lots. Mary Lou is unusually independent & responsible about getting round the boat alone, running errands. She still is the noisiest youngster aboard, but some of the others are knocking some of her deviltry out of her.

All of us husbandless women in the same boat, plus the bad seasickness, have kept me from getting morbid about ever seeing you again. You can't get romantically sentimental under the circumstances. But don't think I don't think of you every hour of the day. I feel very much by myself now, and torn in two parts. But sometime we shall be together again, united as we should be. Till then, my love comes all the time, and my thoughts and prayers, my beloved.

On board the S. S. President Jefferson   *Friday, October 22, 1937*

My dearest –

We got into quarantine outside Kobe by 7 a.m. yesterday and had to go thru the inevitable health inspection & immigration officials' inspection. In the afternoon after our naps, I took the children for a taxi ride. Actually saw women standing on street corners making the thousand-stitch good-luck belts for the Japanese soldiers in China. A group of soldiers was "off for the front" and large groups of women & school children with flags were cheering & demonstrating. A huge department store had one whole window given over to a model of an air raid. War posters on buildings.

Sailed from Kobe 8 p.m. The crew was not allowed shore leave on account of feared cholera, though all passengers were allowed to go ashore. (We had to use special moveable toilet cans all day in port!) This a.m. we anchored at Nagoya about 10 and all day long have been loading "China – with care – Porcelain made in Japan" – headed for U.S. It is enough to make one sick. But it's easier for our government to make speeches than for anyone to give up the imports – so we still sit and load Japanese porcelain as I write this – and writhe. What a mess.

One good stroke of luck today: the cabin next to ours was vacated & I asked to be moved in – and was! It seems twice as large so we can have a chair, move around, put our things away. Have room enuf to get the trunk up from the hold…and get out some warmer clothes…

I'm not a good mother these days. I find my temper so short with Mary Lou particularly for she is so trying in interfering with Carolyn, and I yell at her and hit at her. It's not good for either of us and I do feel bad about it. Then Mary Lou can be so terribly sweet and thoughtful and helpful sometimes that it breaks your heart. I am going to try not to let her irritate me… Carolyn is good as gold, for a wonder, plays joyously with the other children.

Played some cutthroat bridge last night. But I kept thinking how strange and far-away it all was – the luxurious salons, people in dinner dress and dining from menus a yard long, lights, music, security, comfort – and you in Fenchow, driving, lonely, tired, living and working among the "common people" of the earth, concerned for their country and their future. Did we ever share that life with you? And do we seem unreal and distant? Now I'm off to take a pill and try to sleep tonight. I thought too much last night – and thinking isn't good for me. Only loving is good for me at night. And I do love, tonight, as always, only you.

On board the S.S. President Jefferson   *Tuesday, November 2, 1937*

Darling –

Bad luck the last two days. Heavy storms slowed us up no end, and a head sea started the boat pitching again and made me sick. For two days not a thing stayed down and I wanted to die. Today, fortunately, the sea's a little quieter. Mary Lou has been awake two or three hours in the night several times, has fallen out of bed with the rolling of the boat. Poor kiddies, this has been a hard trip and I think they've been unusually good – no tantrums or heavy scenes. It's as bad a sea trip as I'll ever want to take…

I've filled out customs declarations; I've bought stamps and posted all my letters; I've made out my list of tips, will cash an American Express checque for them & my laundry bill, deck chair, etc.… Good-bye for now dear. I think of you so constantly in our war-torn suffering China. God bless you in the things you are trying to do for her and give you wisdom and strength to meet the problems.

> – My deepest love.

6

Return to New Jersey

1937 - 1940

Passport photo for return to USA

Once again, Miriam managed on her own during the journey from Seattle to Montclair, New Jersey. She traveled to Nebraska to visit Walter's father, to the Mayo Clinic in Rochester, and then Detroit on the way home. Throughout it all Miriam wrote letters cheerily describing her trials and tribulations as she visited old haunts and was reacquainted with friends. Miriam finally arrived at her parents' home in Montclair the day before Thanksgiving. She was relieved and exhausted and thirty-three years old.

As Miriam settled in, she sought childcare but only found part-time help. With the loving yet questioning eyes of her parents upon her, she ran out of time, reluctantly leaving her two daughters (ages two and four) with her parents (ages sixty-six and seventy) for two weeks while she was in the hospital giving birth to Eleanor Grace, born on February 14, 1938. Eventually, the differences between her ideas of parenting and those of her parents created some tension in the household.

Miriam wrote long, loving letters to Walter of her longing to hold his hand and feel his touch, marveling at one point: "How deep and understanding our love has grown." Reading my mother's letters from this era, I am struck by her amazing self-reflection and connection to my father, despite the miles between them and the dangers of war. She had a psychic experience during this time. In the hospital four days after Ellie's birth, Miriam had trouble sleeping. She had been waiting for word from Walter, yet none was forthcoming. On February 19, 1938, she learned from a newspaper account that the Japanese had captured Fenchow on the day of her distress. Deeply troubled, she turned to the only solace she had: her faith.

Walter and Miriam were apart for eleven months – a time when she was tending to the needs of her three girls, worrying about her husband's safety, and chafing under the constraints of living with her parents. But she had no money and no choice; she had to stay put. She made speeches to local women's groups about what was happening in China. Finally, the fates smiled on them when Walter treated a Japanese general inflicted with a venereal disease. Once cured, the man said that it was time for Walter to leave Fenchow (likely to keep the condition confidential) – and Walter was only too happy to comply. The ABCFM gave Walter permission to return to the U.S. and the couple was joyfully reunited in Montclair on August 18, 1938.

Though my first language was Chinese, I don't remember any of it. Mother and Dad retained the language for the rest of their lives. They sometimes spoke Chinese together – particularly when they wanted the conversation to remain private from little ears or amidst crowded elevators.

Walter undertook full-time speaking tours about Japanese aggression, joining his voice with other Americans trying to alert President Roosevelt to the threat from the Japanese. With a part-time secretary, Miriam handled his correspondence and travel arrangements, as well as managing her parents' home, making speeches, and caring for the three of us. In the fall of 1939, Hitler invaded Poland. France and England declared war on Germany and international tensions increased.

Miriam was often weary. She stayed up late writing Walter's correspondence and dashing off short notes to him about the daughters. The strain came through in her short temper, at times, with the children. She had seen by now that world events would always interfere with their life together. She wrote privately on August 27, 1939, the day before her thirty-fifth birthday: "Oh what a *Hell* I have been creating for myself and living in these last six months! I have allowed disillusionment, bitterness, cynicism to overwhelm me…" Yet just six days before she wrote about her despair, she sent Walter a long list of things that she loved about him. Like most relationships, it was all human, and very true. She was trying hard to not give in to despair and fatigue; these two letters, six days apart, are the perfect evidence of the depth of her struggle.

But even the most dedicated heart can only stretch so far, and in the spring of 1940, Miriam was near the breaking point. She confronted Walter about his constant absences. She told him that the children no longer knew who he was. And she challenged him, saying that he should consider going back to China – alone. Miriam encouraged idealistic Walter to make his decision based on where he could meet the greatest need. I can only imagine that he made his choice in his typical fashion – with a list of pros and cons. He decided to remain stateside for a few years, speak, and find a medical position.

In April, Miriam moved the family to a nearby rental home, which relieved intergenerational tensions – a great plus. She looked forward eagerly to the family's move to Minneapolis at year-end, where Walter found a post running the medical practice of Dr. Y. T. Johnson while he served in the National Guard. With her hopes rekindled, Miriam prepared to move and begin again in Minneapolis. She was ready for whatever lay ahead.

Seattle   *Wednesday, November 3, 1937*

Mother, dear –

So excited after talking to you & Dad that I can't sleep. It seems impossible that I am really in America.

Yesterday reached Victoria at midnight. I packed this a.m. as we sailed down the Sound. Off the boat in Seattle around 4. A long wait for baggage at customs and a careful inspecting of everything. Meantime had discovered China friends waiting for me, Plymouth Church people, American

Express, and good friends of Walter's. Tomorrow a.m. Walter's friends are coming back in their car to help us do a few errands before leaving at 4:20 p.m. Clergy certificate here O.K. so will get reduced rates on railroads. Will check one small tin trunk, a hat box, a bag, a large black suitcase direct to Montclair, as Dad's letter suggested (four pieces). Four pieces left to bring with us – easy! We'll go to Nebraska [Rising City]. Will see about Rochester. I'm working my way slowly across the continent. I may not come this way again. Can you stand us for the winter? Or longer? How strange to be coming back to my old room, and bringing two sweet little girls. And having a baby there. But not strange to be coming to my own Dad & Mother. Somehow you can always count on them – and how that holds me. Keep hanging on. I'm coming.

Rising City, Nebraska   *Saturday eve, November 13, 1937*

Walter –

We've had a good week here but I do hope it hasn't been too much for your Dad and Olive. I think the irregularity and the children is upsetting to their quiet life. I've washed clothes every day, written over twenty letters or notes, tried to get Mary Lou out every day to let off spirits, went to a church dinner with your Dad. Then your Dad and I have talked lots, and I feel for the first time that he has spoken without any restraint as if I were one of you.

Alvarezes' home, Rochester, Minnesota   *Thursday, November 18, 1937*

Mother, dear –

You can guess how full the days are here with traipsing around the Clinic. Not hard days – everyone is lovely to us – but long ones. Tomorrow I see their doctor for final instructions on how to bring them up. Reports *all* are good.

Please tell the Guild Chairman I will not speak on China. Reason: pregnancy; I do not want to get into a sensational "my-harrowing-escape-from-China" account, which is what people expect. I've refused stories in Nebraska and here, have allowed an item reading "on account of disturbed conditions in China, Mrs. Walter H. Judd and her two —. Dr. Judd is remaining in Fenchow where he is Superintendent —" The Board can send out publicity they want, but none from us.

Tomorrow afternoon Mrs. A. will have a few folks I want specially to see, for tea. She has a girl to look after the children – dress, bathe, feed them, go with us to the clinic & help keep them amused between acts, carry Carolyn in & out, etc. – isn't that just like her! I breakfast in bed, pamper myself, and am getting horribly spoiled.

Just now I'm staying with Betty Thelin's two boys while she has some exams herself. She was so nice to help me on the boat when I was seasick. She's staying in a hotel, so I'm glad I can give her a hand. One of her boys is small, so the two of them look like twins, younger than Mary Lou. Everywhere folks looked at me with these four lively small things under four, and another one on the way, and nudged each other and whispered. I was a sensation!!!

Montclair, New Jersey   *Tuesday, November 30, 1937*

My Dearest –

There's no use trying to describe the blissful beaming at Newark at 7:30. Both youngsters had to be wakened for they were dead tired and were fussy. There were Dad and Mother and Clarke and the car. Clarke was most useful – slung luggage and chased children and unlocked suitcases and trunks and helped with feeding and dressing problems. That was a hectic day, for the kids were cross and everyone was excited, and there was so much that was new and lovely prepared for them that it was bewildering.

What Mother hasn't thought of isn't worth thinking of. Some things have been given or loaned. But Mother has spent herself. People have been rallying around for Lao III; already there is a basinette and a complete outfit, necessitating my buying next to nothing…

Thanksgiving Day. What a riot the cousins had. Mother has a maid who cooked the turkey and mince pies so all we had to do was to straighten out quarrels, award the piano bench to one child at a time, etc. Clarke's two are cute, and lively as they can be.[97] Carolyn made an immediate hit. Mary Lou was shy and yet autocratic. She is disobedient and defiant beyond words, but perhaps if we can restore her sense of security and stability that will go. These two days when there has been no company she has improved tremendously, helped dry dishes, make beds. I'm getting a girl to help with the children. I can't lift them in and out of baths now, or pick up their toys etc. for I'm having pretty severe backaches.

Montclair, New Jersey   *Monday, December 6, 1937*

Dearest –

What a different Christmas this year from last! …Christmases should be in one's own home, with the joyous little children around, and especially with the day expressing some of the inner ideals and foundations and attitudes on which that home is built. I almost dread this year, with the overdoing, over stimulating, over excitement. Not that I can blame heart-starved grandparents for wanting to shower their expressions of love on the two adorables, but it certainly is hard on the little devils – quite aside from the hurt in my heart when I think of the Chinese, known & unknown, who are suffering today for even the essentials of life.

But we will be close together on Christmas I know, thinking of the things that we are longing and hoping for this torn world and of our part in helping to bring them, and of our great unitedness that leaves us free to work even miles and miles apart. You will feel my special love for you that day, even if you never get this letter, I know.

---

97   Clarke and Elizabeth's two children were Betty Lou and Johnny.

Montclair, New Jersey   *Saturday, January 1, 1938*

Dear Folks —[98]

Happy New Year! …We tried to spread Christmas and the excitement out as much as we could for the sake of Mary Lou who was so high-strung – went to a pageant in our church – help Grampa trim the tree – a party at her nursery school – tying up parcels – hanging up the stockings Christmas Eve.

Christmas morning we all slept until seven, dressed before looking into our stockings, breakfast, and then the gifts around the Christmas tree. By this time, the excitement was terrific. So Grandpa took them out for a quiet ride in the car. Clarke and his family appeared and there was another siege of package opening. At our turkey dinner there were ten of us and we had a real home party with all the fixings. We were hardly finished when people started dropping in to say Merry Christmas and there followed a busy afternoon. It was a lovely day.

Today is a birthday, so we had to have a certain amount of recognition. It took the form of ice cream and cake with candles, and a few small gifts for lunch. I told Mary Lou about the baby and showed her some of the things I had ready for it, and that seems to have made almost as much impression as the birthday. We'll be driven to death now with the daily persistent questioning about when the baby is coming, but there are more difficult questions than that to answer that she's already thought up! Wish Walter were here. He's a good talker!

Mary Lou still asks daily when we can start back to *our house*. Christmas night I said, "It's been a happy day, hasn't it?" Quick as a flash she snapped back, "No, it hasn't. My fadder isn't here!" Her adjustment to life in America is going to be more painful and slow than I had at first anticipated, for her foundations and interest still seem to be elsewhere. Hope I'll have the patience to live through some of her contrary moods and disobedience.

Montclair, New Jersey   *Sunday, January 16, 1938*

Dearest –

I am surprised to see how some girls I've known change as they get their families. I wonder if I seem changed to them! I *feel* changed in lots of ways as I get back in my home and don't fit the way I used to. Do you think I have changed these last six years? I wonder if you have any conception of what you have done to and for and with me? I bless you eternally for the joy of these years, for all they have brought me of living and learning…

I went down Jan. 3 to Newark to take my written exam for the new driver's license and discovered when I got down the end of nowhere that I had to take a road test as well. In Montclair they told me *only* a written exam for a renewal, and I had gone on the bus to avoid traffic & slippery roads. The man in charge told me to go out & find the inspector and tell him, which I did. He said, "Sorry," nothing he could do about it. He & I stood on the corner and got into conversation, and it turned out he'd been to China and we got to be good buddies. Two young boys rode up in a rattle trap old Essex to take the test, and he had to rule them out on some misqualification. Then he up and asks

---

them if they'll lend their car for the lady to take her test in. So in I got, with the inspector & the two lads all showing me where was starter, gas, warning me about brakes that gripped fast etc., and off I rattled down half a block, was told to turn in the street and go back – and thus ended my test. Nice inspector! Nice lads!

Montclair, New Jersey   *Sunday, January 23, 1938*

Dearest –

It seems strange to be so completely cut off from your life and interests and activities – I even long to sit across the table from you and hear a good general cuss-out of someone or something – you used to come to in the middle of one and sort of laugh and say half apologetically, "Well, I'm not scolding you!" I wouldn't even mind being scolded by you tonight, argue some on the subject, and then end up – well, close together, as we both dropped off to sleep.

Wish I knew how you are managing, if Fenchow can furnish food for the hospital, what about coal, drugs, & supplies? I think daily of the countless problems you must be having to work at. Why can't I do something? Sometimes I get impatient and heart-sore at the disinterest and unconcern and lack of insight, or foresight, all around me; or even mad at myself for my almost complete domesticity and preoccupation with petty details of "child rearing"; or even madder at the "comforting" platitudes and careless speeches spoken to me by well-meaning friends who want to make a hero of you or a martyr of me. I think I used to be more patient of human nature before I married you. You have infused something of yourself into me – but now I need you at hand to be the steam escape valve. No one else understands.

Montclair, New Jersey   *Friday, January 28, 1938*

Dear Judds –

We have the chicken pox. Isn't that some'pin. Mary Lou came down with it yesterday, has to be out of school for twelve days, and Carolyn is expected to get it after Mary Lou is finished. I was about ready to go to the hospital any day, but now I'm hoping that I will be "spared." If I do have to go off to the hospital before Mary Lou can get back to school, Mother will have to get a nurse to help with the children.

I stay in the house most of the time, try to get my exercise after dark, write a few letters every evening in a vain attempt to get caught up. Last night I listened to the radio for a change. I got so mad at Boake Carter.[99] This business of "Have we forgotten that 'Charity begins at home?' and didn't we think we could find enough people in America who could use the million dollars being raised by the Red Cross instead of sending it to China?" If he thinks we can remain isolated from conditions in China, it shows what a short-sighted commentator he is.

---

99   Boake Carter was a well-known radio commentator in the 1930s. He frequently voiced controversial opinions.

Orange Memorial Hospital, Orange, New Jersey   *Friday, February 18, 1938*

Dearest –

To get to *The Story of The Event*![100] …Monday morning I woke at six and felt sure things were going to happen. At 6:30 pains were coming every 7-10 minutes. I got up, called Mother & the cook, got Mary Lou up & told her to dress herself as I couldn't help her. By a little after 7:30 Mother and I were off in Mrs. T's car, leaving Father at home to run things (with the cook) till Mother should get back. Incidentally, he is grand with them…reads stories by the hour.

I walked in the hospital about eight with pains coming every 2-3 minutes. Dr. Bingham had been in the hospital all night. He came to examine me at 8:30 by which time I was having *the real thing* every minute, and plenty hard. Within five minutes the membranes broke and the jig was up – they rushed me into the delivery room and thirty seconds later I was breathing that blessed chloroform. The baby was here at 8:50 without my knowing anything more about it.

I wished beforehand countless times that you were to be with me to hold my hand, but afterwards I wished you'd been here to see how smart I was to get it over quickly, how brave I'd been, and how easy it was compared with the two you were present at. Not but what the pains are pains just the same. I kept thinking "I wish Walter were here. Then I could cry or yell and he'd understand and love me and help me. But he isn't, and I'm going to be the kind of person he'd be proud of, before all these complete strangers." And I just groaned quietly while a nice nurse rubbed my back, until the membranes broke when I did say some too loud *Ohs* for the two minutes till they gave me the chloroform. It's funny because before, when you were to be with me, I wanted so desperately to be brave for fear you'd think I was a sissy. But this time I *was* brave, but wished you were here so I could cry. How deep & understanding our love has grown.

The little lady is a dear. She had hair and lots of it. Eyes are blue. I've never heard her cry. And does she nurse well!! As for me, I'm 100% O.K. with a short labor I wasn't at all exhausted, and have been feeling peppy. It seems ironical that with this easiest of deliveries I have to stay longest in the hospital – the rules let me go Sunday, Feb. 27, too late for Carolyn's birthday. I'm reveling in the luxury and idleness, making up for the decidedly unrestful convalescence last time.

Montclair, New Jersey   *Tuesday, February 22 , 1938*

Dearest –

Everything going fine. Eleanor lost weight down to 8 lbs. 1 oz., has started gaining now. Carolyn is practically finished with the poxes, is good as gold. Mary Lou went to Mount Vernon for the weekend, had a grand time and felt very big to be away visiting all by herself…[101]

On February 17 came *four* letters from you. One was a December 4 letter that had evidently been sidetracked somewhere. In it were a general letter which went on to your Dad, and the sweetest love note that couldn't have come at a better time to whisper its message to my heart.

---

100   Eleanor Grace Judd was born on Monday, February 14, 1938, weighing 8 lbs. 13 oz.
101   Mary Lou traveled to Mount Vernon, New York to visit Miriam's brother's family: Mary Lou's Uncle Clarke, Aunt Elizabeth, and cousins Betty Lou and Johnny Barber.

You wrote of your psychic experience on January 1 – I know of no interpretation of it. But am I, too, having a sense of closeness to you that feels the strain at certain definite times? February 17 Father & Mother went home from the hospital early in the evening after a good visit. I'd had your four letters and was feeling you near and loving me; all should have been quiet & peaceful with me. But there was a strange restlessness – I couldn't understand or explain it. It wouldn't let me read any of the literature that sits on my bedside table, nor do my inevitable knitting, nor even rest quietly till the baby came at ten to nurse. Later – much later – I slept fitfully and worked at hard problems all night. And that was all day of the 18th for you!! On the 19th a paragraph in the papers – all too brief – presented a possible explanation.[102] Since then I have lived day and night with you. I lie here and go over details of life in Fenchow these days as it very possibly is – until I have to make myself deliberately stop – shut off my mind and heart and try to regain again the peace that I need these days in caring for *our* blessed Eleanor. I remember your saying often that *uncertainty* is the worst thing in the world, and that it's more difficult for those away from a scene, than for those busy in the midst of it. I try to let my faith be strong. It's hard… "As thy days, so shall thy strength be." This helps me, and I believe it for you.

Montclair, New Jersey   *Monday, March 21, 1938*

Dearest –

Little Eleanor five weeks old today… Mother has been trying to keep me from doing too much and make me rest, which is anything but restful for me. So we've had a tense time. We finally got Mother off today for a rest. She went away only under heaviest protest, saying she felt like a shirker deserting me in my time of need etc. And me feeling just fine, able to sleep well at night for Eleanor *never* cries then – and with one full and one part-time helper in the house! If people don't quit feeling sorry for me, I'll scream.

Montclair, New Jersey   *Tuesday, March 29, 1938*

My Darling –

I can't help feeling that some decisive word will come from you. Surely things must soon come to a head…with no supplies or funds, Emma leaving, and under the present circumstances. It's very well for the Board to have a policy of keeping work going, but how do they expect you to do it??? I ache to have you here speaking out as you can and do – but you'd have to expect to find yourself a bit of a leper. You're used to that, but it doesn't hurt any the less to be disapproved of and misunderstood by your own organizational group. It makes me feel so impotent sometimes that I haven't the ability or the detachment or the opportunity to rise and lift my voice as you would. The poor people at 14 Beacon St.[103] have to raise the budgets and cover the deficits, so they must see that no "missions retreating or closing down" word gets out (hence don't want you to close up) and they get their contributions from people on both sides of the fence, so have to keep both groups pacified (hence don't want Walter H. Judd home making too disturbing speeches). I know this won't deter you if you decide it is wisest to come home – but still your loyalty to the Board would make you wish you could help them to see things *as they are*, and act accordingly, so that there would not be need to cross them.

---

102   The Japanese captured Fenchow on February 18, 1938.

103   A reference to ABCFM and their home office in Boston.

There was an incident last week that profoundly stirred my emotions in relation to the situation in our adopted country. In the Union Congregational Church the choir sang Gounod's motet *Gallia*. I sang it with the Holyoke choir more than once. It is a powerful thing. I think it has affected me as nothing else in music ever has. Partly I suppose it was this reminiscence of former emotional experiences that started me off. But largely, I am sure, it was the new significance that seemed to be attached to the words. They might have been written at this moment to fit this situation. As the chorus picked up each phrase, sang it back and forth, answered and reiterated and emphasized and repeated in that beautifully sung music, I finally couldn't stand it and my heart burst. I cried and cried till I thought I could never control myself – a thing I have never done in public before. Don't worry! Mother sitting next to me was the only one who knew – I had to borrow her hankie when I'd used up my own.

Gallia, Motet for Soprano Solos and Chorus, by Charles Gounod

> Solitary lieth the city,
> She that was full of people!
> How is she widowed!
> She that was great among nations,
> Princess among the Provinces,
> How is she put under tribute!
> Sorely she weepeth in darkness,
> Her tears are on her cheeks.
> And no one offereth consolation,
> Yea, all her friends have betrayed her,
> They are become her enemies.
> Zion's ways do languish
> None come to her solemn feasts.
> All her gates are desolate;
> Her priests sigh;
> Yea, her virgins are afflicted,
> And she is in bitterness.
> Is it nothing to all ye that pass by?
> Behold and see if there be any sorrow,
> That is like unto my sorrow.
> Now behold, O Lord,
> Look Thou on my affliction,
> See the foe hath magnified himself.
> Jerusalem, O turn thee to the Lord thy God!

Darling, these days for you are most perplexing, I know – trying to know what step to take next… I will be with you *whatever* that decision is. You are wonderful to be doing the thing you are. There will always be admiration and respect and deep reverent love in my heart for you.

Montclair, New Jersey   *Tuesday, May 24, 1938*

My Dearest –

No letter have I written to you in seven weeks. When I had word that you hoped to leave Peiping the end of April, it did sound so definite that I quit. So these last weeks I've felt more cut off from you than ever. Life has gone too intensely and ruthlessly on in our two separated circles for us to expect we can completely catch up again. For that reason I'll limit myself tonight to recital of events and leave ideas and ideals and hopes and heartaches till I can whisper them in your ear – in the darkness of night.

It was a relief to hear Tuesday that you had actually got to Peiping and were able to be there for Council. You found out you had a charming red-headed daughter almost three months old, and you got some photos of the two little girls and a huge batch of mail – or didn't you?

Montclair, New Jersey   *Monday, August 1, 1938*

My own Sweetheart –

I can't make it seem possible that I'm writing a letter that you'll get in this country. I won't know you're not in Fenchow till I see you – and feel you.

I do want to write of a talk I had with Betty & Harry Price yesterday. A group of twenty friends of China met in their apartment, representing varied interests – labor, church, secular international organizations. From this has grown the "Committee on America's Participation in Japan's Aggression," which they speak of as the "Embargo Group." They are publishing a pamphlet – sixty-five pages or so on "America's Part in Japan's War Guilt" – to go to a list of 25,000. They are getting "sponsors" – Helen Keller…Admiral Byrd, Buell of Foreign Policy Association, Carter of Institute of Pacific Relations, etc. are being aimed at. They have several well-known economists doing research and investigation for them. Pearl Buck may do an article. Luce hopes to have an article in *Fortune*. Wallace wants a fifteen-page supplement in the *Reader's Digest*.[104] They have been to Washington and seen Hull & Roosevelt, and Pittman has intimated there are real possibilities of passing certain legislation in the Senate at the next session, dealing with the sale of war materials to treaty-breaking nations. But Washington claims public opinion still lags woefully in supporting action the government is ready to take. And P. C. Chang, brother of Chang Po-Lin, now lecturing in America, says action by Congress next January is too late to wait for: this next month or two is the most strategic time and the public is waiting for leadership…

What of your plans after landing and what do I suggest you do? I don't know. I feel baffled at having you to consider again in my plans. I have planned nothing, but I have been increasingly determined that we should not live with Mother. The problem of where we're going to settle for now is going to be a difficult one to handle psychologically, even if it weren't difficult to handle practically and financially, which it is.[105]

---

104   Henry Luce was founder and editor of *Time Magazine* and Dewitt Wallace was the founder and editor of *Reader's Digest*.
105   Walter arrived by train in Montclair on August 18, 1938. In the fall, the Barbers moved to a rental apartment in New York City. Walter began full-time speaking tours. Miriam handled his travel arrangements and correspondence, while managing the children and her parents' home during their absence.

Montclair, New Jersey   *Sunday, November 27, 1938*

Dearest –

I've been working all evening without feeling that I am making any intelligent headway with the pile of requests that must have an answer. This fall trip was set up as to definite dates. All I had to do was to follow thru. After January 1 the whole thing is in a state of indecision, and I am unwilling to be responsible for making your decisions for you without having a much better idea than I now have what you want to do – e.g., any student groups? any "repeats" to same groups? emphasize more definitely labor, or church, or what? concentrate on certain geographic section? fulfill certain oral promises? etc. You said once you wanted to consider going with the Student Mission in March and now you seem all booked up (in your mind) in Mississippi Valley. IN OTHER WORDS – Without the information that is in your head, and the approaches and angles and points of view and modifying factors that you *feel*, I can't go on scheduling. And yet letters must have some sort of answers; so I am stalemated.

Montclair, New Jersey   *Thursday, December 1, 1938*

Dear Friends–[106]

Greetings to you all at Christmas time! Walter finally got back to America the middle of August – six weeks less than a year since he put us in the plane in Hankow. Mary Lou was beside herself with excitement but Carolyn gave him the polite go-by for several weeks. Eleanor seemed to approve of him – as she does of all life. She's a prize baby, a joyous, contented disposition.

In September we had a week in Boston, where our resignation from the Board,[107] presented months before, was finally accepted. Walter was free then to say the things he has to say with as little danger as possible of reprisals on our Chinese colleagues, without connecting the American Board with efforts toward political action, which is not its primary function. Our hope is eventually to be back in China, and under the American Board; but our immediate concern is to get the war stopped or there will be no work in China for any of us!

Walter is speaking towards an embargo on American war materials going to Japan. His first weeks were around the New York and Boston areas and everywhere the general response was "Why haven't we known the facts?" People seem amazed to learn of America's part in this mad game. And hearing of it, there are two or three stock reactions. Some say: "Well, the whole world's in such a mess now that we'd better not make a move." Others say: "Thank God for the Pacific Ocean!" They make me boil! But always there is a group keenly concerned, asking "What can we do?" and starting to do even what little they can. They give us hope to carry on.

Now Walter's off on an eight-week trip through the middle west getting back a day or two before Christmas. I'm making the bookings for his tour almost entirely through personal contacts or names

---

106   This was a mimeographed Christmas letter to friends.
107   The American Board of Commissioners for Foreign Missions (ABCFM).

given to us by friends. It's a hectic job. I've put the two little girls in nursery school for mornings. I have a part-time stenographer to whom I dictate most of the morning, between baby-bath-and-breakfast act. Afternoons I housekeep and chase children. Evenings I sign letters, send telegrams, organize the next day's dictation. I have a part-time cook who is slow but faithful. We get enough to eat, but I'm afraid if you dropped in on us you might find the house in more disorder than I like and some socks undarned. Well, if we can save China I'll have an Amah to darn the socks. Furthermore, I'm doing a small spot of speaking myself – five times in the last two weeks. I like it, only I wish I didn't have to sandwich it in between secretarial work and motherhood, as it were. It would be more effective if I could give my whole time to it, but someone has to keep the home fires burning, and I'm elected. I'll have to admit I'm tired most of the time, but with satisfying feeling that it's a worthwhile tiredness.

Montclair, New Jersey   *Saturday, February 4, 1939*

Dear Walter –

There were about 150 women at the East Orange, NJ meeting and I got them all worked up about China. They were a fine group and will take petitions back to their own groups. I got many requests for speeches afterwards, most of which I turned down.

Montclair, New Jersey   *Wednesday, February 8, 1939*

Dear Walter –

Please go on loving me even if I don't do my work right. I'm so tired. There's no way of getting your work done unless I spend long evenings on it. I am getting more demands for speaking than I can accept and I feel I ought to do them rather than go to Holyoke, which others can do who can't do China. (But I've been counting a lot on Holyoke too.)[108] But worst of anything is the children. I'm not fair to them – I've scolded, and slapped and yelled till I hate myself. I've been super-strict and mean and of course it doesn't bring the desired behavior but increases the tension. Think of it! Those two sweet, precious little girls that are yours and mine *together*, that I love so dearly, that I long so desperately to train to be fine strong useful women – and I'm too busy with other things to have time to be decent to them, or affectionate. It's *wrong* as it can be. Oh darling, I'm crying. I love you all so much and I want to be able to do everything for you all and I don't seem to be able to – and I give you up for most of the time and wish you were here, but can't be a decent mother to the part of the family that *is* here. Forgive me, my beloved husband, for this outburst. I should be your strong encouraging support when you are carrying so terribly much load – but tonight I don't want to be anything but a clinging vine – and I have nowhere to cling. I love you desperately – and all there is.

Montclair, New Jersey   *Thursday, February 9, 1939*

Darling –

---

108   There was a Mount Holyoke Alumnae Council Miriam planned to attend.

I am going to Holyoke in spite of my outburst of last night. Partly because I knew if I stayed home I would work and not rest and keep on yelling at the kids – I needed a complete break; partly because I knew you'd feel badly if I stayed home because *your* work was getting me down… Am I too heartless to go off and leave them like this?

Montclair, New Jersey   *Friday, February 10, 1939*

Dear Family –

In January Walter spoke at the Washington Annual Conference for the Cause & Cure of War, where 6,000 women from all over the country seemed much interested in the situation and ought to be able to carry the ideas back to their own regions. He has had talks with William Allen White, Senator Cooper, Colonel Knox whose *Chicago Daily News* had been sold on the idea of embargo of war materials to Japan. This week he is to speak on the nationwide hook-up of the Town Meeting of the Air. He has a tentative invitation to testify before the Foreign Relations Committee of the Senate…

Last fall when he was talking to members of the State Department they told him that they did not need to be convinced on the importance of stopping our support of Japan, but they could not initiate policies. They felt that American public opinion needed to be aroused to a strong and united support of Congressional action. Walter talked to one Senator who said he personally was in favor of some such action, but felt his state would not support it. Later Walter had a chance at that state for two or three days and as a result heard that three thousand letters and petitions had gone in to the Senator. It is all slow work but there are hopeful signs in it.

In this business of helping China, and evidently in all good works, there are too many working groups in the field. The Committee for China Relief is having difficulty raising funds, possibly because people who are interested in China want not only to give to relief but also to see that war is stopped so that relief does not continue to be necessary. Walter advocates doing both relief and efforts to stop the war: personal boycott and government embargo. His illustration is turning off the water in the overflowing bathtub as well as getting the mop.

Montclair, New Jersey   *Tuesday, March 28, 1939*

Darling –

I'm just back from speaking. The meeting was about as poor as I've done – not that what I said wasn't of value but that I left out the most important things. I don't know why. I didn't feel tired when I went – but sort of "stale." Gosh, I hope I perk up before Tuesday. I have the Women's Guild at [Rev.] Black's Congregational Church at 11 a.m., and the Watchung Congregational Church in the afternoon. The group tonight was uninspiring – forty or fifty heterogeneous folks obviously dragged there – with more interest in "the gospel" than in our moral & social obligations as Christians. Not a question asked. It was no responsibility of theirs! Which shows how badly I fell down!

Montclair, New Jersey   *Saturday, April 8, 1939*

Dearest –

This "Easter Bunny" business is a new one. Is it commercial interests that have introduced it? I don't like the idea of giving gifts on Easter – it seems to spoil the significance of the occasion.

The opera was beautiful – Flagstad and Melchoir in the title roles, and the music just plain melting.[109] We had perfect seats – a real treat.

Montclair, New Jersey   *Saturday, May 13, 1939*

Dearest –

Yesterday was a good meeting. They had done a lot of work, invited in women from other churches, put up lovely Chinese hangings, served a simple tea and rice cakes, had a dignified impressive meeting. Every one was complimentary in their remarks – even Mother on the way home said she thought it was a good speech – "good material, well organized, well presented." But I wish I had somebody, like your wife, to light into me after a speech and criticize it and make suggestions. Perhaps sometime you'll do it for me.

Montclair, New Jersey   *Monday, August 21, 1939*

Why do I like you, Sweetheart? I don't know. Funny things you do. Unexpected reasons –

Because you felt so terrifically chagrinned over the torn shirt.

Because you genuinely enjoyed two hours watching Eleanor, even the "cleaning up" process.

Because you can't ever be bothered blowing off at me even when I —, or — and —.

Because you're so loveably inconsistent at times.

Because you can hate to <u>waste</u> money yet never hesitate to <u>spend</u> it.

Because you thought, and spoke, of how you may have appeared ungracious to the P's…

Because you like pretty silk nighties.

Because you hate to shave.

Because you like me to help you buy clothes.

Because you don't expect as much of me as you do of yourself.

Because of hundreds of things as important as these that I think about and glow over from time to time and never have the opportunity to say to you – little, homely, quiet things that are bonds of love and affection just as truly as the larger or more important or more obvious things. Funny, isn't it? But I do think about them. They're all a part of my love for you.

---

109   Miriam attended *Tristan und Isolde* at the famed Metropolitan Opera with her parents. Kirsten Flagstad and Lauritz Melchior were the premier Wagner interpreters of their day.

– Private Writing –

August 27, 1939

Oh what a Hell I have been creating for myself and living in these last six months! I have allowed disillusionment, bitterness, cynicism to overwhelm me. I have tried to interpret all life in terms of the evil and unhappiness and suffering that exist in my world. I have let doubt rule me in all my contacts, and fear, with all their deadening and paralyzing effects. And I have consciously denied the efforts of the true and the good and the noble to break thru and recreate or govern my daily living. I have felt that I must bring suffering and unhappiness to him for all the unbearable misery he has brought to me, and that I could do this by remaining miserable myself. But the hatred that I have nurtured, I could not keep confined to this situation in my life. It will not stay in its own compartment.

And so my whole life in its other relationships has become much less than I have wanted, so ineffective and dragging and weighted down. I have denied God, really. I have dashed busily, madly, from one thing to another in an effort not to think, to forget, to escape fear and hate and personal insecurity. I have allowed my personal pride and vanity, wounded inestimably, to dictate my attitudes. And I have insisted on seeking an explanation for what will never be explained, seeking to punish another Soul, and so my beloved daughters, those three sweet growing trusting lives, and my loving parents, my family and friends, have all been victims of this wrong attitude that has dominated all my living. And he most of all.

Forgive it all, and help me forget it, and wipe it out of my life in its blackness and throttling despair. Help me to conquer it way down deep where its roots are – by not setting up myself as the judge of another, as the administrator of punishment. Gradually may I be able again to dwell with him in love, and perfect forgiveness, and trust, and faith. May I stop seeking a perpetuation of my misery and unhappiness as a way of inflicting suffering on him. Tear out all hatred, that it may not be found in any realm of my life, for when a tiny speck exists it colors everything. Oh how I know the moods of depression, boredom, disillusion, inactivity that have paralyzed good impulses to action. Oh how my stubbornness has refused to allow expressions of love and affection to break thru. Clear out the debris and start again, slowly, painstakingly, deliberately to build a life based on faith and trust and confidence and courage and suffering that leads to strength and not to death.

And I can do it because I want to, and because "ye have not chosen me but I have chosen you!" God chose me for definite tasks he wanted me to do. My first allegiance is to Him, was to Him long before the other took such a large place in my life, and He will not let me down.

Only believe and thou shalt see – That Christ is all in all to thee. Tomorrow is my birthday – and today!   August 27, 1939

Montclair, New Jersey   *Monday, August 28, 1939*

Dearest Mother & Dad —[110]

Congratulations on your fortieth! Your example of forty years of love and problems and joys and difficulties is a beautiful one. I hope when we reach our fortieth we may have lived with as strong faith and courage in the face of hardships and difficulties – for I think our life is to be full of such. My birthday has been a happy one. Last night my girls and Walter got ice cream for our supper celebration and a large box of candy for me. Walter had to leave at 7 p.m. for Cleveland.

Montclair, New Jersey   *Monday, September 4, 1939*

Darling –

I read the papers – I listen to the radio[111]…and think of everything, and back always to you and the tremendous disheartenment this is meaning to all you have been doing and saying and living these years. It seems that nothing is good for easing this sick pain we have to bear, but if we could cling to each other in the night, and perhaps cry out some of the bitterest of the anguish and hopelessness – perhaps – would it strengthen us to go on with what we must do? Our suffering, too, must be borne separately. But you will know now, even more than ever before in our separations, I am with you in the increasing difficultness of your days, and that in the nights I am close beside you, crying on your shoulder, for the easing of our heart.

Montclair, New Jersey   *Sunday, September 9, 1939*

Dearest –

Last night I sure felt like the clean-up squad at an orphan asylum. I bathed and shampooed the three, and the two older had haircuts earlier; then I cleaned five pair of shoes. But they looked nice today – all ready for fall. The mouse situation is getting worse; two more in traps today. Mother is having fits that Father gave them to Mary Lou and allowed her to bury them, after showing them off to the neighborhood. I don't mind her burying them if she can stand it – I rather admire her fearlessness. But I'm standing up strong against Mother who feels children should be spared these details – after all, it's one of the common-places of life!

Montclair, New Jersey   *Sunday, September 17, 1939*

Dearest –

I was on the point of writing you an extremely depressed letter last night. Instead I went to bed at 9:15. And today's activities have been stimulating and re-creative, so that tonight I feel quiet and happy and hopeful in my heart (a quiet spirit where deep fundamental faith and confidence triumph over pessimism and cynicism and depression in setting the mood)…

---

110   Her parents were vacationing in Ottawa, Canada.
111   Hitler invaded Poland September 1, 1939. On September 3, the United Kingdom and France declared war on Germany.

I haven't taught Sunday school in twelve years and I look forward to the year with real eagerness. [112] My eleven girls are bright and quick and it will be good to get the outlook & stimulus that a different age group brings. I did ask all who could to see *Stanley & Livingstone* before next Sunday, as a point of departure for our discussion of "Heroic Lives" and "Adventurous Living." This sounds like "progressive Sunday school teaching" with a vengeance! We'd have been shocked at such teaching in our childhood! Dr. Vincent quoted from Robert Louis Stevenson's letters – "I've been to church, and I was not depressed. Hurrah!"[113]

Montclair, New Jersey   *Friday, September 22, 1939*

Dearest –

Mary Lou is increasingly wild and rude and unmanageable – partly perhaps because school regiments her and controls her and she reacts when she gets out; partly I'm sure because of her reaction against Mother (and this is easy for me to understand for Mother makes even me feel like doing exactly the opposite of what she suggests); partly because my fear lest *your* work will suffer, makes me impatient and quick tempered and too severe and perhaps not always just, and she naturally revolts against this in the only way she can. This child-raising is surely a full-time job and I know I'm not doing credit to it now.

Montclair, New Jersey   *Monday, September 25, 1939*

Dearest –

Work here is practically at a standstill with folders piled high with unanswered letters. I've even lost interest in writing letters with tentative dates, or offering several possibilities for them to explore. When even the ones you try hard to get straight have to be cancelled, it doesn't leave much incentive to make new ones to be cancelled, or set up a tentative itinerary only to have a whole area or block of dates changed. Don't please think I'm unsympathetic of the unbelievable demands on your time, or unaware of the terrific schedule you're working under. But it does seem the height of inefficiency and wasted effort not to take the time necessary to sit down and make sane and reasoned decisions as to *what* you are going to do and *what* you are not going to do, and not allow yourself to be dragged into messes by either well-meaning friends, promoters, aspirers, or nit-wits – or your wife!

I'm busy too – and since you don't have time to read letters asking for replies or invitations or dates, even less answer them if you do read them, there's no use my doing busy-work sending date requests or information on schedules. It only piles up into confusion for both you & me. I'll desist until such time as you may have time to read and consider, and let me know beforehand.

After writing this I thought I'd not send it as you might feel horribly discouraged with the engulfing of demands. But it's written in cold reason, unemotion, seriousness, and *love* – so here it comes. You are a wonderful person, you know darling, and with all your inefficiency do as much as three efficient folks – I guess I'll keep you – and I *have* to love you. Your own – Secretary

---

112   Miriam was teaching a sixth-grade Sunday school class.

113   Dr. Vincent was the minister at the Montclair Union Congregational Church.

Montclair, New Jersey   *Wednesday, September 27, 1939*

Dearest –

I felt terribly today when I got your letter of Sunday night – partly because *you* are feeling so overwhelmed and licked, but more because of the note I wrote you. To think of my criticizing *you*, and writing as I did when you are working on an impossibly full schedule & suffering so intensely. Darling, please forgive me. You know it was my desire that you do the most effective groups that led me to urge haste and decision – for I, too, want people to be roused to demand the right. It *is* an impossible situation, my Dearest, but *you* must go on for there is no one who sees it so clearly and tells it so convincingly and vividly. Everyone bears this out. So forget and forgive my letter – knowing that I'm for you.

Montclair, New Jersey   *Sunday, October 29, 1939*

My Dearest –

I know that the conflict between your family and your work is a never-settled hurt in your heart. I would not want you to do anything but what you are doing, Dearest… It's the old story of "he whom a dream hath possessed shall not again know peace." I am convinced that for you and me there will never be the "peace a calm heart knows" – but only snatched, rapturous moments together (like our Boston trip) and stabbing partings that eventually dull to endured separations, punctuated by letters and such unexpected sparkling moments as your phone call tonight. How strangely Life treats us! I had asked a lot less of It than this. But I like to think that somehow I was considered able to cope with the problems and responsibilities that go along with the *greater* happiness Life wanted to bestow. So for myself, I am content. God grant that our children may not bear scars in their lives because their parents' lives have not brought them peace nor taken them along the common paths of men.

Montclair, New Jersey   *Friday, November 3, 1939*

My dearest –

Father & Mother are all packed up with the car loaded.[114] I will miss them a lot – for I am essentially a social creature (in case you may not have noticed!) and like to have someone around to visit with – if and when I want to visit!!

Montclair, New Jersey   *Thursday, November 9, 1939*

Gosh, Sweetheart –

I want you tonight. I hadn't realized how deep down inside I am weary and lonely, for this continuous effort to appear calm and contented to fool the public sometimes fools even myself. But after you phoned tonight I just couldn't seem to get hold of myself or stop crying. It had the unexpected result of sobering up the children and getting them snapped out of a long day's fussing, whining, complaining, quarreling – but I wouldn't exactly have chosen that way of quieting them!…

---

114   Miriam's parents were driving to Florida, where they would winter for several years and eventually move.

That's one thing I always marvel at in you (and in our early days I was scared about it) that with all your amazing strength and power you can yet understand, and not despise, another's weakness. Most of the time I try awfully hard to be strong because you are strong and I admire it in you, and I know you want me to be strong – but tonight I want to be weak. Why couldn't I have been made a pure delicate clinging-vine type and not be troubled with this drive for action and strength. Well, maybe I wouldn't have got *you* then, so I guess the Lord knew what he was doing.

I felt ashamed all evening for nagging at the children. If I went out in an auto accident I'd hate for them to have today to remember me by. We are so obtuse and clumsy in the way we deal with our loved ones – and then one day they're gone and we're left with sick regrets at precious hours with them wasted in needless nagging. I've *got* to do differently, Dearest.

Montclair, New Jersey   *Thursday, November 16, 1939*

Dear Folks –

I am following Walter's example and traveling around the countryside. On Tuesday I drove to Bound Brook Congregational Women's Guild luncheon and spoke on China. It was a good meeting. When I got back I found a report of three little angels and no misbehavior, which strengthens me in my decision to go on the road and let someone else take care of the children!

Tuesday night I went to the high school to hear Pearl Buck. She explained the philosophy that motivates the Chinese actions and gave an excellent insight into their cultural and historical background… When someone asked her about the boycott, she said she herself was opposed to it because wearing lisle hose[115] was not worth the effort and would make no noticeable impression on the whole situation and was, therefore, too small an effort; and in the second place, because a boycott could not be effective without hatred for the peoples being boycotted. That's an argument many people hide behind, but I think it is not valid. I wonder if she cannot restrain and discipline her own children without hating them…

Her attitude seemed detached and almost superior, as if she were a spectator reporting events she had witnessed but was not particularly concerned about. Perhaps this is a characteristic she has absorbed from the Chinese for they tend to be objective and not get excited about anything. *I* am used to a different lecture on China, which in true American fashion exhibits concern and enthusiasm and excitement and urgency. All of these were lacking in her calm comments. She said, for example, that China's major defense was in deciding to just stay alive. Incidentally she used Walter's David and Goliath illustration, which he puts in his speeches but with a different point. She said David refused the heavy sword of Goliath which was offered him, and preferred to fight by a method he was familiar with – his sling – with which he knew he was a good shot. So China is refusing to use the Japanese modern war methods and is wearing out the Japanese in its own way. I felt she gave entirely too little credit to the modernization of China and its turn to western material and methods, but her strong point is interpreting old China.

---

115   Lisle was an alternative to silk.

Yesterday I went to the State Conference on the Cause and Cure of War and it was one of the most stimulating experiences I have had in a long time. The best speaker of all was the only woman, Mrs. Dean of the Research Department of the Foreign Policy Association. She made a splendid address on the present situation in Europe. Only one of the speakers mentioned the Far Eastern situation. It seemed too bad that the whole day's discussion ignored a part of the world that's so definitely our responsibility to deal with, particularly when all speakers were saying we are so closely knit together that what happens in one country affects our own country.

In the afternoon there were four speakers discussing attaining peace through world government. They ignored Russia and seemed to confine all their attention to England, France, Germany, and Italy and how to safeguard small nations. There must have been 2,000 women. I got home at six and found the family better again for my absence than my presence.

I couldn't help feeling: Why do I try to do something that I don't do well (raise children) when I might make a contribution toward war and peace in working with adult groups?

Montclair, New Jersey   *Tuesday, November 21, 1939*

Dearest –

Your letter came tonight. I have read and re-read it. It is so lovely, the most revealing you have ever written concerning yourself. But there is no "answer." If you were here we would talk and talk – and your facial expressions and your warm rich tones, and your nearness, might help to explain things that do not seem clear to me now… In spite of what you have said about me, I feel that I understand infinitesimally little about the whole realm of human relationships, and I have been schooling myself not to try to understand what has seemed unfathomable to me, but to accept, and to love without understanding. Tonight I shall not try to write comments on your letter which might or might not be pertinent. Only this – I love you beyond all reason.

Montclair, New Jersey   *Monday, December 11, 1939*

Dear Judds –

Walter is to broadcast again on the Town Meeting of the Air on December 14 at 9:30. The subject is "America and Japan – Embargo or New Trade Treaties." He never likes to do a thing of this sort because he is limited to ten minutes and cannot give reasons or qualify statements for opinions he expresses, and second, he feels how terribly important what he says could be because of the vast audience listening and thus feels he doesn't do as well as when he is not under such special strain.

Montclair, New Jersey   *Friday, December 15, 1939*

Dearest –

I phoned NBC to see if I could proofread the Town Hall speech or the discussion. They have a deadline of six o'clock tonight with the publisher and they get galleys on the speeches at three o'clock and on the discussion at 5. That gives only an hour to check or make corrections. I have agreed to go to the office at 4:30 and read through the speech and discussion.[116] I will drive in and maybe take Mary Lou to keep her out of mischief.

Montclair, New Jersey   *Monday, December 18, 1939*

Christmas excitement is great in our house. Today we are driving into the country to get greens. Tomorrow we are making candy for gifts. Wednesday Mary Lou is helping me make cookies and Christmas gifts. Friday we have two school parties at the same time at different schools (Walter will have to attend one and I the other) and that afternoon special Christmas programs in the music studio. Mary Lou and Carolyn have planned a concert for Christmas Eve when they are going to play their own pieces and all of us sing carols, and I am to tell a Christmas story. This is their own plan and they have selected each item. If Eleanor contributes, it will no doubt be "Old McDonald had a Farm" because she knows the song and can sing the words "E-I-E-I Oh."

Montclair, New Jersey   *Monday, January 22, 1940*

Dear Folks –

Walter left yesterday for Florida and points south leaving a schedule planned to keep him away from Montclair all but two days between now and the end of April. The hectic days before he goes away leave me almost too tired to know that he's gone. This time the hecticness was worse than usual but it wasn't his fault, and there was one good break that came out of it all.

The Prices (executive secretary of the American Committee for Non-Participation in Japanese Aggression) asked to be allowed to schedule some important meetings for Walter in New York while he was here at Christmas time. Betty Price asked two friends to invite "influential" friends to their homes to meet Walter and informed us of the engagements at 11 a.m. of the same day. Worse than this, we were actually going out the door in the mid-afternoon to get the train for New York for the five o'clock tea when she phoned again to say the evening date required evening clothes! Were we mad! I cussed all the way to New York about the necessary accessories to evening clothes I had forgotten in the rush and that my dress wasn't pressed.

The tea was in one of the old-fashioned aristocratic homes, uptown, brownstone front, maids and butlers, ornate furniture, high ceilings, mammoth mirrors, and tons of heavy wrought silver on the tea table. The hostess was a tall, dignified elderly lady. All of her twenty or thirty guests seemed to be heads of corporations or presidents of banks or leaders of society! Walter talked about three-quarters of an hour and then they asked questions and exclaimed over the terrible picture he painted, which seemed news to most of them and promised to write to their Congressmen, and wanted Walter to speak to their private clubs in New York. We got out of that melee about 7:30, had a bite of dinner and I changed into my evening clothes in the offices of the American Committee and off at nine o'clock to our second junket, feeling quite ill at ease.

This time it was to the apartment of Mary Kennedy, actress and author of light novels, ex-wife of

---

116   The NBC office was in New York City.

Deems Taylor, the noted music critic. It was off Central Park, complete with butler etc. Only this time it was all smart and modern, everyone introduced by their front names, no one quite sure who anyone else was, all milling around trying to be cheery and pretend they were glad that they had been asked to meet Walter, whom, I suspect, most of them had never heard of. Our hostess had been in Peking once to gather atmosphere for one of her stories, so had lots of Chinese furniture. I was surprised to find there Celestine Mott, Helen Mencken the actress… Of the twenty present, most of the women were in evening clothes and only two of the men.

Most important of the guests (for our purposes!) were Mr. and Mrs. Roy Howard, owner of the Scripps-Howard newspapers. He was a dapper man…sort of hard-boiled but friendly and keen, and I couldn't get a good look at her because of the diamonds and lorgnette. He used to be in China reporting, years ago, is sympathetic with the situation there now. I think he had his fingers crossed on Walter for he looked bored when Walter started talking, but after a few minutes he slipped down onto the floor from his uncomfortable chair, reached for a pillow, took out a note tablet and pencil and made notes all the time the speaking was going on. Then started the heckling: everyone there knew all the arguments on the other side of the fence and wanted to hear Walter knock them down. One lawyer was trying to figure out how you could legally get an embargo passed with the Neutrality Law as it is; Helen Mencken was trying to insist that the silk hose boycott was too unimportant to bother with; someone wanted to know what would happen if Japan took the Philippines; and after a while Mr. Howard asked if he could make some comments.

He claimed that the psychology of China and Japan was too confusing, the situation too involved, the background too complex for the "average man" to be able to know anything about what was going on or to be able to form an intelligent opinion as to what U.S. should do now; he wanted to know how it could be "spelled out in words of one syllable" for their benefit, claiming that there were few people who could get much out of Walter's speech – "present company excepted, of course!" He thought we'd never get anywhere going round to one group after another with this message; he thought we should go to "the fountain head, drop the coloring in the water there and let it color the whole thing as it flows down and out over the country in tiny streams and rivulets." Someone suggested that they didn't think Walter would object to going to the "fountain head" if he could get there, and then Howard said he was sorry he didn't own the most influential paper in the country, the *New York Times*, but that he would be glad to do whatever he could in his papers. The party ended at one o'clock with everyone cordial and friendly and Mr. Howard saying to let him know if he could do anything to help. It was 2:30 by the time we got home with the last bus gone and trains running infrequently and the coldest night of the year, and me with evening dress and wrap on and no hat. I still get cold thinking about it.

(Intermission in the story: Saturday morning Walter decided we should get family pictures taken. I called up half a dozen people, finally got one to come to the house and take pictures. The proofs haven't come yet, but in time you may have the privilege of seeing how I look after a late night, and how the girls look when they are still, which is seldom.)

This is a better picture than Miriam feared!

Saturday, supper time: Mr. Jack Foster phoned, a stranger to us. Said he was with the *New York World-Telegram*, Scripps-Howard paper; said he was going to do a series of articles on China, and wanted to interview Walter. Walter was sorry, he was leaving for Florida the next day, couldn't change his schedule. Good bye! Fifteen minutes later Mr. Foster again: If Walter was leaving the next day, why couldn't he interview him tonight. After some discussion, Walter invited him out. Fifteen minutes later Mr. Howard phoned. Hoped Mr. Foster had been in touch with us. Said he was one of the top men in the chain, was beyond writing such articles and doing such interviewing, but because he had been in China, was definitely sympathetic with China, knew his stuff.

Walter has been working on an article for the *Saturday Evening Post,* with no assurance that they'd publish it, though one of their editors had written asking Walter to submit one. Walter didn't want to spoil his chances for that by getting the stuff out across the country first in the Howard papers. But Mr. Howard told us frankly he thought these articles would be a build up for a possible *Saturday Evening Post* article, and not an obstacle to getting it published; and furthermore, he said when this series had been published containing all the latest facts released by the State Department, and gathered by the Foreign Policy Association, the Institute of Pacific Affairs, and other such scholarly bodies, and all woven into anecdotes and incidents and quotations from Walter, he himself would be able to comment editorially and thus set the editorial policy of all his papers across the country, in favor of the embargo, which he is glad to do but can't do out of a clear sky without some news stories to be commenting on. He further said on the phone that he wasn't used to handing out compliments or soft-soap to people (and I can well believe that) but that he had never heard anything before like what Walter had given the night before, and he was all sold on it, and wanted to see that this series got into print as soon as possible after January 26, the day our treaties with Japan expire, and the time when the Senate Foreign Relations Committee takes up the discussion as to whether to make new treaties or put on an embargo. So wipe out all my comments on the cold and late hours of the night before, and hooray for Mr. Howard!

At nine-thirty Saturday night Mr. and Mrs. Foster arrived, and both were exceedingly nice people.

Mr. Howard had been so enthusiastic about the things Walter had said the day before that he had taken a full hour that morning to repeat many of them to Mr. Foster, from his notes, and help him plan the series. He wanted to know everything Walter knew, and that gave Walter free reign to talk. Was he in his element! I learned many things about what had gone on in Fenchow after I left that I'd never heard before. Both the Fosters made penetrating comments, asked pertinent questions. About twelve o 'clock I thought it was time to reinforce our guests if Walter was going to talk all night, so I went into the kitchen and made coffee and ham and cheese sandwiches. At one o'clock they left, taking lots of printed material, some pictures of Walter, pages of notes.

We really liked them for they seemed genuine, friendly, definitely interested in promoting public opinion toward the embargo. Today I got a note from her asking me to lunch on Wednesday and to go in the afternoon to a matinee – *Life With Father*. So I'll go with pleasure. Meantime, they hope to get this series of articles into print within a week, so watch your Scripps-Howard papers. If they're as good for our cause as we hope they will be, and have every reason to expect, they can do untold good. Meanwhile the *Saturday Evening Post* article will get written between speeches; and tomorrow should come the *Readers Digest* with Walter's Town Hall speech in it so we may gradually be getting before a larger public.

Father and Mother have both been in the hospital in Florida. They are better now and are at home again but aren't feeling too cheery. I would like to go down to visit them, if I can get most of the important arrangements for March dates made in these next few days, and if I can make the necessary plans to leave the children here.[117]

Montclair, New Jersey   *Friday night, March 22, 1940*

Dearest –

In your yesterday's letter you said, "the next few years at least of my life are to be spent in my home." If you should feel that it is likely that after the "next few years" the circumstances may be such as will again take you away for long periods of time, then I think it's infinitely preferable that the next few years of your life *not* be spent with your family. The children are not now used to you or your discipline or restraining influence or points of view, etc. They are too young now to miss you seriously, to feel any loss because of dependence on you, etc. But if you'd been with us for some years, being a part of their family and dependence and discipline and reliance, and adding the masculine element, and then were gone indefinitely, I think it would be extremely difficult, perhaps disastrous, tearing at their roots and foundations, not to mention making infinitely harder my task of taking on their management alone then, than the difficulties I would have of continuing alone to manage them from this present point. These last 2½ years of our being apart have inevitably seen us building defenses and developing techniques for living separately – we have got *used* to living apart (whether we like it or not) and it would be far less demanding on all to continue, than to have an interlude and then to have to readjust again – when we are older and changes come harder.

---

117   Miriam did go.

Which makes me wonder if you had not better consider seriously going back to China now alone, to do whatever seems best. I won't find it easy, and I won't like it, and I'll probably fuss about it on occasion forever after – but the same can be said from one point of view or another, for any decision you might make. There is no ideal solution. Why not make the decision again then on the basis of where there is the greatest need that *you* are able to meet?

Montclair, New Jersey   *Monday night, March 25, 1940*

My own Sweetheart –

Your Easter letter today made me cry. Love is overpowering sometimes, isn't it. You are right – it is too beautiful to be sacrificed to a desire to avoid the difficulties of life. I knew that even when I was writing you. But I am so completely dominated by Fear – I think you would be amazed if you really knew all the fears that rule me. That's why I love and admire your strength so deeply – and some times even fear that. But I am struggling with them. And your love and confidence and belief in me help beyond words. I want and need them desperately and yet am afraid to trust myself to them too completely for fear someday they will be gone. Be patient with me – and know that you are the only one that can ever meet my needs, and that I am *always* wanting you, even thru my fears.

262 Claremont Avenue, Montclair, New Jersey   *Monday night, April 22, 1940*

My Loved Husband –

Still haven't completely conquered the question of order and "place-for-everything" in this house[118] with the result my pens are missing tonight. Can you forgive pencil? I worked till after midnight on Sunday school stuff… We're getting a new Frigidaire – on the "rental basis" – $3.10 a month, about 75 cents to run – and it will cost no more than our monthly ice bill, which in hottest months went to $5. It is infinitely more convenient, furnishes ice cream as often as desired for the kids who love it – whenever we stop paying they'll take it back. Price is $100 + $17.50 carrying charge.

Montclair, New Jersey   *Wednesday, May 1, 1940*

Dear Folks –

His Royal Highness is due this evening, after ten weeks absence, and we have a full five days planned till he leaves for his six weeks trip to the coast. As for our new house, we like it immensely. I shouldn't use the word *new*, as it is anything but that, but the wallpaper is fairly good, the floors hardwood, the cracks and peeled paint not too conspicuous, and the whole thing in keeping with three lively and careless young ladies.

Montclair, New Jersey   *Sunday, June 16, 1940*

My Lover –

Come back to me! These last three weeks have been indescribably beautiful… So many things

---

118   On April 1, 1940, Miriam moved her family to a rental house half a block away from her parents' home. The Barbers didn't discover this until they returned from Florida on April 12.

you've done these last days to please me. Your last morning when you needed to store up extra sleep you got up and came down to eat breakfast with us. You've watched children, come promptly to meals, done errands – little things, but they make up a Great Big, in telling me your love. Thank you, Sweetheart.

Montclair, New Jersey   *Tuesday, October 7, 1940*

Dearest –

Worked about three hours in office last night – but before that Mary Lou asked me to lie on her bed and she'd rub my head. It was a stall to have to go to sleep – but still in the dark & quiet she often gets reminiscent and I learn things. She was telling of school and incidentally happened to remember that when she walked to school yesterday afternoon some boys in her class were hiding in the bushes on Valley Road where she turns onto the school property – and they jumped out and caught her and held her and first Wallie kissed her (on the cheek, I discovered!) and then Kenneth and Robert. (No racial discrimination – Negro, Italian, U.S.!) They made her walk to school with them and said she was their Girl Friend – "but I'm not!" She seemed to think nothing of it, went right on to talk of something else. I attached no significance to it, just said they must have been trying to tease her.

Montclair, New Jersey   *Sunday, December 8, 1940*

Dear Mother and Dad–[119]

Walter got home Thursday night, and lots of things have been decided since then. He goes off tonight for eight days – which ends his speaking. He says there's no doubt about our coughs being whooping cough. They're not severe, as the disease goes. But the quarantine rules mean Mary Lou cannot go back to school before Christmas.

The decision to go to Minneapolis is made and we are negotiating about a house. Walter saw two in good locations either of which will suit us fine if we can't get something at a bit lower rental.

---

119   The Barbers were wintering in Florida again.

7

Minneapolis Years and the First Campaign

1941 – 1942

The Judd family moved to Minneapolis for Walter's new position, after stops in Buffalo, Chicago, and Rising City. His office was adjacent to the right-field stands of the Minneapolis Millers baseball team at Lake Street and Nicollet Avenue, and we loved watching the games from his back office windows. Walter worked long hours seeing patients and making hospital visits, combined with a still-rigorous speaking schedule. Sometimes he would give two speeches over the lunch hour, racing between locations.

Miriam devoted herself to family life, with occasional speechmaking on the side, and was free to pursue some of her own interests, or at least as much as she was able, given her full-time parenting duties of three girls, with another child on the way by the fall of 1941.

I don't have many memories of this era of our lives. I do recall that after the December 7, 1941 Japanese attack on Pearl Harbor, we were swamped with calls from newspapers for comment, as well as even more requests for speeches. The fear level rose four days later when Germany declared war on the United States. We were all worried, especially Walter, as he had desperately warned of these potential realities. He continued to speak at churches and meetings, launched a Chinese relief organization, while balancing the demands of his clinical practice and family obligations.

In January, we children found out, joyfully, that Miriam was expecting a baby, but twin girls were born more than two months prematurely on February 1, 1942. Both babies died the next day in spite of heroic efforts to save them. When Walter came home to tell us, it was one of the few times I ever saw him cry. Miriam's recovery was complicated and prolonged by phlebitis requiring a nurse and extra household help. She was brave and sad during weeks of inactivity. A two-week respite with the Barbers in Florida lifted her spirits, and she returned to oversee music lessons, Brownies and Girl Scouts, neighborhood spats – while also taking sewing lessons, speaking occasionally, entertaining out-of-town guests and accompanying Walter to some events.

Several groups began pressuring Walter to run for Congress. Miriam was not excited by the prospect, and even Walter had misgivings about giving up his clinical practice, which he loved. But he was eventually persuaded and Miriam acquiesced. He made it clear, however, that he would run to represent the interests of the country as a whole, not just Minneapolis. An organizing committee was formed and an intense campaign began.

Miriam again turned to her private writings after Walter filed for the position in that fateful election. Reading her pieces, I can only begin to imagine the apprehension she felt as her already over-scheduled Walter faced a life in Congress. How much of his time, attention, and love would she have? When Walter won the September primary and then the November election with 64 percent of the vote, her reservations returned after the exhaustion of the campaign wore off, which she expressed in a private writing concerning how to make their life in Washington, D.C. satisfactory. Though she could not know it, she was about to embark on a fulfilling period in her life.

Editor's Note: Many of the following letters do not have salutations as the originals no longer exist. Miriam destroyed some of these original letters after she used them to compile a selection of letters about her daughters' growing up years. On Miriam's eightieth birthday, she gave these compiled notebooks to Mary Lou, Carolyn, and Eleanor.

205 West Rustic Lodge, Minneapolis, Minnesota   *Wednesday, January 8, 1941*

We arrived as scheduled. Walter left Rising City the afternoon of the 31st, because the weather and driving looked bad. We ladies left Columbus, Nebraska at 6 p.m. on the 1st after a noon birthday party complete with a cake we baked with a tiny one for the dollies. Having supper on the diner was another treat for the birthday. They had delicious dinners for 35 cents apiece. Sleeping was impeded by the shunting and backing and stopping and delaying of the train. The two older, who behaved most creditably in the upper berth, finally got to sleep when the train left Missouri Valley about 11:30. Not long after that, Eleanor had to wake up and spend the rest of the night till 5 a.m. peering out of the curtains, tickling Mummie's toes and climbing on her to play horsie, singing "Silent Night" in a Kate Smith contralto to create anything but a silent night for the passengers. We eventually got to Minneapolis a little after 9 a.m. and were glad to be met by Walter and the car.

Minneapolis, Minnesota   *Sunday, January 26, 1941*

We're beginning to feel as if we'd always lived here, and I suspect it's largely because Walter has plunged into his work headfirst. His two weeks at the Mayo Clinic he greatly enjoyed, watching operations, studying, having conferences, attending lectures and staff meetings, working on x-ray. Last Monday morning he went to work. The schedule so far has been to leave between 8:30 & 9, back for a 12:30 lunch most days. Then he's gone till 9:30 or later. Another night he was called out at 3:30 for a baby. Today – Sunday – he left before we finished dinner at noon, got back after the children were in bed, went out on calls and is still gone as I write this at 11. Mary Lou found school a bit difficult. I am working with her on reading.

Last Sunday we had a full but happy day. Got home from church about 12:45 and I scurried around getting things finished for dinner as Dr. Johnson was coming.[120] Mary Lou and I cleaned up the mess from the meal. By that time phone conversations had transpired and I found myself with a supper party on my hands and practically nothing left in the house of the essentials! So I tore around and made and iced a cake, made salad dressing and a salad, threw together enough for everyone. The "everyone" was: Cliff Domke, a Carleton boy who taught in Fenchow. He had taken movies of China and wanted us to see them. We had no projector so asked to borrow Dr. Johnson's, and then invited him, and he brought along the office receptionist; I asked Grace Keen because she had met Cliff in Hong Kong, and Laura Cross of Peking who also knew Cliff and Grace.[121] The pictures were excellent and we had a swell time talking them over. We let the girls see one reel – of the baby panda Cliff escorted home from China to be put in the St. Louis Zoo. It was Eleanor's first movie, and she tried to pick up the "teddy bear" and to pat his "soft furry" – and was put out at the results.

We finally succeeded in locating help – a California girl about eighteen. She's to come two to seven daily, and on alternate Sunday mornings, will iron, clean, watch the children when I'm out.

They have the half-year promotion here and a new term starts tomorrow. Carolyn is two days under the age for admittance. They gave her an achievement test and decided that she probably had intelligence enough to grasp Kindergarten, going from 1:15 to 3:15 p.m.

Minneapolis, Minnesota   *Wednesday, March 5, 1941*

We had a blizzard with a foot of snow, and since then below-zero temperatures. The streets are slippery and our car got hit twice within eight blocks as Walter was going down to the office after supper. They are working on new fenders and grill.

Walter is *working*. But he loves it. He's been getting in a few speeches on the side and a broadcast. Next week I get back into the speaking game, which I haven't done for six months, with three speeches in the next two weeks. I'd rather keep house but feel I ought to do a bit.

We went to a nice dinner party last Saturday, given by one of the ladies who is a most active member of the local committee on the boycott. There were fourteen people, from the head of exports for Pillsbury Flour to a man who covers ten states selling ladies millinery. An economics professor from the University here disagreed radically with Walter and we had some fireworks. He knows that education will take care of all the troubles in the world today, given time, so we should not be perturbed, nor pessimistic. He objected not only to Walter's arguments, but to his vocabulary and his analogies and his illustrations. But you know Walter and his "rather-be-right-than-president" —! In a fight like that I'd give in and be president. But it was a good evening.

Sunday night we had nearly twenty high school kids from our church here to sit around the fire and ask Walter how he came to choose medicine and missions and how he liked it and how it had worked out. It's part of their course at the church on vocations.

---

120   It was Dr. Johnson's medical practice that Walter was to handle while Dr. Johnson was mobilized with the National Guard.
121   Grace Keen, in whose Hong Kong home Miriam and the girls had stayed, had moved back and was living in Minneapolis.

Minneapolis, Minnesota   *Thursday, March 20, 1941*

The Blumers, who have transferred from Buffalo, came to see us last Sunday. [122] They don't know anything definite about this business of General Mills making "bullets instead of bread." The man I sat next to at dinner the other night said that because of General Mills branching out into cereals and other products in the last few years, they had a good set-up in engineering for making machines and setting up factory equipment, which is likely why they got those contracts from the Navy. But exactly what it is to make no one seems to know, or at least won't tell – not even Fred Blumers who is working on it.

The girls are certainly full of life these days and so interesting and fun. Carolyn is growing noticeably. I wish you could see her sit down to the piano and pick out almost without error and with correctly harmonized cords in the bass, almost any tune that may be in her head – "Old Kentucky Home," "My Country Tis of Thee." Mary Lou is reading music well. Eleanor is in the cutting stage at the moment – cuts everything she can get her hands on including her own clothes, and is having a series of severe punishments. But the little monkey is overflowing with pure animal spirits and energy and joy. Her eyes sparkle, she laughs continuously, and is a most appealing youngster. We are all so happy here. Walter likes his work, the surroundings are congenial, the girls like school, and it seems like a treat to have Walter in the house every day, even when breakfast is the only meal he eats with us.

If you get a chance, read the lead article in last week's *Saturday Evening Post*, called *Alcoholics Anonymous*. We are hearing in detail from Jim who has joined the group in Los Angeles. It seems to have performed a miracle, for it has done what nothing on earth yet has been able to, for him. His personality is completely changed; from chagrin, shame, and disheartenment, he has become calm and quite open in talking of his struggle, has not touched a drop since he joined the group six months ago, writes home of his progress, and is working with all his strength in the group. No one dares say that it will work permanently, but we are all hoping and Mr. Judd is so happy.

P.S. You asked about the missionaries coming home from China. It is hard to say how we feel. But when their presence there has become a liability to the Chinese rather than an asset, then they help the Chinese by coming home. All our British friends were driven out of Shansi two years ago because their presence was detrimental to their Chinese Christian colleagues, and they have not been able to return. Last November American Brethren Missionary friends in Shansi left our Province because the Japanese took fifteen of their Chinese colleagues including one of their Chinese doctors and beheaded them. The missionaries left in twenty-four hours because their presence was harmful to the Christians as long as the Japanese regimen persists. Our own Chinese Congregational North China Council, two-thirds Chinese members, voted for most of our group to go home, and voted for a few to stay. I think we should listen to them. It may be more good could be done by staying; I know there is room for honest differences of opinion. But when the *Christian Century* suggests that those who come home do so because of political motives rather than spiritual considerations, or because they are soft and fearful, or because they are not caring how they desert their Chinese colleagues in this moment of great strain – that is just plain crazy.

---

122   The Blumers were friends of Miriam's brother Clarke, in Buffalo, New York.

Minneapolis, Minnesota   *Thursday, March 27, 1941*

Dear Folks –

I think we're in the messiest season for Minnesota, for spring is trying to come, and warmish days melt the snow and leave rivers of mud in streets and sidewalks. The children come in with soaked feet, for the big lakes and puddles are too tempting, and their winter coats begin to look shabby, particularly when covered with mud. But there are robins and pussy willows and spring clothes galore in the shop windows, so we keep hoping.

One evening we had seven "China" folks for a Chinese dinner. It was the first time I had attempted cooking "Chinese food" for anyone outside the family. It was a lot of work for the Chinese style of cooking requires detail work, adding a little this or that, browning, or searing, or warming two minutes before adding, etc. – which is what makes it so good, I suppose.

Our other event was going to the Weyerhaeuser's last Saturday night. They are a great lumber name here. They live in a huge old house in St. Paul, sent their car and chauffeur for us. It was fun to see a place with butlers and maids and high-ceilinged rooms, and art treasurers, not to mention the dowager herself. She wore a funny dull blue dress with a train, and on her vast expanse of bosom was planted a couple of boxes of pansies, all of which had wilted before the evening is over and if you know how a dead pansy hangs you have a good picture of the "The Collapse of Corsage." She had heard Walter speak recently. I guess sixty were there, most all in evening dress. Walter talked a good hour, answered questions almost as long, then we got fed while the ladies had the chance to do the gush act over Walter, about how wonderful he was, and how simply terrible it was that he had had to come without any dinner and how could he possibly hold up and talk so well on an empty stomach, and couldn't they get him a lamb chop. Of course, I hadn't had any dinner either, as I'd had to hurry the children thru their supper and baths and bed after we'd returned late from a children's party, and then I'd had to dress, so I was all for taking them up on the lamp chop; but we modestly refrained and stuck to the eggnog and a canapé – and virtue must have been rewarded for yesterday came a note with "unspeakable thanks" for the marvelous thing Walter had done, and "never can repay you but here is a little check to buy toys for the children." It was for $100. She threatens to invite us for dinner sometime soon to make up for Walter's missing out his meal that night.

I've done two speeches myself. At one I was invited to speak to a group of business and professional girls who met in the evenings. The "girls" turned out to be all between fifty and eighty. I'll be careful the way I interpret "girls" in the future!

We've been putting in quite a few spare moments house hunting. We'd like to get into a house we could call our own, with our own things, small enough to be able to run fairly easily but large enough to allow for a good guest room and also a maid's room, for we find we'd save money if we had a full-time maid, rather than this half-time person plus paying out nearly three dollars a week for someone to sit evenings with the children when we're out.

Minneapolis, Minnesota   *Thursday, April 17, 1941*

We have a house, but what an ordeal it has been. One morning I had eleven phone conversations with agents between 9:00 and 9:50. I neglected the girls, the house, we ate mostly out of a can for ten days, and nights I was dead and fell into bed. It's a stucco semi-bungalow type with two bedrooms and bath down, and three bedrooms and bath up, only two blocks from the lake.[123]

4626 Emerson South, Minneapolis, Minnesota   *Thursday, May 8, 1941*

Dear Folks –

I'd like to say that we're all settled in our new home, but this settling process seems unusually slow this time – or am I getting old? It's livable and roomy and well arranged, and has good features. Unfortunately, we find it isn't in as perfect shape as we'd like. We've had an endless procession of repair men. We're going to like it– liveable, roomy, and well arranged, has many good features.

Walter continues to practice medicine and talk on China. I'm not sure that he knows yet that we've moved!! We had another Saturday evening soiree at the Weyerhaeuser's when she had invited a number of Army people this time from Fort Snelling here. I wore real flowers – it was the same evening that I had spoken at the annual meeting of the Minneapolis branch of the State Federation of Women's Clubs at their noon luncheon and they had given me a corsage.

Minneapolis, Minnesota   *Tuesday, May 13, 1941*

We've been looking at secondhand cars. He got one for my Mother's Day present and nicer than most of the $200-300 ones we had been confining our attention to. It's a 1938 Plymouth deluxe, radio and heater, four-door, grey with red wheels and trim, only 2,000 miles. So we're all ready for you to come now!

I know you wouldn't be happy unless you thought I were anticipating your coming in terms of work for you both to do – ahem! – so I'm starting to save sox for you to darn, Mother, and am making a list for Dad. His major problem is to be the brains behind engineering a swing onto a high branch on one of our lovely tall trees.

I spoke last week in a town thirty miles away. Also went to a nice luncheon where the ten ladies were all interested in doing worthwhile things and all active in organizations for peace, etc. It did me good to be with this bunch. There are so many ladies who just play bridge, or putter, and don't know what's happening in the world.

Sylvan Lake Hotel, Custer, South Dakota   *Saturday, June 21, 1941*

Dear Folks –

Walter and I left Minneapolis about six p.m. yesterday. We took an airplane to Huron, South Dakota. It was fun to have this little jaunt together –our "summer vacation." I have never flown in the U.S.

---

123   The house was near Lake Harriet in Minneapolis.

before and the box supper served aloft was good. In Huron we saw a good movie while waiting for our Pullman train that brought us overnight to the beautiful Black Hills. Then a lovely drive thru the hills and along the Rushmore Memorial Park where we had enchanting views of the Gutzun Borglum carvings on the high mountain of the four great American leaders: Washington, Lincoln, Jefferson, Theodore Roosevelt. It's the Methodist University Girls' National Biennial Convention with 200 officers, leaders, and sponsors from fifteen State University Methodist Kappa Phi groups. Got here before ten a.m. when I was scheduled to lead the Hilltop Devotional hour. It was an outdoor worship for which I had arranged songs, poems, scripture, etc; and I talked on the need of students in these strenuous days for (1) seriousness in attitude and approach to life, (2) courage and daring in action, and (3) serenity in spirit. After this, Walter spoke at their regular morning worship. We start back right after supper, ride tonight and all tomorrow on a train back to Minneapolis. Riding a train is pure joy to Walter, and any way out of reach of that phone pleases me.

Miriam leading worship at Sylvan Lake in the Black Hills, SD

We had a good time with Grampa Judd and Jim when they drove up last week. Saturday they and I went to a double-header baseball game, sat in box seats, while Walter watched out his rear lab window overlooking the ball park, whenever he had no patients. Grampa bought us a jungle gym apparatus. The girls were beside themselves with joy, and it did Jim and Mr. Judd good to pick it out, and see the genuine joy and gratitude of our girls – and the neighborhood children.

Minneapolis, Minnesota   *Wednesday, July 9, 1941*

Dear Folks –

Today has been my "day off." I left at 9 a.m. to drive three new friends seventy miles over to Wisconsin to a summer cabin where another Minneapolis friend had invited us for the day. The drive was fun and the cabin, lake, quiet, and out-of-doors were all lovely. It was a congenial group in ideas, tho' ranging in age from younger than I to a "Grammie" – interested in international affairs and how to bring up children in this kind of world...

The other night Carolyn prayed spontaneously, "Help the hearts of the war people to stop thinking to fight."

Minneapolis, Minnesota   *Tuesday, September 23, 1941*

Dear Folks –

One night we went to the home of the Morris Robinsons, the minister. They had eight couples – all ministers and wives except us, and we had a hilarious time playing games. One crazy one was: line up two sides opposite (men and women alternating in line) and give each person a toothpick to be held in the mouth. Put a life saver on the toothpick of each Captain, to be passed from toothpick to toothpick down the line without using hands. See which line wins. We nearly went hysterical for the facial contortions are beyond description. After refreshments they got telling true stories of embarrassing moments in the pulpit – delightful.

Minneapolis, Minnesota   *Monday, October 6, 1941*

Mary Lou seems to have got through her first week in the advanced half of second grade. She likes the new room and teacher, and from her reports she's as good as any of 'em! Today the teacher asked her to bring chopsticks and Chinese dolls in costume and give a talk in class on China and she seems to have survived that ordeal.

Carolyn seems to be in the testing stage in school. They were having articulation test this week to see if any have speech difficulties. They were asked to repeat "take a bite" for fifteen seconds. Carolyn with great glee informed us that she said instead "chih fan ba" – which means in Chinese "eat your food" – and which we are always hollering at her when she pokes along at the table! Carolyn's sense of humor seemed to think it was a rare joke on them!

Went to my first sewing class last week and got shown how to work on fur. I find it neither so hard to cut or to sew as I had feared and came out with quite a passable collar.

Carolyn and Eleanor seem preoccupied with death, burial, etc., at the moment. It may be because we drive past the cemetery every time we go down Dupont Avenue – for church, music lessons, downtown, whatever. One day Walter and I drove them all through it and it is beautiful. Carolyn asks; "What happens to the 'wonder part' of you when you die?"

Minneapolis, Minnesota   *Friday, October 17, 1941*

Dear Folks –

Walter and I have been going in circles that have touched each other only occasionally. He had been trying to attend sessions of the International Post-Graduate Medical Association here all week, around his work at the office. I've had three speeches in a week: one to the College Women's Club, which had me worried because I thought they might be more critical than the church women I'm used to, but I find they know as little about China as anyone.

There have been several luncheons; one today with Mrs. Alvarez, up with her husband from Rochester. Another day at the swank Minneapolis Club with several other doctors' wives, some from out of town, all connected with the conference. Today both Walter and I managed to get free at the same time and go through the medical exhibition together and collect a few free samples, and attend a couple of lectures.

Monday night we went to our first P.T.A. meeting at school, a dinner for about 150 at which Walter spoke. A couple of the ladies had had to listen to me that same morning at the College Women's Club and it happened that we used a few of the same stories and illustrations, so I suppose they wondered which of us was giving whose speech! …

I went to the University to the special dinner put on by the Chinese students in celebration of their *Double Ten* – Tenth Day, Tenth Month – the day they became a Republic, like our Fourth of July. Over a hundred there, many friends we had known in China. There were good speeches and good movies of China. But I sat in a draft, and that's where I caught my cold.

Rising City, Nebraska   *Sunday, October 26, 1941*

Here we are at Rising City. It seems they had Teachers' Convention in Minneapolis and gave the children holiday the last two days. So we bundled everyone into the car. We had clear, bright October sky and sun and all were vibrating over the prospect of a trip together – and I think Walter most of all. He had spoken at Duluth the night before, came back on the night train, spoken at noon that day, cleared up cases and we finally got started about 3:30 Thursday; leaving behind phone calls and requests for speeches and patients. Walter was like a boy out of school. We drove until 10 that night, stopping at a tourist cabin for the first time in our lives and slept comfortably – two cabins, total $3.00. Off after breakfast and were in Rising City by 11 a.m. and found all fine here. One afternoon we went to Olive's brother's farm and the girls milked the cows, watched two-week-old pigs nurse, hunted for eggs, and all the rest.

In Rising City, Nebraska

Minneapolis, Minnesota   *Sunday, November 9, 1941*

This past week seemed terribly long – partly because Eleanor was sick. Now we're waiting for measles to break out for Carolyn has been exposed to them at school. Another thing is the discouraging task of looking for a new girl, for Bernadine told us she was going to leave. She can go into the new defense industries that are going up here and earn more money and live at home, so off she goes. I'm depressed over the whole thing.

Walter and I attended the Nebraska game. After he'd insisted that he could never leave his Saturday p.m. office hours, he phoned me before noon and we dashed over to the stadium where the game started at 1:30 and was over in time for him to be seeing patients again by four. It was a good game. No sun and thirty-degree temperature made it nice and brisk. Score: MN-9, NEB-0

I had one speech last week. Have two this week, as well as a Holyoke Club business meeting at which I must preside, being the President for Minnesota. Have done sixteen letters for Walter so am afraid my mind isn't very fresh for this one.

Minneapolis, Minnesota   *Wednesday, November 19, 1941*

Helen Smith arrived last Monday.[124] What experiences she had getting out of China – the story is unbelievable. The Japanese officials held up their passports seven weeks in Foochow, then took them by Japanese boat to Formosa, caused all to land, forced all passengers through *two* sets of disinfectant baths in *public* – Helen and ten other women including two Catholic nuns and a Congregational Missionary lady nearly seventy and extremely straight-laced, all made to bathe together after fifty men had used the same bath, then walk completely naked before these fifty men passengers to the second bath, etc., while their clothes and every belonging were fumigated for several hours – all this in roasting July weather!

The book Grace and I are trying to do is for children, say under ten, showing the courage of a Chinese boy under war conditions. No bombings or atrocities to be described, but a family trying to find food, shelter, clothing, work, a lost father in a strange city when they have had to move because of the war. Our plot keeps making it too complicated for the elementary needs of children in this country who know nothing of China. Then Grace's South China background and my North China are different enough so that we stick on simple things as how a man peddles water from door to door, or what a Chinese boy calls his mother. But we're having fun.

Minneapolis, Minnesota   *Monday, December 1, 1941*

Midst this entertaining the domestic problem did not go smoothly. Now I'm alone: sent out the laundry, had the best time digging out the unbelievably filthy kitchen. I shall get a cleaning woman once a week, go slow about maid-hunting again. I have no heart for it, and don't know where to turn.

One of the main reasons we want to get this help problem settled satisfactorily and permanently is because we're expecting to complete our quartette of girls in April. You see, we read an article in the paper that said four was the ideal family of children and we believe all that we read in the paper! The girls have kept clamoring for a baby, so we of course believe in granting their every request! At any rate, the baby is due sometime around the middle of April.

I felt sorta punk most of September but am feeling fine now. I thought I'd get my speaking over before I told you or anyone else. The only hitch was that this time I spread much earlier and had to dash down and get a girdle fitted and buy a good dress to speak in, and a hat to match. The dress I made in sewing class was also a maternity dress. It's perfectly obvious to anyone who knows me now, but I'm banking on the children's not being observant and being preoccupied with Christmas, to keep them in the dark till the first of the year if possible.

I am to take Mary Lou and Carolyn to the University to see the opera Hansel and Gretel, and the girls are excited. I've been over the music and they can play some of the themes.

---

124   Helen Smith was a close college friend who had taught in China. They were frequent correspondents.

Minneapolis, Minnesota   *Tuesday, December 9, 1941*

Just a note tonight to say we're well and going along normally in spite of the strenuous days since December 7.[125] Walter has been swamped by telephone calls from newspapers and friends, and requests to speak, for all want to hear his comments. If people had listened to him two to three years ago we might not be at war.

Saturday I took my life in my hands and took the three down to Dayton's to see Santa Claus, ride the merry-go-round, see the toys, have lunch. They adored it and didn't mind the jams and waits. Mary Lou is so helpful, held Eleanor tight and came close behind Carolyn and me.

Minneapolis, Minnesota   *Wednesday, December 17, 1941*

Walter is feeling the war situation keenly and doesn't sleep much nights. Sunday when he preached in our church he was splendid. A jammed church was thrilled at his message. Today he is apprehensive about a noon luncheon to launch the China Relief Campaign here to which have been invited the Governor, Mayor, all the Pillsburys and Daytons and "big names" in town. He doesn't know what sort of things to concentrate on to get their interest for China. He started last week a ten-week Sunday evening forum series for college students at Dick Raines's church.[126]

This is to be our *Merry Christmas* letter. Things are certainly dark everywhere in the world and we do not intend to forget or minimize others' suffering with our own merry Christmas. Yet to have children in the home with their natural joyousness and delight in Christmas, and with the challenge to try to help them see their responsibility for building their world better than we have built ours, is a release for our sore hearts and tense emotions. We try to help them sense the true meaning of Christmas, and in this sober spirit, send our love to you all.

Minneapolis, Minnesota   *Tuesday, December 30, 1941*

Our Christmas was a happy one, though not entirely as planned. Walter had a lady in labor forty-eight hours, finally had a forced delivery the day after Christmas. Then poor Grace had gone to pieces over the fall-of-Hong-Kong news.[127] She did come for dinner but was nervous, hadn't slept for days, etc. After the girls were in bed I fixed her a bed in the study, talked her out a bit so she could try to relax, gave her hot milk, a sedative, alcohol rub, and she did sleep and looked better when she went off to work. No one knows when casualty or prisoner lists will be published out of Hong Kong by the Japanese, so she has nothing to do but wait.

We had agreed on 7:30 a.m. for the "opening hour," and the girls were dressed and downstairs on the dot. Then we tore loose. What fun it was to watch. Eleanor wanted to take one gift and go off in a corner and play with it, never mind any others. Mary Lou was impatient, Carolyn was methodical, and all were thrilled. The girls were so excited – Xmas tree, parties, presents, church pageant. It is a joy to be with them.

---

125   The Japanese attack on Pearl Harbor was on December 7, 1941.

126   Hennepin Avenue Methodist Church was one of the largest churches in Minneapolis.

127   Kenneth, Grace Keen's husband, manned one of the big guns when Japan was attacking Hong Kong.

Sunday after Christmas we had the Holyoke alumnae tea here. We had about fifty altogether, including several men – papas or husbands. The last handful stayed on from six to seven to ask Walter questions about the war, so it was a long afternoon. Fortunately the girls were invited to a birthday party which kept them away till the festivities were over here.

Minneapolis, Minnesota   *Tuesday, January 13, 1942*

Dear Mother and Dad –

I got a girl, a twenty-six-year-old Norwegian from a farm home in the country, conscientious, hard-working. She should be able to take all responsibility in April when I'm away as she's a bit older. Her name is Helen.

Our "cold spell" is over. Fortunately, the fuel pipe of the furnace waited till yesterday to break. The house was at fifty all day. I sent Eleanor to a neighbor's, gave Helen the day off, took Carolyn and Mary Lou to a restaurant to lunch, let Carolyn play with a friend while I took Mary Lou to her swimming & rhythmics classes at the YW, and I had my hair done. Collected the girls by 6:30, got home to find the house still cold as they were having trouble getting the fuel pipe repaired. Started a fire in the fireplace and found someone had jimmied the draughts so what had given perfect service before now smoked us out. What a mess! So I stuffed them in bed, & Walter came home and fixed the fire drafts. By ten p.m. the furnace had us all hot again – so glad that day is finished.

I went to see my doctor, Paul Larson, who was in Walter's class of Fellows at the Clinic. He is friendly and fine and I feel confident with him. Paul was apprehensive over my abnormal increase in size. He sent me to an x-ray specialist, and today the report comes back – TWINS – developing normally, good position. It's a relief for all of us. The earlier x-ray on Walter's machine was either too soon for a diagnosis or the x-ray not powerful enough, or one twin hidden behind the other. When they believed there was only one baby, my size suggested some abnormality, and I have been worried. So my mind is greatly relieved – though I'm somewhat stunned at the idea of having *five* children!! Walter will have to register next month, but will be deferred with all the children he has![128]

Minneapolis, Minnesota   *Sunday, January 18, 1942*

Dear Mother and Dad –

We told the girls today – not about the twins, but that we were going to have a baby. May Lou wiggled and jiggled and danced and pranced, but Carolyn just threw back her head in a hearty laugh of joy and delight. Eleanor accepted it matter-of-factly and walked off to get her baby doll to show us how our baby would be. There were surprisingly few scientific questions, mostly what to name it, and how to get rubber pants for it because of the rubber shortage (we're trying to make them conserve their rubbers and boots). All scientific inquiry originated with Carolyn, like where exactly was the opening for it to come out (we told her) and was that why my tummy was so big and I kept asking *her* to pick up so many things these last weeks (what an observing tyke). Mary Lou said she hadn't noticed. Ye heavens – I'm an elephant! …

---

128   There was a draft in effect in the U.S. at the time.

We changed the girls' rooms around. Mary Lou's room has been immaculate ever since – unbelievable! Carolyn's teacher told me Carolyn was changed since vacation, *much* more approachable, less "defiant" or "stand-offish," freer, joyous: asked if any home situation had made the change. I told about changing rooms & she felt that helped. Carolyn doesn't have to defy dictator Mary Lou any more, is now the responsible and loving *big* sister helping little sister.

Minneapolis, Minnesota   *Sunday, February 1, 1942*

THANKS FOR YOUR MESSAGE TWINS LIVED ONLY NINE HOURS WALTER WILL DRIVE RISING CITY FOR BURIAL TUESDAY AFTERNOON MIRIAM DOING FINE AS ALWAYS MIRIAM AND WALTER[129]

Minneapolis, Minnesota   *Thursday, February 5, 1942*

Mother & Dad –

You dears – I am semi-sitting up today so will try to write. I am feeling fine and everything is going splendidly. I may get home on Sunday as I can rest more at home with no baby responsibilities to take my strength – but may have to wait till Tues.

Your letters have been a help & comfort and everyone has been so good to us. My room is a bower of flowers and I have had many notes and phone calls. The girls call once or twice every day and that has been nice, to be able to keep in touch with them or answer their questions. Wasn't it thoughtful of Walter to have a phone put by my bed! Eleanor has been staying at Peg Blumers a week now. Their Freddie is six months younger than Eleanor but all boy, and they had become fast friends. Eleanor has no playmates her size near home and is lonesome with Mary Lou and Carolyn gone all day at school. Eleanor is beginning to get homesick now for the novelty has worn off. She talked to me on the phone today and said "Mummie, I've never seen you for a long, long time. What day are you going to be better?" Wasn't that sweet? Helen seems to be doing well at home from all reports and it's easier to have just the two to manage out of school hours. Friends have taken them on Sunday & Thursday afternoons when Helen is off, and have taken Mary Lou to her swimming.

Now about the babies – I have had since the early months a hydramnios complication which means too much water in the uterus. No one knows how these things come, tho' they are more frequent with twins. It was what was making me so terribly big – *not* the twins. Carrying around this excess water gave rise to stretching of muscles and back and front aches, and cramped my stomach till there wasn't room to eat or digest normally. At last discomfort was so great they decided to put me in hospital for a few days rest, sedatives, relaxation, etc. Walter bro't me over about 10 p.m. Saturday evening, January 24. I got good care, made up lost sleep, pain relaxed and was set to go home on Wednesday and take life easy for a month. They knew my size would not allow me to go to full term, but a few weeks extra would protect the babies. (At twenty-eight weeks, 2% of babies born live; at thirty weeks, 50% live. Ours were twenty-nine weeks! Identical twins!)

---

129   This was a telegram sent to the Barbers.

But Tuesday night started up pains, which continued on & off two days. They didn't know if this was false labor and to quiet it with morphine, or if it was to be true labor giving morphine would ruin the chances of the babies living. They called John McKelvey in consultation – our good Canadian friend, once at P.U.M.C. now head of OB at the University here and smart as they come. They agreed to try all sorts of things to delay labor as long as possible, and none of them was much fun and I was not comfortable while I had a stomach tube down my nose several days, and intravenous liquids, and no food. But the pains were stopped and it looked as if all were going O.K. when suddenly, without warning, about 4:45 p.m., Saturday, January 31, when the doctor and head nurse were standing in my room making regular rounds, the membranes burst and that huge gush of pent-up waters escaped. Nothing could have been more providential than having Dr. Larson right there.

Walter was called and there within ten minutes. I was put at once in the delivery room, the babies were born with little pain or effort, one in twenty minutes, one a half hour later. First weighed 3 lbs. 1 oz., second 2 lbs. 8 oz. They had a baby specialist on hand who worked steadily for hours with them in the incubators, and later called another specialist from the University. I went to sleep after talking to you and Grampa Judd, but Walter stayed right with the specialists, special nurses, and twins until they were gone, within twenty minutes of each other, about 3:30 a.m. Then Walter went home to bed.

How he got thru Sunday I don't know, for it was a terrible day for him. First in the morning was telling Mary Lou and Carolyn who had heard the night before that twin sisters were here. Mary Lou rushed to her room alone and sobbed and sobbed and this upset Walter worse than anything. Carolyn sat and thought about things and asked questions. Then Walter came over here by 7:15 a.m. to tell me, and we had to make plans what to do. We had a mortician whom Walter had as a patient take the babies, and I phoned Mary Lou to select two tiny dresses from our supplies and they were taken to the mortuary en route to Sunday school. We phoned Mr. Judd & wired you our first plan. But he got thinking and phoned Walter that *he*, Mr. Judd, would be glad to do everything he could at that end – that Walter had done all he could now for the tiny twins and that he ought to stay and care for me and the girls. This was his usual thoughtful way – we didn't want to ask him to manage things down there, but he offered – and Walter was *awfully* far behind with patients for he had spent so much time with me the preceding week, and had slept at the hospital three nights so I could call him in a moment. So Walter didn't drive down.

At 4 p.m. Sun. Walter went & got Eleanor and tried to explain to her what had happened. She listened wide-eyed, thought about it a while, then seemed to take it in. Then he picked up Carolyn and Mary Lou at home and drove to the mortuary chapel just before 5 and took the girls in. They had the tiny twins at each end of a white, satin-lined casket and they looked like rosebuds, so natural and perfect and so beautiful and pink. Mary Lou couldn't do anything but cry softly but the other two touched the tiny cheeks and looked at the little hands and asked questions. Then Dr. Beach[130] took Eleanor on his knee & the other two sat on a settee with Walter and Walter said he had the most beautiful service – short, and planned for the girls mainly – talking about tiny flowers that hadn't

---

130   Dr. David Nelson Beach was the family's minister at Plymouth Congregational Church in Minneapolis.

had time to unfold in their world but would go on and develop and grow in another world. When it was over they phoned me and Eleanor said – "Mummie, never mind about those little dead babies, I'm going to send you my twin dollies that Grace gave me for my birthday" – her most prized possessions. How things like that warm your heart – and how grateful I am to have those three wonderful girls to go back to.

The mortician brought the casket over to the hospital for me to see before he put it on the train that night – and it was beautiful – such a perfect, lovely picture to remember always. Grampa Judd got us a lot in the Surprise, Nebraska cemetery not far from their own and the lot of the Greenslit grandparents. We are such roamers on the face of the earth that is does us good to think of belonging somewhere. The Barber family has nowhere such a sense of *place attachment*, does it? There is something strengthening in it.

Walter had to speak Sunday evening, do an emergency appendectomy at 2 a.m. on a six-year-old child, speak twice Monday, try to catch up on calls and cases. He is terribly fatigued, but thru it all so tender and thoughtful that it hurts. How did I ever get such a husband. He is wonderful.

Your thoughts and prayers and loves and notes have helped so much. After all, *family* is the only thing that really counts in a war-torn world like this… Deepest love to you both –

P.S. Grace bought me a tiny radio in the hospital. She and the two office girls of Walter's all went to the hospital to have their blood tested as possible donors, were waiting to help out if needed – but fortunately I didn't need to borrow any. Walter was disgusted that his didn't match. Our good Peking doctor friend John McKelvey offered to do *anything* to help, including giving blood, and said in his dry way he thought it would improve the Judd stock to have a little Scotch blood in them!! Also, to shock your good prohibitionist hearts, he and Dr. Larson both ordered champagne for me when I couldn't keep anything else down – except the stomach tube thru my nose! So poor Walter had to spend his hard-earned money on expensive champagne. What a nuisance I am.

Minneapolis, Minnesota   *Thursday, February 12, 1942*

Dearest Mother & Dad –

I came home Sunday – which was a bit early. I had promised to stay in bed a week at home – and how convenient this first floor bedroom & bath have proved… I didn't do too well the first days – ran a fever, and scared my doctors with the possibility of a phlebitis developing – So I've behaved strictly according to instructions. It was *so good* of you, Mother, to write to all our family for me. I didn't feel up to it. I did up all the checks for the monthly bills one evening – about twenty – but haven't yet attacked a pile of nearly fifty of *his* business letters. Walter gave up a speech last night (his evening off) and stayed home with me.

Minneapolis, Minnesota   *Sunday, March 1, 1942*

Mother & Dad –

This phlebitis I don't understand. A week ago I still had a back ache & pain, so they decided to keep me flat longer, especially as Walter was to be in San Francisco and didn't want me trying tricks while he was away. He got back Friday and that day I sat up in bed the first time in two weeks. Today he carried me to the table for Sunday dinner and possibly in a day or so I'll have "bathroom privileges" restored. Miss Petersen, the practical nurse, is here 8 a.m. to 8 p.m., is fifty-ish and helpful with everything. She's sewed & mended & darned, washed the girls' hair, bathed & bedded them, cleaned, cooked on Helen's off days, taken girls to Sunday school – all this on top of my daily bed bath, two twenty-minute back rubs daily, hair brushing on my scalp dirty from seven weeks without a shampoo, etc. I am spoiled, lying still & letting everyone wait on me. I have baby things to return to stores – like the bathinette – but they can wait.

Minneapolis, Minnesota   *Tuesday, March 10, 1942*

This getting back into the former schedule is a slow process. The nurse left a week ago. I went to all meals last week but stayed in bed the rest of the time, till Friday when I dressed.

The Shrine Circus was here last week. The local Shriners sent us complimentary reserved seats for the closing performance. It was too good to miss. Walter was free after a grinding week and he loves a circus. I was rarin' to get out. So we went. The seats were on the ground floor, no steps to climb (I'm not doing stairs for another week) in front with all the celebrities so we were conspicuous. Eleanor adored everything, had never seen elephants before. The questions she asked, and her loud comments were amusing to everyone. Mary Lou didn't miss a thing, told Carolyn every detail the next day.[131] I greatly enjoyed being out after six weeks even though I was a bit shaky on my legs.

Sent out fifty letters last week, all written in bed on typewriter. Made a wash dress with bolero and panties for Eleanor and am at last developing some confidence and a little know-how, if not skill, in my sewing. Am now working again on the three sister "party dresses" for spring, which are coming along nicely. I'm still not to drive the car for a week. I have been helping Mary Lou drill on her arithmetic and working for accuracy. Small hints show she thinks frequently of the little twins. I think this has been a hard thing for her; I am trying to give her a little extra love and attention. Yesterday she went downtown alone on the street car to her swimming lesson at the YW and felt very grown up.

Minneapolis, Minnesota   *Thursday, June 11, 1942*

After weeks when we thought this Congress issue had died down, suddenly several groups approached Walter again, each unknown to the other, saying they hoped he would do it if given a chance. He had to give an answer and believe me it was not easy, as it may turn out to be the end of his work in clinical medicine, which he would hate to give up. As he says, why would anyone give up a satisfactory profession and a fairly respected position in a community, to go into Government

---

131   Carolyn had a cold and couldn't attend.

at a time when to be a Congressman is more of a joke than an honor, when it's fallen about as low as at any time in the country's history. Well, there are lots of folks who want that situation changed, and he has crystallized their ideas and expressed their thoughts, and they are demanding that he go and do the kind of thing he has been talking about. Then there is the business of the post-war settlement that will be coming up that will need clear thinking and courageous action. He'd like to be able to help then. So he finally told them he would consider it if they would come to him with a proposition. There are a lot of folk who will feel he has not been in the state long enough to be aware of all Minnesota's interests which he would be supposed to foster in Washington. And he will not run unless it is clearly understood that it is not Minnesota's interests which he is primarily concerned with, but the country's. When he gets thinking what a sap he is to consider going into that grief and pettiness and disillusion and hard work, he reminds himself that people are giving up their homes and families and professions today to go into places almost as dirty and difficult as Congress!!

Minneapolis, Minnesota   *Friday, June 19, 1942*

This business about Congress is like a merry-go-round that starts slowly and for a while you can keep track of individual faces on it, but soon it is whirling so fast that you can't make out who's who. We're beginning to whirl!

The various separate groups that have been working on Walter have kept pushing for action till it was obvious there had to be some sort of an organization to get them all together. Sunday night two men took the lead, the editor of the paper and the General Mills Vice President. They came around to ask all the important questions from the simple name & birth date of all the family to Walter's ancestry, what organizations he had belonged to, if he had ever been a member of the Communist party! They have a chairman (honorary) for the campaign, a paid executive, office space, are circulating petitions, are raising a campaign fund. Two men gave $1,000 each without hesitation – Russell Bennett and Walter James, the Chinese owner of Nanking Restaurant. They are calling on the influential people in this district to "sound them out," are attending the ward caucuses…getting ready to burst the bomb on the public.

Technically Walter had till the end of July to file for candidacy; the primaries are September 8. This is the largest district in the state, and many feel it will mean a great deal to get the incumbent from here turned out, if Walter can do it. He is Oscar Youngdahl and filed this week for a third term so they want Walter to file as soon as all is ready, likely early next week, and then it will be in the papers and public property.[132]

So we're in pretty deep now. We both feel *sad*, we *dread* giving up individual freedom in the sense that as long as we are "public servants" we can never quite be free agents again. We talked about definite things he had been saying in his regular speech, given hundreds of times. But after his public announcement as a candidate, those same statements will sound like, or be construed as, a bid for office. You know how Walter would hate not being able to say what he thinks, how he refused to be

---

132   Oscar Youngdahl also was a Republican.

tied to any organization all that time he was speaking in 1938-40. He will never be the kind to temper his convictions for politics, and we are prepared for stormy days ahead.

This step is not easy for us to take, and is against our personal inclinations. But we feel it is right, like some of the other hard things we've had to do. However, I'm sure many people will never understand this feeling, but will think of us as seeking personal glory, or money – though this step will be a financial loss to us definitely. But as long as *you two* know and understand how we feel this as a deep Christian mission to improve our country and its relations to the rest of the world – as much as the imperative that sent us out to China, then we feel strong…

Walter has said that if it is the sincere desire of enough people 'round here for him to go to Congress, they have got to get out and elect him, while he debates the issues. He will not go and campaign himself, or put his own money into it. He'll continue speaking as he has been right along and they can figure out exactly his philosophy of government from that, and they can like it or leave it. He doesn't know the political game so someone else can run the campaign for him.

We typed off a list of about sixty organizations and groups and churches before whom Walter has spoken in this district. They are going to get folks from that to go around and ring door bells in each block. He is unusually well-known for a non-politician, for he has addressed Jewish and Catholic groups, most of the churches, American Legions, and business groups; and then he has such a large group of poorer, Scandinavian patients who know him firsthand.

They all tell him if he can get Youngdahl defeated on this Republican Primary, he can have the election, as this has always been a Republican district. Also, if he files, the Democrats will not put up any strong opposition. One of the men just back from Washington said Stephen Early told him the President was anxious to have men returned to Congress this fall who would be concerned most of all to get on with the war, get it finished, and work for a real peace, regardless of party, and had given orders for Democrats not to put up opposition when a good man of such a kind was nominated by the Republicans.

I'll stop this Congress discussion now and get on with the important matters in the Domestic Department! Mary Lou went to camp last Monday for the week and seems to have been enjoying it. Taking advantage of Mary Lou's absence, I gave a luncheon for ladies we have long-owed dinners to; I had despaired of ever getting Walter free for any entertaining of husbands and wives, so took on seven ladies. Had a tuna fish roll made with rich biscuit dough and served with mushroom sauce and a ring mold of seasoned cottage cheese surrounded by chopped Harvard beets that looked very pretty. Everyone seemed to have a good time and I'm glad it's over; but I wish there weren't so many more we still owe. Eleanor has been sick and we are wondering if she is at last coming down with the measles, though it is a month since Carolyn got them. She is heartbroken at missing friend Freddy Blumers' big birthday party tomorrow – such an important event for a youngster!

– Private Writing –

Minneapolis, Minnesota   *Wednesday, July 1, 1942*
Darling –

Sometime in the years ahead you may look back on your life before you went into public office and say, "That is when I lost her. My taking up the torch for my country, which I felt was a sacred obligation lost me her love. It was one of the prices I had to pay for my devotion to the ideal, one of my sacrifices." Oh, no dear. It only accentuated my loneliness, which has been growing more and more complete in the last ten years. Now at last I have acknowledged to myself that my life with you will always be fundamentally lonely. There will be joys in it, and satisfactions and achievements, but the hidden spring that feeds & nourishes it will be a steady, quiet stream of aloneness.

You will say – Why didn't she tell me? But oh, My Darling, I have broken and bruised my pride and my poor love trying to speak to you. You tell me you want to listen but you do not listen to, you cannot understand my heart. You always say – "If my life could have been different so that I could have been with her more, if circumstances had not necessitated the long periods of absence" – not understanding what I have tried again and again to make clear, that my deepest loneliness is when I am <u>with</u> you, that when we are apart my heart feels closer to you.

There is no blame in this. I shall not hate you. There is simply acknowledgment of what I had hoped for ten years might be temporary, might right itself. Always I shall respect and admire and honor and work for you, trying in some measure to make my life worthwhile and useful thru you and your great gifts as my dear Dad has also done.[133] But always there must be a small wistfulness, a yearning for what might have been and cannot be.

– Your Wife

Minneapolis, Minnesota   *Sunday, July 19, 1942*

Dear Dad & Mother –

I find myself looking forward to your being here more than anything else, and I do want you to stay as long as you can and as long as we don't wear you out. The girls are through their YW activities July 30 and their music soon after so we're ready to spend long lovely days with you. Canned six quarts of raspberries this week.

Minneapolis, Minnesota   *Saturday, August 22, 1942*

I'm sitting in Walter's office while Mother is having a physiotherapy treatment for her arthritic hip. Life has been hectic. Elizabeth (visiting with daughter Betty Lou) got a bad attack of asthma, and I had her in bed on the first floor at our house (she couldn't climb stairs). She was depressed to be sick when she was away. I was out to lunch every day but one, which didn't help matters much.

---

133   Benjamin Barber, Miriam's Dad, was the personal secretary to John R. Mott, visionary and founder of the International YMCA, co-winner of the 1946 Nobel Peace Prize.

The girls themselves pulled what turned out to be a neat stunt. They decided they wanted to give a play, and they asked girls from across the street to be in it. So I was in for coaching and costuming and stage managing with seven small girls under twelve yrs. They learned their parts fast, and were always hounding me to have a rehearsal with them just when I was dashing off to a luncheon, or typing a manuscript for Walter. I managed to scrape up all the properties and improvise all the costumes, and as I dashed out Wednesday noon told them they could have the play at our house that evening after supper and could invite their mothers. When I got back in the late afternoon I discovered they had gone up and down the street and invited all the neighbors, most of whom had never been inside our house and many of whom I knew just to nod to. They seemed to have had an argument about whether to tell people admission would be two cents to help them raise money to buy their war stamps; or if they told them it was so much people would stay away! And Mary Lou informed me they had asked them to bring the money, but had softened the blow by adding that there would be refreshments! A blow for me!

By 7:30 our house was a riot! We were trying to get the dining room cleaned up and chairs set up for the performance; I was constantly called to the porch, which was the dressing room and where they needed pins and belts and hairs combed and fairy wands adjusted, and then rushed back to the living room where I was improvising sheets across the end by the fireplace and piano, for the stage, and making a false fire in the fireplace with red paper and lights. In came the neighbors and friends; actors weren't quite ready, Walter played some of our Chinese records at first; the play began; Eleanor refused to say her part because someone had forgotten to hand her the golden ball as she went on the stage; three of the actresses had to go to the toilet between scenes; the Frog Prince's big eyes, made of powder puffs and stuck on with adhesive, came off four times during the performance because, as I learned later, I had used some old stuff Walter had had for years with the stick-up all gone; someone tripped on the electric cord and put out the witches' fire – and all in all we had a most successful play. At the end they made Eleanor go around with a tin cup, and were terribly upset that some of the august gentlemen contributed a quarter and didn't want any change!

Then while I was serving ginger ale with blobs of homemade lime ice in it to almost thirty people, someone asked to see our movies of our town in China, and first thing I knew Walter was setting up the projector and the screen and giving a lecture with pictures; and then they went on a sightseeing tour of our Chinese things in the house, wanting to know what the Chinese scrolls said, and asking Walter why he started to run for Congress and he started telling them, by gum, and before they all left it was 10:30 and they were so pepped up that they have got up a big "Neighborhood Party" for next Thursday in a big backyard with hamburgers to be cooked, with a Swiss band to play in Tyrolean costumes, and with Walter H. Judd, there to "talk" to the neighbors. I was pretty limp after it was over, for I had to keep building up the hype between scenes, getting children started to bed in spite of the political meeting still going on in the parlor, and try to put away the discarded costumes and properties and sceneries.

I've been stalling off commenting on the Campaign, because when I get into that subject, I feel infinitely tired, and I don't know what to say. They tell me the official betting is three to two for Walter, but the few people whose judgment we respect think there is hardly a chance, for the opposition is getting so scared about losing the campaign, on the basis of merit and ideas, that they are now beginning smear tactics, and will stoop to anything to win. Whether this will ultimately lose them more votes than it will gain them remains to be seen. They have implied that Walter's education is unreliable, have said that he did not even vote himself in 1940 (we hadn't lived here long enough to vote yet, but did, in 1941), have called him "that Chinese missionary" as if that were something derogatory and not a badge of honor, and we understand have picked out some half-sentences from his testimony before the Senate in 1939, which they intend to use completely out of context to prove that Walter is a worse isolationist than the present incumbent. None of this bothers Walter, for he's clear on all scores, and besides loves an argument. But unfortunately many of our adherents and helpers get mad at the accusations, and don't know the best answers to them, and we're afraid there are going to be a number of petty brawls, when we've been trying to keep the whole thing on the level of *ideas.*

Walter will not be having evening office hours from now till September 8, the day of the primaries. He has two or three meetings every evening, mostly ward or precinct meetings, some small, some on a large scale in High Schools. He has three big broadcasts, one last week at 9 p.m. right between Lady Esther[134] and Campbell Soup, which they say is an excellent spot, and which some enthusiastic businessman paid for. It was a wow and though he was terribly depressed because he went a minute or more overtime and was cut off the air before the climax of the talk, it turned out to be a good thing, for everyone thought he was addressing a big studio meeting (which was true; there were 300 there) who were going on to hear more of his talk, but only part of it was to be broadcast; they called in till the radio station switchboard was swamped asking when his next broadcast was, or where they could hear him in person or why he was cut off.

He hates these broadcasts mightily; they are insisting now on manuscript submitted twenty-four hours ahead and rigidly adhered to, for the studio doesn't like to take the complaints for cutting him off! So after this he will have the manuscript to talk from (I hope) and avoid this extemporaneous stuff, and if he is so tired he can't even stand up, at least he can read the manuscript and not have to stutter around as he does when he talks freehand and is tired…

I went to my first true political meeting last Wednesday. It was a Republican rally in one of the Wards and a dozen or more candidates, mostly for local offices, were speaking. It was upstairs in a funny hall, on a sizzling night, with an odd cross-section of people there, including some negroes, mostly laborers, but a few higher-ups. Youngdahl and his wife were there, and she was friendly, came voluntarily and introduced herself to us, said she had heard Walter at the state P.T.A. Convention, told me to cheer up, I'd get to like these fights a lot – she did – said she thought we might as well be friendly enemies and took us over to meet her husband, who was not at all cordial. He says he has faithfully done the errands his constituents have asked of him! After the meeting I got brave and went to talk to anyone, giving out leaflets with Walter's qualifications, and trying to feel natural and pleasant when I was neither.

I've spent part of each day in the Campaign headquarters working on a couple of Walter's manuscripts for local church magazines, etc., and keeping my eyes and ears open to check whatever gross mistakes I could detect. We have been able to catch a few things.

Walter I scarcely see. He always has a luncheon date with a group or some individual who wants to

---

134   A cosmetics brand.

see him; comes home after I'm asleep and tears off in the morning without much time wasted. He's terrifically tired, and isn't planning any rest after September 8, which I think is a mistake. His big keynote "opening" address is on Tuesday in the Hotel Nicollet ballroom, and will be a discussion of the platform. He also has a big A.F. of L. meeting with 2,000 expected, this week. How can he go quietly along taking out tonsils and gall bladders? He's amazing!

Minneapolis, Minnesota   *Monday, August 31, 1942*

Dear Mother & Dad –

We miss you dreadfully. The girls talk of you all the time. Thanks for the birthday tho'ts. Am glad you are keeping in touch with Washington regarding the missing plane.[135]

Saturday evening Emma Noreen phoned – she was on her way thru to her home north of here. She was with us three hours and we heard plenty about conditions in Fenchow, and the vicissitudes of internment. The burden of her feeling was – as it is of *all* who have seen anything of the war firsthand – that America is *still* asleep, *still* doesn't know what's going on, *still* hasn't begun to suffer & to sacrifice – as she must. It wasn't a pleasant evening – to hear details of our Fenchow friends – but it was good to see her and to get renewed strength & stimulus to keep putting before Americans the facts we know, that affect us so deeply. My own speaking engagements start September 16 – your birthday, Dad – I have one a week average signed up for all fall. Things Emma said will help.

The campaign went "dirty" the day you left. That evening the opponent broadcast for half an hour in a tone of voice guaranteed to make anyone who didn't know Walter H. Judd *hate* him violently (so we were told: we didn't hear the broadcast). All sorts of innuendos and half truths and misquotations, and taking sentences out of context from the Senate Testimony of 1939 – "We can stop Japan, I believe, without firing a shot" – leaving off the rest which said "NOW, if we will use economic means. And if we don't, and quickly, then war with Japan is inevitable." We wanted to ignore the attack but our Committee wouldn't allow that. So at the Tuesday evening Nicollet Hotel rally where the place was jammed with about 1,500, Nygaard[136] gave ten minutes of answer, Walter spent five minutes quoting from his Senate Testimony to clear up one point and show what tactics had been used, mentioned it again on his Wednesday evening broadcast & challenged Oscar Youngdahl to public debate on *issues* (which he so far hasn't accepted) and gave it a final going over for fifteen minutes at a big Ward rally on Friday evening. It has been a "dirty" week and I wish I were far from here.

Our neighborhood party Thursday evening was a success. Mary Lou worked with bigger children, distributing 2,000 handbills at every house 40th to 52nd Street, and Lyndale to Lake Harriet. They earned five five-cent tickets to be spent for hamburgers or pop or ice cream for their services. They must have had 400 to 500 folks in those two back yards – sold nearly 700 hamburgers. Had tables & chairs, some sat on grass, had community singing led by Mr. MacPhail, who shook Mary Lou's hand and remembered her playing the piano concerto in May when he conducted the orchestra at MacPhail. Walter gave a talk on the Far East – not one word of politics.

---

135   Miriam's younger brother, Charles, was the radio engineer on an Air Transport Command DC3 plane, which had disappeared over Alaska on August 16, 1942. The plane, and Charles, were never found.

136   Harlan Nygaard was the Campaign Committee Chair.

Minneapolis, Minnesota   *Thursday, September 24, 1942*

Dear Folks –

I'm sure you'd like to hear the final score[137] and unfortunately I can't tell you what it was, but it was a lead of between nine and ten thousand. Walter was glad to hear from each of you, even though he'll never get around to writing you. As you've probably seen in *TIME, Newsweek*, newspaper editorials and the rest it seems to be considered quite an accomplishment for Minneapolis to have turned out its isolationist Congressmen, for few other states were able to do it.

We took a short vacation after the election. Left here with the children in mid-afternoon to drive to a resort sixty miles away on beautiful Clearwater Lake. As we drove along we could see the storm clouds brewing and we had been at our destination five minutes when the wind and the rain started and we had the chance to see at least the edge of the tornado. Trees came down around us and broke wires so we were without electricity, which meant water also, as it was electrically pumped, and phone for twenty-four hours. It did tremendous damage in lots of towns with 75% of the barns down, buildings and churches destroyed.

We had a two-bedroom cabin right on the edge of a lake, and with no lights we went to bed at 8:30 and 9 the two nights we were there. We went fishing in an outboard motor rowboat and Walter caught one sunfish, which we named Oscar and ate joyfully for breakfast on Sunday. It was a lovely spot and quiet, but we had to get back for an afternoon speech of Walter's. I suppose we should be thankful for small favors!!

We had freezing weather and a snowstorm today so I suddenly had to pull out of mothballs the winter coats and mittens, etc. What unseasonable weather for Mother to arrive in! She came this afternoon to stay a month. It was her suggestion and I accepted. She will take over the sewing, which will be a real lift, and will also be here when I have to go out with Walter.

Last week I started my speaking again. Haven't done any since last year and was apprehensive about my ability and my material, and more conscious of being Mrs. Walter H. Judd with the recent notoriety and publicity. I did spend time on reading and working out my outline, and after the first pretty awful effort seem to have got something that sounds O.K., for I've had ten new requests come in. I'm going to stick to my plan of one speech a week though.

Walter is busier than before, if possible. Tonight he ate supper with us because Mother had come but that was the first meal, except Sunday dinner he's eaten with us in two weeks. He had medical work piled up, operations, and special cases that he had postponed during the campaign. There were the regular speaking engagements he'd booked last spring. And millions of new requests from groups and persons who want him to understand their pet project or pet peeve so he can do something for them in Washington. Sometimes I let the phone ring – better than burnt food! Tonight he's sitting dictating to a gal he brought home after office, trying to get caught up on congratulatory letters from leading Republicans in the state and in Washington. He hopes to get some doctor friend of Johnson's to help out so maybe he'll become human again – I doubt it!

---

137   Result of the primary vote: Walter H. Judd—34,835; Oscar Youngdahl—25,699; Sheridan Stevens—2,144.

Minneapolis, Minnesota   *Sunday, November 1, 1942*

Dear Folks –

The end approacheth, and that pleaseth me plenty. Last week was hectic, with two radio broadcasts, political rallies, and speeches as many as three and four times a day. I went to two luncheons, two dinners, four evening meetings, had one speech on my own account and another on Walter's account. This latter was a joke. As Walter went on the air Monday they called me from the hospital that he was wanted for a baby. He broadcast fifteen minutes, then dashed to the YW where about 100 school principals and superintendents had had dinner and were waiting for him to speak. I got him on the phone there just before he went into the dinner, he dashed off to the hospital, I dressed and looked over my notes and herded children thru their supper in the fifteen minutes it took two lady principals to drive to get me and leave one of them to stay with the children, and before I could catch my breath I was speaking to the group at the YW, telling them I was no substitute for Walter in any capacity, but that I'd rather try delivering a speech than delivering a baby. He came in before I was finished, which completely unnerved me, so I quit and let him carry on.

Minneapolis, Minnesota   *Monday, November 9, 1942*

Dear Folks –

Well, the die is cast[138] and while I'm terribly proud, at the moment I'm too weary to be enthusiastic. The phone has been ringing solidly for days. I was out for three lunches and four dinners, which surely leaves the poor youngsters wondering if they have a mother or not (they have about got used to not having a father)… Walter and I each went to a pheasant dinner but they were different dinners and different people and different nights. I had to speak the night he was free and he had to speak the next night when I could go to dinner. We're getting used to this separate existence. I generally go by myself to the teas, dinners, or meetings where he is speaking, but he nearly always says hello to me if he sees me at them!

We're going to Washington Wednesday morning, and at least on the twenty-one-hour train trip there will be no phone calls! We will stay with the Joe Balls,[139] and Walter will get introduced around and tend to business matters, like choosing an office and the West Point appointments. It's up to me to interview the real estate people and make the rounds of houses. We won't decide till we see what we can find, whether I'll stay on here with the children or all move down at Christmas time. We've had helpful letters and suggestions from friends that may give us some leads. We expect to be gone a week for Walter has to return for speeches November 17. The girls will be all right with Helen and kind neighbors are near enough to help out if necessary.

Minneapolis, Minnesota   *Sunday, November 29, 1942*

Dear Folks –

We gave a dinner party last night – the second since we came to this city. I wangled this free date out

---

138   Walter received 60,883 votes, or 64 percent. Gilbert (Farmer Labor) received 18,566 votes for 19 percent, and Ryan (Democrat) received 15,976 or 17 percent of the vote.

139   Joseph Ball was a U.S. Senator from Minnesota.

of Walter when we were on the train to Washington. We had the six couples (one more couldn't come) who had done the most hard work during the campaign. Shipped Eleanor out, had Carolyn in bed with a cold, so Mary Lou did the honors passing the hors d'oeuvres and serving the coffee in front of the fire at the end. We got the silver cleaned and the best linen laundered once for this year. I 'spose I'll have to do this in Washington and I certainly hope I can find a good maid for I don't like to do all the planning, *and* the cooking all day long, *and* ride herd on the children and their engagements, and then come up trying to look bright and fresh in the evening. All went well this time…

Friday morning the girls and I drove into the country to visit the Children's Ward of the tuberculosis hospital. Mary Lou had been writing for eighteen months to a youngster there about her age who has practically no relatives and no visitors. Our girls had spent time making Christmas chains and decorations, as well as fixing a Christmas card for each child, and assembling toys and gifts for the stockings. We wanted to take them out before gas rationing. Our little protégé, Ludean, came back from the examining room, she was beaming from ear to ear, for the doctor said she could get up now on crutches – after four years on her back. She and Mary Lou were a bit shy but soon were telling what they ate for Thanksgiving and how they hated the sevens in multiplication, etc.

I know it did our girls good to have this firsthand contact with suffering and misfortune, among children, and to see how cheerfully they accepted their necessary disciplines. The kids hear a lot about the war suffering, but that is far away and unreal. Here is something right close to home for them to remember.

We're behind on our gas rationing as we were away on the days we should have registered. Tomorrow I'll have to go and stand in line half a day to turn in our blanks. We got our fuel ration, and were assigned 1,300, tho' last year we burned 1,750 gals. Don't have any idea on what basis they made the cut. We have to turn in this when we leave here and get another one in Washington, so it's all a gamble. Meantime we're burning up our fireplace wood to finish it off before we leave and help keep warm. It has been down to 10-20 above zero for several days.

Miriam and daughters looking at Chinese robes at the Minneapolis Institute of Art

Girls are having double-breasted, gold-buttoned flannel jackets to go with their plaid skirts, for travel. Mary Lou's is red, Carolyn's navy, Eleanor's dark green. Found some good blouses at a sale, so they are all set – and laundry will be simplified for travel. To bed now, as it's late. I'm glad we're moving *nearer* you. Your room will be ready anytime.

– Private Writing –

Minneapolis, Minnesota   Thursday, December 5, 1942

Dear Walter–[140]

I use this method as a hope of getting to you – tho' I do know you leave letters unread for days. I use it too because it can bring a quiet, considered idea without the distraction of an argument which personal encounters inevitably bring, and without your having the chance to discount it. – Poor girl, she's having another one of her low moods! – or what have I done <u>now</u> to hurt her? – and without the chance to conclude the discussion with your telling me how much you love me.

The other night when you thought I was "just tired" when I said you have a mania for speaking – that was just an attendant factor. Because I still think you have. And oddly enuf, two of your good friends have said that exact same thing to me. If you don't have a complex about the speeches, you at least have the reputation for having one, which has come from your actions. For I can't make it seem right that you should make yourself so completely unavailable to certain individuals and groups, thus making yourself available to others.

First of all it's a matter of taking on more things than even you can possibly do and then making everyone mad by not being able to do credit to your commitments. The fact that the boys on Bataan[141] can't take a vacation doesn't seem to me a logical excuse for your inefficiency and lack of good judgment in trying to do what you can't do.

Well, if you can't do <u>everything</u>, it seems to me you ought to make intelligent choices, not take on the thing most immediate to your hand, or telephone, or personal contact. The announcement that you're a one-track guy, however true it may be, doesn't help when you've taken on a job that has as many tracks as the St. Louis railway station. If you could think out as clear a basis of accepting engagements or making appointments or writing letters as the one you long ago thought out for your life work, and stick to it, it would be easier for you, and for me, too, to answer the hundreds of messages and demands that come daily. Perhaps it might even help your secretaries for they may soon be as puzzled and baffled and confused as I in trying to help you.

Another thing I think would help would be to recognize the element of "circumstances" that comes in and always will delay or change plans – and then <u>allow for it</u>! You know that a doctor's time is never his own because of unexpected demands and you pin all your sins of omission and commission on that but from now on you're going to find something else to lean on. If you could only remember that the unexpected will <u>always</u> happen – then allow extra time, take on one less item of business, I think you'll get along better, and I know the strain will be less on me. This is what you call my pessimism, looking for the worst – but I feel it is intelligent realism based on past experience.

---

140   This letter was filed differently from the rest of her sent letters. It is unlikely that she ever sent it to Walter.
141   Bataan was an island in the Pacific that saw particularly fierce fighting in World War II.

You may be tempted to say all this is none of my business, you can run yourself well without my help. I know you can. But you've <u>asked</u> for my help. I still feel that I'd much prefer to stay here with the girls when you go to Washington. Because I don't seem to be able to stand the sort of disorganization and pressure and confusion and strain that your life these last months has made on me. I might adjust to it if I felt it were necessary or achieving a great end (like the war) but I don't – I feel it's unnecessary and wrong. The Bible says if your hand or your eye offend you – are causes of your offending – cast them from you. What if your husband is such a cause?

Now I wouldn't write this if I didn't think something could be done about it. Here we go into a new and difficult situation with all sorts of problems and demands. I can't either be a help to you, or live in any sort of peace of mind or usefulness to the children, unless you and I have worked out some sort of "modus vivendi." (For heaven's sake don't mistake this for a request for you to come home to lunch. How many times I've heard of your virtue in doing that!) But it does seem as if two mature, loving, intelligent human beings could talk over their <u>mutual</u> life and arrange it for the greatest usefulness of each to a common cause.

I considered going to talk with Dick Raines[142] about this, feeling that he as a third person could perhaps help us both more than we can (or have seemed to) help each other. But once before you asked me not to. So this is my bid for another chance for us to work things out together. Just saying you love me won't answer this problem. Remember the quotation – "We sin against our best loved not thru lack of love as thru lack of imagination."

Yours – Miriam

---

142   Dick Raines was the minister of Hennepin Avenue Methodist Church and a friend of the Judds.

8

Navigating
Washington Life

1943 – 1947

The family moved to Washington, D.C. in early 1943. Miriam found settling into a new home and community both invigorating and challenging, especially in the midst of wartime. She struggled to find and keep household help. She entertained, navigating her way through the ration booklet limiting food supplies. The family faced typical health challenges. But she enjoyed the new community and the growing daughters and meeting new people and seeing old friends.

My sisters and I were busy with school and activities, and Miriam with settling in and attending events, including visits to the White House, various embassies, and organizations. Miriam and Walter had brunch with First Lady Eleanor Roosevelt. Miriam heard Churchill address the joint session of Congress. She saw ailing President Roosevelt sworn in for a fourth term, wondering if she would "… sometime tell grandchildren, 'We saw Mr. Roosevelt take the oath…shortly before he died.'"

After World War II was over, the Judds anguished over the limited US response to the civil war in China. Due to Walter's harsh personal experiences with Communists in both the mid 1920s and 1930s, he worked tirelessly to educate America to the dangers if Chiang Kai-shek were to be defeated.

Miriam found time to help in Walter's office and traveled in the fall to Minneapolis in even-numbered years to help with campaigning. In the midst of the international tension, she still kept up with friends, her parents, China connections, classmates from Mount Holyoke College, and parenting. After four years they moved to a more comfortable home, one they would remain in for forty-one years.

Miriam built a community for the first time in years. Her activities and home life were a fulfilling period of her life. Her private writings disappear in this period; one could simply say that she was too busy. Or that Walter was at home more occasionally. Whatever the reason, Miriam was enjoying her opportunities, despite the daughters' spats, the endless searching for household help, and a desire for more hours in her day to do everything she wished to do but could not fit in.

Washington, D.C.   *Friday, January 1, 1943*

Dear Folks –

We got safely to D.C., tho' driving was *very* icy, and later foggy & Walter went into the ditch once; and our trains were all late. Our furniture van is delayed, first by icy weather, now in the floods in Pennsylvania. We are disgusted with having nothing to do but stay in an expensive hotel. The house, bought by Mr. Judd for us, is fine. We ache to get in. School starts Monday. No oil for our furnace yet. No maid in sight.

Washington, D.C.[143]   *January, 1943*

This is wartime and rationing. Men in government have gone off to war, or into war-related agencies. Women move in to take over these vacancies. Schools are poorly manned. It is a tough time.

First, Flimsy, Feminine Flashes from Washington.

- No bacon, no butter, no bananas, no cocoa, hamburger @ 65 cents, eggs 70 cents, steak $1.
- Laundryman says, "Don't send our laundry anything good that you don't want spoiled!"
- Lady-in-waiting on the telephone – sit hours waiting for the desired extension. The Capitol has just one number, then hundreds of extensions – one bureau has over six-thousand extensions.
- Anti-aircraft guns in public parks, on the roof of the two-story garage of our dairy.
- Congress – New members of Congress, taken out on the Capitol steps to have their pictures taken, were delayed twenty minutes by the military guard patrolling the steps who had orders not to let *anyone* have his picture taken on the steps and Congress was "anyone." They finally got special permission for the picture. Here's the Army running civilian life – symbolic?

Washington, D.C.   *Sunday evening, January 17, 1943*

Dear Dad & Mother –

The first day to catch my breath and glimpse a chance of normal life. Had electricians two days this week. Two different cleaning women didn't come. With clothes all sprinkled for ironing I finally ironed till 12:30 one night. House is beginning to look homey and we like it. I may make drapes or curtains myself, and save money. Walter got for my Christmas an electric Singer Sewing Machine in a walnut "desk cabinet." I hope I'll have courage to use it. Sunday Walter and I went (by bus) to a Republican reception for new Congressmen & wives. We were gone 5:30-7:30 leaving the girls all alone as we could get no one to stay.

The Marion Anderson concert was one of the loveliest pieces of music I've ever heard anywhere.

---

143   Several letters in this chapter, including this one, came from Miriam's notebook to her daughters and do not have salutations.

That great historic auditorium opened to negroes at last – and a negro singer leading the singing of the Star Spangled Banner at the end – wow![144]

Walter's work is slowly getting caught up. Had a half-hour fruitless appointment with Hull.[145] Had a good evening with the Chinese Military Adviser Shiung (just recalled by Chiang Kai-shek) the night before the President's speech, so he *knew* the word of our being so *united* in spirit with China, and the sending of so much material over the Burma Road, was all BALONEY. Whoever said they could hear Walter cheering at FDR's remarks was sadly mistaken. He sat on the floor facing me in the gallery and we looked at each other and simultaneously shook our heads.

China hasn't been treated right either in quantity of war goods shipped, or in being taken into United Command planning or strategy. The Chinese are getting bitter & disheartened. All China folks here (like ourselves) consider it a *grave* danger, for China may easily be forced – or force Chiang Kai-shek – to make terms with Japan because we won't *fight together* – and if she did this, we'd be in the soup for sure. There is to be a bill introduced to give China another sum – five – perhaps million. They don't know that that is less use than taking Shiung into the United Nations Council. He has sat here since *April* without being received by the President, or being taken into the planning councils. It is a disgrace. Walter will speak on this before long, I'll bet. It's too important to America's future, to keep still.

Washington, D.C.   *Thursday, January 28, 1943*

Walter started out Sunday with a dinner engagement made for every night this week. I'm glad for it, for if, as seems possible, he isn't able to make a great deal of contribution thru the regular channels of Congress, he can relieve his frustration by getting some things off his chest in these small, informal, invited groups in the evening. If the Law of Seniority is so sacred here that only the Bearded Ones can do anything, then he's going to get to the Bearded Ones and convert them.

He didn't get on the Foreign Affairs Committee (twenty-seven Republicans applied, and there were five vacancies, and no "freshmen" were appointed). He did get on Education, and Insular Affairs, which deals with our island possessions and may be quite important after the war.

China's Rear Admiral Liu gave a swell dinner at a Chinese restaurant. The Chinese guests were commenting on this being the first time there had been a Chinese-speaking Congressman! We went to a dinner where Ray Moyer, close friend in Shansi, spoke. He was an agriculturalist, got caught going thru Hong Kong, was interned with the Americans six months. He says the starvation was the worst thing they had to endure – and the Human Element – having to live closely under extremely irritating conditions with many sorts of people. He spoke without bitterness. We people in this country still don't know what Conquering Japanese are like.

The government gave us a travel item of 40 cents a mile from Minneapolis here, to cover a round

---

144   Constitution Hall was desegregated at the request of President Roosevelt specifically for this concert, which was a benefit for the Red Cross.

145   Cordell Hull was the Secretary of State.

trip, which I believe is all the travel money we get for the two years. It is expected to cover the Congressman and whatever of his family he can squeeze in on that allowance.

Sunday we are going to have two bunches of flowers in our church, for our little twin girls. We are not having any memorial notice put in the church calendar, as we do not care for the publicity, and this is just a Family Occasion of our own.

Washington, D.C.   *Sunday, February 21, 1943*

Activities this week have been largely on the minus side. The oil burner started acting up, we couldn't get immediate service on it. While we waited it kept running and used up all the oil, without warming the house, so then we had to wait a coupla days for oil, with the house at 40. I kept busy eating breakfast at drug stores, lunch at school, supper at neighbors, or in the kitchen with all gas stove burners lighted, making it quite livable.

None of this prevented my being among those present when Madame Chiang appeared before the House of Representatives. She is lovely, "to the manor born," as Speaker Rayburn remarked to Walter, a LADY every inch. We wondered if they who clapped so loud knew the full import of what she was saying. If they did, why couldn't they do something about the China situation? To hear her talk so movingly about China's heroic resistance for all these years and its significance for the world, made me want to cry, and Walter said he felt the same way.

I delivered my maiden speech in Washington to the Girl Reserve Mothers and Advisors and High School Principals, the same day Walter testified before the Foreign Affairs Committee.

Washington, D.C.   *Wednesday, March 3, 1943*

Dear Folks –

The past days might well have been "Madame Chiang week." …Last night we heard her in Madison Square Garden, New York, and her speech was erudite, and confused, and complicated by long sentences and longer words and historical parallels that were too much for my feeble brain to follow completely. The occasion itself was thrilling. The auditorium was beautifully decorated with Chinese flags and bunting, and the lantern parade was lovely – Chinese children carrying the lighted Chinese lanterns, all lights off and colored spotlights revolving on the procession. Mildred MacAffee gave a dandy speech as President of Madame's Alma Mater,[146] and Dr. Coffin,[147] representing the church, read parts of Madame's tribute to the help and heroism of Missionaries in China. One of the most thrilling parts was the singing of the Chinese National Anthem, led by the nearly 400 voices of the Westminster Choir – and entered into by the thousands of Chinese, and friends of China there. Walter and I sang along lustily in Chinese. In spite of the disappointing speech, it was fun to see the pageantry of that big meeting of 17,000, fun to talk to China friends, fun to be in New York, fun to get away from the routine here. We came back on the night train, were back on our jobs by eight this morning.

---

146   Madame Chiang Kai-shek was an alumna of Wellesley College.
147   Dr. Henry Sloane Coffin was the head minister at Riverside Church, New York.

What I enjoyed most was going to church with the Madame on Sunday at the big Foundry Methodist Church whose pastor is also the Chaplain of the Senate. The Chaplain invited us to sit in the pew with her, representing the House. The Vice President and Mrs. Wallace were on the other side of her, from the Senate. The church was covered by Secret Service men. In the chancel was a huge basket of lovely red carnations and on it a card which the pastor read aloud, dedicating the flowers to the Generalissimo and Madame, in honor of all the Christian sacrifice they made to help build a strong nation, etc. There was no announcement made that Madame was worshipping there, tho' he prayed for China in the prayer, and his sermon was a regular one. Just before the benediction he asked everyone to remain seated till the "distinguished guests" had left, and we all went out the side door, where photographs were taken, we shook the Madame's hand, she got in her car and drove off.

Walter finally got his first speech off his mind, last Thursday on the floor of the House. He had a fairly large group – over 100, which is considered good when often there are only fifteen or twenty men who stay after the regular bills are discussed. He got quite an ovation when his thirty minutes was up, and has been hearing compliments ever since. He gave them a general explanation of background factors in the Far Eastern conflict – historic, economic, political, etc. He plans to speak again on what are the implications for America of this analysis of the struggle.

Had the children home all last week on account of the rationing in the schools. I went down and helped with the rationing one day. Then I took the girls on an educational tour one day, to see the Declaration of Independence and the Constitution, to see the House and the Senate, and Dad's office, and sandwiched in a lunch in the House Restaurant. Another day we had to have Carolyn's birthday party, with eight girls and quite a noisy and satisfactory party.

Washington, D.C.   *Wednesday, March 17, 1943*

Dear Folks –

I have joined a five-week class in household engineering, so I can learn how to change electric fuses, repair toasters and irons, fix electric light cords, put new washers on leaky faucets, and small things you practically can't get a man to do for you now.

Have gotten busy in the speaking line again. Addressed the American University Chapel, and wives of our new Congressmen. Hope I get a maid soon, as I can't do credit to either the speaking or the housekeeping-child-raising if I do both…

Had a big meeting at famous Constitution Hall (one of a series of Five United Nations Discussions) where they had Governor Stassen speak on his post-War Plan.[148] They had a panel of four – a Democrat and Republican Senator and Representative – on the stage to ask questions and discuss afterwards. Walter was one of the four – quite an honor for a Freshman. There must have been 3,000 present… Walter is received with respect and interest everywhere, for he always has something to say that's worth saying.

---

148   Harold Stassen was the governor of Minnesota, who resigned the following month to enlist in the Navy.

Washington, D.C.   *Monday, March 21, 1943*

Dear Folks –

The first day of spring started with a snowstorm, and today we have a beautiful world. Hot days last week brought out the forsythia and magnolia, and now the yellow stalks stick through the white snow. It won't last long, and the cherry blossoms on the "Oriental" cherry trees (not "Japanese," please) are to be out in two weeks. We have winter and summer.

Walter and I went to Sunday dinner at the White House yesterday; though the invitation called it "lunch," it was plenty good enough for a dinner for me. The invitation went to Walter's office on Friday, was written by Mrs. Roosevelt's secretary, said it would give her great pleasure if Dr. Judd and his wife would lunch with her at one o'clock, enclosed a small ticket with the White House printed indistinctly on its background and printing authorizing them to admit – our names filled in – to the White House, north entrance on – date and time filled in. The White House has guards all 'round now, and no one is allowed to walk along the sidewalk next to the street, even outside its picket fence.

We got to the wrong one of the two north gates, were sent to the other, proceeded along the forbidden sidewalk, were challenged by a guard further on, presented our ticket, were allowed to pass, though he promptly shoo-ed off another couple who tried it. Negro butlers took our coats, a secretary showed us the seating plan for lunch, then ushered us into a small reception room and introduced us to the other five guests (we were the last to arrive, but not over thirty seconds late – a record for us).

We sat and visited about five minutes and then the secretary announced Mrs. Roosevelt and she greeted us all, the secretary helping with introductions. She wore the inevitable blue, was gay and effervescent with her high-pitched nervous laugh, looked well. We stood chatting a minute, then went across the hall to a small dining room. Eleanor sat in the center of the oval table in a highbacked, carved chair, Walter on her right. She explained that "Franklin" was sorry he couldn't lunch with us as he had a conference, but we'd see him later. Three negro butlers served the meal: oysters on the half shell, roast beef & Yorkshire pudding, string beans, rolls without butter, ice cream with butterscotch sauce & cake, coffee, mints. Nothing was passed twice, no salad, nothing to drink but water…

As soon as we were seated she turned to Walter and said she had read in the Congressional Record his speech before Congress and was impressed with it, but was sorry he hadn't finished it, said she had sent for extra copies to send to friends; said it was her Sunday job to clip all the newspapers and magazines for interesting bits to send to "Jimmie," now again in an island in the Pacific, this time in charge of 1,000 men, and to "Frankie," both of whom depended on her to keep them up-to-date on things; said she had sent them W.'s speech.[149] Said Elliott had never asked her to send him any clippings, as he had always resented his father's public life. Went on to talk of Madame Chiang being her guest and of her beginning to realize how little she understood the Chinese, their

---

149   "Jimmie" was James, the Roosevelt's oldest son; Elliott was another of their four sons who survived infancy; "Frankie" was Franklin Delano, Jr., their second-to-youngest son; John was the youngest.

fundamental philosophy, their ideas of hospitality, etc. This gave Walter an opening, which he took and we were off!!

Actually, Mrs. Roosevelt kept the conversation pretty well in her own hands, asked the English girl a few questions about her concentration camp experience, read aloud a "ballad"…which Franklin is going to read aloud on one of his broadcasts… After lunch, we all stepped into the elevator opposite the dining room, went upstairs, and sat talking a few minutes in Mrs. Roosevelt's sitting room. Then a secretary came to tell us the President was ready for us, and we went down the hall, with large oil paintings of Presidents on both sides, to the Lincoln or oval study where he sat behind his desk, an aide having just carried out lunch trays. He looked well, perhaps because he'd slept late and had breakfast in bed, Eleanor told us. We were each introduced and shook hands. He told Walter he wanted to have a "long talk" with him about that speech and the Pacific situation. He laughed a lot, then got talking intimately with the Browns and we drifted out of the room, stood talking in the hall with Eleanor who then said goodbye to us, and we went down in the elevator escorted by aides to the door and were out in ordinary life again. So that's that! (May I please be permitted to wonder with pardonable pride how many freshman Congressmen are invited to dine informally at the White House within the first three months, on the basis of intelligent speech made before the House of Representatives???)

Walter has seen Nelson Rockefeller a number of times and likes what he is doing and the man himself. Nelson is close to Mrs. Roosevelt, and I guess said a good word for Walter. They think Mrs. Roosevelt will take another trip outside the country before long, and Walter is going to write her today, with our thanks for the lunch, and suggest that she seriously consider going to China, for the good it would do their whole morale over there, not to mention the good that might come from our country's better understanding of their people and problems.

Washington, D.C.   *Tuesday, April 20, 1943*

Dear Folks –

I seem to have been in a daze of no maid, no heat, sickness, and company. After our White House dinner Walter and I were both ill, and tho't it might have been the oysters, till two of the girls got ill with the same symptoms. After being completely out of oil we finally got an additional 100 gallons assignment but are using it frugally and wondering if spring will ever come. Then we've been having a lot of company: ten overnight guests in seven successive nights last week, and three guests coming over Easter. I do like company and entertaining, but making beds and buying groceries and washing dishes gets a bit thick, in a big house like this, and with no help.

While Walter was in Florida I went to dinner with the Leon Pearsons. Present was his brother Drew Pearson of the "Washington-Merry-Go-Round."[150] I never had any association with such a columnist, didn't realize that they are eternally looking for dirt until I heard him listening intently to a story I was telling about one of the Congressmen, heard him ask who it was. I quickly said, "I forget his name," got a laugh from the group. I've been watching the column ever since, was surprised to see this

---

150   "Washington-Merry-Go-Round" was a controversial column in the *Washington Post* written by Drew Pearson.

item, under the heading DR. JUDD'S CRITIC: "'I've heard lots of good things about your husband,' remarked a friend of the wife of Minnesota's Congressman Walter H. Judd. She joshed back: 'Do you want to hear some bad things about him?' Dr. Judd has made an impression on Democrats and Republicans alike, who regard him as one of the ablest new members of Congress." Well, his report was accurate, but he must be hard up if he has to record trivial dinner chat. I've learned to watch my step if I'm going to associate with columnists!

Washington, D.C.   *Tuesday, May 4, 1943*

Dear Folks –

I had "brunch" with Eleanor Roosevelt ten days ago. She was a guest at the Congressional Club, the beautiful Clubhouse for wives of Senators and Congressmen. There must have been 200 there. Mrs. Roosevelt spoke on what the women of Britain were doing in the war effort. She stated plainly that she had no intention of making a comparison between them and our women, as we faced quite different circumstances. Then she spoke for nearly an hour, without notes, most informally. And as she described the things the women there were having to face, and finding they *could* do, I kept seeing our Chinese friends and what they have been facing all these years, and wondering if America would ever know *firsthand* all the sacrificing and readjusting they have learned across the oceans. It's considered naïve and unsophisticated to admit you are impressed with Mrs. Roosevelt, and particularly if you are a Republican! But I was touched with her talk and I wish people would listen to her and get a few good ideas about what we may be up against, rather than criticize her endlessly. I thought she was splendid.

Last night we were at dinner in the swank apartment of President and Mrs. Quezon of the Philippines, on the strength of Walter's speech on the Japanese execution of our flyers – another standing ovation in the House. Also there was General Chennault. His face was seamed and his teeth bad and he was deaf, but he was a real guy, and what he doesn't know about China isn't much. He's trying to get some of his "Flying Tigers" to go back with him to China. Why couldn't Roosevelt for once listen to one who's been doing the fighting, and knows the score?

The General and the Judds were the only "white" folks in the party of fourteen. By the time I'd talked all evening with those Chinese and Pilipino accents, I'd practically developed an accent myself. My English sounded so odd in that company. After dinner the ladies sat in the living room while the gentlemen, darn it, went off in a study to hear Chennault. Madame Wei[151] had discovered that I could speak a spot of Chinese, and as her own English was poor (she talks fine French from her fourteen years in France), whenever she got stuck for an English word in her long rambling stories of her life, she would shoot the Chinese equivalent to me and expect me to produce the English. This was a bit of a strain on my poor Chinese! She is an interesting person, being the first woman lawyer and first woman judge in China.

It was a good evening. Walter was tickled to have a chance to talk to Chennault firsthand, and I

---

151   Madame Wei was the wife of the Chinese ambassador.

enjoyed seeing how the other half lives. These foreign diplomats who aren't subject to our ration laws wear the most gorgeous American shoes and dinner clothes – the Chinese wore Chinese gowns with real jade jewelry, but the Philippino ladies had extreme American styles. Walter says he isn't doing as much for China and the Philippines now as he was in those earlier days when no one paid much attention to him, and now they feast him because he's a Congressman! Well, if you come to visit us you'll still find us serving baked beans to guests.

Washington, D.C.   *Thursday, May 20, 1943*

Dear Folks –

I heard Churchill yesterday at the joint session of the Congress. I guess I'm by nature a "neck-craner" for I enjoy the pomp and ceremony of visiting celebrities – as long as all the fanfare doesn't get in the way of getting the quickest and most lasting victory and peace. The speech itself was good – now all we want is action on the promises and we'll be satisfied.

Monday I went to the White House to a garden party given by Mrs. Roosevelt and the Cabinet wives for the Congress wives. It was informal. I did say hello to Madame Perkins[152] since we're both Holyoke gals, but she was embarrassed to be there as she was *not* a "Cabinet *wife*" and isn't the punch excellent. It was.

Washington, D.C.   *Sunday, June 6, 1943*

Dear Folks –

We had a terrible thing happen here Wednesday. I was keeping five-year-old Juju Alexander. At 5:30 I stepped next door but one to say hello to the neighbor whose two-year-old son has mumps. At that moment the girls decided to pour boiling water on the ants crawling in our yard, to kill them. In the confusion, and quite by accident the boiling water got knocked onto Juju. The next few hours were a bad jumble of neighbors, doctors, screams, and a few terribly sobered little girls. They put her in the hospital. She was burned, but fortunately it was only a second degree, so she will be O.K. and is at home again, but still bandaged. Mrs. Alexander was wonderful about the whole thing. She said after the family had all been imprisoned by the Japs nine months in Shanghai – they are our British China consulate friends now stationed in Washington – a little burn was nothing. But still you can imagine how I felt.

---

152   Frances Perkins was the Secretary of Labor, the first woman appointed to the U. S. Cabinet and a Mount Holyoke graduate, class of 1902.

Washington, D.C.   *Tuesday, June 15, 1943*

Dear Folks –

Walter spent thirty-five minutes with the President, at Franklin's invitation, supposedly on a matter concerning the erection of a temporary Army hospital in the Twin Cities, but the President chatted breezily on all subjects under the sun before he got down to business. Walter promised to dictate a family letter on the subject…

Am finally getting at the Singer sewing lessons due me on my new machine, and hope I'll garner more confidence. I'll have to if I'm to go on clothing three growing girls.

Washington, D.C.   *October, 1943*

Dear Helen –

Two mishaps while I was in Minneapolis. Eleanor broke two bones in her right arm, was in a cast over six weeks, is O.K. now. (Good she's left handed!) And I lost what we'd hoped would be "Little Brother." We didn't tell the girls about this. They were in New Hampshire (on the Rinden's Farm) and Ellie was staying with a friend. I wasn't too peppy for a while, and when we were in New Hampshire, to retrieve the older two, I had to send an SOS for medical care. I'm feeling quite O.K. now though a bit snowed under…

Washington, D.C.   *Sunday evening, October 24, 1943*

Mother dear –

What do you think about the immigration bill passing so well?[153] Walter is pleased.

Washington, D.C.   *Sunday evening, November 7, 1943*

Dearest Mother & Dad –

It seems too bad not to be free to do things Walter wants me to do – he's home so little and when he is here, there are things that seem important for us to do together. These are important days in our world's history. I would have given my eyeteeth to have been able to attend the Senate debate and vote this week on the Conally resolution, O.K.ing the Moscow statement proposing "a general international organization."[154] Walter spent the week in the Senate listening to debate, calls this the most important decision in America since the Declaration of Independence!

Friday night *we* had a dinner here for ten. Bought a whole ham, completely cooked, gave $5 and 115 points for it, and then a dog took it off the back porch ice box and gnawed it to bits. If I'd known which dog, I'd have served roast dog for my dinner! I had to start over again, with a $10 turkey. Our dinner was on the day the Conally bill passed, and with Joe Ball there and all the work he's done for the international organization, and Walter elated over the vote, you can imagine what a festive occasion it was – if expensive!

---

153   The Magnuson Act of 1943 allowed Chinese immigration for the first time since the Chinese Immigration Exclusion Act of 1882.

154   The resolution was a preface to the founding of the United Nations, strongly supported by Minnesota Senator Joseph Ball.

Washington, D.C.   *Sunday, November 21, 1943*

Dear Folks –

On our train trip to New York for the *Tribune* Forum, we did the inevitable last-minute super-perfecting and retiming of the manuscript. At the Forum, held at the Waldorf Astoria I thought Greer Garson[155] who spoke shortly before Walter might throw him off, but Greer seemed to speak with great emotion a rather mediocre bit, making up in looks what she lacked in ideas. Forrestal and a couple of the educators were good, and Mrs. Roosevelt said what she had to say briefly, made a real point, and sat down, which was all in her favor. She came onto the stage in time to hear Walter's speech, and as he sat down shook his hand and said, "Splendid." Walter was the only member of Congress on the two-day program…

We went to the Annual New York City YMCA Membership Dinner at which Walter gave the main speech. I saw many of my Dad's old friends and fellow-workers among the 600 present. I liked it, too, when Walter was introduced as an intimate friend of the YMCA and a particularly close member of the family because his wife was the daughter of their long-respected and beloved co-worker, Ben Barber! We took the midnight train back to Washington that night.

This was Parent's Visiting Week at the schools and I had to go three different days. I was not impressed with teaching job I saw. They are all doing well, but I don't think the teachers make much use of their boundless energies and mental possibilities. I spoke once, an evening forum at a large downtown church – men and women. Have also taken on a Sunday school class.

Washington, D.C.   *Sunday, January 2, 1944*

In spite of illnesses, we did have a happy Christmas season, starting with Mary Lou being the Virgin Mary in both the school and the Sunday school pageants, wearing a beautiful blue sari that I brought from India. The Monday before Christmas we were invited to have a "family lunch" with Ambassador & Madam Wei at the Chinese Embassy. Mrs. Wei is a dramatic person, not tall but wearing extremely high heels, fairly stout. She never seems to walk, always runs on little tripping steps, which look comical. So she comes bouncing in, completely surrounded by her little white Pekinese who is leaping all over her and to whom she keeps yelling "Seet down, seet down" between handshakes and voluble welcomings in English-Chinese-French mixture. Shortly, when the dog refuses to "seet," she takes him out, locks him up in the bathroom.

In a few minutes, Ellie, who has been looking over the Embassy, comes in and says in a significant whisper: "I need to go to the toilet." Madame leaps up, trips across the room clapping her hands, calling servants, pulling bell cords, pushing buttons, hollering, "Ze poor leetle girl, he is hungry. We not wait for the Ambassador to come. We eat. Serve lunch."

Madame tells us in un-understandable English and fast Chinese where she wants us to sit, but she doesn't remember the girls' names and Ellie being somewhat confused thinks its safer to stick to me so plunks herself down in a chair next to where I'm assigned, only to have Madame shout, "no,

---

155   Greer Garson, a British actress, was nominated for five Best Actress Academy Awards, winning one for *Mrs. Miniver* in 1942.

no, no. Zat is for ze Ambassador. Move over."[156] But Ellie doesn't see an Ambassador anywhere, likes that seat, and sits placidly on. Gosh how I wanted to laugh! Then the soup is brought in in a deep bowl with a whole chicken floating in it, but so tenderly cooked that the chopsticks can easily tear bits of the meat off to put in the individual soup bowls. Madame starts to serve the bowls, stops precipitously, summons all the servants in her fast, high-pitched voice, says the bowls are too small and orders them all off the table. Larger ones are brought and she starts to serve again, stops suddenly again when she decided that the little girls should have the smaller size after all and orders some of them back on the table again.

The Ambassador came in while we were eating. The girls managed their chopsticks well, Walter helping Ellie whom he now had over by him. Carolyn didn't like some of the stuff too well so when the Madame urged more on her, she replied in a small, polite voice, "I'm almost entirely filled up." …For dessert we had fruit and Chinese fortune cookies, which the girls enjoyed so much that after they'd eaten all they wanted, they decided to reach over and smash the rest to get the fortunes out to read. To prevent this, Madame ordered a large box for us to take home.

After lunch we played ping pong on the recreation porch. Ellie smashed two of the ping pong balls, but I thought as between a ping pong ball and a priceless Ming vase in the sitting room, I'd better keep them in the ping pong room till the last minute. When we started the homeward dash and Madame discovered we didn't have our car, she was insisting it was too cold for us to walk, and the girls were loudly reminding me that I had promised them that on the way home we could stop in the Embassy gardens to see the pond on which children were skating. They dashed off to the pond, I, realizing that it had melted enough to be dangerous dashed down the hill after them, Walter hovered at the door doing the courtesies, the Madame insisting in true Chinese style in coming out to the car to see us off, finding us at the pond she called for a huge Chinese coolie sun hat that ended in a pagoda peak and came along laden with the box of fortune cookies, a large box of candy – tripping in her high-heeled shoes over the irregular ground. Ellie took one look at her and remarked conservatively, "You look funny in that hat!" Strike three, Ellie!! I laughed all the way home as we whirled along in the limousine, surrounded by gifts and fur robes, the little girls in the "extra" seats running the glass between them and the chauffeur up and down, Mary Lou trying out all the radios in the rear seat. What a luncheon!

I must brag about the two dolls I made – 26-inch rag dolls, stuffed with three pounds of cotton batting, with braids made of wool, one brown hair, one redhead. It is the cutest McCall pattern and makes a huggable, lifelike doll in a size you can sew clothes for. I had knitted wool sweaters for them, made plaid skirts to match those I'd made for Car and Ellie, panties with lace. Really, I went nuts about this project. Walter was most uncomplimentary while I was working on them in the evenings, thinking I ought to buy the girls "decent" dolls. But he's converted now. The girls adore them, take them everywhere. Mary Lou doesn't play with dolls so she didn't get one.

---

156   Ellie was six years old.

Washington, D.C.   *April 11, 1944*

Helen Dear –

Your cable had a sentence in it that gave me a good feeling. You said "We are *out* of the mainstream but life is challenging." You'd better thank someone for that. We may be *in* the mainstream but life is sometimes depressing. The political outlook is bad, and no one is interested in what happens after we get the war won militarily, and there is so much pussyfooting and lack of aggressive and challenging leadership that it leaves you sick. Walter has filed for reelection… He feels that if he left his profession to do this job, he'd better stick to it till it's done. But he does long to get back to his practice. I believe that, discouraging as this job is, it's the place for him at the moment. If we can't do something more constructive than we did after 1918, then surely our civilization deserves to perish. But we *will* do something better.

Washington, D.C.   *Monday, July 17, 1944*

We had tonsils and adenoids removed from the two younger gals when school closed. The gals have all made progress on their music. The two-piano work has been a stimulus to Mary Lou's practicing. She and Shelia Vincent gave a recital this spring and earned money for the Red Cross. Mary Lou has become the pianist for our Sunday school, since she can do the hymns, play for the choir, and do the preludes and offertories. Carolyn has wanted to do two-piano work too. I'm anxious to have my two stimulate harmony instead of the eternal competitive, which leads to much bickering. Ellie will be right there pretty soon…

The Moral Rearmament people have been hot on our trail this year and have proved a nuisance.[157] From the start they made it evident that if they could land us, they would consider us a "big catch." One evening the Moral Rearmament visitors tried to force me into a statement as to what makes Walter tick, "the secret of his success," what is the source of his inspiration. I refused to answer for Walter (he wasn't home), so told them I didn't know, had never asked him.

So they turned on me: what did I have to go on, to get through the days, to solve my problems. At first I was thoroughly annoyed with their ruthless, prying methods, seemingly untouched by love and understanding and friendship. I was going to be cold and uncooperative and refuse an honest answer. Then I thought it was too bad someone didn't tell them that there were convictions and beliefs different from their own, and yet compelling and satisfying. So with difficulty I opened up and wrenched from my inmost being some of my deepest convictions and suggested what I thought would work for me and for the world, as briefly and as humbly as I could. When I finished, F.R. said to F.B. "Not bad, is it?" The condescension in her voice nearly finished me.

Because I had said I had never asked Walter, I found myself the center of an earnest plea for greater unity in Walter's and my married life, where each knew the other's every thought so that they could create a strong family, and how *their* way was the only way to achieve this. I had to smile inwardly for though Walter and I are far from perfect, and there is much we could do to improve our family

---

157   Moral Rearment was a worldwide movement for moral and spiritual renewal founded by Frank Buchman.

life, our personal relationships and mutual understandings are eminently satisfactory to ourselves, and we are extremely happy in our work and lives together.

Leamington Hotel, Minneapolis, Minnesota   *Friday, October 27, 1944*

Dear Mother and Dad –

My air trip out here was perfect. It's good to be away from the household problems for a bit.[158]

Schedules –

Baker – comes to back door Monday, Wednesday, Friday. On Friday tell him what is required for weekend, and he leaves on front porch Saturday a.m. – has good cakes…breakfast rolls or sweet buns – charge account

Dairy – leaves six quarts of milk every other day, a dozen eggs every fourth day and one lb. of butter either Monday or Tuesday of every other week. Put 20 red points out for him under a milk bottle on Tuesday, October 24, and again on Monday, November 6. If you need more or less of anything, telephone the order the day ahead to MI 1011 Chestnut Farms – charge account

Music Lessons – Tuesday, after school: Eleanor 3:15 at Mrs. Young's; Carolyn at 5:30 here (following week reverse the order); Friday, 5 p.m. – Mary Lou at Mrs. Robbins: Saturday, 10 a.m. Mary Lou at Mrs. Young's

Dance Lessons – at Dance Playhouse, 1742 Church St – Each Saturday allow half hour to get there on bus – 10:15 Eleanor – 11:30 Carolyn – 2:15 Mary Lou. Need two tokens apiece

Sunday School – 9:40

Day School – *9:00 a.m. & 1:00 p.m.*

Scouts – Mary Lou – Thurs. at school, 4:00 to 5:30

Bed Times – Eleanor – 7:45: Carolyn – 8:00: Mary Lou – 8:30. This means *in bed* at these times. If greatly delayed one night, then earlier to bed the next night

Breakfast at eight o'clock

In the house – every evening at 5:30, or earlier if it is dark

Piano Tuner – Mr. Edwards due here November 9 to tune two pianos alike. Leave or send bill.

Girls may bring friends here to play after school but Carolyn & Eleanor may not go to play elsewhere while I'm gone except: to Jean Hollander's if they ask permission, to Mrs. Gray's if she phones here and makes arrangements, to any birthday party, if arrangements are made satisfactory to Miss Martindale. Mary Lou may ask permission to go to play at Joan's, Eleanor's, Kitten's, Anne's etc., but not oftener than two days a week, and must be home by 5:30. No skating during my absence.

---

158   Miriam joined Walter in Minneapolis to help in the election campaign while the girls stayed in Washington D.C. with the housekeeper. Miriam left schedules and instructions.

Leamington Hotel, Minneapolis, Minnesota   *October 31, 1944*

Dear Girls –

(I suggest that Mary Lou read this aloud at table one meal, and Carolyn read it aloud the following meal – as I want you to read it twice and think about it – Mother)

Dad and I were terribly disappointed at the reports about your behavior and attitudes. We had expected that you would understand that by cooperating in making it easy for Mother to be away, you were doing *your* part in the thing Dad and all of us are working so hard at – trying to get the war over, and to make sure we don't ever have another one…

We knew you had been taught to obey and to have *some* manners and to stick to *some* rules, and we were unhappy that you have not been doing what you *know* is right. It only makes for unhappiness when you do what is wrong – you're unhappy yourselves, people around you are unhappy, your parents are unhappy, and your world will be unhappy if you go on that way.

Let me tell you something that happened yesterday here in Minneapolis. We were going to Willmar and since the Governor had to speak there, too, he and Mrs. Thye had asked us to drive up with them in their car. When they came for us at the hotel, they told us they were delayed by seeing a boy killed. Three boys about ten- to twelve-years-old were on bicycles and were hanging onto the back of a big ice truck and getting pulled along – a thing *all* safety rules and *all* traffic rules and *all* bicycle rules say *never* to do. The Governor's car was right behind the ice truck. The ice truck driver didn't know the boys were there and he wasn't in any way responsible. He turned right, at a corner, and the boys' bicycles were knocked into each other, and one was knocked down and the rear wheels of the truck went over the boy's chest and crushed it. The other two boys came to where their friend was lying in a widening pool of blood, and told him to get up. But the Governor was there and told them – that boy will never get up again. They got terribly scared and ran off. The Governor and the truck driver waited till the police ambulance could come.

Now *there's* disobedience and breaking rules leading to a *lot* of unhappiness. Not just because a boy is dead and will never have a chance to grow up. Not just for the parents who are not only lonely for their boy today, but more sad that he died because he broke rules. But sadness for the boy's friends who realize that *they* were breaking rules, too, but only their pal got killed – and that will worry them for a long time. And sadness for the truck driver who even though he wasn't breaking rules, probably has children of his own and is unhappy to think it was *his* truck that killed some other people's boy. And sadness to Governor & Mrs. Thye who had to watch it and try to help, and he didn't feel much like going on to Willmar and making his speech. And sadness for Dad & Mother who heard about it, and remember their own little girls breaking rules.

All breaking of rules and disobedience leads to unhappiness – even if you're the only one who knows, you get an uncomfortable feeling inside, because you hate yourself and wish you could get away from the feeling. You just *can't* do wrong and get happiness out of it.

If you aren't yet able to think what's right and do it, we're going to have to go on *telling* you what's right and *making* you do it. That's why we asked Miss Martindale to keep a list of each girl's disobedience or rudeness or rule breaking, and plan to punish you when we get home…

I must go now and do some letters for Dad. You know we both love you all very much, and we know you are swell gals when you want to be – so please be swell gals.

Washington, D.C.   *November 15, 1944*

Dear Mother & Dad –

Back in the regular routine, and it seems good, in spite of the interesting three weeks away. When there was nothing more pressing on tap in Minneapolis, I showed up at Walter's office and answered many of his letters on the typewriter, and answered one of the two phones, which were continually ringing, and talked to friend or foe, in an effort to smooth out difficulties or take messages or keep Walter from being bothered by every Tom, Dick, and Harriet. At the Ward Rallies he spoke for Dewey, the rest of the time mostly about the China situation, at no time about his own candidacy.[159]

Got home to find the house and children in complete chaos. The lady in charge turns out to have been about the worst person I could have chosen. She was a conscientious but rigid New England spinster near sixty, full of negative virtues. I guess she was half scared to death by them, and showed it, and when the kids discovered how indecisive she was they set out to lead her a merry chase. She had no sense of humor or imagination in dealing with them, would stick her neck out with commands demanding rigid and instant obedience. When I got back two of the gals had not been in school in three days, because she couldn't decide whether they were sick or just fooling. She had the knack of bringing out everything bad in the girls – and there's bad there. She thoroughly irritated them, and I can't blame them, for her personality irritated me before she left.

I've been having fun getting things back to rights. I've kept the gals working, washing windows, raking leaves, cleaning up their rooms, straightening bureau drawers, mopping floors. They have been cooperative and helpful. It encourages me to know that I *might* do worse at raising children than I do, and to hear them say that they're glad I'm back because I know how to punish them when they do wrong and Miss Martindale doesn't! Walter, who wanted me to help down at the office, is going to have to wait until he finds someone else who will manage his gals.

Washington, D.C.   *Thursday, December 28, 1944*

Dear Folks –

They called from New York to ask Walter to be on a Town Meeting January 4 on China, and he was puzzled as to what to do. The situation is extremely tense in our relations with China now, and Walter is one of the few people who can speak out freely – Army people aren't allowed to tell what they know, and *all* news correspondents are heavily censored by the War Department, but a Congressman can't be censored. Almost anything could be said on such a broadcast, and with two

---

159   Thomas E. Dewey lost the presidential election to Franklin Roosevelt. Walter won his election for the House of Representatives with 81,798 votes or 57 percent. Edgar Buckley, the DFL candidate, had 62,761 votes or 43 percent.

sides being presented folks are left with no positive impression, and Walter has avoided speaking even before his colleagues on the floor, fearing misunderstanding, or political implications that would make the result worse than if he had said nothing. He has been to see Wei[160] confidentially to get his slant, and the feeling is to say as little as possible publicly to avoid confusing things more. He talked to the Town Meeting people and got them to postpone for the present a public program on China, in the interests of letting some delicate situations work themselves out. Walter is mulling over whether he should speak before the new Congress and how much he should say, and when. It's hard to know what is right.

Washington, D.C.   *Sunday, January 21, 1945*

We've got Mr. Roosevelt started on his Fourth Term! I couldn't help wondering as I stood in the garden looking up at the porch, watching him take his oath, if we'd sometime tell our grandchildren, "Yes, we saw Mr. Roosevelt take the oath of office on his last term shortly before he died."[161] He certainly didn't look well. He was wheeled out onto the portico and then Elliott and his aide helped him stand. People were saying he has had a slight stroke and I wouldn't be surprised. The ceremony was moving, and his speech impressive, except that I couldn't help feeling that he knew how to put noble ideas into words but didn't know how to put them into deeds. I didn't catch a glimpse of daughter Anna, who they say is the closest advisor the President has, and he turns over stuff to her and asks her opinion on all weighty things.

There have been a number of Congress friends asking Walter about his trip to China, and we decided to ask a small group that has stuck together this last two years, with their wives, to come and let Walter talk to them.[162] It's the first time we've entertained any Congressmen so I wanted the house fixed up as well as the children. Served them hot wassail, which is spiced cider with fruit juices. They all seemed to like it though they were used to something stronger, I'm sure. Walter kept answering questions and talking "off the record" till long after eleven, and though we were both tired afterwards, it was a profitable & enjoyable evening.

Walter was not put on the Foreign Affairs Committee, and there are folks who are pretty sore about it. It is disappointing that the Republicans are being shortsighted in concentrating on the Old Guard, overlooking the younger progressives. They'll never win an election again.

Tomorrow I go to a "ladies' school on post-war planning" run by the League of Women Voters. I'll leave sandwiches, salad, and dessert on the kitchen table for the girls' lunch when they come home from school and let them eat unchaperoned, and fight it out if they like.

Washington, D.C.   *Thursday, March 8, 1945*

We've been carrying a heavy social schedule so I'll run through it:

---

160   Wei Tao-ming, the Chinese Ambassador to the U.S.
161   Franklin Roosevelt was in poor health. To accommodate him, the swearing-in ceremony was on the south portico of the White House rather than the then-traditional east portico of the U.S. Capitol. He would die April 12, 1945.
162   The "small group" was fully twenty-two strong.

February 22, Thursday – …Walter phones from New York City at 2:30 to say a document he needs to quote from that evening on his Town Hall Broadcast is on his office desk and can I bring it up to New York City to him! I rallied friends & neighbors, got Walter's secretary to spend the night with the girls, leaped into clothes and a taxi and the four o'clock train, having collected both cash and manuscript en route. I reached Town Hall at eight. Walter and I came home on the midnight train. Got home in time to get breakfast and go on from where I'd left off.

February 24 – Walter was out of town so I had dinner at the Statler Hotel with one of our constituents and strong booster – Art Strong. All very pleasant, but my missionary background makes the delicious lobster stick in my throat when the bill for five of us is fifty dollars. There wasn't even a fifty-cent idea expressed all evening. It was nice to come home and find Clarke and Betty Lou. They were driving to Orlando, Florida where he has a new job building up the YMCA.

February 27, Tuesday – Walter spoke at the Nebraska alumni dinner. We left this place about 10:30 p.m. and went downtown to the Stage Door Canteen where they were dedicating a new Lounge and had invited Celebrities and Important People – ha! ha! We watched the soldiers dancing with the hostesses, and stayed till closing to see their show, some of the talent imported from New York, as Washington is too low on theater to supply enough talent… It's a nice job they're doing for the men in this old theater, with painted murals showing life-size caricatures of Franklin & Eleanor laughing uproariously – enough to make anyone laugh.

Mar. 1 – FDR made his report to Congress.[163] I held a seat next to a Pathe News man who took pictures continually, learned a lot about moviemaking, and he had a manuscript he was following to get pictures at the right place, so I read off his manuscript and kept up with the whole thing. I had a good view of FDR who didn't look as bad as he had in the Yalta movies. We wonder why he never mentioned China by name. Lunch afterwards with Walter, then to Mary Lou's class where I talked on the rural work and improvement of village life in India.

That night to a formal dinner dance at the Congressional Club – the first time we've broken down and been frivolous since we got here. I meet the wives a lot, and Walter sees the men in business, but this was all pleasure. The Navy Band was unnervingly loud, to drown out any incipient political fights on the dance floor, they said. It was really fun!

Mar. 3, Saturday – Mrs. Roosevelt and the Ladies of the Cabinet entertained at the White House. Tickets to get in, a sea of hats, a receiving line, and then tea in the State Dining Room. Home from this gala function in time for the arrival of our new pup, Shadrack, a full-bred, all-black cocker six months old. He is lively and playful and we love him.

Mar. 5 – The Chairman of Walter's Volunteer Committee in Minneapolis came to town with his wife, and as she had never been to Washington, I was elected to show her the sights. We went to the famous Monday session of the Supreme Court, with all its solemnity, as Monday is Decision Day. Lunch with Walter and then to my surprise were in the gallery of the House when he made a fifteen-

---

163   President Roosevelt, Churchill, and Stalin met at Yalta to discuss Europe's post-war reorganization.

minute talk on the Draft Nurses Bill. First time I'd heard him down there, and I was plenty proud. He was the only one on the Republican side allotted time to speak on the bill, and he was opposing it. He felt that the voluntary signing on of nurses would fill the bill, if some of the confusions in the whole matter were cleared away, like their not taking male or negro nurses, or many who have already volunteered and heard nothing from their offer, etc. They did improve the bill before the vote, and some of his amendments got in, but he wanted the bill passed as of a future date in case voluntary enlistment didn't fill the needs, and this was defeated.

Mar. 7 – Last night to the Chinese Embassy to a small formal dinner with General and Mrs. Wedemeyer, who succeeded Stillwell in China-India-Burma command. Walter got a good talk with him and was much pleased with the man, and with the reports he brings from Chungking.

Washington, D.C.   *Saturday, May 5, 1945*

Mother, dear –

Wednesday a.m. I had the program for our women's meeting at church – "A Day in a Mission Station in North China." I discussed by telling illustrative incidents, such things as personnel of missionaries, building up native support for the institutions, difficulties that differences in their and our culture make, comments on servant problem, "squeeze," food we ate, my typical day. It was chatty, informal, full of humor – a real idea of some of the aims and principles of mission work.

Washington, D.C.   *Saturday night, May 12, 1945*

Mother dear:

The trip[164] did me no end of good: partly the vacation from the girls and home, partly seeing old friends, partly the grand meetings and the ideas I got there. The girls seem to have fared all right with nothing more than a rat in the kitchen to upset the equilibrium. Since I'm on the curriculum committee of our Religious Education Department at church, I spent a lot of time talking to various churches about their curricula and got good material and pointers.

Washington, D.C.   *Sunday, May 27, 1945*

Mother dear – Dad, too!

A good Sunday dinner at the Chinese Embassy. Dr. Wei got back from the San Francisco Conference yesterday,[165] and he & Walter wanted to talk. The general feeling among Chinese one of optimism and encouragement, I gather. Hope you have Walter's speech by now – on The Truth about China. Clare Luce asked for fifty copies, which she sent to influential newspapers.[166] She told Walter Henry spent 5 hours working on it – getting something to use in *Time* or *Life*.

164   Miriam had traveled to the annual meeting of Middle Atlantic Congregational Churches in Montclair, New Jersey.

165   He was part of planning for the United Nation's charter.

166   Clare Luce, wife of *Time* founder and editor Henry Luce, was a congresswoman and a close friend and colleague of Walter's.

Washington, D.C.   *Friday, June 22, 1945*

We are in the midst of a "slumber party." Six girls ages eleven & twelve cooked hot dogs in the back yard, spit watermelon seeds, played croquet, have come in and are "catting" in the sitting room to records, as I sit and type. "Catting," I discovered by inquiring, is a form of jitterbugging. We have just had the elevating record "I boogied when I should have woogied." Walter is on the couch concentrating on an issue of *Life*, since he can't start dictating till the noise settles down (it records on his dictaphone – the secretaries tell him they have heard Shadrack's barks…).

We took the little girls out to the farm in Laurel, Maryland, and they look forward to a grand summer. They are twenty-five miles from here, with three other girls and a total of five dogs, including our beloved Shadrack. School closed Wednesday. Mary Lou had to be Master of Ceremonies at their farewell assembly, for her sixth grade. Mary Lou is to go to Sidwell Friends School in the fall. It has small classes, emphasis on academic work. I think she will thrive there, for she can study when she wants to, but lately has been majoring on having a good time and doing well at it. It will do her good to get into the regulated life of camp next week.

Walter is to be on Town Meeting next Thursday discussing the San Francisco Charter. About this $2,500-dollar expense money raise voted to the Congressmen, the *Judds* are refusing it.

Washington, D.C.   *Monday, July 2, 1945*

Mother dear –

Walter's *Time* article has brought amazing amount of congratulatory comment, requests for the whole speech. Requests for 800 copies came in Friday. Forrestal called Walter & wanted to talk to him on it.[167] Today Nelson Johnson, former Ambassador to China, came to Walter's office to congratulate him. So maybe we'll get somewhere. Walter expects to see Truman this week.

Rising City, Nebraska   *Thursday, July 26, 1945*

Mother & Dad –

We've been having a good restful time here – exceedingly hot at first. The first day the girls were all gone in D.C., I had a *bad* day. The house was so empty, so quiet, so desolate, unalive. I realized how much the children make life for us. I went to straighten their rooms, take time to look thru school papers and evaluate how they were progressing mentally. As I was putting books in their bookcase, I picked up Dad's typed loose-leaf book and read thru much of it – the descriptions of events that had made up his life as a boy and the poems that express his beliefs and his strong conviction. I thought of the deep faith that has guided *all* his living thru the years, and made him the person everyone loves and depends on.

The same thought was repeated about Mother's life. I had wanted to share with Walter what you had written of your own life and thought, but knew there would never be an occasion in the kind of life we live in D.C. But when we got driving across Ohio the second day out, I got out your manuscript,

---

167   James Forrestal was the Secretary of the Navy.

Mother, and read it aloud. It was a wonderful time we had together, Walter getting to know about your early life he's never had time to listen to, the relationships to your friends and relatives whom he hears about now but hadn't understood the earlier ties. But the most outstanding feeling in it was your complete dependence on a loving, guiding God.

Walter and I talked a lot about the parents we both have, the faith and conviction they have built into us. Now we are to build it into *our* children. Walter's childhood was so immeasurably different from our children's eastern large city, sophisticated, nation's capitol environment, that many of the techniques that helped him grow into the strong person he is today won't operate in their cases. It sets me to wondering: what are the forces that will operate, *for their day*, and *for their environment*, to give them the faith in God's love and power, that was the only thing that carried our parents thru the problems and trials of their life, and on which we too are dependent for meeting difficulties in the strenuous days *we're* living in.

That last is just a rhetorical question. It is a putting down in ink of a persistent desire, an aim, of my life. There is no answer to it – except to keep working along from day-to-day dependent on God to guide, and trusting that he will show us ways to lead the children, or use our feeble attempts, to build a strong faith in them.

Washington, D.C.   *Wednesday, January 16, 1946*

I went to a tea the Congressional wives gave for Mrs. Truman the other day.[168] She was more at ease and friendly and warm than press reports had led me to expect. The talk is that now that the war's over and restrictions on entertaining and society are to be lifted, Mrs. Truman is about to declare opened the social season. That means, so they say, calls on Supreme Court wives Mondays, Congress wives Tuesdays, Diplomats Fridays, drop cards at the White House, tails for formal dinners for the men, etc. If anyone calls on me Tuesdays, they'll find it's my ironing day, and I'm likely to set them up for a half-hour's work while I rest, and converse!

On return from my four-day's visit in New Jersey I was informed by Walter that everything was going beautifully, that the girls had behaved perfectly, and that the difficulties of running a house & raising girls had been greatly overrated, it was simple! The fact that I'd spent a week preparing and more than a week getting things back on strict schedule doesn't enter into his computations. I had a good time away, and it was good to get back, and all said they'd missed me.[169]

Washington, D.C.   *Sunday evening, April 21, 1946*

Dear Mother & Dad –

Hope you've had a lovely Easter Sunday as we have here… Our Sunday school special service I had complete charge of. It has to reach children from 5th grade thru high school, which is too wide an age range for the best interest-holding. I'd put a lot of time on it, and I like doing it – but only a handful

---

168   Harry Truman had become President after the death of Franklin Roosevelt on April 12, 1945.
169   Miriam had gone to New Jersey for another Congregational Church meeting.

ever are at Sunday school & no one else seems to work hard at getting students, & I get discouraged. I am pushing hard for a religious education director for our young people's work. It is a crying need.

Washington, D.C.   *Wednesday, May 29, 1946*

Last Saturday was one of those days when everyone was jumping on one horse and riding off in all directions at once – and I felt like the horse! Started Friday when Truman announced his plan to address the special session of Joint Houses of Congress Saturday afternoon…

Saturday afternoon Carolyn had her annual dance recital and I saw her part in the program before I had to dash down to the Capitol – where I had a reserved seat in the gallery for the Joint session. The atmosphere was tense, the place was jammed. I still get a thrill each time the Senate is announced by a handsome, deep-voiced Clerk of the Senate, "Mr. Speaker, the Senate of the United States of America," and with everyone in the room standing quietly, they file in with dignity and take the front seats. Shortly after, the buzzing conversation stops and we stand again, "Mr. Speaker, the Members of the President's Cabinet." Then four Senators and four Representatives are named to escort the President in, and I see them forming outside the rear door. While the Clerk announced, "Mr. Speaker, the President of the United States," I watched Truman in the doorway, serious, taking deep breaths, then walking quietly down the aisle without his usual smiles and bows to pals on both sides of the aisle. And then the speech, interrupted for the announcement of the settling of the railroad strike. It is interesting to look down into the faces of the members and watch their expressions. A whole bloc of extreme left-wing Democrats sitting nearest me sit stonily silent, without applauding where the rest of the members burst into prolonged clapping. Some of the most conscientious members, particularly the few I recognize as coming from strong Labor districts, sit there with puzzled furrowed foreheads, concentrating on what is said, making notes, nodding assent or disagreement. It was a most solemn and serious atmosphere.

It was over quickly, the Senate retired, the House had a ten-minute recess before they were to take up the already-drafted Bill for this emergency legislation. Rules allowed them only forty minutes debate on the bill, which came up "out of order," and no permission for any amendments. That put them all in the hole, for you can imagine how little can be said in forty minutes, and what a spot you're in if you have to take all or nothing of the emergency legislation the President tells you is essential in avoiding civil war.

Walter sat with me in the gallery while we listened to the debate, and there were lots of things he didn't like, but on the whole he didn't believe you ought to refuse the request of the President at a time like this. So when the roll was called he voted yes from the Floor. And then we leapt into the car and dashed like mad to the local NBC station which he reached five minutes before the six o'clock hour he was supposed to be on the Forum of the Air program. I went on home, but there was some difficulty with transmission, and it wasn't too successful and the cards were stacked against Walter by the left-wing producer of this program plus his two opponents, but he felt he wanted to give his side, and you never knew him to dislike a scrap anyhow, did you?

Walter's cousin wanted to see us, so I'd written asking them for supper. When I got home after six they were in the back yard playing croquet with our girls, and Mary Lou had invited one of her friends for supper and to spend the night! Fortunately I had my potato salad and ice cream made and in the icebox, and it wasn't long before ten of us were eating picnic style on the front porch. Just got cleaned up from that debris when Walter came on the scene and had to be fed. Then they took their two girls and put them to sleep in their car on the street, which they say they are accustomed to, and brought out all their kodachrome slides and gave us a show of lovely scenes in the Northwest. Then our girls had to put on the dance ballet they had composed and do the dishes. Then we adults had to sit on the porch and solve all the labor disputes. They left about midnight, and I still had to type some checklists on "your attitude toward prayer" that my high school girls' Sunday school class had to discuss the next morning. What a Saturday!

The Russell Bennetts' home in Minneapolis, Minnesota   *Summer, 1946*

We're all staying in Minneapolis this summer where a friend loaned her house right on Lake of the Isles. A canoe, a gardener, cook, laundress go with it – but it is too swank to suit our style. But "housing" is a real problem, with no available space so we are glad to be here. The polio has cut down the girls' activities completely. The camps they were to go to were cancelled, and while they hadn't been swimming in the lakes anyhow, now we hardly allow them outside the grounds, and don't allow them to play with other children. We still go riding on our bikes, and I go along with them to herd them past any other kids, and we have gone to Lake Calhoun to watch sailboat races at spots where no one else was sitting. But movies, picnics, concerts, shopping, church is out for them. We cut out the lettuce, radishes, celery, raspberries, cherries, and other raw foods that couldn't be boiled and peeled. Since no one knows how this polio is carried, we can do this and feel we're doing something to protect our children.

Walter arrived here tired after Congress closed. The closing days were long and hot and confused. They did vote that Congress should hereafter adjourn not later than July 31. This seems to mean that Walter should be in Minneapolis the latter part of each year, but I have to be in Washington as long as the girls are in school there. We seem to be fated to live apart – and I don't mind admitting that I don't like it! Nor do I like living in the "goldfish bowl" where the public know better than you do what you should do, and whatever you do is wrong from someone's point of view. I'm either too dressy or not dressy enough; enter too much or too little into my husband's affairs; spend too much or too little time on the children. I'll go on being myself the best I can, and to heck with them all!

Washington, D.C.   *Sunday, September 22, 1946*

Our trip home in the new car was most enjoyable. Drove late into the night, finally finding a good tourist home at Bloomington, Indiana. The next night it was a funny little non-modern cabin with a smelly outhouse and no running water, which we had to laugh at the third night when we found ourselves in all the luxury of THE HOMESTEAD at Hot Springs, Virginia. The College of Obstetricians, Gynecologists and Abdominal Surgeons was having a conference in those beautiful surroundings, and Walter was to be the guest speaker. We got the gals all foxed up and took them to the hotel dining room where we left them to order everything on the menu (our expenses were all paid!) and eventually betake themselves to bed in their luxurious rooms, while Walter and I went on to a cocktail party and to the dinner.

Not sure I'm glad to be back. I wished I'd never let those two Wellesley seniors use our home for six weeks. I never saw such filth, disarray, mold, disorder any place. And to think that these are the educated leaders of the future, down here doing a seminar on labor and politics, and the Far East. The one value of the whole experience – I hope! – was for our girls. They were disgusted particularly after the way I made them step around and clean up the house we had been using all summer. By Friday morning when Dad & Mom arrived, we had a nice house. I quickly got out the winter sewing so she could start work on hems and mends and remodeling…

Walter was in town twenty-eight hours last week, and we had a Birthday dinner to help celebrate my Dad's seventy-ninth and Walter's forty-eighth next week. Couldn't buy a roast so had to be satisfied with a meatloaf. I can't get any sugar here even though I have the stamps, so there's no chance of doing up any peaches or pears or applesauce from our trees, as I'd hoped.

Washington, D.C.   *Sunday p.m., November 17, 1946*

Dearest Mother & Dad –

The last days in Minneapolis were hectic. Walter and I felt those of our committee on the inside displayed a too-sure attitude, "Judd can't lose" and the men, especially, talked big and worked little. The women did the heavy work, and saved the day. But the opposition got a bigger vote than the "big talkers" had expected. I hope it scares 'em enough so they'll *really work* next time.[170]

Washington, D.C.   *Sunday, December 29, 1946*

Coming back on the train was restful.[171] I was here in time for the Church pageant in which all three girls had parts. The family in my absence had bought and trimmed the Christmas tree, put up the manger scene and decorated the mantelpiece with angels.

I'm taking the two smaller girls to their beloved farm in Maryland, so they will be away during the excitement of the BIRTHDAY PARTY. Mary Lou is to have her first girl-boy party New Year's Eve, with fourteen youngsters from school. Walter promises to be here to help, and we are to chauffeur them in two cars downtown to see a movie, *Uncle Remus*, then back here for a roast ham and ice cream dinner. Mary Lou is so excited about it, that the problem of preparing the house and food is infinitesimal beside the problem of who shall sit by whom, whether to pair off at the movie or sit boys and girls separately, whether to dance or to play games or to sing popular songs after dinner, whether to have the boys or girls clear off the tables, and on and on. Every few minutes she calls another of the girls to get advice on how to run things. It is terribly important that her home or her food or her parents or her customs shall not disgrace her with HER GANG. If I survive this introduction to present-day teenagers' parties, I'll write again.

---

170   Walter won the election with 66,837 votes or 58 percent. Douglas Hall, the DFL candidate, received 47,777 votes or 42 percent.
171   Miriam had visited her ailing parents in Winter Haven, Florida.

Washington, D.C.   *Monday, January 27, 1947*

I had a good time last week at an experience new to me – an auction sale. I read that art goods, antiques, household goods were to be sold by Sloan Auctioneers, and would be exhibited previously, so I went down and looked the lot over, found exactly the thing I wanted – a Chinese rug the exact color and all-over cut pattern as our sitting room one and the exact size we needed. The day this was to be auctioned found myself jammed in tighter than the New York subway in rush hour, but a good-natured crowd of Washington society ladies, dealers, antiquers, collectors, cheap skates, and some who go to auctions 'cause they're cheaper than movies (and more fun?). I got scared at once, though I'd read the rules carefully and thought I knew what was going to happen. I found that bidding went extremely fast and no one was given time to think. I decided in my own mind that I would go as high as $150 on the rug, as we needed it and it was so perfect a match.

The auctioneer started it at $200 and my heart sank. But there were no takers, and he came down $25 at a time till at $100 someone jumped in – and I followed after. The thing leapt up by $5 bids between me and someone else I couldn't see, and I got scareder, till at $140 my opposition upped by only $1 and a negro attendant standing near me whispered, "Stick to it, lady, you've got it." A second later and the auctioneer was hammering and hollering "sold to the lady in the feather hat (the remains of the pheasant dinner I ate with friends in Minneapolis) for $144." The whole auction was such fun that I may have acquired a new vice.

Carolyn's sixth grade studied China, and last week gave a closing demonstration of their work. Carolyn felt practically personally responsible and carried no end of our Chinese things to school to be exhibited. Walter took off from work and came to see it. We had a couple of musical treats last week: Carolyn went with her violin teacher to hear a negro violinist who played beautifully. Mary Lou and I went one evening to hear the Brazilian woman pianist, Novaes, who was exquisite.

Washington, D.C.   *Monday, February 3, 1947*

When I wrote you about buying a rug, I didn't have the faintest idea that I was going into bigger and better purchases. I've bought a house. Here's how it happened!

Bea [Brown] Hanson, who was with us in Fenchow, teaching in the school, now lives here. She sells real estate. I had lunch with her, chattered along about keeping busy running this house, with all its drawbacks, and the next day she phoned to say she had found us a swell small house. I looked at it, described it to Walter who's out of town, and now Bea is trying to sell our house…

It's seven years old, red brick, looks deceitfully small from the outside, because it is so economically built that every corner is used. There are no steps up from the street. We'll be tickled to have a garage for our new car, a place to put the girls' bicycles, which now get lugged up and down all those steps,[172] the extra baths with showers, the recreation room, and such a compact, easy-to-care-for house. It's just four blocks from where we are now.

---

172   There were twenty-five steps!

I'll admit that I'll miss this big old house, and the fruit trees, for the new place has only evergreens at the front. But there are houses on only one side of our new street and children in every one of them. We think it will be more neighborly than this older, more settled section where there are no children. We surely ought to save on heating and servicing.

We were supposed to dine tonight with Crown Prince Otto of Austria, but Walter called it off (on the pretext of my health) in favor of talking into the Dictaphone all evening. He won't be home for dinner with the girls again for a week, and then he's off to San Francisco. He has to go to New York for speaking this weekend, and I'm going to sneak in a trip with him, since one of Mary Lou's schoolmates has a mother who offered to come stay. It's midnight now. I better crawl into bed and leave Walter talking to his darn Dictaphone.

Washington, D.C.   *Wednesday night, February 12, 1947*

Dear Mother & Dad –

Our house is sold! …We'll move the end of March. I attended a luncheon to launch the YW World Reconstruction drive here. Mrs. Moore, Henry Luce's sister, was down from New York as the chief speaker and was marvelous. Next to her sat Mrs. Woodrow Wilson, then Admiral Nimitz who spoke, and at the head table wives of many ambassadors here, a number of whom spoke of what YW reconstruction would mean in their countries. It was a fine program – 900 women ate lunch – and I hope they get lots of money.

Washington, D.C.   *Monday, March 17, 1947*

Mother dear –

I'm packing. I'm sorting. I'm disposing. I'm filthy. But I stop in the midst for a note to you. I've been emptying out my desk. These letters of Walter's to his Dad & Mother, written from China, came to light. The one to his mother came a day after her death and was quoted from at her funeral. At his Dad's funeral the other day the minister quoted from his letter to his Dad. [173] I was struck in re-reading them with the similarity in idea and ideal between his expression to his mother of his (our) aspiration to raise strong Christian children, and the letter you sent me recently to read, written by your Dad to you up in the India hills in the summer of 1904 about your aspirations for *your* children.[174]

3083 Ordway St. NW, Washington, D.C.   *Saturday, April 12, 1947*

Mother dear – and Dad –

This week seems to have been too busy –with Carolyn & Eleanor home from school, inevitable settling to do, and reduced energy and working hours. I'm at the Zoo, writing in the car while three little girls look at giraffes and peacocks. I've been going to bed with the children as I still tire a bit easily…

---

173   Walter's father, Horace Henry Judd, died in early March, 1947. The family traveled to Nebraska for the funeral.

174   Miriam was born August 26, 1904, in the hill town of Simla, India.

I got a little black straw hat with varied-colored poppies to wear with all my things and aside from that will not buy *one thing* – dress, gloves, bags, or shoes – this year. My hospital experience was expensive![175] Also moving and buying a house! But on the whole, we look & feel fairly settled, and *love* the new arrangements.

(Continued next day): Walter had a complete physical check-up at Mayo Clinic, is fine. However, one little cancer on his lip was developing fast and they are to take it off tomorrow, perhaps do some skin graft. He will enter the hospital tonight, if all goes well will fly home Tuesday afternoon, but will wear a facial dressing six weeks or so, may cancel his speaking engagements.

Washington, D.C.   *Sunday, July 20, 1947*

Dad & Mother are happily established here.[176] She lives a quiet life, but she does help about the kitchen, tho' mostly she sews. Dad has failed more noticeably, but keeps busy doing jobs around the house. The girls are having a grand time at camp. Eleanor is fun to have around the house – she has decided she wouldn't want to be an only child.

We had a delightful time the Fourth of July weekend. Walter had to give a patriotic address at Ocean Grove, New Jersey, so we drove up. Both Walter and I got blisters and peeled in spite of the advertised excellence of suntan lotion. Ellie had no fear of the giant waves, and we spent hours jumping them with her. I enjoyed the delicious meals in the hotel, which I didn't have to plan or cook, nor Walter pay for! Next Sunday we all leave for our trip to Nebraska, Estes Park, Yellowstone, back through the Black Hills to Minneapolis. It will be more than seven weeks before we get back here, living out of suitcases, and I have to pack for four females. Walter can't see why it can't be done in half an hour. I wish *he* had children, as I do!

Denver, Colorado   *Friday, August 8, 1947*

What a grand day's drive we had that Friday we left Rising City. As we got into the canyon and began to climb, it felt really cool. We got to Estes Park after five. Walter spoke five times in three days. We found Washington friends, and Minneapolis friends, and ex-Nebraska friends. I don't see where Walter gets any vacation. He was tired in Rising City, but he's mapped out a whole "vacation" with speeches & people & visiting. I'm frank to say it's no rest to me and I'm not much caring whether I push on or not.

Hotel Leamington, Minneapolis, Minnesota   *Saturday, August 30, 1947*

Our Rochester visit gave both Walter and me good reports. The girls were with various friends while we were at Mayo… Between chauffeuring the gals to and from their engagements, the subject that took most attention was Walter's plans for a Congressional trip.[177] He leaves D.C. airport September 5, with the Voice of America joint investigating Committee of House and Senate, four Senators, four Congressmen. They will be taken to every European Capital (not including Russia and a couple of

---

175   Miriam had miscarried.

176   Miriam's parents came to stay in Washington, D.C., during the summer.

177   Walter was finally put on the Foreign Affairs Committee in the 80th Congress, 1947.

her babies) by the same Army transport. Isn't that a grand chance to see things firsthand that they constantly have to deal with?

Washington, D.C.   *Monday, September 15, 1947*

Dear Folks:

Walter spent Labor Day at the State Fair in St. Paul, where he was one of those who received and breakfasted with Eisenhower, lunched with him with other dignitaries, and attended a dinner with him at the Minneapolis Club that night. I was packing up the girls and all the extra belongings and getting the picnic basket ready for our trip home.

We pulled out about 7:30 a.m. after Labor Day. We have fun driving along as a family and Walter enjoys it as much as anything. We read aloud (this time it was *Robinson Crusoe*), we play geography games or naming the state capitals or the presidents or we listen to the radio. Always eat breakfast at a restaurant, and the other meals out of our basket at wayside tables. Were home by 12:30 Thursday and took Dad and Mother out to lunch.

We all went to the airport with him the next a.m. They let us go thru the big A.T.C. plane that is to take this group all over Europe, see the four berths (suppose the Senators get those!) see the kitchen and lavatory facilities, oxygen supply, parachutes, life belts, table for bridge playing or writing reports or typing, etc. Then it was time for the briefing that every transoceanic passenger gets, military or civilian, and they let the assembled wives and children sit in. There was a fascinating movie, which explained in detail what to do in an emergency – how to "ditch" in the ocean, how to inflate life rafts, how to repair same, how to use first aid kits, concentrated food, how and when to drink the water supply, how to fish for food, use fish oil for sunburn, how to use the emergency radio. The children were delighted, particularly when the parachutes were given out and Walter had to climb into his harness for the required takeoff and landing. The movie alarmed some of the wives, because it talked of emergencies, but had just the opposite effect on me. I was pleased to think they had provided so expertly for every vicissitude.

Washington, D.C.   *Sunday, October 19, 1947*

I'm sending along the bits I have of Walter's letters from Europe. I got few details at all, the four nights he was home. One I went to a PTA meeting because he said he had to dictate anyhow; one I went up to New York for my Board meeting on a 9 a.m. train and home at midnight; the last night he worked at the office till 2 a.m.; and the first night he showed the coins he had brought home from nineteen different countries and souvenirs he had picked up. This is the first time he has ever bought anything for the girls, so I was quite impressed…

He had a difficult time getting the schedule he wanted to go to the Orient. He is simply appalled by the sheer inefficiency in the State and War Departments here. In Europe he thinks the Consular service is good. He finally went alone, for the other men fell by the wayside as the Europe trip had been extremely strenuous. He is to be transported in Army planes, reach Tokyo today. Will go thru Korea to Peking, Nanking, Shanghai, leave the 4th for the flight home.

Bill Herson weekly radio show, "Coffee with Congress,"
in the Judd dining room

Washington, D.C.   *Sunday, December 7, 1947*

Pearl Harbor day, six years later, and what a sorry mess still!!! Walter flew to Texas Thanksgiving morning for a teacher's convention, so we gals had a simple lunch and went to see *Firefly* in the afternoon – first musical for the two small gals. Walter was back in time for us two to go to Philadelphia Saturday to the Army-Navy game. Special trains from Union Station and jams of people reminded us of war jams. Had fun seeing the President in a box close to us.

Monday evening Walter was struck with a sudden and severe cold, and Tuesday he felt too miserable for words, but the Emergency Aid bill was on the fire. He had a 10:30 p.m. broadcast on Aid to China in the bill, and in the interest of being able to stagger to this, we skipped the formal reception at 9 p.m. at the White House.

Washington, D.C.   *Monday, December 15, 1947*

Dear Mother & Dad –

I can't get to letters on the weekends when the girls are home and clamoring for attention, or using my room for the phone, or wrapping gifts, or asking help on their Christmas lists or accounts, or wanting to get the decorations and start with them, or needing help with their music. I love this being needed by them – gives me a sense of usefulness, and great joy. I must add that I have to give Walter *some* time! We were out together four nights in succession, and I love going with him, hearing him talk with people about the China situation and watching their interest, and their respect for him. How did I ever get such a great guy, and how comes he seems to like having me for a wife, even after sixteen years? Don't answer! I'm willing to accept it without knowing why!

9

Busy Times in D.C.

1948 - 1952

As her daughters rounded the corner into adolescence, Miriam continued to do an extraordinary job of juggling increased lessons, activities, and social lives while also contributing her time and talents on the volunteer front. The home in Washington, D.C. was always open to visiting Minnesotans, many Chinese and college friends and visitors.

The 1949 victory of the Communists in China was a hard reality for Miriam and Walter, as they feared totalitarianism spreading in Europe and the brutality of oppressive governments as they had personally witnessed. They suffered with their friends impacted by these difficult developments. Walter's efforts supported the successful Marshall Plan and a strong defense during the Cold War.

Miriam's commitment to support the Sunday School and youth activities at Cleveland Park Congregational Church necessitated hours of meetings, some travel, plus her own teaching. Miriam also went to New York for meetings and events, to California for the Pacific Pact signing and Japanese Peace Conference, and to Florida to visit her parents. When Walter increased his overseas travel and national political speaking at two National Republican Conventions, and especially on Dwight Eisenhower's behalf, Miriam sometimes accompanied him, but usually she oversaw their daughters and worked to "train them up in the way they should go." She kept the home fires burning and tried to maintain "decorum" amidst the antics and angst of teenagers.

The Barbers visited in D.C. in the summers, and we had several driving trips to see them in Florida over spring vacations. Miriam's mother suffered a severe stroke in 1950 necessitating extra time and care. Miriam continued attending unending historical, social, and political events with Walter, in addition to giving support during three more fall reelection campaigns in Minneapolis.

How she had the energy to do everything contained in these pages is astounding to me. I think she was running on adrenalin, fueled by a devotion to family and a sense of excitement and purpose as history unfolded around her.

∼

Washington, D.C.   *Friday, January 2, 1948*

Walter left December 27 for Kansas, but the two weeks before were certainly China dominated in our lives. One thing that has been personally disagreeable as well as difficult to combat is our local *Washington Post*. Since Thanksgiving it has made an open and desperate attack against aid to China, particularly in editorials and news items. It has thrown dirt all over Walter, by name, heading one of its editorials CHINA'S JUDD, calling him well-meaning but misguided, calling his testimony and speeches in Congress "fairy tales" and more that is less polite! Walter doesn't mind these attacks on him except that it is confusing the entire issue here in the Capitol, and friends are asking him to refute them. This they will try to do next Tuesday, January 7, when Walter and Bill Bullitt will be on Town Meeting of the Air against Owen Lattimore and a newspaper man. Bullitt is a likeable and extremely brainy guy, and a Democrat, so hope we get somewhere.

Washington, D.C.   *Sunday, February 1, 1948*

Dear Mother & Dad –

A number of things have complicated the schedule: the extra cold here, combined with oil shortage so I try to keep furnace shut off all day till 4 p.m. when girls start coming in; the heavy-for-D.C. snow, requiring shoveling, & of coasting & lots of wet clothes to dry; Walter in, and out, and in, and gone again and only one car running (we put the other up during the bad driving).

Harriet Hardy came Friday on her way to Los Alamos, New Mexico, for a year's work with the atom bomb commission.[178] She hated to be connected with the bomb, but they are using beryllium, and she knows more about beryllium poisoning than any U.S. MD. She discovered and exposed a horrible disease among workers in Massachusetts. She thought she might find out more regarding industrial diseases with new products they are using in the atom bomb project and so could help humanity. She is a fine person, well-read, deeply religious, such a balanced judgment and good sense of values – as well as sense of humor. Her visit did me good…

Wasn't the news about Gandhi shocking.[179] There is a memorial service for him in our big Congregational Church tonight. Poor, poor India!!

Washington, D.C.   *Thursday, February 12, 1948*

I took on a couple of extra activities the first of the year. One is to prepare each week a worship service for our Sunday school that the youngsters put on themselves – choose hymns and scripture to go with whatever theme is selected, dig up (or write!) a short story or illustration. Takes a batch of time, but I like doing it.

The other activity is an eight-week (2½ hours per week) dress-designing course by Magda, a New York couturier who is opening her salon in Washington. It is disillusioning to find Magda's name is Mrs. Johnson, and she isn't glamorous looking! But she does know her stuff, and it should give me ideas and experience as I try to sew for my girls through their expensive teen years. She's had us

---

178   Harriet Hardy was a longtime friend from Miriam's camp days in Maine.
179   Mohatma Gandhi was assassinated in New Delhi on January 30, 1948.

take careful measurements and make ourselves a basic pattern on heavy unbleached muslin, for she shows us how to make a full or swing skirt from the slim pattern, how to vary sleeves, necklines, etc. We each designed a dress, are to go ahead and make it! [See picture on page 213.]

I also had fun and a new experience in upholstering an old chair with a lovely heavy brocade Walter brought from Shanghai. I refinished the woodwork first. I'm so pleased with myself that I've ordered material to put new chair seats on our dining room chairs.

Social activities have been fairly limited because of Walter's absences. We did go to a big Minnesota State party for Stassen where we had to stand in a reception line and shake over 500 hands. I drove to Richmond with Walter one night last week when he had to speak. We had a good visit, and a nice dinner en route. We enjoy getting together occasionally!!!

Washington, D.C.   *Tuesday, February 24, 1948*

Thursday I left early for New York to attend one of my regular Board meetings, leaving Ginny to bring Carolyn up to New York after school was out.[180] Carolyn has looked forward to this twelfth birthday treat ever since Mary Lou had such a trip two years ago. We started out sightseeing Friday morning: The Art Museum, the Natural History Museum, the Planetarium, which simply fascinated Carolyn, dinner at the English Grill on Rockefeller Plaza where we grown-ups dined and Carolyn preferred to skate to music and moonlight, coming in with skates on (the accepted procedure) to snatch a bite or two and back to skate, while we watched out the wide windows. Then on to Radio City to see the Rockettes and the movie. Saturday we climbed to the top of the Statue of Liberty, which my stiff legs cause me to remember vividly! It sure was fun to see New York through the eyes of a twelve-year-old.

Yesterday Walter spoke at the Nebraska Alumni Dinner, and I heard him for the first time since he's returned from Europe give a political talk, about the Marshall Plan, mentioning talking with Cabinets in Europe on what they would do to get their people to work harder if we undertook to help them out – events I never would have heard of if I hadn't got to hear this speech…

Sunday Ellie is to play at the Washington Children's Music Club and I'll help her get ready as her music teacher is at a clinic being checked for cancer… How we mortals tear around and where does it get us? I wondered that when I sat in the Planetarium in New York City and saw the stars and planets, the order in the universe and the dinosaurs who lived millions of years ago and are extinct now – it makes my recital of this week's activities seem ridiculous and man quite insignificant. But I still have to buy groceries for dinner, so I'll stop this philosophizing.

Washington, D.C.   *Friday, March 5, 1948*

Mother dear –

Walter is terrifically preoccupied these days with the strenuous activities in the Foreign Affairs Committee. But he patiently & doggedly pushes for the right and got a chance for Bullitt,

---

180   Ginny and Ronnie Welch were long-time friends and active Republicans.

Wedemeyer, Chenault to testify – MacArthur couldn't come home but sent a magnificent statement – his prose reads like Shakespeare. Walter doesn't know anything else is going on. So I have to keep the home balance just as if he were out of the country.

Washington, D.C.   *Monday, April 5, 1948*

The idea I'm struggling with is how I can work into regular housekeeping and family raising the fantastic number of unexpected visitors and unscheduled events that push you around. It's unbelievable the number that called in the last twenty-four hours. Not but what all are good friends and I do want to see them.

Last week Walter was not home for dinner one night, Mary Lou was out every evening for dress rehearsals for *Pirates of Penzance* that her school gave, and had to be taken and fetched, we had Minneapolis friends in town who had kept our gals with their own five last summer, so I had to take them sightseeing to Mount Vernon, Arlington Cemetery, etc., and gave the father my seat to hear Truman address Congress, which thrilled him to go and me to stay away.

I invited a Minneapolis friend to go to the Congressional Club to hear Walter and at the last hour he decides he can't get away from writing the committee report, and sends instead the famous Jimmy Yen.[181] Dr. Yen did a bang-up job, spoke well, answered indirectly and in narrative form and subtly some of the things Walter would have hammered away at with a ten-ton sledgehammer. I was glad to hear him, but it still was embarrassing, and besides, Walter had ducked a speech there once before and at only thirty minutes' notice.

Well, Walter's so tired from running the world and I'm so tired running Walter (and his daughters) that we haven't either of us got good sense. I didn't realize I was worrying much about Walter till a Minneapolis friend said yesterday at dinner Walter told him he came in one night about 3:30 a.m. and I sat up in bed and said "You damn fool!" and lay down and went right on sleeping – and I never remembered a thing about it next morning.

Washington, D.C.   *Sunday, May 30, 1948*

Dearest Mother and Dad –

Walter is delighted that his WHO bill finally passed the House. He has put much time talking to men who might have opposed it – to join the World Health Organization.

Just heard the eleven o'clock news: "Congressman Walter H. Judd had use for his medical training today at Albright College, Reading, Pennsylvania when the bleachers collapsed as he was to give a commencement address. One hundred fifty were hurled to the ground but not seriously injured. Judd attended four women till ambulances arrived." Gosh, D'ya 'spose he gave the address after all that? If not will he collect a M.D.'s fee? Wish he'd call up and tell me!

The thing that is on Walter's mind now – and hence on mine too – is that he received a wire from Harold Stassen marked private & confidential and asking that Walter put his, Stassen's, name in

---

181   Jimmy Yen was a prominent Chinese educator known for his work in mass literacy and rural reconstruction.

nomination at the Republican Convention. This is a tremendous responsibility, for a convincing nomination speech might swing many undecided delegates for Stassen. Think of Walter this week as he tries to write his speech.

Washington, D.C.   *Sunday, July 4, 1948*

As to my first experience with a Convention, I'd just as soon it would be my last. I was depressed by the Hollywood influence – klieg lights, television, makeup, sweater girls, noisemakers, balloons, Indians, parades, bands, sirens, elephants, confetti, banners, and buttons. They say this Great American Circus element is part of our democratic process. But I rather tremble to think of our being Governed by Circus. If we do have to have the Circus, I wish it could carry the broadcasting while somewhere else in a quiet, cool room, delegates of intelligence and integrity could be thoughtfully expressing opinions, ironing out differences, and choosing a candidate. I'm told this is the essence of political naiveté. So be it!

Washington, D.C.   *Friday, September 25, 1948*

Mother & Dad went back to Florida Monday night. It was grand having them here, but I'm frank to admit that when they are mixed with the children it is a strain on me. I feel I have to protect each extreme in age from the other. I find Dad & Mother can take less of the noise and confusion and activity that seems to be the normal life of these healthy active girls.

En route to New York City   *Late September, 1948*

I'm on the train to New York for a meeting of the Congregational Board of Directors for our Middle Atlantic Association. Since Walter was to speak Saturday noon to NYC teachers, he said he'd come up Friday if I'd stay over. I'll window shop tomorrow, we'll go to dinner and then to see *As the Girls Go*. Getting ready to leave home for three days is a major undertaking. They have to discuss all their *possible* engagements, and I have to foresee contingencies and forestall most of them. Carolyn particularly is wanting to do weird things to show how independent and grown up she is. We're going to have to hold a tighter rein on her and therefore expect more explosions. No telling what she'll do, but we all know what she's expected to do.

Washington, D.C.   *October, 1948*

The girls seem to need attention more than ever, albeit a different kind now. Saturday Mary Lou went downtown by herself to get a wool dress, didn't want help from me, thank you. She lost her wallet with $25 and came home just sick, too upset to go back to counters where she had been looking. She and I went downtown, crowded or not, and by George we discovered it turned in at a shop where she had bought a sweater. She was lucky to get it back, money and all!

As for my going to Minneapolis for the campaign, there was a time in our negotiations when I told Walter I wouldn't come. The gals are too unpredictable, too unsure of their own dawning freedom. But Walter felt it was important, and Minneapolis friends arranged for a widow to come down and stay with the girls, so I'm going. Still have a million things to do before I leave...find new Sunday school teachers, make brownies for a tea, attend Deal Jr. High PTA meeting because

Carolyn is playing in the orchestra, go to a Scout Mother's planning session, type the list of rules and regulations for the girls to give the housekeeper, clear out my bedroom for her, etc.

Washington, D.C.   *Tuesday, November 16, 1948*

Dear Mother and Dad –

The last days in Minneapolis were beautiful as to weather, hectic as to engagements and depressing as to results.[182] Walter had predicted this result last June in his nominating speech for Stassen. He said, "The fall election is *not* in the bag. We cannot ignore the people's choice in June and expect the people's support in November, etc." Now he is extremely depressed at the thought that this new philosophy that has taken the country, that the Government will take care of everyone and do everything for you, is bound to end in disaster. It makes him ill to think of having to sit in Congress for two years and see the other side passing legislation, which he feels to the core of him is against the best interest, even the survival of our country and our world, and not be able to do anything but vote opposition. It is extremely frustrating to contemplate.

And now to have the China situation finally come to a climax – he thought last fall it would come within six weeks, but the brave Chinese have held on beyond belief – and to know how much our iniquitous China policy has had to do with their suffering and their disaster, and not being able to hope for a change to a constructive China policy in January under a new administration keeps him awake nights, and I mean literally. I've never known him so depressed, so beaten, so hopeless.

It sure is good to be back home where you can see some anchoring of the enduring values in life. But I admit that present-day insecurities beat hard on our children and make life difficult for them. Perhaps they will be stronger for the struggle, if they survive at all.

Washington, D.C.   *Sunday, January 30, 1949*

We couldn't get up much enthusiasm for the inaugural activities this week. So much money is being spent and everything else stops work – the girls have two days' holiday. We did attend the GALA in the armory the evening preceding and saw only two Republicans we knew. We thought the applause was feeble and sporadic and the show drawn out. We did enjoy the four bands that played the hour before the affair while the 5,000 people were assembling and we were waiting for the President's party – the Army, Navy, Air Force, and Marine Bands.

Inaugural Day was a beautiful, clear sunny day. Mary Lou & Carolyn made their own way to the two seats we had in the stands in front of the Treasury, right next to the White House, where they had a good view of the parade. Eleanor & I went down to the Capitol Plaza to seats in the section for Congressmen's families, and fortunately saw not only all the swearing-in ceremonies but had a good vantage point for the parade. Walter was in the Congress stands – but we all got cold feet and moved round, and I went in the office building for a while and drank hot coffee. Ellie was thrilled

---

182   Harry Truman, Democrat, won the presidential election over Thomas Dewey, Republican. Walter won his congressional election with 76,313 votes or 54 percent. Marcella Killen, DFL, had 65,113 votes or 46 percent.

with the whole thing, bands, costumes, floats, governors, drunks, cadets, aircraft display, crowds etc. The parade was late starting and long drawn out, and we munched sandwiches we'd taken along and survived till we got home at 5:30.

Mary Lou and friends attended fourteen sorority rush teas this afternoon.[183] It's a wild, stupid system, illegal in high school, and Walter says she may not join one but could attend the teas. So — !

Washington, D.C.   *Tuesday, February 21, 1949*

Walter and I went to a dinner for Dorothy Thompson last week.[184] Only twelve there, formal, beautifully served. The Chinese Ambassador, Italian Ambassador, the Robert Tafts were among those present. Dorothy was most interesting. Told us that she had recently discovered that she employed for five years a Communist lad as research worker on her staff. Says a year ago she would have sworn before all un-American Activities Committees that he was not a Commie, but now she knows he is. He resigned and is in Europe, blasting her for her writings.

Her conscience hurts her badly that she has been so duped, deceived, and used by the Reds when she is a supposedly intelligent and experienced and informed leader of public opinion. She has asked her writer friends if she should write this in her column, so people will know the insidiousness of the Reds, and they all tell her No, why be a dope and ruin your following, and besides, she said, five other leading columnists (she would not let us guess their names) came around and whispered to her that they also discovered Communists on their staffs. So I ask you what are we to believe of what we read in the newspapers? We all urged her to admit it in her column, and that might be the opening for others who have been so used to break down and admit it, too, and we can begin to get a clean break on this business.

I had been asked to be the Chairman of the Holyoke Alumnae Committee to sponsor a benefit concert of Burl Ives in March for the College Endowment Fund. Just as they were to sign the contract with the Concert Bureau they read in the *Saturday Review of Literature* that he is a Communist, so they cancelled the contract. Now it seems that the *Saturday Review* is about to retract its allegation, so the Bureau wants us to take on the concert again. But I've done some private investigating through "channels" (first time I ever called Walter H. Judd that, I'll bet)… I can't reveal the sources of my information to the Concert Bureau and they are mad that we are cancelling, so things are in a mess. Meantime College writes us they are glad we cancelled, as their faces are still red from having used Alger Hiss[185] last summer as their chief authority at their United Nations month on the campus. What a political climate we live in!

---

183   Mary Lou transferred to Woodrow Wilson High School for her sophomore year.

184   Dorothy Thompson was a prominent journalist. *Time* called her the second most influential woman in America after Eleanor Roosevelt.

185   Alger Hiss was a U.S. State Department official convicted in 1950 of perjury concerning his dealings with Whittaker Chambers who accused him of participating in a Communist espionage ring.

The China mess seems to be making a lot of people fighting mad.[186] If only they wouldn't expect Walter to do their fighting for them. They phone, write, and call here and at the office constantly. One dame phoned him from Los Angeles, then ranted that Walter simply must do something to rouse our government to action, because thousands of good people in this country loved China, and we must not let it down. She lived there thirty-five years. She's just one of scores. Saturday afternoon it was a lady doctor of some note who's just retired at sixty-seven from having been in China for years and knows whereof she speaks firsthand. Said she wrote a letter to the *New York Times* trying to give a more firsthand and balanced view of recent events, and had it returned to her: "Sorry we are unable to use this material." She made five speeches in one day this week.

Washington, D.C.   *Tuesday, February 22, 1949*

Dearest Mother & Dad –

The matter that has been taking my thought these weeks is Mary Lou's relation to the sorority system at the high school. Walter and I oppose them strongly and at first forbid her joining. But I felt the decision should be her own instead of ours, if she were to learn to make judgments, so we allowed her to do as she liked. Then followed days of uncertainty and debate with me and all her friends, until she was in a highly emotional state. I am sure the whole system is iniquitous. They do not have the experience to give them perspective, and cannot take *our* way in this process of their attaining selfhood. I put *many* hours on this, including visits to the school, talking to mothers & to school authorities, and hours of talks with Mary Lou. She was so upset she could think of nothing else, could not go to school one day, and I had to give her a sedative one night. Finally, she joined one and with her indecision relieved she is immediately herself, and happy.

But the strain, and the decision, have left me low in mind. Where have I failed, in bringing up the girls, to help them want to choose the *best*, instead of the *good*, to want to build their lives around the service motive instead of around selfish pleasure? Sororities are insignificant and trivial, with no purpose other than amusement and requiring more in monthly dues than she gives to the church. Has she learned no other values in her fifteen-years' association with this family? I can only hope that this is a temporary thing, that it looked glamorous and she had to try it out, but that she will see its faults and eventually leave it. Meantime I feel discouraged over a job poorly done. Only I am sure God can teach her, his own way and in his own time, so I'll have to trust.

Washington, D.C.   *Wednesday, March 9, 1949*

Saturday we attended a most interesting event; a lovely lunch (squab) in the Library of Congress for forty eminent (!?!) Minnesotans followed by a large reception and speech by Humphrey[187] to open the Library's exhibit of Minnesota, celebrating its centennial as a State. Humphrey's speech was researched and written largely by the Library and was excellent. All Humphrey did was to read it. He was in the men's washroom before time to begin, reading it over, and asked Walter how to

---

186   Chaing Kai-shek resigned January 21, 1949 as President of the Republic of China, after the advance of Communist troops against his military forces.

187   Senator Hubert H. Humphrey of Minnesota.

pronounce the Rune Stone.[188] But I'm wrong when I say *all* he did was to read it. He emphasized, interjected asides, interposed, till you could believe it was a most personal talk he had written just for you, mah friends! When there would be a cold statistic about the flour production of Minneapolis, he would serve it up with an "and I'm sure a former Mayor of Minneapolis will be pardoned a little personal pride in this figure." When it would mention North Dakota, he would add, "that State I love so well, where I was born." When it would mention the number of institutions of Higher Learning, he would add, "in one of which, Hamline, I was privileged to be a professor." Almost every phrase was twisted and turned to reflect honor on Humphrey. He is an FDR the Second, for sure!

I've been drawn into an editorial job under the National Federation of Women's Republican Clubs. We will get out a bi-monthly newsletter to local Clubs, so they can get a feeling of warmth and closeness to the Republican setup in Washington, and so they can get some true reporting on what goes on in Congress. I've written the lead article on the China Aid Bill. We have to oversimplify and condense. It's fun working with these intelligent ladies.

Washington, D.C.   *Tuesday, April 12, 1949*

The Atlantic Pact signing is the thing that's caused excitement on the Washington scene recently.[189] Saturday Walter and I set out about 5 p.m. all dressed up, to meet the Foreign secretaries in the Embassies. Went first to the Italian. From there to the huge British Embassy where Lady Frank was receiving alone since Acheson[190] had suddenly summoned Bevin and Ambassador Frank[191] for a conference. We floated round and drank tomato juice till the honored guests arrived. Then a few words with stout Mr. Bevin, and the charming Franks, and we were off to the French Embassy. Everyone was making the rounds and you kept bumping into friends either going in or coming out or parking cars or checking coats. The French party was more exclusive, perhaps because champagne is too expensive for a crowd. We visited with Premier Schuman, and the charming Madame Bonnet, Ambassador's wife. From there we checked in at the house to see that the girls were alive and kicking, and to get a fresh supply of Kleenex and nose drops (I'd been having a bad head and throat infection). Then on to a Chinese dinner at the home of General Pee, the military attaché. One Chinese just landed here had left Chiang Kai-shek only three weeks before, and said he was in excellent health since he'd rested a bit, was calm and poised and keen and interested – very little the picture of a defeated politician, I'd say. Bullitt was there and he got up a breakfast for nine the next morning in his home (Sunday) for Walter and these newly arrived Chinese, but what they talked about I never did learn.

Monday Walter and I got to go to the signing of the Pact Ceremonies, receiving engraved invitations because he is on the Foreign Affairs Committee. It seems the State Department issued invitations only to heads of committees in Congress and the Foreign Affairs Committee of each House, and all Congressmen omitted are pretty mad, feeling that if they wanted Congress to ratify it, they might at least have invited Congress to attend. They had to ask all the diplomats in town, and loads of

---

188   The Kensington Rune Stone is a carved stone, found in Western Minnesota in 1898, and is a source of ongoing controversy as some people claimed it was proof that Scandinavian explorers reached mid-America six hundred years ago.

189   The Atlantic Pact established the North Atlantic Treaty Organization (NATO) for mutual self-defense.

190   Dean Acheson was the Secretary of State.

191   Ernest Bevin was the Foreign Secretary for the United Kingdom. Oliver Frank was the U.K. Ambassador to the U.S.

State Department people, but they sure slipped on Congress. I felt the news cameras, television with its glaring klieg lights, and other paraphernalia of the media was too conspicuous and too noisy. The lights bothered the Foreign Ministers on the platform so that the Danish Minister put on dark sunglasses after he'd made his speech. Others held programs over their eyes. While we were waiting for Truman to come – he was not there for the sixty minutes of speeches by the twelve signers – the Marine Band played "I Got Plenty of Nuttin'" and "It Ain't Necessarily So," from *Harry & Bess*, as some wit said.[192] Can you imagine any more inappropriate titles of selections? It didn't take long to do the signing and the historic moment was over.

Washington, D.C.   *Monday, May 9, 1949*

Two days after we got back from Florida,[193] Walter phoned from Detroit and told me to hop a plane and come out for a couple of days. I thought he must be in an asylum but it seems he was in the Presidential Suite of the Book-Cadillac Hotel. I finished putting dinner on the table for the girls and caught an eight o'clock plane and was in Detroit before midnight. And was that suite something. But when you think that someone was paying $65 a day to put us there two days, and that someone was the Wayne County Medical Association – you wonder if they don't deserve to get socialized medicine! It was their hundredth anniversary, and they were celebrating with a dinner at which Walter was the speaker. It was fun having this little interlude with Walter.

I was home long enough to find out that the girls had done well entirely by themselves – the first time I'd left them *overnight* without someone in the house. Then I was off on the midnight train for my New Jersey Board meeting. Walter flew up Friday after Congress quit fighting on the Taft-Hartley bill and arrived in time for us to see *Where's Charlie*. Saturday got home in time to get dinner for the girls before we went out to a dinner some Chinese were giving…

Do you wonder the girls gasped, "Mother you're not going again!" when I told them Tuesday of the plans and menus and foods cooked ahead, so I could be gone Wednesday. I left before 8 to drive with a group from our church to a Congregational Conference in Dover, Delaware, getting home after 3 a.m., as I felt I'd better settle down and start raising children again.

Washington, D.C.   *Sunday, June 5, 1949*

The gals have been stepping out. Eleanor went down to Suffolk to visit a camp friend – her first trip alone on the train. Finishes sixth grade in two weeks. Carolyn's away this weekend too. Mary Lou went to a formal dance, complete with gardenia corsage. I had to fix her strapless formal; also alter a new dress she bought – her first real silk "tea" dress. The occasion was the sorority tea given for parents. I went and loved it. They had put time into fixing a garden and had lovely food – a good chance to meet the mothers. They looked so pretty – a bit wobbly in new high heels they are learning to walk on, but so young and fresh and enthusiastic.

---

192   The original operetta was *Porgy and Bess*, jokingly referred to here as *Harry and Bess*, to kid President Harry Truman and wife Bess.

193   The family took a week's spring break drive to see the Barbers.

Incidentally, Marcantonio, the one Labor Party Member in Congress and admittedly and openly pro-Communist, sat down beside Walter in Congress the other day and said, "It's too bad for you, Judd, but we've finally got China. And we'll have India, too, in a few months." Defeatist Christian Americans follow leftist propaganda and line of least resistance and set back immeasurably our Christian work and influence. What a defeat. Our only hope is our knowledge that God is not defeated. He will win ultimately, but man's stupidity makes the cost so great.

I am going to help out in the office during July… It will be cool down there with the air conditioning, and I will get to see Walter during our drive to and from work! Walter is taking us all to the baseball game tomorrow night – a great joy to the girls for they are real ball fans, and our Washington team has been doing right well this year.

Washington, D.C.   *Tuesday, July 5, 1949*

Monday night I went to Cleveland and the Christian Education Conference at Lakeside, Ohio. It was the first joint effort of our Congregational Churches with the Evangelical and Reformed Denomination with whom we will formally unite next June. I learned a lot. Four days like that can pep me up and start me off for a new year of Sunday school work.

Washington, D.C.   *Wednesday, September 28, 1949*

For the first time I have no one coming home to lunch. Eleanor is adjusting well to the new school – 1,100 pupils – perhaps because though only in seventh grade, she has Carolyn to advise her, and Carolyn does plenty of "advising." Mary Lou is working awfully hard, which won't hurt her, but is a change from last year when she mostly floated.

I'm busy with the fall clothes – having to make skirts, corduroy – Also a beautiful dark blue and black taffeta to make for Mary Lou. I've given up the Sunday school superintendency and am quitting on the Republican Newsletter… The demands of the girls are great these years.

Washington, D.C.   *Sunday, December 11, 1949*

I finally achieved my League of Women Voters trip to the U.N., with a large group of women and a carload of high school kids. Had a good briefing in the Security Council Chamber, a talk on the Human Rights Commission, and the plenary meeting of the Assembly was in session. I'd like to go back when there is time to study the intricacies.

Mary Lou had sorority meeting here Friday night, and I washed curtains and bed spreads as well as baked twenty dozen cookies. Even so we ran out of cookies and cokes – 4½ cases of twenty-four! The thirty girls met 7:30 to 8:30; then the boys start arriving for food & dancing, ping pong, cards. She thinks 160 were here – not all at once! The entire football team came, stayed the evening and were still singing Christmas Carols round the piano at 1:15 a.m. when I put them out – and it's really BIG STUFF when you land them. I'm glad it comes only once a year!

Washington, D.C.   *Monday, January 2, 1950*

Two things this past week were a real strain and have left Walter and me weary.

For Walter, it was the China situation, which he had been discussing with the Moyers who got back from China before Christmas, and with other Chinese recently come from there.[194] He decided to try to talk to President Truman again – never having been successful in these last two years' tries. They wouldn't let him see Truman, but with insistence, they let him talk to him on the phone, and Walter said it was the most discouraging thing that's happened for some time. Truman was belligerent, rude, shouted, interrupted, said he didn't want to hear anything more about the corrupt China regime who weren't even trying to fight and wanted us to do their dirty work for them, and on and on, leaving Walter without a chance to get across the points he wanted to make and even without a chance to finish one sentence. Walter feels Truman is dominated by his advisors and isn't given opportunity to listen to anything on the other side.

The thing that took a lot out of me is that our Church Youth Director, Mat Condo, resigned suddenly. I felt there was misunderstanding in the situation and insisted on going to see the minister and having it out with him, which was not easy. We persuaded Mat not to drop the whole year's work in the middle, for there is no one who could carry on with either of the young people's groups. Walter and I offered to pay the salary of a part-time office secretary till June, to allow Mrs. Condo to work with the youngsters full-time, which is her forte. In the course of all the "frank discussions" I think it was made clear to the minister that his manner and approach is not pleasing to the young people and that he had better leave them alone. Feelings have been hurt, everyone is tense, and I feel as if I'd been run through a street roller.

Miriam speaking to a group of youth at Cleveland Park Congregational Church

---

194   On December 10, 1949, Chaing Kai-shek retreated to Taiwan with his followers.

Washington, D.C.   *Wednesday, January 25, 1950*

Sunday Walter preached at Howard University Chapel and the whole family attended. The music was superb. It was a good experience for our girls to see so many fine negroes. They know only the kitchen variety in D.C.… Also good to hear their Dad speak.

Had to go to a Congressional lunch, a Sunday afternoon reception, and a Women's Colleges' meeting last week, and this week a formal dinner with Walter – so the social race is on. I like it much better before Congress opens and the activities start.

Washington, D.C.   *Sunday, February 12, 1950*

Eleanor and I went to New York for her twelfth birthday treat. Carolyn & Eleanor were in two plays at church given by young people to raise money for a movie projector. Some of the cast came here afterwards. Fortunately, I'd made a cake, which soon disappeared. I love having them come.

I've been up at school talking to the authorities about Carolyn and some of her escapades and companions, and feel more reassured about her final outcome with this particular group. The school is aware of a difficult situation and are working at it. I feel more confident in my attitude toward her, and I sense a response in her. Keep carrying us in your hearts.

Washington, D.C.   *Tuesday, March 7, 1950*

This last week has been as "society oriented" and untypical as any for a long time. Out to dinner six times & each time I've had to cook a dinner here for the girls before we go.

Walter has gone to New York tonight to speak at Riverside Church. He was terribly disappointed that his "books" bill was defeated last week, the one authorizing the use of over a million dollars that has been paid into the treasury for the work done in private industry by certain conscientious objectors during the war, to restock the destroyed or depleted libraries of Europe with new scientific and medical and professional texts. The objectors have asked to have the money used this way, but since the money is in the Treasury, there would have to be a bill authorizing it. The Congressmen are getting fed up with sending money to Europe, fearing we won't have enough for our expenses; and not being realistic about stopping the Communists, they stupidly vote down anything for Europe, even tho' this money cannot be used for general budget.

Mary Lou's sorority is putting on the 9 a.m. worship service at the Veterans' Hospital. They have been practicing their anthems every afternoon after school. I am interested to see what kind of things this group of girls do, and some of their ideas, for they have no adult supervision. I think Mary Lou has matured a lot, and seems to have a good evaluation of the good and bad in sororities, which she might never have achieved if she had not been allowed to join.

Washington, D.C.   *Tuesday, May 2, 1950*

Our headline news of this issue is that Walter is going to attend the World Health Organization meeting in Geneva as delegate from the House of Representatives. Walter was the one who got the

U.S. into WHO in the 79th Congress, and got the appropriations for it. This year the Democrats on Foreign Affairs want him to go, possibly as a bribe to stop beating on the State Department, and you know how successful they will be in that hope! I hope the change in pace and climate and in continent may give him a needed rest and pepping up!

Spring has come to Washington! I'm not meaning primarily the beautiful dogwood trees or the green everywhere. I mean partly that I'm having spring cleaning done. I'm meaning further that the spring influx of visitors and sightseers to the Capitol is in full swing.

Washington, D.C.   *Wednesday, May 17, 1950*

No letter from Walter, only postcards, but on Mother's Day he phoned from Geneva. Carolyn was disappointed, I think, that she couldn't hear the waves beating on the undersea cable, but they were thrilled to be talking to Switzerland, and I was thrilled to be talking to Walter! He is due back in Boston May 24 to speak to the Baptists' National Convention.

Washington, D.C.   *Thursday, May 25, 1950*

Walter came home completely exhausted as he brought a six-year-old German girl over on the plane with him for some Americans who are going to adopt her. I had to laugh at him recounting his adventures, saying "You really have no idea, Miriam, how lively a six-year-old youngster can be, and how many times a minute she can ask *why*."

Washington, D.C.   *Wednesday, June 21, 1950*

Reunion was a great deal of fun.[195] I refrained from calling my classmates "the girls," and we laughed with each other over the three Bs: Bifocal, Bulges, and Bridgework; and we got swelled up with pride over the achievements of some of our number who told stories of working with the Czech underground during the war, or being in the Manhattan Project, and doing cancer assays on rats surrounded by Top Secret Documents, or being the only woman department head in ECA in Washington.[196] The girls as a group were nicer than I'd remembered them – or could it be I'm more tolerant and less priggish than when I graduated, I wonder?… Ah to be young again!

Mary Lou went for a ten-day house party to a Maryland beach with her sorority, and after the other gals & Walter left,[197] I drove over to a quiet little inn in the country outside Annapolis and slept and ate and slept again and sat in the sun on a tall bluff and watched the sea craft and knitted and read & didn't speak to a soul for two days.

Hotel Leamington, Minneapolis, Minnesota   *Friday, July 21, 1950*

Tomorrow is the opening of the Aquatennial and the big parade. The girls are to ride with us in the open convertible with Walter's name on the banners. I imagine they'll get a kick out of it – I'd gladly miss the conspicuousness of it. We're taking the girls to the Aqua Follies – a gorgeous outdoors spectacle.

---

195   Miriam was celebrating her twenty-fifth college reunion at Mount Holyoke College.
196   The State Department's Bureau of Educational and Cultural Affairs.
197   Carolyn and Eleanor were off to camp Danworthy in Walker, MN and Walter to Minneapolis.

Washington, D.C.   *Sunday, September 24, 1950*

Mother is back in her house in Florida.[198] She was improved enough to travel, and Dad needed to get back to his home and friends. An R.N. went with us on the train, and everything was as comfortable as possible, but all the moving was difficult and confusing for her, and the heat in Florida plus a small hospital room she went to for a few days didn't help. I wish I could have seen her safe at home. I wonder if she will ever be able to do anything for herself again.

Leamington Hotel, Minneapolis, Minnesota   *Saturday, October 28, 1950*

Still goin', but I won't say "strong." Frankly, I'm weakening a little. Two mornings I stayed in bed till noon, too bushed to push. And I'm not going half as hard as Walter, with all the speeches he has to do each day, and the interviews and the pressures and the business with boys wanting military exemptions and auto dealers wanting terms liberalized and people wanting rent controls lifted and on and on. He's tired, too, but he still is hitting hard and answering the questions about how did we get into the Korea mess and how are we going to stop the Russians, and are we going to seat the Communist Chinese in the U.N., etc. How he does it I frankly don't know.

We don't cross our opponent's path too often but today she and Walter were together… Walter spoke on policy. She raved and ranted against Walter, yelled and said in answer to a thoughtful question that the questioner didn't really make sense and was a lot of "hogwash" and she wouldn't answer it. Last time she appeared on a platform with Walter they asked her about the Brannan Plan[199] and she answered she wasn't a farmer but just a housewife, and they really hooted at that one.

You'd think such a person wouldn't have any chance at all. But somehow the public likes to see women wrastlers– besides, labor is working her, and she is pedaling their papers. She is an incessant worker and has rung more doorbells and shaken more hands and passed out more flyers than there have been words in Walter's speeches. I'm cynical enough to believe we have about an eighth grade mentality in the electorate, and they will vote more on the basis of a personal contact and smile than on the basis of a reasoned intellectual approach. So anything can happen!

Another row has been with the negro press where a sportswriter said that it looked like victory for Killen because many Republicans were sore at Judd for voting against the Marshall Plan, Point Four, and voting to reduce aid to Korea!!![200] Walter wrote protesting the falsification of his stand, and the embarrassed editor gave him a front-page spread for explanation & apology. Meantime we had one meeting in a negro home with neighbors invited in to talk to Walter; and we have another meeting next week in a negro cafe called DREAMLAND, where the proprietor is giving us the use of his place for all the free advertising it will bring him.

This week I made my one speech of the campaign to a group led by Mrs. Pollard who was so nice in taking our girls in for a couple of weeks after camp when I couldn't get out here.

---

198   On August 5, 1950, Miriam's mother suffered a stroke in the Judd home in Washington, D.C.
199   Secretary of Agriculture Charles Brannan's plan was to provide federal support for farm income while allowing the prices of agricultural commodities to be determined by market forces.
200   All of these reports on Walter's positions were incorrect and the exact opposite of his actual votes.

Leamington Hotel, Minneapolis, Minnesota   *Monday, November 6, 1950*

It's about over but the shouting. We've had a couple of days with six meetings! Friday he had two radio broadcasts on two different stations on two different subjects at 7:15 and 9:15 p.m., with a meeting in between. I drive him while he keeps the light burning inside the car and works on the manuscript, or his notes for the next meeting; while he speaks, I grab the manuscript and slash some more, and count lines & insert transition words; then he's thru, and we're off to the races again. Sometimes while he speaks I grab a carton of coffee and a ham sandwich at a drug store and have it for him to eat while I'm driving to the next spot. I feel breathless…

Last Saturday we relaxed a bit. Went to the football game. Then to a homecoming reception of a couple of hundred and saw many friends. After that we went to the Symphony and had a chance to hear Piatagorsky on the cello, and it was relaxing. Sunday he had two speeches…

He has one radio broadcast tonight, which he's working on and I'm waiting to type, and one speech with veterans. Tomorrow we'll vote, & he will see people who have waited with personal matters till after the campaign. I'll sort the office stuff and prepare things to be sent back to Washington. In the evening we'll have a big open house in our volunteer headquarters, with coffee and sandwiches and doughnuts all evening and radio and returns and general excitement. Wednesday we have a luncheon of our inside committee and workers, and leave for Rochester where he will speak in the evening and have some spots on his face burned off next morning. On to Milwaukee for a Thursday night speech, and home by Saturday, driving our car. Walter is off Monday for a week of speeches in Maine, one a day, a rest for he can relax in between times.

Washington, D.C.   *December, 1950*

The election was gratifying after all the hard work everyone put into it.[201] There was a larger vote in most wards than is customary in an off-year election, which shows that people are concerned. We were terribly tired, but enjoyed our drive home. The family had twenty-four hours together before Carolyn had to return to her school.

I went down to Florida to see Mother, whom I found comfortable and glad to see me. She is cared for exactly as a six month old is. She visits along speaking with more vigor and clear enunciation than she did, but many of her ideas are fanciful. She is a good, happy patient. Dad clings with dogged determination or sublime faith to the idea that she is going to get well.

Returned to D.C. Thanksgiving Day, and we went to a hotel for our family dinner. Then after only five hours in town, Walter and I left for Minneapolis. We had decided that for the first time we would give a reception for all the faithful block workers and doorbell ringers and members of our committee. We'd sent out 1,400 invitations to an informal open house in the ballroom of the Calhoun Beach Club, had a string trio play, had a caterer supply a pretty table with flowers and candles and

---

201   Walter won the election with 71,243 votes or 60 percent. Marcella Killen, the DFL candidate, had 48,759 votes or 40%. Grace Carlson, the Socialist candidate, had 1,323 votes or .1 percent.

sandwiches and fancy small cakes and coffee, and girls to serve. We didn't reach the Leamington Hotel till about 2:30 in the morning after engine trouble with the plane in D.C.

That day I shopped for a new dress, attended a Judd committee luncheon, got my hair done, and we managed to get to the reception only ten minutes late, without dinner. Got the reception line formed and proceeded to shake hands and try to remember names and faces for two solid hours while 1,100 folks passed by. Then both Walter and I made remarks, thanking them for all their work and emphasizing that we were all in this cause of better government and a better world together, explaining that this reception was put on not from campaign funds but from the generous and unexpected check the *Reader's Digest* had sent Walter for the article of his they had condensed. Then we mingled and shook hands, and it was after twelve before they were all gone, after a very good evening. Boy, were my feet tired!

Washington, D.C.   *Wednesday, December 6, 1950*

Dear Betty and Helen —[202]

Last week I was at the constituting convention in Cleveland of the new National Council of Churches – it was thrilling. Everyone felt the enormous significance of our unifying direction in the Protestant group of the Church when the rest of the world was pretty well divided up in actions and convictions and disturbances, etc. The great procession of voting delegates the opening morning marching singing to their places, in academic robes, was most impressive. I rented a gown and a Columbia University Master's hood, first time I'd ever had one on.

Washington, D.C.   *Sunday, January 7, 1951*

Dear Gals (My College Round Robin) –

For the sake of the girls, I could have wished that we might have been defeated this fall and moved from Washington. It is not my idea of a place to raise children, from point of view of schools, recreation, social life. Walter said it was the first time he had really wanted to be reelected, for things are so horribly bad in the Far East, and he has background that others can't have and is a fighter, and they need people who will keep persisting that we get a proper foreign policy. Many of the men who came when Walter did, fine people, are too tired bucking the opposition and politics and bureaucracy. A number were so frustrated that they didn't run this year.

Washington, D.C.   *Thursday, May 3, 1951*

My meeting at the Congressional Club went beautifully. Our Minneapolis Mail Carriers quartet were nice, fresh, wholesome-looking fellows, sang without accompaniment, had a selection of songs they dedicated "to the ladies from Texas" (Tumbleweed) "to the ladies from Carolina" (Carolina in the Morning) "to the Irish ladies present" (Galway Bay) "to all the ladies" (When You Wore a Tulip). Dozens of ladies told me they loved this program as a change from the more stuffed-shirt kind of things we'd had. The quartet kept calling to each other, "I wish the boys back home could see us

---

202   Two of Miriam's college classmates.

now," or "I sure will hate to go back and put on the old sack and start pounding the pavement." Walter had them over for lunch at the Capitol.

I've been to the Annual Luncheon of the YWCA where over 700 members and friends shook hands with Mrs. Truman & Barkley.[203] I was elected that day to the Board of Directors of the YWCA of D.C. for three years.

Washington, D.C.   *Friday, June 8, 1951*

This week I was in Evansville, Indiana, with Walter, and now he is on his way to England. He left today with sixteen Representatives, half and half Democrat and Republican, and home in eleven days. The idea is to see what Eisenhower thinks is needed for the defense funds in Europe. They are going to hold hearings soon for legislation on this, but Ike didn't want to come to the U.S. to testify, and I think he's smart. So this was set up instead, and Walter was pressured into going. He will miss four commencement addresses and receiving two honorary degrees; he will miss Mary Lou's graduation. He hasn't been over in nearly four years and this will help dispel the accusation that he is interested only in China, and will give him good, fresh material for his speeches.

Leamington Hotel, Minneapolis, Minnesota   *Wednesday, June 27, 1951*

Dear Folks –

I am in Minneapolis – put Carolyn and Eleanor on their camp bus this morning and glad I have four days to myself – except for dentist appointments and dinners with friends – before I head for Florida for three weeks helping with Mother and cheering up Dad.

Walter got back from Europe the 19th and left three days later. I heard little about the trip. They were kept *very* busy, leaving their hotels at 7 a.m. to be taken to inspect bases or installations. He brought me the most gorgeous antique silver tea and coffee service from London – something I have long wanted.[204] I am delighted to have this "thing of beauty" for my sideboard.

As for Mary Lou's graduation activities, even the continuous rain couldn't dampen the festivities. The night of the Senior Prom it poured great guns. I attended in evening clothes, as a chaperone. I had fun watching the youngsters and examining the dresses. I had made Mary Lou's. A crowded Sunday followed: recognition of the high school graduates at church (and Eleanor joining the church), arrival of my niece from Florida to share Mary Lou's bedroom for two weeks and in her wake several Amherst boys who flowed in and out of our house at all hours the next days, the baccalaureate service at the big Cathedral in the afternoon.

Ellie pushed in a long-promised "slumber party" for six of her friends. It is a form of torture I do not especially relish but they adore it. They all slept (?) on the recreation room floor on mattresses and shrieked much of the night because of a few water bugs that shared the floor with them. Eleanor said they were the thing that gave her party a flavor and made it memorable!

---

203   Jane Hadley Barkley was the wife of Vice President Alben Barkley.
204   Miriam mentioned a silver tea service in an earlier letter to Walter, dated January 18, 1935 in China.

Washington, D.C.   *Saturday, September 29, 1951*

Dear Family –

The day before we left for San Francisco, August 30, was the signing here in D.C. of the Philippine Mutual Defense Pact. I was frantically getting the house running after a partially closed-up summer, getting the girls' trunks and duffels back from camps, fixing fall suits and hats to take on the trip, so I didn't go to the ceremony at noon with Walter. Gertrude was glad to use my ticket and to be in on all the ceremonial doings.[205]

Walter had done more pushing and fussing about this Philippine thing than anyone. He wanted them in on the Pacific Pact signing in San Francisco, but this is the best they could get thru the State and Defense Departments. Walter got invited to the President's stag State luncheon for eighteen at the Blair House following the signing. Here an amusing incident occurred. Senator Conally, head of Senate Foreign Relations, had a couple of cocktails too many before lunch and was quite talkative, if not belligerent. He started in to attack Walter, across the table from him, as soon as they were seated. "Weren't you a missionary once?" "Yes." "Why'd you come back here?" "Because I thought Congress needed a little missionary work!" He didn't like that. "Well I was in China once, and I didn't get a very good impression of the missionaries." "Why not?" "They had too many servants." "Well, any of the missionaries would be glad to have traded some of their servants for your services. You pay for plumbing, electricity, telephone, etc. They pay for servants to do those things." "Well, I don't like the churches taking the money we hardworking people give for the Chinese and using it to pay for your servants." "They don't. We paid for our servants out of our salary." "How much did you get?" "Fourteen hundred dollars a year."

Conally had gotten louder and more belligerent and the whole table had stopped and were listening. Walter tried to stop the discussion, but Truman kept egging him on, saying when he made some dirty crack about Chiang Kai-shek, "You aren't going to take that lying down, are you Walter?" and urging Walter to answer Conally's attacks. Walter was embarrassed to be the center of the conversation, when the President of the Philippines was on Truman's right, and the Ambassador, and our Ambassador to them, and other dignitaries including Acheson and Dulles.[206] But when he was leaving the luncheon and shook hands with Truman, Harry said to him, "Gosh, Walter, I was so g.d. glad Conally was taking it out on you. I was terrified he'd start in on the President of the Philippines." High-caliber men guiding the Foreign Relations of our country, what? So Truman was deliberately egging Walter on, to save America's face with our Philippino guests.

Next morning we all went to the Airport in time for a ten o'clock plane the State Department had chartered and forty-nine of us went on it, mostly State Department functionaries, military advisors. Also aboard were the Achesons, the Dulleses, the Cowans (our Ambassador to the Philippines), and other Senators and Congressmen, and Chip Bolan who is the Russian interpreter for our State Department, and who was the one who had to translate Roosevelt's promises to Stalin at Yalta, which nearly made him sick when he heard them.

---

205   Gertrude, Walter's sister, was visiting and stayed with the daughters while Walter and Miriam were in San Francisco.
206   Dean Acheson was the Secretary of State 1949-1953. John Foster Dulles was the Secretary of State from 1953-59.

The plane had hardly taken off when Acheson came forward from the back, greeted me cordially, said he'd asked the pilot if he were prepared to make the supreme sacrifice and take "all of us" (meaning "big shots") out of public life together, and the pilot had told him he thought that was… beyond the call of duty – ha, ha, ha! Then he proceeded to compliment Walter on his patience and good humor and quiet handling of Conally at the President's lunch – and later Dulles and Cowan did the same at separate times, so I guess it was a noteworthy event!…

We were quietly reading up front, when one of the State Department fixers came to invite us back to drink with the Hi Hats. We went, so as not to insult them, but we didn't drink. I found myself the only lady around a table with Acheson, Dulles, Cowan, and Bolan, and they got telling jokes about previous boners Conally had pulled with crowned heads of Europe and elsewhere and it got terribly hilarious and matey and we were one big happy family, and I don't see how Walter can ever again call for Acheson's resignation, but he says he can!

We landed at Reno for re-fueling. As Walter and I stood watching, Acheson walked over to visit with us in a fascinating, friendly manner. The plane was called, we walked slowly back to the steps together, photographers ran up to ask for a picture, Acheson said, "Here, take me with Mrs. Judd," then Dulles came along and joined in and a couple of others and there I was photographed with all these dignitaries – I was sure roaring inside. Dulles kidded me and said he'd bet Reno never saw one woman get so many men before!

We came down in San Francisco before dusk, and cool it was. After a session with newspaper and photographers – they kept asking us wives weighty questions as: "Do you intend to attend the sessions, or shop, or sightsee?" – we roared into the city in official cars with a sirening motorcycle escort and gaping crowds, to the Palace Hotel where the American delegation was housed.

The first official function was the signing of the Pacific Defense Pact with Australia and New Zealand at 3:30 on Saturday. We received instructions from the State Department to be in the lobby of the hotel at 2:51(!) and what order we were to ride in to the Presidio. They sure had everything arranged like clockwork, but we went sirening thru a coupla the red lights too fast, evidently, and had to pause about 2¼ minutes outside the Presidio to allow for our simultaneous entrance with the Australian and New Zealand officials. What a lot of red tape and protocol in officialdom! Acheson presided, the speeches were short, the Australian and New Zealand Ambassadors signed, followed by Acheson and a couple Senators, while Walter and several other alternate delegates, appointed by Truman, looked on. Then we went to a reception…

There was an 8 p.m. formal dinner for several hundred Australian, New Zealand, and U.S. delegates and friends, with us "signers and alternates and wives" at the head table. Again Acheson presided and the talks were informal and witty. Sir Carl Berendsen, the New Zealand Ambassador is a salty and vociferous guy, kidded Australia in his speech, and the Australian Ambassador threw back a few tart remarks in good humor, and when Acheson got up right after this he said soberly "I can see that this mutual defense pact has come in the nick of time" and brought down the house with laughter.

When Dulles spoke he said he'd been worried to death ever since this afternoon, as he made his living for thirty-four years urging people never to sign till they knew what they were signing yet he sat down and put his signature on a blank page and never turned back to see what it was he had signed. It was a delightful evening. Tuesday started the meetings of the American Delegation to the Japanese Peace Treaty Signing.

Washington, D.C.   *Monday, October 15, 1951*

Dear College Classmates –

The chance to go to San Francisco with Walter for ten days was a thrilling event. I went along but not at Government expense. Being in on the sessions of the Peace Conference in the Opera House, where each of the fifty-one countries had an hour to express its feelings about the treaty, and then to hear the dignified speech of the head of the Japanese delegation as he accepted the responsibilities of Japan's rejoining the brotherhood of nations, it was really moving.

I enjoyed the hot sessions, listening dutifully with my ear phones to the translators, while Russia tried to insist on late amendments to the treaty; while she tried to postpone the conference till China should be invited and their delegates arrive; when Poland refused to sit down when his time had expired and defied Acheson, and Acheson called the next speaker, Britain, to the microphone who spoke for a few moments in concert with the loud-expostulating Polish delegate shouting about free speech; when Gromyko walked out, probably for a smoke, but Poland and Czechoslovakia not being sure of their signals, hesitatingly got up after him, and all three returned in about five minutes, perhaps having been given "instructions." It was dramatic, and Acheson with his cold, calculating, quiet manner was exactly the right person to preside, where nerves were jittery over what Russia might do to try to break up the conference.

I loved it when Sir Carl Berendsen, with keen wit and insight, laid it pretty straight on the line, after Gromyko had put out a lot of poppycock about American imperialism and our starting the third world war and about his coming to the conference under false pretenses thinking they could still make a treaty of peace. Berendsen said if U.S. was so imperialistic, wasn't it strange that New Zealand, a comparatively small country with small defense wasn't in the slightest degree afraid of our intentions; and if Russia had come there under false pretenses, it must be her own fault for she had had exactly the same chance as every other country to read the preliminary draft of the treaty, to make modifications and amendments and suggestions and to approve the later draft, and if she didn't like it, she didn't need to stay. He sure got wild applause. I was sitting close to Gromyko and he didn't even bat an eye.

Washington, D.C.   *Saturday, November 3, 1951*

Most of my time recently – except for a siege with flu, has been spent in my Red Cross Class. I'm hoping to do volunteer work one day a week in their Home Service Division. We'll have twenty-two hours of training before we get our pins and uniforms and become "Social Welfare Aides," carrying our own caseloads. About thirty-five in the class. The work will be entirely with service men and their families, case work, counseling, helping them fill out forms for benefits and compensation, making or refusing emergency loans or grants, securing health and welfare reports for local doctors when emergency leaves are requested for family illness, etc. There's a lot to learn about Army regulations and Red Cross procedures.

My *big event* was meeting the Princess and Philip at the British Embassy reception. Six of us "recess widows" went together. We were in sight of Princess Elizabeth about fifteen minutes. She looked tired but her smile for each guest was genuine and radiant. She's petite, 5 feet 2 and small-boned, dainty. I hadn't heard much about her dimples in the press, but they seem prominent. People were shaking her hand, not stopping to speak, the British women curtsying, the names of each guest called out by the Aide to the Ambassador, Sir Oliver Franks, first in line. When the Aide called my name, Sir Oliver said as he shook hands, "I'm so sorry your husband can't be with you today." Then he turned to the Princess next to him and said "Congressman Judd is one of the better known and most useful of the Congressmen." Holding my hand she said, "I'm sorry not to meet him. Where is he?" I answered, "Back in his district in Minnesota." By this time Philip, standing next to her, joined in the conversation with "Oh, Minnesota. We know. We went right by there when we were in Winnipeg. It's sort of up there at the north, isn't it?" I said yes, and how clever he was to know our geography and he said, "Oh, well, I remember hearing about it when I went past there."

Then I went out of the line to where my Congressional friends were frantic to know what the royalty and I were so chummy about as to hold up the whole line. Well, if that poor dear had to stand there and shake 1,400 hands I guess a break in the monotony helped, and she sure knew how to say and do the right thing when anyone gives her an opening, to say nothing of Philip's quick uptake. The British Ambassador I consider to be a man of rare discernment and judgment!! I told this incident to the gals when I got home and after I'd gone upstairs, I heard Ellie saying, "Mother's lucky to have such a famous husband, isn't she?" Sometime I'll tell her it wasn't luck, it was hard work!

Washington, D.C.   *November 22, 1951*

Thanksgiving Day – Walter is in Strasburg – will be in Paris next Saturday hoping to see Eisenhower. Yesterday I cut his weekly fifteen-minute broadcast record for Minneapolis use, making it an interview with the Congressman's wife, about official functions, meeting the Princess, luncheon for twenty-four when the State Department officially farewelled the Indian Ambassador, Madame Pandit, and unofficial functions like Red Cross work, being on the YWCA Board, chatty and feminine for a change from Walter's weekly official reports.

Carolyn's and my Armistice Day weekend colleges' trip expanded to include Walter and Eleanor, which made it much fun. Mary Lou is fine, loves her friends and surroundings.[207] We went to Amherst to a football game interspersed with a trip to Smith. Sunday while Walter went off to make two speeches we went to church and Sunday dinner with Jim McClure (Betty Lou's fiancée) and drove to Wellesley. A trip like that relaxes Walter more than anything, and it's good for the gals to see him occasionally.

---

207   Mary Lou was a freshman at her mother's alma mater Mount Holyoke College.

– Private Writing –

OBJECTIVE STUDY OF FAMILY AND PERSONAL RELATIONSHIPS – WHJ –
MBJ –[208]

Contributions Walter has made to my life for which I am deeply and
continuously appreciative and grateful:
Name – fame – position
Children
Physical satisfaction
Zest – joy – enthusiasm
Wide acquaintances
Travel – adventure
Money – possessions – security
Intellectual stimulus

I. Lacks in our life that occasionally rise to thwart, frustrate, or depress me:
    Companionship on my level
    Evidence of personal attention or affection
    Development and discipline of the children
    Interest in the house, physical equipment, etc.

II. Suggested minimum requirements that would help to remove above:
    <u>Once a month</u> – an evening together with "the arts" – play, concert,
    music, lecture, something creative
    <u>Once a week</u> – an hour with the children – dinner together, a game,
    reading aloud, listening to their interests, a movie, a trip, something
    especially theirs
    <u>Once daily</u> – "a kind word"

III. My estimate of my responsibilities or duties, which I should like to have
     Walter number in order he considers them important for our happiest
     and most useful life, underlining those most important from his point of
     view:
     <u>Housekeeper</u> – care of house and grounds, repair and upkeep;
     employment of help; food, planning, purchase, preparing; clothes,
     cleaning, repairing, making, buying; finances
     <u>Mother</u> – nurture of the children – reading aloud, music lessons,
     dancing lessons, educational trips, concerts, supervision of school
     and Sunday school, physical health
     <u>Wife</u> – satisfaction of physical demands; attendance at dinners,
     meetings, other engagements, entertaining his guests; assisting with
     official or professional work
     <u>Individual</u> – self-development: reading, lectures, church, clothes,
     beauty parlor, friends
     <u>Community demands</u> – requests for speeches, individual and personal
     correspondence, dinner engagements, Red Cross, PTA

---

208   There was no date for this private writing. It was most likely from the early 1950s, as Miriam mentioned the Red Cross.

> *IV. Specific suggestions from Walter as to actions, activities, habits, restraints, processes of thought, etc., in which I could indulge or toward which I could work, that would, from his point of view, definitely make our life together happier and more useful*

Washington, D.C.   *December, 1951*

Dear Mother and Dad –

The girls are taking more responsibility and asked to fix the stockings. They took charge of all the day-before-Christmas excitement of answering phones and doorbells and marketing and arranging gifts under the tree, etc. That allowed me to work at Red Cross all day, for the paid staff there was on vacation, and there were emergency requests for aid: servicemen just granted holiday leave and no funds for transportation, wives with delayed allotment checks and no funds to supply Christmas dinner. The girls begin to get a feeling for their privileged position when I tell them bits about the cases I have. Walter even rose to the occasion by inviting us all out to dinner. I think Walter was a little proud showing off his three beautiful blessed brats, all taller than I now. Then to the airport to get Gertrude and Jim.

Christmas morning, Car & El fixed scrambled eggs and cereal, coffee, fruit & toast, then called on the phone – some trick way whereby they can make the upstairs phone ring, about 8:30, a professional-sounding voice said: "This is room service. Your breakfast will be up in two minutes." And it was!! All the family together in our room on Christmas morning.

The gift opening went all morning, while we kept smelling the eighteen-pound gift turkey cooking. We all went to the movies together in the early evening and came home to eat turkey sandwiches and listen to some of our new Brahms symphonies and Wagner music on our new three-speed victrola, and an occasional boogie-woogie thrown in!

The rest of the week was spent in many social engagements for the girls. We did some sale shopping and some sewing. One night Car & Mary Lou had an open house and we baked 625 cookies. At 1:45 a.m. kids were still playing ping pong in the recreation room with a coal fire glowing and the victrola blaring, when I called down and gently suggested good night. Walter was in Chicago. I doubt if he'd have been as patient, or lenient, or do you call it stupid?

Orlando, Florida   *Saturday, January 5, 1952*

Mother had another severe stroke on December 29 and I came down on the overnight train New Year's Eve, having worked all day on emergency financial aid cases at the Red Cross, and having had a hurried-up birthday dinner for Mary Lou.

Perhaps she [Mother] hears and knows we are there but she is unable to respond, and all her movements and expressions seem to be random. It is a good sign that she is as well as this after a week. I will go back to D.C. by plane tomorrow, for Walter has been able to keep his eye on home things, but next week Congress starts and he'll be all agog. Ellie starts school Monday but has been in charge of housekeeping during my absence. Carolyn started school the second, Mary Lou went back to college the third, all without my help. They are growing up.

Well, we're into another election year and I shall likely be attending the Republican Convention in Chicago in July, where we expect to nominate Eisenhower. I don't look forward to these next months. I'm a pacifist by nature and have enough ostrich blood in me to wish to find a wide desert to hide my head in and not come up for air until December. Walter assures me that is not the way to preserve our freedoms or our democracy, and I tell him I'm lucky to have a husband who'll fight hard enough for us both. But he wants me present when he fights.

I met Churchill at a reception for 200 given by Acheson. His speech before Congress was "a remarkable example of fancy figure skating on thin ice" as one of the Senators said. I told Walter I'd be glad if I could use the English language the way Churchill does.

Washington, D.C.   *Easter Sunday, April 9, 1952*

Mary Lou was here ten days beginning March 28, and she had a classmate for a coupla days and two others for sightseeing one day. While Mary Lou was home I had access to the car only by petition. Two days she and I went shopping, and then I had altering to do. Also got started on her bridesmaid's dress for Betty Lou's wedding.

Walter still lives here, I think, as I see his shirts in the wash each week. He seems to be busy making short sprints outa here evenings to speak for Eisenhower. I have attended a couple of official dinners with him, but at one of these he had to duck out before the steak to be on television for Eisenhower and got back in time for the speeches, so we finished up the evening with bacon and eggs on the kitchen table in evening clothes. They drink so long before these things that Walter and I never plan to go till an hour after the time we're invited.

Chicago, Illinois   *Saturday, July 12, 1952*

Hi, Folks:

The tumult and shouting dies, the captains and kings depart. We will be pulling out shortly, driving to Minneapolis. Walter is sorting papers and telegrams – he got over thirty. It was a great convention. I'm glad I was here, after all my previous remarks about preferring not to come. I attended practically all the sessions, and they were uneven, sometimes wildly exciting and tense, sometimes long-drawn-out and boring. Got a lot of knitting done. Had a good seat, close to the platform where I looked over the heads of the huge Press section right to the speakers. Walter sat with the Minnesota people on the floor.

To me the most exciting session was not the nominating evening with the carefully planned "spontaneous" demonstrations but the evening the report of the credentials committee was presented, and after debate by the delegates they voted to throw out the recommendations of the credentials committee to seat the pro-Taft delegates in Texas and Georgia, and instead seat the pro-Eisenhower ones. It was this which probably turned the tide for Ike, so people felt strongly about it. The Taft people had put out reams of dirty stuff and untruths to mislead the public. It was unbelievable the scurrilous printed stuff that was in our mailbox at the hotel every time we got in. But it backfired, for even their own best folks were ashamed of their vile attacks. Everyone says that it was Walter's summing up of the case at the end of the debate on seating the Texas delegates that was the high point of the convention, and I'm perfectly willing to agree. It came at 12:30 at night, when people were tired. It came after Senator Dirksen had spoken in favor of seating the pro-Taft delegates, calling on the Bible and the Flag and quavering his voice and putting out pure corn that disgusted almost everyone.

Then Walter was introduced and started wading in for the brief seven minutes he had, and suddenly the place was quiet – at least comparatively! – And everywhere they listened, and gave him a huge burst of applause at the end. And we haven't moved two feet anytime since then but what perfect strangers come up and shake his hand, from the girl at the drugstore who waits on us for our 2:30 a.m. suppers, to several taxi drivers, the maitre d'hôtel at the Blackstone, and dozens of people we pass on the streets who just yell, "Hi, Congressman, great speech!" The delegates and gallery people have stopped him with comments, and someone put out the idea of making him Vice President and his friends started kiddingly calling him the Veep.

That was a great night when the American people, the delegates, stood up and said we're not going to be kicked around by a few stuffed shirts who try to control this party, and when we get the facts, we're going to be able to tell right from wrong. Great country, America.

Walter's other speech was an anti-climax. Not that it wasn't an excellent speech and things that needed saying; but the first one came bursting out because he was so mad, and was unscheduled and unwritten and unrehearsed. He's had responses galore on this second speech too.

I don't intend to give a play-by-play account of the sessions. After the enormous excitement and joy of the balloting for Eisenhower, we dashed in town – and when Walter talked with Brownell (Ike's manager) about the silly rumors about him and the Vice Presidency, Brownell said, go on over to Ike's apartment and congratulate him. So we went.

We had been there the first night when he received the Minnesota delegation in his sitting room to answer their questions on his policies and ideas. He and Mamie had been cordial to me. When someone asked about foreign policy and he talked a few minutes about cooperation, etc., he suddenly stopped and said, "Here I go on talking about foreign policy with Walter Judd sitting right here. But I know if he disagreed with me he'd say so." And Walter said, "I sure would."

When we went over to the Blackstone Hotel where he was staying about an hour after he'd received the nomination and had returned from Taft's apartment where he had asked for his support in the campaign, you can imagine the mobs 'round the place. We pushed in and finally got an elevator to 5th floor where his headquarters were. No one wanted to let us in, but suddenly someone who knew Walter froze onto him and shoved us both thru all the security folks and into a back bedroom where Senator Carlson (Kansas) his closest advisor, was sitting with a couple of the speechwriters and inside guys. Everyone was grinning completely round their heads. Carlson said, "The General isn't seeing anyone, but he'll see the Judds," and he took us past a locked door with huge security men, to the sitting room where Ike and his five brothers were watching the baseball game on TV.

He leapt up, shook hands with me first and then Walter, accepted our congratulations and thanked Walter profusely for the great speeches, and for a few minutes they discussed the Vice President. He was relaxed, and wanted to insist we sit down and watch TV with him, but we left at once, and ran smack into Nixon getting off the elevator and all the photographers jamming up to get his picture and trailing him in to see him shake hands with Ike. When Walter and I held our hands out to congratulate Dick Nixon, he grabbed Walter and embraced him – everyone so darn happy they couldn't see straight.

The evening session when Ike and Mamie and the Nixons each made short speeches to the convention was an excellent climax to the whole thing. By then everyone could relax, so we got cleaned up and dressed up and at 9:00 went to get Ginny and Ronnie Welch to take out to dinner – first real meal in three days. Ginny has sat constantly as receptionist outside the Eisenhower suite. As we went to get her, Ike stepped out and said "Hello Judds, come on in and sit," and shook hands again, bless him. He really is wonderful. But people were waiting to see him by the score, so we pulled out for an evening of celebrating and dinner and postmortem and fun. Now I must quit, paper finished, Walter waiting, Chicago ended, campaign begun!!

Silver Bay, New York   *Sunday, August 24, 1952*

Dear Barbers All –

We are at Silver Bay & having a swell time![209] The cottage is perfect. It's right on Lake George, comfortable, convenient, quiet, rustic. This a.m. after church we had quite a reception of old friends all of whom asked for the Ben Barbers and sent love. Last night we did a jigsaw puzzle together. Tuesday Johnny is coming to dinner with Mary Lou. The younger girls have found new friends – are keeping busy. Tonight we hear the *Elijah* – What a restful recreating time.

Washington, D.C.   *Thursday, October 9, 1952*

I've got things in good enough shape to leave for Minneapolis on the 13th to stay until the election. Mat Condo will stay with the girls as she did two years ago. Poor Car and El are fighting the battle of Republicanism and Ike in their school classes and with their friends, as almost everyone around here is a government worker or administrative appointee. Every night I feed them ammunition for the arguments, and help Car with her Government Class assignments.

Leamington Hotel, Minneapolis, Minnesota   *Sunday, October 19, 1952*

Walter left town to go to New York and help on Ike's speechwriting for the New England tour. As for Walter's campaign, no one hears any activity from Rolvaag. Reports say he isn't expecting to make any dent this year but wants his name promoted and known so that next year when Walter is supposed to be going to take on Humphrey in the Senatorial race, he, Rolvaag, can get Dad's congressional seat!

Leamington Hotel, Minneapolis, Minnesota   *Saturday, October 25, 1952*

Thursday was an exciting day. The Nixon train was starting in the north of the State, doing whistle-stopping and speeching, and reaching here before evening. Republican officials went up by bus, two hours away, to ride down with the Nixons. Since Walter couldn't go, I went in his place, and did I have fun!

---

209   Silver Bay is a YMCA Conference Center in upstate NY. All three Judd daughters worked there for a summer during college in the 1950s as did Betty Lou and Johnny Barber. Ten of the next generation's daughters did the same.

Our chartered bus left about noon. Crowds of country folks were out in the little town of Litchfield, including hordes of children let out of school, with their homemade signs for Ike and Dick. The train is beautiful and most efficient. Nixon and Pat spoke off the back platform and received the usual roses, which were afterwards distributed to all the lady guests in the train. We got on the train when it arrived, listened to the back platform speeches from loud speakers in the club cars. When the train got going, the Nixons came through and visited. I thought they both looked terribly tired but were doing a fine job of being friendly to everyone.

Arrived at St. Paul there were the usual crowds, photographers, signs, yelling. The evening rally was held at the armory with much excitement and balloons and bands. Nixon did a swell job. After a short reception, they were off for their train and Wisconsin. Walter and I were glad to get home and take off our shoes. One day of leaving the hotel early in the morning clothed for the entire day till late at night, with an extra pair of nylons in my purse, talking all day to officials and importants and hurt feelings and pompous stuffed shirts, and "what does Walter think?" and "meet my friend, Blank," shaking hands and smiling and waving at a public that doesn't want to see you but can't see who they want to see, and grabbing food where you can and hunting taxis to get to the next place and freezing a smile on your face even if you're dying to find a W.C., and remembering to freshen the lipstick before they turn on the cameras – boy, I was ready to quit. How in heaven's name do Pat and Mamie stand it, not to speak of Dick & Ike?…

This next week I'll have my first glimpse of our opponent when he and Walter are to appear together at a forum to make statements and answer questions. I've not heard of any public activities of his, meetings or radio, and Walter is so busy for Ike that no one is bothering much about his campaign. Hope we don't get fooled.[210]

Washington, D.C.   *Friday, November 14, 1952*

Back less than a week and picking up loose threads, which seem a bit looser this year. We finished up things in Minneapolis and drove back. En route, Walter read accumulated mail three hours each day while I drove, and answered much of it before he took off for more than two weeks as far as the West Coast.

We're tired. It was a strain, particularly for Walter who had put all he had into it for so long, but it's a good sort of tired. I wish more places had elected Republican Congressmen so the margin wouldn't be so tight. Walter was elected by the highest majority he's ever had. That's good, considering how he neglected his own district for the Ike speeches and broadcasts and trips.

Walter talked on the phone to Ike the day he left here on his trip. Each contact he has with the guy he gets even more enthusiastic, says Ike has the grandest intuitive grasp of human nature and common sense in sizing up individuals and feeling into situations and proceeding cautiously but with understanding. He'll start slow, but it may interest you to know he is already thinking into things he wants to do two years from now.

---

210   Walter won the election with 99,027 votes or 59 percent. Karl Rolvaag, the DFL candidate, had 68,326 votes or 41 percent. Dwight Eisenhower won the Presidency, the first Republican since Herbert Hoover.

10

The Emerging Leader

1953 – 1957

Miriam and Walter celebrated the inauguration of Republican President, Dwight Eisenhower, with great excitement and hope for the future. The change enhanced Walter's influence in Washington, where he was increasingly seen as a key leader, one who was admired on both sides of the aisle. He was reelected twice and was appointed a delegate from the House of Representatives to the United Nations. Ever the practical wife, Miriam did their laundry in the bathtub of their New York hotel while they were at the United Nations.

They moved from active parenting to an empty nest. Carolyn enrolled at Mount Holyoke College and I graduated, to Miriam's delight, and set off to "grow as a palm in a desert" in New York City, just as she had done thirty years earlier. Ellie graduated from Sidwell Friends and headed off to Pembroke College. Miriam supported us unstintingly, providing encouragement during difficult times and rejoicing in our successes – always guiding us along. She bid farewell to both parents, oversaw my wedding, and always continued her full life in Washington.

She did some traveling with Walter, working through three campaigns and her own volunteer positions. Her leadership style was emerging as she steered the YWCA by chairing their major events, as well as planning the weekly Congressional Club programs – assignments she found especially stimulating and sometimes taxing. Miriam was energized by contributing to successful organizations and dedicated her prolific energy to worthwhile causes.

Washington, D.C.   *Sunday, January 25, 1953*

Dear Folks –

We've just survived one of the jamdest, excitingest, wearyingest, movingest weeks ever… If I can whip my weary brain, I'll jot down a few impressions.

Left Florida Saturday a.m.[211] Walter got back from Rochester, New York Sunday noon and the festivities opened that afternoon with the Governors' Reception. Took half an hour standing in line outside the Statler Hotel to get inside the door. But the weather was good. Once past the receiving line, which consisted of the D.C. Inaugural Committee, we got to the ballroom where each Governor had a box with State insignia, and where his friends elbowed their way to greet him. The California box was mobbed with folks trying to get Nixon's signature, so we passed it by.

The Nixons had all been in our church that a.m. tho' they are Quakers, and they spoke to the minister at the door, then walked slowly down the steps while the entire congregation gawked. I was ashamed at the lack of friendliness, so as they came along past me I stepped up and shook hands and said my name (Dick knows Walter well, but Walter wasn't in town) then introduced Car and El. Nixon said quickly to me, "I'm delighted to see by the calendar that you teach in the Sunday school here" and to El he said, "I know you're the girl who, with Dale Rogers stuck up for me against the Democrats at the Friends School this fall." That thrilled Eleanor. Nixon knew about it because Dale Rogers' father is his good friend, counsel for his Senate investigating committee.[212] Not another soul in our church greeted the family outside, but everyone stared and whispered. What Price Glory!

After the Governors' Reception, Walter and I went to a smaller, private party given by the Eugene Meyers, owners of the *Washington Post*. Here they had a delicious buffet. Their assortment of guests was just as elegant: we visited with Clare Luce; the John Dulleses, with Mrs. Oveta Culp Hobby.[213] (Her ball gown, shipped from the designers in New York City got stored in the icebox by mistake with boxes of her cut flowers, after frantic search was unearthed at the Statler, where she was staying, frozen stiff, but none the worse for the experience when it was thawed out!)

Left the Meyers' (parking a headache, in spite of special police) to dash home and into evening clothes for the special symphony concert in honor of Eisenhower and Nixon, at Constitution Hall. Ike didn't attend, but Nixon's box was three rows in front of us, and the American public made a spectacle of themselves jamming the aisles and mobbing the box to get him to sign their programs – and this was not teenage autograph hounds, either. The concert was lovely with Beethoven and "American in Paris," James Melton and Jeanette MacDonald singing solos and a duet, and Yehudi Menuhin doing a beautiful concerto. Walter Pidgeon introduced the numbers.

Arrived home we found our house guests, the Ronnie Welches, had arrived, to use Mary Lou's room. She was disappointed that her semester exam schedule wouldn't let her come down for the festivities.

Walter went to the office Monday to fight the battle of the TICKETS: confusion in the inaugural arrangements office had many ball and parade tickets not mailed out or assigned, and everyone in town was phoning to see if they could pick up extra tickets. Minneapolis folks made Walter's office their headquarters and meeting place, left messages, transacted business, changed their minds, drove everyone pleasantly nuts. I got my hair done, took Minneapolis BIG WIGS to lunch, home to check on my housework, groceries, maid, and family before we dressed and went off to make the rounds of

---

211 Miriam had visited her parents in Florida, returning for the inaugural activities for Eisenhower and Nixon.
212 Dale Rogers was Ellie's classmate. Her dad, William P. Rogers was later Attorney General and Secretary of State.
213 Oveta Culp Hobby was the first cabinet Secretary of Health, Education, and Welfare.

as many of the parties as we could attend. One was given by Mrs. Mary Lord, successor to Eleanor Roosevelt in the UN. She's a Minneapolis Pillsbury, before marriage, so we met Minneapolis friends there, as well as a goodly number of UN people and foreign Ambassadors. Greeted the Omar Bradleys, the George Marshalls. Must stop here to say that at all these public functions, everyone seems to know Walter. I like to see the confidence and respect with which people approach him.

We squeezed in time for the Minnesota Party at the Shoreham. We had to get in evening clothes again for the two big gala celebrations. Walter and I had to go over in a motorcade procession with the Nixons and police escort, enter the Uline Arena mid spotlights. Then the Hollywood and Broadway show went on and was fabulous, partly because of its unprecedented four-hour length, partly because of its amazing assortment of talent: Tony Martin, Fred Waring, Hoagy Carmichael, Bert Lahr, Abbott & Costello, Edgar Bergen, Ethel Merman, Esther Williams, New York Opera and Ballet, Walter Winchell, etc. About halfway through the program they stopped for introductions. As each name was called he was spotlighted in his box, stood for applause. Walter had to introduce the Congressmen, was up on the platform for this part. After we finished, all the "Honored Guests" filed out to our motorcade, and dashed thru the city to the big Capitol Theater, where the overflow of folks who couldn't get tickets at the Arena were having an overflow festival of exactly the same acts, but it started at 10:30. Walter had to do the introductions again. This entertainment was going on too late and some people did leave, but we felt badly for the entertainers who were scheduled toward the end, for many of them had given their services at no cost or cheaply, and deserved an audience after waiting so long and having to play to two places in one evening.

So Walter and I stayed till it was over, 'bout 2:30. Then we went to the Mayflower Hotel where some wealthy man was giving a breakfast for all the actors and distinguished guests. We were frankly a little beat, and hungry, too, having had no dinner but only the cocktail party snacks twelve hours before. We dug into the scrambled eggs, fried potatoes, fresh strawberries, etc. Esther Williams was at the next table trying to figure out with Delores Gray and a coupla boyfriends what the show would have cost to produce at regular commercial prices (I believe they decided on $500,000). I finally persuaded Walter I was about to fall flat on my face, and he took me home around four a.m.

Tuesday was a lovely day. The sky was blue and it was mild. We packed ham sandwiches and set off for the Capitol Plaza where special inaugural tags on our car (one now stolen by souvenir hunters) let us into the special park place. We got in about 11:15, enjoyed hearing the Marine Band play, the Defiance College choir sing, and the celebrities file in. The Senators and Justices came in two groups, various cabinet members and wives, and eventually the Trumans with Margaret, the Nixons whose in-laws were holding their little girls on the front of the platform, the Barclays, and finally the young Eisenhowers and Mamie. Congress wives I sat with had glasses so I got good close-ups of everyone. It was sunny, silent, and solemn when Eisenhower spoke. People seemed to have a feeling it was momentous; I will remember it for a long time.

Afterwards we all made our way back to meet at the car, and I joyously farewelled the Achesons in their chauffeur-driven Cadillac as they passed a foot from me. We ate our sandwiches in the car as we drove along roped-off Pennsylvania Avenue and only our special tag admitted us to park back of the White House and come to excellent seats right in front of the White House. The parade was too long, but terribly interesting with all of West Point and Annapolis marching, with thrilling divisions of armored trucks, tanks, Korea veterans, as well as the traditional state floats. Our gals were excited because some of their high school boyfriends were driving some of the official cars, getting $15 a day for the four-day period.

Parade was still going after six in the dark when we left to get a steak dinner at the Shoreham. Then home to dress for the balls, which started at ten. Eleanor went with a Congressman's family whose son is in school with her, and they were assigned to the Ball at the Armory. Car stayed home (her cold was bad and besides, said all her boyfriends were Democrats!) Walter and I went to the Ball at Georgetown gym, and Walter got me a white orchid for my navy blue taffeta and pink lace dress. The place was too jammed to move, and too hot to endure, but we got seats in the box of Minnesota's governor to wait till Eisenhowers appeared in the balcony at midnight, and enjoyed the music. After they left, we enjoyed people and gowns and visiting, till about two.

Home to coffee and sandwiches on the kitchen table and our shoes kicked off to relieve our aching feet, to discuss with El what celebrities she'd seen at her ball and which band she liked best; to tell of meeting Mary Lou's West Point guy who was singing with the choir for Ike at our ball; to hear of Ronnie[214] breaking thru police lines to greet his friend Jim Haggerty, press man for Ike, and finding himself talking to Mamie who said she was tired and wanted to get to bed;…and finally to fall into bed for our first deserved and gratifying night's sleep in the New Era, wondering how the bed at the White House would suit Ike. What a day!

I let myself get talked into being the program chairman for the next two years for the Friday afternoon programs at the Congressional Club teas, which means a lot of hard work to land topflight celebrities and interesting programs and be in charge of introducing all the speakers and escorting them thru the whole afternoon. Fortunately, our season goes only from January thru May, and with a good committee of both Democrats and Republicans, from all over the country, we ought to have wide variety and plenty of talent. Back to the Red Cross tomorrow.

Washington, D.C.   *Sunday, February 1, 1953*

I got in to see Ike in his private oval room office at the White House this week. Stassen asked Walter and me to come to his swearing in.[215] Walter was to be out of town so he insisted I come anyway. I went. Took a taxi to the front gate of the White House where a guard said I was "cleared." First I visited with Mrs. Stassen and ten-year-old daughter and officials in the Cabinet Room till Stassen came in, piloted us all into Ike's office, introduced his wife, then Senator Thyes and me to Ike who shook hands all round, said to me, "Isn't Walter coming in today?"…

Walter had lunch with Ike a couple of days later, with Senators Duff and Carlson, just the four. Said he was easy and jovial, apologized for having lamb stew but said he liked it so he ordered it, had a good visit and no official statement as to what they discussed. Walter did say Ike commented, "This is a heck of a job. They make me go through doors ahead of the ladies!"

---

214   Ronnie Welch and his wife Ginny were houseguests of the Judds for the inauguration festivities.
215   Stassen, former Governor of Minnesota, was being sworn in as the Director of the Foreign Operations Administration.

Washington, D.C.   *Sunday, February 15, 1953*

Eleanor's birthday yesterday we celebrated according to her wishes with a formal luncheon with her school friends *and* their mothers. The girls I know as they come in and out, but none of the mothers know each other. We had a total of thirteen to seat at our dining room table and one bridge table. We did ourselves proud with best linen, silver, menu, flowers. Eleanor loved the whole thing, was delighted the mothers seemed so congenial, I think she hoped that I would get new ideas or standards about bringing her up, and relax disciplines. I didn't!

We went to the Henry Luce formal 8 p.m. dinner for the speaker of the House, Joe Martin. They had 150 guests, including practically the entire cabinet, Congressional leaders, bigwigs, and some news, radio, and press people. Wonderful food, decorations, orchestra, and entertainment. Rosemary Cluny [sic] and Gladys Swarthout to sing, and Edgar Bergen with Charlie and Mortimer. That Bergen is a genius, the way he worked out his patter for this group!

Washington, D.C.   *Wednesday, April 8, 1953*

The morning paper said Walter talked for an hour with Nehru, and that's all I know about it. Think of it! Gone less than two weeks and all the way to India and back. Mary Lou got home for vacation and had a tonsillectomy 8:30 a.m. the day Walter left at 2 p.m. I've been cooking custards and broth and jello and playing bridge to relieve her boredom.

So with the hospitalizing, visiting sister-in-law, absent husband, usual spring sewing, daughters on irregular vacation schedules, we've had the Cherry Blossom visitors, some friends and some constituents…six sets of people for suppers. Why does everything come at once?

I did Walter's fifteen-minute weekly broadcast (played three days and times in Minneapolis), talked about my work with Red Cross, about celebrities, my going to the White House in the past and again tomorrow when several of us will present Mrs. Eisenhower her honorary membership in our YWCA. I was also on a local TV broadcast called "The Modern Woman," with other Congress wives and we told about the Congressional Club, had a birthday cake with forty-five candles for its anniversary, and got as prizes, samples of the stuff being advertised.

Washington, D.C.   *Tuesday, April 21, 1953*

In Calcutta Walter went around specially to see 5 Camac Street and 25 Chowringee and 86 College Street (addresses where our family lived when I was a child). He was encouraged with the progress India is making and with its official awareness of the Communist danger. He talked with Nehru, with Prime Minister of Pakistan (whose problems he feels are simply gigantic) and saw Frank Laubach for an hour.[216] I've been elected one of three Vice Presidents of our YWCA Board with responsibility in the Program Department, such as Teenage, Health & Recreation, Adult Education, Music, USO, etc. It's a real challenge but they have fine women to work with.

---

216   Frank Laubach was a leading pioneer of the adult literary movement and founder of Each One Teach One.

Ocean City, New Jersey   *Sunday, July 12, 1953*

Here we are at this lovely Methodist seaside place again with Car and El. We all love the ocean and relaxing. Walter speaks tonight in the big evening service in a boardwalk theater. Last night he spoke in nearby Seabrook where twenty-six Issei (Japanese immigrants, parents of American-born Japanese) had become naturalized American citizens, thanks to Walter's work on immigration legislation.[217] These people were brought to Seabrook ten years ago out of the concentration camps USA had put them in, to work on the farms and in the processing plants of Mr. Seabrook, the largest grower and producer of frozen fruits & vegetables. This is the largest group of new Japanese citizens and they were given a banquet honoring them, and Mr. Seabrook, and Walter.

Washington, D.C.   *Monday, September 28, 1953*

Dear Folks –

I've had my four-day jaunt, taking the girls to Holyoke and now the house seems quiet, and El and I rattle around. College was beautiful, fall weather, trees turning, the campus lovely.[218] I was impressed with what marvelous opportunities college offers and wistful as I remembered that at eighteen and twenty you don't always appreciate or make use of the privileges, and ever after wish you could do it all over again.

Yesterday the USO in our YW building had its twelfth birthday party. I had to head the receiving line and greet the top brass from Pentagon. Top honor guests were Admiral & Mrs. Radford; he made a few remarks, and she cut the huge birthday cake midst popping of flashbulbs. I enjoyed talking with lonely and lost-looking young guys who find a home in our building. One thousand come for Saturday night dances, with square dancing other nights, dramatics, glee club. A number of couples who had met at the USO came back to celebrate. A great affair and a great service.

Washington, D.C.   *Sunday, October 18, 1953*

Dear Folks:

Sunday afternoon and Walter's going to do eight hours of dictating at the office before he takes the night plane for Minneapolis. So I'm down here ;with him to get caught up on long-overdue letters, and being fascinated ;with my first ;use of the new electric typewriter which keeps throwing in extra semi-colons, I'm not sure why.

Keep busy working on household details of replacing and renewing, and it was good I elected to thoroughly clean out the third floor "dump room" last week. Bob Hunter and his pregnant wife and two small children stayed with us on their way back to Costa Rica after leave, and they used the whole third floor. It was Bob's parents who took me in with Mary Lou and month-old Carolyn, when we fled to Peking in 1936. We were glad to help out Bob.

The week before had the interesting experience of attending a twenty-four-hour conference of the Women's Advisory Committee of Federal Civil Defense, representing the National YWCA. An

---

217   This had been the first civil rights legislation since World War II.
218   Carolyn was joining Mary Lou at Mount Holyoke College.

interesting bunch of about fifty women representing University Women, American Legion Auxiliary, AMA Auxiliary, the Press, Salvation Army, President of the Women University Deans of U.S., DAR, Jewish Women and Catholic Women's organizations, PTA. We met first in the headquarters here in D.C., then out twenty miles to Olney, Maryland where they have a Federal Civil Defense Staff Training College where they put up overnight guests, and have our all-day sessions. They gave a vivid presentation of what they have done planning and preparing for any war or natural disaster – made me feel more confident, till they told us folks around the country wouldn't believe it was important to be informed or prepared, they can't get the necessary volunteers for training, and they can't get people to use the excellent materials. Federal Civil Defense only coordinates what the States are doing, but many of the States are disgracefully behind at even starting a program.

Washington, D.C.   *Tuesday, November 17, 1953*

Dearest –

I see by the papers that you dined with the Chiangs and that you addressed a Nationalist gathering "in fluent Chinese."[219] Good for you! Bet you're having fun, as well as keeping busy. El is going crazy because you are not here to tell her what to think about the Truman-Brownell-Harry White Case[220]. Today after Truman's speech they fought it out in one of her classes, and she came home full of Democratic & New Deal bull: Why raise dead issues? Why don't Republicans be positive? Why try to discredit the past, etc. I tried to stem the tide of stupid platitudes but she wouldn't listen. Then they rebroadcast tonight Brownell's prepared speech[221] before the Committee today, and she listened one hour and decided he really knew something about it and perhaps there *were* some Communists in our government, so she's changed her tune a bit. But she *longs* for your convincing and authoritarian voice. So do I!! YW meetings Monday, Red Cross today, and now I'm getting ready to moderate a YW staff forum tomorrow for 40-50 on what YW *really* is and does, where it serves community, how it is a *Christian* Association. It ought to be fun and is challenging. Then Thursday evening is Sunday school teachers' monthly meeting. Off to my lonesome bed now, thinking of you, and hoping you're well.

Washington, D.C.   *Monday, January 11, 1954*

I was in the gallery when Ike made his State of the Union speech, and as always had a grand time watching famous people on the floor react to different parts, like Benson on the farm situation, and McCarthy and Mamie, of course. That morning I had been at the Red Cross for an hour's consultation with Dr. Saltzman, the psychiatrist who gives six hours a month for specially difficult cases. You make an appointment and present a brief written summary of the case in person to pose your problem and get advice. My poor woman he decided was mentally retarded – It was interesting to watch him work.

Friday the Congressional Club opened its season, and I had Dulles for our first speaker, thanks to

---

219   Walter was on a Foreign Affairs Committee trip to Asia and the Middle East, November 6-December 17, and they had stopped in Taiwan, where Chiang had moved the Government of the Republic of China after the 1949 Red Communist takeover.

220   Harry White was a senior U.S. Treasury Department official who was accused of espionage in 1948.

221   Herbert Brownell was US Attorney General from 1953-1957.

Walter's assistance. The place was mobbed. I enjoyed sitting three feet from him and watching his mind work and marveled at the orderliness of his progress thru an informal talk with no notes. It was magnificent. Eleanor and a friend of hers went, and as usual she surprised me at her easiness and naturalness with THE GREAT. She seems to have no embarrassment, and I found her chatting gaily with Mrs. Humphrey and others. She's the best of our three at that. I guess my introduction was all right. Yesterday someone phoned to ask me to be the guest and critic at a public speaking course as they had heard I was "one of the best Republican women speakers in Washington." I declined, but you know the old story, "thank God for the rumor."

Washington, D.C.   *Saturday, January 30, 1954*

Yesterday was another big day at our Congressional Club. We had Nixon give an off-the-record report on his trip, and he was excellent.[222] He had turned down my original invitation on the basis of having to make official talks on the subject, but Walter pointed out to him that they were all for men, that it was a matter of good public relations to talk to the Congressional wives with all the influence the women carry. He had an excellent map, which he used to advantage to make points about the dependence of those nations on each other, a sort of travelogue discussing the weakness and strength in each country, their outstanding leader, what the U.S. relation to them is. As I stood in the receiving line with him and Pat afterwards, I heard literally dozens say "I'm a Democrat, or I'm from the south, but what you said sounds right and I'm for it." I think he did himself, and the Administration, and our Far Eastern policy no end of good. Pat is friendly and easy. She tells me she does her own housework; that the elderly white woman there is mostly to keep her little girls in order. They left at 5:15 after tea, and Pat then had to go to shake hands with about 500 women for a woman's Patriotic Societies Forum. What a life they live…

Last week Walter and I went to a formal dinner for twelve… I found myself sitting next to Joe Alsop.[223] We got into a discussion of higher education and I got telling him about the question Mary Lou had for midyear exam for her public administration course: Assume you're Secretary of State. Write your plan of organization based on proper functions, major budget items, personnel policy. Well, the words "personnel policy" gave him the springboard he wanted, and he launched into a tirade about curtailment of freedom because of congressional investigations. I'm afraid I sorta laughed at his inflated fear and told him I knew he wasn't really frightened, before the conversation switched me to Walter Robertson on my other side. Next day I got a handwritten letter from Joe saying he was sorry he got so heated but that he was really frightened, and one of the things that made him most terrified was that intelligent people like myself [sic] didn't sense the impending disaster in curtailment of freedom, and enclosed one of his columns on the subject. I'm still not frightened. These people open their mouths to yell to the world that McCarthy has closed their mouths! Ideas are still able to circulate freely in this country. I say let's not switch the attention from Communism, which is a serious threat, to McCarthyism, which is a passing phenomenon.

---

222   Vice President Richard Nixon had just returned from the Far East.

223   Joseph Alsop was a famous syndicated newspaper columnist who had been investigated by Senator Joseph McCarthy's controversial "Committee on Government Operations," which was seeking information about possible communist sympathizers among government personnel.

Washington, D.C.   *Wednesday, February 24, 1954*

First weekend in February I went to Holyoke as a delegate from the Washington Club to the Alumnae Council. Saw a number of friends & old professors; attended interesting meetings and chaired one for the 160 alumnae present; attended a political science class with Mary Lou and a Bible Class with Carolyn; visited with their friends, met some of their dates, heard Mary Lou sing in chapel choir, and generally enjoyed the four days.

That Friday night while Walter and Eleanor were attending the Lincoln Day dinner at which Ike, Walter, and other celebrities spoke, people broke into our house, and did a thorough job of ransacking the second-floor bedrooms. When Walter and El got back about midnight, milk bottles sitting on the kitchen counter were still cool so couldn't have been out of the icebox long, glasses they'd used had paper napkins round them to prevent fingerprints. They had torn out everything from bureau drawers and desk and closet, heaped in piles and pawed through, torn apart jewelers' boxes, dumped all my earrings, gloves, letters, torn open all my purses, etc. Nary a cent did they find, but they took two watches of Walter's and a new billfold. They brushed aside watches of mine, my jade, the Japanese real pearls, etc.

The police thought it must have been boys, for they spread intimate feminine things around in the girls' rooms. By the time Walter had had the police and detectives here and the beds had been cleared off so they could get to bed, it was close to four. When I got back from my blissful weekend, I had a very un-blissful several days cleaning up the debris. Police found no clues, but two other houses were done the same evening in a similar way… I thought of Mother's saying, "Blessed be nothing."

El and I went to New York City as her birthday celebration and had a wonderful time. Saw two Broadway shows, a TV Broadcast, the UN, and the planetarium. What happened while we were away this time was much nicer. Carolyn came home from college, entered the competition at the Minnesota State Party and won. She will be Miss Minnesota in the Cherry Blossom Festival activities in April. She was duly crowned, had millions of pictures taken, had a thrilling time, and went back to college next day. Now I have to cope with the problem of clothes needed.

washington, d.c.   *tuesday, march 2, 1954*

dear folks:

(i'm tired tonight so decided to save energy and not make capital letters – quaint, eh?) i'm at the office using the electric typewriter to send the family letter, while walter dictates in the other room, and eleanor is at the library of congress working on her term paper.

the white house reception is cancelled because of the shooting yesterday.[224] …walter just finished a phone call in the cloak room and stepped back into the chamber and raised his hand to be counted in a vote, when he saw the fireworks in the gallery directly facing him. he says the expression on the face of one of the men shooting was that of a fanatic, intense hatred and a wild insane look. everyone thought at first it was firecrackers, but when walter saw members down under their chairs, and one

---

224   On March 1, 1954, four Puerto Rican Nationalists opened fire in the House of Representatives. Five congressmen were injured, one seriously, but all recovered.

stumbling out bleeding, he knew it was the real article. he dashed down to where bentley[225] was, and it was lucky he did, for they were trying to hold him in a sitting position and he was in shock and quite pulseless. walter put his own coat over him, got him laid down, and when the young md arrived evidently had to suggest blankets, stretcher, morphine, etc., to one who had never seen a gunshot wound before, or acted as if he hadn't. walter helped carry him to the ambulance, then was rushed right out to a tv station where they had him give his account of what had happened. by this time the office had got hold of me by phone and told me to watch tv which I did. walter said exactly where he thought the bullet had gone in bentley, and when the operation was done last night and the diagnosis given out, he was pleased to find he was right. we sure hope the guy will pull thru…

walter had to do a number of other broadcasts. eventually he got el from the library of congress and they came home to a hot dinner, which was the best thing i could do to fill time till i got firsthand reports, as telephones into the capitol were jammed and i couldn't get thru. today the city is rushing about madly putting on extra guards every half inch and special precautions to congress visitor galleries – locking the barn after the horse is stolen.

YWCA 49th Anniversary Luncheon. Director of Foreign Operations Harold Stassen is at the podium; to his right are Mamie Eisenhower and Miriam Judd.

Washington, D.C.   *Wednesday, April 7, 1954*

Want to tell you about the big annual meeting and luncheon of the YW two weeks ago, of which I was chairman. We had 1,200 present. Mrs. Eisenhower was guest of honor along with several Cabinet and Supreme Court wives and lots of Ambassador wives from countries where the YW is at work. They had a good chance to see and hear what our local Y is doing to meet the needs of the Capitol, as well as the National and International YW. In several countries YWs are cooperating with Mr. Stassen's FOA[226] work so it was appropriate to have him give the speech. Mamie is easy to chat with. She genuinely likes people and it shows. We got talking about her schedule and how she

---

225   Representative Alvin Bentley was from Michigan's 8th District.
226   FOA was the Foreign Operations Administration.

gets in all that she has to do; then we shifted to Ike and all that he is carrying, and she said naturally and quickly that although he has a magnificent physique she knows he couldn't carry all that he's carrying without some help from an outside power. She said she didn't understand enough about prayer and how it worked but she knew it did work and that prayer made all the difference with Ike. Said people came down receiving lines every day and said as they shook hands that they were praying for her and Ike, and she told them, "You just keep it up. We both need it." And she meant it.

Washington, D.C.   *Saturday, May 8, 1954*

Please don't anyone ask me what Walter thinks about Dulles or Indo China. I have no chances to speak with him. He just got in from speaking in Texas, is catching up on sleep and will suddenly go off in a terrible hurry to catch up on his work at the office, work late because he has slept late, and I'll be asleep when he gets home – so it goes. He was called in by Dulles the day he got back from Europe, and I guess those Congressional leaders got the works. When he did get home just said things were bad and didn't sleep much that night.

As for McCarthy, I won't watch TV or listen to radio or read papers on that subject. I know there is so much misrepresentation in the reports and papers, that it only gets me worked up, and there's not a thing in the world I can do about it, so no use getting myself into such a state that I can't do the things I have to do. So I'm playing ostrich.

Orlando, Florida   *Monday, June 28, 1954*

Hi Family –

It meant so much to me to talk to Car & Dad. Just wait till you find yourself in real emergencies, or where you are facing essential facts of life, like illness and old age and possibly death, and then you'll understand more clearly that in the last analysis your family is what really counts. Sat a long time with my Dad in the hospital yesterday, mostly thinking and listening to the things he wanted to tell me as his mind wandered mostly over his past. He seemed to feel he was in some sort of confinement – the oxygen tent, no doubt – and he kept assuring me that his conscience was perfectly clear and that he had nothing to report or to regret and no cause for any criminal action.

It made me wonder what kind of things might come out of my wandering mind at some future date. How wonderful to live eighty-seven years and have nothing to regret or fear! And then sick as he was, and nurses working on him – he never forget to say "Thank you, Nurse." What you *really* are comes out at a time like this, and he's a grand old gentleman, bless him.

And the rest of my family's pretty good, too, I thought: Car coming home earlier from Ocean City, keeping the house running smoothly, and cleaning up after the general exodus. And cards and letters from the other two who are caring and sending love. As for their Pop, I don't dare say what I'd like as it would embarrass them, and El would call it mushy! But may I say, Gals, that it's deeply, beautifully wonderful to have a guy that it makes you feel better to talk to on the phone, and one that makes you know he cares deeply for you & for all you care about.[227]

---

227   Miriam's father, Ben Barber, died July 10, 1954 at age eighty-seven. Miriam's mother was moved to a nursing home in Washington, D.C.

Friday, January 14, 1955

In 1955 the YWCA of the World is 100 years old, and the YWCA of Washington, fifty. Everyone is planning centennial celebrating special events, membership drive, a birthday gift. I am Chairman of Centennial and have been getting committees and campaigners and publicity lined up.

We opened our activities Tuesday with a wing-ding luncheon for 1,300 at the Mayflower (and 350 turned away). I had sent handwritten letters inviting wives of Cabinet, Supreme Court, Ambassadors from abroad as guests, and we had a head table of forty-five. They filed in in order of their seating, after others were seated, and I introduced each one as she went by the microphone. Had to practice hours on such names as Notewigto (Indonesia) and Gunarwardene (Ceylon) and Tran van Chuang (Vietnam) and van Rojen (Holland), etc., after I had phoned Protocol and gotten briefed on the correct pronunciation. Mamie was introduced, and she came in as the Marine Band played her march. Much time was spent with the White House security as to which entrance we'd meet her at, who'd be seated near her, above her in the balcony boxes, exact minute of her arrival (she must not be kept waiting), what we wanted her to do and say at lunch.

I sat next to Mamie, conversation easy as always. We talked about the gorgeous cake Mamie was to cut. We'd negotiated that for a month for there had to be conferences on design, decoration, architect's drawing, samples of the color of the icing to see if they matched our YW blue. The result weighed 250 pounds, was five feet high, forty inches across the base, had 100 electric candles around the platform, which had first to be wired, then iced to match the cake. Whew!

Before dessert I talked to the guests about ten minutes, welcoming, thanking band, florists, press, etc., and explaining our aims for our centennial. I was proud that we were already 200 over our 20,000 membership quota, and hope we'll do as well in our financial campaign, which started day after luncheon. I explained our coming hook-up with the YWCA National Luncheon in New York at the Waldorf, where they had 1,800 celebrating at the same time, with Dulles to give their main speech. We were to be connected by direct wire for three minutes, when I would introduce Mamie (one minute), she would rise and say Happy Birthday and Good Wishes, etc., and push a button which would light our cake candles and also those on the New York cake, and Mrs. Laurence Rockefeller as chairman of the New York lunch would thank her from there (third minute).

We'd had nine electricians and AT&T men working twenty-four hours to install all the needed wires and speakers and phones to get this three minutes cared for, and I'd tried voice levels and timing devices and height of microphone. Everything went perfectly, friends at the NY luncheon wrote that my voice came over perfectly in the minute of introduction, and Mamie's brief words also. Mamie was darling about the slash in the cake with a decorated knife I handed her, which she made again and again while news reels crowded in for pictures. I hear people have already seen me on the silver screen laughing as Mamie snitches and tastes a bit of icing that cracked off when she slashed. The cake was then carried out by four professional cake cutters and quickly cut up and served to each guest with dessert, a real achievement…

---

228   There were no letters for the rest of the year until 1955, but Walter won the November, 1954, election with 69,901 votes or 56 percent. Anders Thompson, the DFL candidate, had 55,452 votes or 44 percent.

YWCA 50th Anniversary Luncheon. Mamie Eisenhower is about to take the microphone. Behind the cake, Miriam is taking charge of the day.

We had five-minute greetings from Sir Roger Makin of Britain for the World, Nelson Rockefeller for the Nation, President of the D.C. Commissioners for the Community, each of whom I'd personally invited and had to introduce with a two-minute introduction, and we closed with our efficient and glamorous Executive Secretary, Mabel Cook, giving a moving talk about the past of the D.C. YWCA and our hope for the coming years of service to the community.

It took a terrific amount of planning and work to get the millions of details into smooth running order, and to prepare all the introductions, welcomes, remarks, presentations, etc. But it was worth it for everyone felt it went off like a dream, and we have received loads of comments and complimentary notes, and not a few contributions from quite unexpected sources. I've just finished hand-writing ten thank-you notes to Mamie and others who took part, and I've been interviewed on TV and radio programs about our activities, so the work goes on.

Congress got underway in the midst of this, with Congressional Club starting. For our opening tea, Walter got us George Allen, retiring Ambassador to India. Today we had the wife of our former Ambassador to the Philippines who talked beautifully about a Diplomat's wife's experiences abroad… One program I will interview the author of *Flicka* and *Thunderhead*, Mary O'Hara. Do you wonder I gave up my Red Cross and Sunday school work for this year?

Washington, D.C.   *Monday, April 6, 1955*

Dear Folks:

Clarke and Elizabeth were here Monday, March 21 for a day of work, doing lots of business details. Mother must have had another of her attacks for we were called quickly to the Home nearby, and one of us stayed with her for several hours till she seemed to be resting more comfortably. Clarke and Elizabeth left next morning to drive to New York to sail for Cairo[229] after hearing from the Home that

---

229   Clarke and Elizabeth were moving to Cairo to lead the YMCA there.

Mother had a good night. But from then on she did not seem able to swallow, ran a high temperature. Walter decided to cancel his Tuesday speaking engagement in Minneapolis. I went several times each day to be with her, and I had no thought that she knew I was there. Still it comforted me to sit by her. Monday night when Walter and I were there she seemed to be making a real effort to say something, her lips moving as they had not in months, unintelligible sounds coming from her throat. Tuesday Eleanor dropped me off at the Home after school while she went to her music lesson, was to come by afterwards to pick me up and see Grammie. I was glad I was there for that last half hour, holding Mother's hand. I do not think she suffered, and it was a blessed release.[230]

Mother was cremated as was her wish. We had a simple family memorial service. The minister read from Mother's Bible, starting by saying he had never held a Bible that was so well used and that showed more signs of reading and study, with its underlinings and profuse marginal notes and dates, and quotations and outlines of talks she had heard. He also read several short passages from the autobiography she had written over ten years ago, showing her strong faith during some of the difficult decisions of her life, and the confidence and joy her trust in God had brought her. His closing prayer was beautiful and included the memory of Charles[231] who must now be happy in the reunion with his Mother. It was intimate and beautiful, as I think she and Father would have liked.

The girls have gone back to college after spring vacation – how fortunate that they were home just at that time, had all been to see Mother in her last few days, were here to bring a closeness of family feeling that is so reassuring at a time like this. I am feeling lonely and let down but most grateful for the way things happened and for the expressions of love and sympathy and support from so many friends.

Washington, D.C.   *Monday, May 9, 1955*

April 21 I went to New York for a week's National Convention of the YW with 3,300 delegates from all over the country and from foreign countries. It was a stimulating as well as strenuous session. I kept bumping into friends from everywhere, mainly a large delegation from Minneapolis YW with whom I had dinner one night. Most of the time we attended sessions voting on policy or public affairs for the next triennium, or listening to speakers. There was a breathtakingly beautiful worship service at Radio City Sunday morning at 9 a.m. with the place jammed – who says Protestants won't get up for early mass? The Rockefellers had made the place available for us; they had the 120-voice Westminster Choir school choir in gorgeous bright red robes, and the cathedral windows in color, high altar and tall candelabra from the Radio City Easter production; Mrs. John D. Rockefeller, Jr., was a strong worker on the National Board, as was Mrs. Laurence Rockefeller's mother, Mrs. French, who helped found the Board in 1906 and served on it till her death in 1951.

Last week I flew to Cleveland where I had a lively twenty-four-hour visit with my good college friend Helen Smith who then drove me to Elyria where I talked at their church breakfast with 250 women present. I talked on Christian women and Public Responsibility. I don't do these public appearances easily any more. I worked hours on writing the speech, even though it was no Gettysburg address, and got tensed up beforehand, but it's good for me to do…

230   Miriam's mother, Miriam Loretta Clarke Barber, died March 22, 1955 at age 84.
231   Charles was Miriam's brother whose plane disappeared over Alaska during World War II.

One social event this last week was glamorous: The Congressional Club Brunch for Mamie. They had all the decorations like a Pennsylvania farmhouse kitchen with red-and-white checked gingham tablecloths on each table. They had a low picket fence across the front of the head table, and a life-sized model hen on a nest that was full of golf ball eggs.[232] You can imagine how heartbreaking it was that Mamie couldn't attend, since her doctor made her cancel all engagements for the week. But IKE, bless his heart, came over and greeted all the 600 ladies, said it was the first time he'd ever substituted for a lady, said Mamie was much better and he'd tell her all about the decorations, and was wonderful. So it was a gala day.

Washington, D.C.   *June, 1955*

The graduations were lovely. We drove up[233] in time for the Dramatic Club play Friday evening on which Carolyn was working makeup and staging. Mary Lou looked impressive leading processionals, standing in receiving lines, making several short speeches, particularly at the alumnae meeting. All my class was at the event, about fifty of us. Chief Justice Warren gave a good talk at graduation.

El's graduation was lovely, too, with the girls in long white dresses and carrying four dozen red roses. Elton Trueblood gave their commencement talk and was excellent.[234] El had exciting events the whole graduation week, including prom, and staying out all night for parties and breakfast, which seems so essential to growing up. She's gone to her camp in Minnesota where she is earning money as counselor, the only earning member of the girls, and looking forward to Pembroke in the fall.[235]

Washington, D.C.   *Sunday, July 17, 1955*

Congress isn't going to get thru in time for us to go on our Scandinavian trip. I was counting on it; but suddenly members of committees got itchy and decided to bring out bills at the last moment that they hadn't worked on all session, and then other committees fought with rules committee and both stubbornly refused to give in hoping one would yield, because it's so near the end of session, so here we sit stalemated. Anyhow, cancel all your hopes of my Christmas shopping being done this year in foreign lands!

Minneapolis, Minnesota   *Saturday, October 8, 1955*

Dear daughters –

The event of the week was the testimonial dinner for Dad Wednesday evening. They had 1,300 people at $5 apiece, could have sold 500 more if Radisson could have fed 'em. Ballroom looked gay with red, white, and blue helium balloons, high in the room but weighted to each table. Reverend Howard Conn gave the invocation. Chuck Mayo was a wonderful toastmaster, kept everyone in stitches and kept the whole thing from being too syrupy, for they spent a lot of time saying highly complimentary things.

---

232   The Eisenhowers had a farmhouse at Gettysburg, PA where they "retreated" and retired; it's now a National Historic Site.

233   Miriam's Mount Holyoke class of 1925 was having their thirtieth reunion. Mary Lou was senior class president.

234   Ellie graduated from Sidwell Friends School. Elton Trueblood, Quaker theologian, President of Earlham College, was the speaker.

235   Pembroke College was a women's college and has since merged with Brown University.

Chris Herter[236] gave a thoughtful, incisive speech about ideas and early experiences of his own that had drawn him to Dad. Governor Thye was cordial and grammatically incorrect. Dr. Paul Larson

Miriam receiving the Paul Revere silver bowl at the testimonial dinner

said wonderful things about Dad as a doctor. Then Mrs. Stevenson from our church who has visited our mission work abroad gave a swell talk on Dad as missionary. They wanted to give us a remembrance of this occasion and their deep affection– a *beautiful* Paul Revere silver bowl, plain but exquisite. Pictures of me receiving it look like a startled ox. Then I had to go to the mike, saying that it was twenty-four years ago that Walter asked me the $64,000 question, and I was glad I had answered correctly and gotten the reward. Said what this had meant to me in broadened experience, enlarged circle of good friends, etc. Ended by thanking them for the gift and all kindnesses, closed saying "I feel like saying tonight, 'All this and Walter too!'"

Dad was *really* the eloquent one of the evening! He thanked Chris for what his words meant to him, thanked Chuck who had to take the night plane to New York City, then sweetly mentioned how pleased he was they recognized me, as I was often "home with the family, in the background," said how *proud* he was to represent Minneapolis and the fine people, etc., brought down the house. We adjourned to the reception room to stand in line and shake hands till 11:30.

As he said in his speech, it's a great tribute to have while you are still alive! Forgot to say that Harlan Nygaard spoke about Dad in politics. They presented him a handsome album with letters from Nixon, Stassen, local leaders. Naturally, Dad was overwhelmed and embarrassed, but it did him good, too, for he *has worked* like a dog, and he deserved every word. Next day people were talking about running him for Governor, making him a "favorite son" at the Republican Convention, this latter to keep Minnesota delegation from splintering up over Stassen, Eisenhower supporters, and anti-Ike groups here, formerly pro-Taft, who are smallish but vocal.

My own time here has been crowded. Among other things, spoke to a Professional sorority on "Washington, Your Capitol City." Spoke to a church group, the YW, and a ward Republican Women's Club all on different subjects, so I had to work. Went to meetings with Dad the rest of the time. Now I'll go back and settle down to plain living and no Dad. He'll be back to D.C. the 15th and goes to New York City next day to take off for his trip abroad.

Washington, D.C.   *November, 1955*

The gals have all called today, Mary Lou not even collect (!)[237], other two from Providence where Car had gone to spend the weekend with El – or was it with a boy in BETA? It's thoughtful of them

---

236   Chris Herter, former Governor of Massachusetts, was then the Under Secretary of State.
237   Mary Lou was working for IBM in New York City and living with four other girls in an apartment

when they know I'm alone. I don't have any word from Walter – three weeks out of the country now and not a line. I know he must be frantic in the midst of this Arab-Israel fracas and probably worries all night when he should be catching up on rest. They go a terrific pace with every minute filled. The papers said their group had an hour and half talk with Nasser in Cairo, and the State Department has had cables that the group had arrived safely in Bagdad and Tehran, this week, so I know he's alive!

There's such a lot to think about with the girls that I wish I had someone to talk to. Mary Lou is genuinely puzzled about whether she is in love. I've talked to her, but no one can decide for her. And El is seeing at close view so much drunkenness in the fraternities on the weekends. She writes that it is shocking even to one who had two older sisters who tried to prepare her.

Carolyn, bless her, is still struggling with the conflict in her mind set up by her enormous love for the theatre and all that goes with production, and with the, shall we say, relaxed moral code she found prevailing this summer among most of the acting and producing people.[238] She doesn't come right out and tell you what's on her mind, and she had to argue in a defensive way that theater people are perfect. I told her to talk to Walter about homosexuality cases he's had, both in medical practice and in Congress (to get dishonorable Army discharges changed for constituents,) cited a few instances, and I think she was surprised that Walter and I knew what the word meant.

I maintained a detached and jovial attitude in the whole discussion (which is hard for me, for I felt strongly she was wrong and ignorant) because I knew she needed to get it off her chest; only to find out later that Mary Lou was shocked both by Carolyn's assertions and by my not refuting them more vigorously. But Carolyn is torn, for she wants a job in summer theater. She is not going to go on with the nursing. Such an intense youngster, and there seems to be nothing to do but stand by and be ready if asked. These are the things I think about when I can't sleep.

Washington, D.C.   *Monday, January 9, 1956*

Dear Folks:

I came through the holiday & vacation period nobly, with all the extras it entailed, then quietly folded after I got five teeming youth started in three different directions last Tuesday. For example: Monday evening January 2, everyone in the family out (Walter & I went to see Grace Kelley in *To Catch a Thief*); a pad in front hall for everyone to sign as they came in, last one to fix lock, lights, heat. After Johnny's signature, in parenthesis, "much too late!"[239] But Mary Lou still not in, came in 8 a.m. off a sleeper from New York City after partying late, though expected earlier. Everyone got up late, started madly packing, radios blaring loudly, conversations screaming from floor to floor: "May I take some of your cotton dresses to Florida?" "Who wore my earrings last and didn't return them?" "You got a spot on my blouse when you borrowed it; you'll have to have it cleaned." "Mom, the pilot in the dryer went out and the clean clothes are still wet." "I'm dashing over to pick up Vickie and her bags as her mother can't drive her to the station so she's going with us." "Well hurry back; I need the car to go to the bank." "Take the other car." "She can't. I'm taking it to mail the suit boxes I've packed back to college as I can't get everything in my cases." "Mom, would you make us lunches for the train? We haven't any allowance left to eat on the diner." (I start making

---

238   Carolyn had a summer internship at Cape Cod Musical Theater.
239   Johnny was Clarke & Elizabeth's son, Betty Lou's brother.

sandwiches. Walter comes down for late breakfast, thinks sandwiches look good, eats same. I make more. Am called to phone; Johnny comes down & eats second batch. I make more. Mary Lou comes down, says her Florida plane is two hours late & carries no food, so she'll need a lunch and these sandwiches taste good, eating one, so please make her some.)

Then the discussion as to who will go in which car with which chauffeur where. Walter has to be at Capitol at noon for opening of Congress. Girls want to take noon train for Holyoke & Pembroke, want to get there early to get good seats for the BIG BRIDGE GAME. Johnny wants to go to bus station, via Statement Department to pick up passport application for trip to Cairo. Mary Lou doesn't know when her plane will get in. Can't you just hear the clamor of suggestions & counter-suggestions, plans made & revised & discarded midst phone calls and dashings in and out and wild confusion. But finally they're all gone and I'm left with a long list of suit boxes to mail, forgotten cleaning to pick up, "left-behinds" to mail, errands to complete, phone messages to deliver, and messy rooms to clean. Now don't think I'm complaining! It's worth every bit of it to have them here, and we had the nicest vacation ever. I'm just trying to explain my slowness in getting at my letter writing!

Washington, D.C.   *Tuesday, June 19, 1956*

Dear Folks:

The situation in Walter's office has kept me from writing. I started work June 1 and have been at it regular hours, coming sometimes by 8:30 in the morning and leaving after six, or working late evenings and Saturday and Sunday. Things were in such an unholy mess and filing so far behind and many things piled high that I am continuing to work, but coming only when I have free time from YW meetings and household duties that have been badly neglected. I am determined to get things in decent order. Meantime, Eleanor worked a good ten days on the monotonous card file corrections and did a grand job. We were pleased with her persistence. She and Carolyn went to hear Walter when he testified before the Senate Internal Security Subcommittee on the references to himself in

Miriam assisting Walter with correspondence

the Morgenthau240 papers – testimony that was badly misquoted in the papers…

Eleanor has gone to Silver Bay, New York for her table-waiting job and Carolyn has been sewing, meeting friends, getting shots and passport for sailing for Europe next Saturday.

Meantime we have been having a busy time with social events. The biggest was the visit of President Sucarno of Indonesia. We were invited to the fancy dinner he gave for President Ike and Mamie and that was the most elaborate and formal of any event I've attended. There were about seventy-five seated at a horseshoe table in the Mayflower

---

240   Henry Morgenthau was the U.S. Secretary of the Treasury from 1934-1945.

Hotel ballroom. I was seated between two Indonesian members of their Parliament, one of whom spoke little English, so it was a tax on my imagination and my pantomime.

First night the girls were home Walter took us all to see *Teahouse of the August Moon*, which makes us wistful for the orient again and tonight are going to the Congressional baseball game when we hope the Republicans will roundly trounce the Democrats, all for the benefit of the poor children's camp fund. Before that we will go to a small reception for Danny Kaye when some Ambassador is going to decorate him for what he has done for the UNICEF Fund.

We went to one formal dinner at the Greek Embassy, about twenty present, and it was exquisitely good French food. As folks were starting to leave, the Ambassador whispered to Walter to remain after the one Senator and two Congressmen had left, and then before the guests had entirely gone, he presented Walter in the name of King Paul of Greece a medal and an Order of the Phoenix for Walter's help in aid to Greece. It was a beautiful gold and enamel cross on a gold and blue ribbon. Walter had to turn it in to the State Department to keep for him till he dies or leaves the government, because the Constitution says no government official may receive a gift or decoration or present, etc., from any foreign government.[241]

Washington, D.C.   *Sunday, July 29, 1956*

Dear Folks:

Thursday I had a ladies' luncheon for eight. First time I've entertained all year, so it was overdue and gave me a chance to get my silver tuned up and my best linens washed and ironed.

That evening Jim drove in. It being the night before adjournment of Congress, and Walter having been all afternoon in a hassle on the House floor, he was involved at the office till midnight correcting his testimony for the Record. So Jim and I ate a meal that was strangely reminiscent of the ladies' luncheon. Next day Jim and I went to see what Congress was doing in its last hours. Sat in the gallery and watched, ate steak dinners with Walter in the House Restaurant, and the two of them stuck it out till the end, sitting part of the time in the Senate gallery listening to the hot air, while the House was waiting for the final draft of the housing bill to be brought in for their approval.

People were making farewell eulogies to members who would not return for the next Congress; they had a little singing, a general air of high school graduation, "who cares now we're through," bidding their pals goodbye. Walter says as much legislation was passed in the last two weeks as in the previous months, enough so that you couldn't know what was in it and that's not good. They got home after eleven p.m. and the Eighty-Third Congress has expired.

Minneapolis, Minnesota   *Monday, October 29, 1956*

Dear Robinettes:[242]

I'm snatching a moment from the most exhausting, nastiest, meanest campaign we've ever had. Our opponent is a labor-promoted, ruthless lawyer, who as of now has not made one positive statement

---

241   Walter also received medals from Turkey, South Korea, and the Republic of China.
242   A term invented for Miriam's college round robin letter circuit.

of what he would do if elected to Congress. Before nomination, he had to sign a pledge of the labor groups that he would at all times protect their interests and vote in their favor. Our District has always been majority Democrat, but it is increasingly labor dominated, and has changed in nature since we first ran fourteen years ago. The Labor Unions will not invite, nor permit Walter to speak to their members, and they have been told in no uncertain terms how they must vote. Fortunately, some of these stubborn Scandinavians don't regiment too easily, which is the reason we have won in the past. But the pressures and distortions this year are unbelievable.

Opponent has put out and widely circulated a JUDD REPORT CARD attacking eight of his votes as "against social security," "against building schools," "against the veteran," "against labor," etc. In each case he gives number of the bill and date of the vote correctly, then says "this was a vote against disabled veterans" or some such explanation, when most of the time it was a vote to recommit the bill to committee with instructions to enlarge the coverage or appropriations and return it to the House, and when it returned within ten to thirty days, Walter voted for it. Reminds one of the thief before the judge who justified his behavior by quoting Scripture: "Let him who stole, steal," and forgot to add the last two words, "no more."

We have a poor blind man carrying a sandwich board in the busiest downtown section that says DEFEAT JUDD: HE'S AGAINST THE BLIND. The guy is slightly cracked, has picketed Community Chest, has a personal feud with the local Society for the Blind, which does an excellent job here and which Walter helped get $120,000 federal funds on a matching basis, to establish a Northwest Regional Blind Rehabilitation Training School. Blind man wanted the money in relief handouts. It is amazing how people who don't know the facts don't try to find out but phone indignantly to our office to ask why Walter H. Judd is opposed to the blind.

Catholics, especially in opponent's parish where his eight children go to parochial schools, have started an immense letter campaign saying Walter appropriates federal funds for World Health Organization to teach birth control in foreign countries, so defeat him.

Walter met opponent in a debate in a negro church supposedly put on by NAACP, where less than ¼ present were negroes, rest labor supporters, negro moderator a member of the opponent's election committee. Each candidate was given twenty minutes for a statement before general questioning. Walter was loudly interrupted by boos, catcalls, hisses, yelled remarks during the entire twenty minutes. Opponent was heard in respectful silence and loudly applauded. In question period opponent got excited and profane, snarled, threatened, shook his fist in Walter's face while supporters in audience screamed, "Punch him in the nose."

They have trespassed on citizen's private property to tear down and destroy VOTE FOR JUDD signs by the hundreds, and in some cases poured gasoline on them and burned them, calling for the arson squad of the police department. These signs were asked for by the residents, and where in other years we have printed and put up 500, good citizens this year have got so aroused by gangster actions that the demand for Judd signs has soared, so that we have had to print over 5,000, of which 1,000 at least are replacements for indignant destroyed-sign owners.

I have learned, direct from a member of the trucking union here, that I was married once before, to a man names Gates, was either widowed or divorced but left with gobs of money, which is why Walter H. Judd married me and which is providing for the "exorbitant finances" poured into our campaign – in spite of the fact that Walter has sixteen minutes of TV time per week, his opponent three times as much.

I've often said that I wouldn't mind being defeated and leaving this job. But I can't bear to think that we would be defeated by such a man. I still believe in the fundamental American way of allowing each side to present its differing ideas as to ways to achieve a strong, free America, and let the people chose. But this guy does not honestly represent the Democrat point of view, nor does he allow us to represent the Republican side or defend our own record. I know he represents only an infinitely small part of the Democratic Party, but their organization is so strong that their people will vote for the *party* most of the time, and many of them unquestioningly. I hate to see gangster tactics take over any party or segment of American life.

Then that skunk Drew Pearson coming out with a bold-faced lie about the President's "relapse" while in Minneapolis, appalls me. Walter and I were with Ike & Mamie every minute of their 2½ hours in the Twin Cities, motorcade and all. The thousands who saw him here, and all the newsmen, are aghast at the misstatements in Drew's column. While the story can be completely discredited in the Twin Cities, where only thousands saw the President, it can make enormous headway among the millions in the country who are so trained and constituted by our moral standards that they simply cannot understand or believe in the technique of THE BIG LIE: Drew couldn't have said it unless there were *some* basis for it, is the reaction. Well, he did.

We've been having an average of five meetings a day, with three on Saturdays and Sundays. Some I have addressed without Walter attending. We've met with Negroes, Jews, Catholics, laborers, masons, fundamentalist church people, Indians (there are 10,000 in the Twin Cities), postal & civil service employees, veterans organizations, and all kinds of people from our American life. The most heartening thing is that by and large they are substantial, good, friendly, common sense individuals. I've seen a cross section of what at least a part of America is thinking and wanting.

– Private Writing –

October, 1956

I've been objective and maintaining lofty detachment and working impersonally for the candidate to the best of my ability. Last night I guess I was too tired to keep up the armor and the whole sickening, lying, deceitful, dirty campaign overwhelmed me with hatred and frustration and despair. Walter is in a fair way to be defeated, they say. This I wouldn't mind, for there is plenty for him to do yet in this poor world. But I hate for this…man to triumph, even temporarily. Walter is so strong, and so fair, and so decent – and so tired. Ike must be too. I ache, and weep, and kick my heels in agony and frenzy and frustration.[243]

---

243   Walter won the election with 82,258 votes or 56 percent. Joe Robbie, the DFL candidate, had 64,602 votes or 44 percent.

Washington, D.C.　　　　　　　　　　　　　　　　*Saturday, November 24, 1956*

Walter, Dearest –

Sure have been missing you like sin – I'd give anything in the world to turn over in the dark in bed and find your comforting presence and pour out everything and nothing, and feel your understanding and your reassurance! Not that anything special has gone wrong. In fact, many things have "gone right." But there has been a great flow of personnel in and out these last five days, with the countless irregularities of sleeping and meals and telephoning and dishwashing and laying in fast-consumed supplies, and messages and coordinating cars. I'm dead… Well, I've let some of the conflicts and complications out to you and that always helps. Each has her own plans, activities, tensions, and I am the coordinator, or the one they "dump" on, and I'm not up to it. I'll keep on keeping on, with the wish I were wiser and stronger and more rested – and closer to my Beloved.

Washington, D.C.　　　　　　　　　　　　　　　　*Monday, January 11, 1957*

Hi Everybody:

Things run madly & delightfully on. Interspersed with THE WEDDING,[244] I try to keep up with YW activities, or social engagements. The latter included a formal dinner given by Republican members of Foreign Affairs Committee for Democratic members plus the Dulleses, Radfords, Hollisters. It was *much* fun, buffoonery throughout the whole meal. Sample: Questioning of the ICA witness Hollister asked him to distinguish between the ICA and the CIA[245] and explain why there was no "cooperation" in ICA and no "intelligence" in CIA? Another fantastic party: formal dinner at Burma Embassy, for sixteen, for MacArthurs before they leave as our new Ambassador to Japan.[246] After dinner the ladies having coffee in a small drawing room, Mrs. MacArthur got demonstrating calisthenics because Chinese Ambassador's wife, Mrs. Tong, at *seventy* cannot just touch fingers to toes, standing & bending, but can put both palms flat on floor. We were all trying it, except shy dignified Japan Ambassador's wife.

Then Mrs. MacArthur says "Here's a trick to really reduce you" – put small ashtray on her forehead, head tipped back looking at ceiling; then without holding it, she got down carefully on floor, sat, lay flat, got carefully up again. I made the mistake of saying – "A good trick, but I don't see how it reduces you." "*Try it*," she shouts, claps ashtray onto my forehead. I slowly get down to floor, achieved the flat-out position on my back – when in walks the dignified uniformed butler with more coffee, takes one look at me flat in the middle of the small space, holds his head high and steps over me as he fills the cups, then exits, without a smile while everyone else is shrieking. After I stopped laughing, I managed to get back up safely – and if *you* try it, be sure you have on a *long, full*, heavy brocaded evening dress with full petticoats! When the men joined us they wanted to know what the laughter was about and Mrs. MacArthur told them in her inimitable style.

Washington, D.C.　　　　　　　　　　　　　　　　*Saturday, April 13, 1957*

Dear Folks –

It can't be that it was seven weeks ago that we were enjoying the festivities of Mary Lou's wedding!

244　Mary Lou's wedding to Norm Carpenter was scheduled for February 23, 1957.

245　The ICA is the International Cooperation Administration, and the CIA is the Central Intelligence Agency.

246　Douglas MacArthur II was the nephew of General Douglas MacArthur.

How wonderful it was to have Gertrude here, and Elizabeth too. Never could I have gotten thru everything, and never can we thank them adequately for all the help: dishes washed, food served, errands in cars, ironing, vacuuming, gift opening and arranging, messages taken, guests greeted and served and entertained. It was a busy, exciting, wonderful time, with the happiest of memories of their being here to share the gaiety.

After the wedding, I started back to my YW job. On March 15 I gave a President's tea for Board and Staff, here at the house, with ninety invitations, all written and addressed by Elizabeth, and about seventy-five present. I was determined that they shouldn't feel that this was secondary to the wedding, so I killed myself packing away and labeled all the gifts in the recreation room and setting up an exhibit of our Chinese things that would give an idea of old China's culture and philosophy and life. It took time to type up the labels for dolls, hangings, embroideries, art work, books, etc. – but they seemed to enjoy it, and the native Chinese music I had playing on the Victrola. I made the cakes and cookies, but ordered the fancy sandwiches. Had received lovely flowers for the 25th wedding anniversary two days earlier so the house looked beautiful.

The YW Annual meeting and luncheon came off last Monday with nearly 1,000 present, at the Mayflower Hotel. We had greetings by Chris Herter, an excellent twelve-minute inspirational talk by Walter H. Judd (*not* my idea, needless to say, nor did I introduce him!) and a meeting that added up to a gay, excellent, moving affair, according to all reactions. That out of it should have come a nasty piece of "yellow journalism" doesn't distract from the meeting, but reinforces my distress that we holler for a "free press" in this country but don't necessarily get an "accurate press." The *Washington Post* woman writer seized on Mrs. Eisenhower's inability to attend our lunch as she had hoped to do, as a means of discrediting the Administration, centered her entire story on "party mix-up" and "Mrs. Eisenhower disappoints 'hundreds'" – when word had been sent to all news agencies two weeks before that Mrs. Eisenhower would *not* be there. The story describes Chris Herter as a "fill in" for Mrs. Eisenhower, which he was not, and which was discourteous to him when he took time from his schedule to come. The writer gave nothing of the spirit of what I know was a moving and meaningful occasion. Ah me! We are prisoners of our information agencies in this country. We are only lucky if our prison guards are trustworthy men of character – and they are not all.

New York City   *Tuesday, September 17, 1957*

Dear Carpenters & California Judds –

This is station Walter H. Judd coming to you from Two Park Avenue, the office of the U.S. Mission to the UN.[247] I'm typing in Walter's office, 19th floor with a lovely view out to the East River. His secretary, sent up from State Department in D.C., sits outside his door typing.

We drove up Sunday, bringing Car who is now looking for a job and an apartment.[248] We have a nice suite at the Vanderbilt Hotel, which is right next door. Lots of cupboard space has allowed me to set up my "breakfast nook" – the plug-in coffeepot, the cornflakes, canned and fresh fruit, crackers, cheese, soup, cocoa, cookies, plastic dishes & spoons from our picnic basket, all very convenient. Our suite is paid for by State Department and Walter H. Judd gets $7 a day for food, which won't go far at New York City restaurant prices.

---

247   Walter was appointed a U.S. Delegate to the United Nations.
248   Carolyn, often referred to as Car, had graduated from Mount Holyoke College in June.

Walter had orientation meetings yesterday, meet-the-press, delegation meetings to plan strategy on how to block moves to get Communist China into UN, etc. At 8 p.m. we went to the Cabot Lodge suite at the Waldorf Towers with official U.S. cars taking the eight of us from Vanderbilt Hotel. Was intrigued that as you enter the Lodge apartment, there is over the door a big coat of arms and sign, Official Embassy of the USA.[249]

Close to 40 were there, all from our U.S. Mission, including permanent heads of various Councils… Tho' it was called a "black tie" affair, none of the ladies was as formally dressed as would have been true or expected in D.C. First hour spent getting acquainted, and we were glad to talk with Irene Dunne's dentist husband, who no longer practices. I know Irene quite well now, since standing in two long reception lines with her, one in Washington and one here Sunday afternoon, so up and asked her to be the guest of honor at our first United Givers Fund report lunch in D.C. October 9.[250] She was gracious, will have to check her schedule.

Dinner was a plate-on-lap affair, and I sat on a couch with Mr. Dulles and Mrs. Lodge. There was a man giving soft background music, and after a while he went around with an accordion playing special request numbers. When all had finished eating, Cabot Lodge got up and said no one had asked him nor urged him to sing, but he was going to do so anyway, and he gave us a real racy ballad, in fine voice and accompanied by the piano gent. Next he urged Delegate Dr. Wells, President of Indiana University and about five feet square, to come to the piano and sing with Cabot "Back Home in Indiana," which Wells did.

Then we got into Princeton songs for Dulles, and Yale "Whiffenpoof" for some other guy, and soon Delegate Irene Dunne was at the piano singing "Just My Bill" and "Smoke Gets in Your Eyes," and before you knew it Walter H. Judd was at the piano accompanying himself for the uplifting rendering of the bull frog and ladie froggie classic, and Mary Lord[251] got up and gave a yell of a girl's college in 1890, and then she and Walter H. Judd did a Minnesota cheer, and by this time Congressman (and Delegate) Carnahan, who once was a music teacher, had got warmed up and sang a coupla Irish songs, and not to be outdone, George Meany, who weighs only slightly under his wife's possible 250 pounds got to the piano for a Boston ballad, and soon we were all doing ancient and modern stuff in barbershop, and after one special harmonious and blending bit someone shouted, "Bring on Gromyko[252]," and it was the gayest and most relaxed "official" dinner I've ever attended. Everyone was in great shape, and Cabot reminded us this was the first and last time we would be together as a U.S. group alone, for from now on we have to entertain and be entertained by the other national delegations, so we might as well let our hair down, which we did. It was great.

In a few minutes Walter and I will taxi over to the UN building for the opening session of the General Assembly. I have to go back to D.C. tomorrow. My campaign work[253] will quicken pace, and I have numerous meetings, but will be up here on Wednesday, September 25 to celebrate Walter's birthday. They say these speeches made by each of the eighty-one countries that wish to speak

---

249   Henry Cabot Lodge was the third U.S. Ambassador to the U.N., 1953-1960.

250   Irene Dunne received five Academy Award best actress nominations (1931-1948) and was awarded the Kennedy Center Honors Lifetime Achievement Award in 1985.

251   Mary Lord was born in Minnesota to the Pillsbury family, and was an active civic worker and delegate to the United Nations.

252   Gromyko was the Minister of Foreign Affairs for the Soviet Union.

253   Miriam was chair of the Residential section of the Washington D.C. United Givers Fund.

may take till mid-October, before they get on with the work of the committees. There are seven of these latter, and Walter has been put on the Economic and Social Committee (or ECOSOC, as they call it familiarly), which deals with Technical Aid to Underdeveloped Countries, World Health Organization, International Labor Organization, all International bank, loan, credit stuff, etc.

Washington, D.C.   *Tuesday, October 22, 1957*

Dear Folks –

All regular activity hereabouts has stopped for the Royal Visit this week,[254] and it has been gay in the whole city, flags, welcome signs, photographs of the Royal Couple in shop windows. I was lucky enough to be at the lunch the Nixon's gave for them at the Capitol. About ninety people were there, and we all walked thru the line that had formed and that had in it the Prime Minister & Foreign Minister of Canada and their wives, as well as the royal guests and the hosts. Then we all proceeded down police-lined corridors to the old Supreme Court room where the honor guests sat up on the dais in the seats that used to be occupied by the Nine Men, and the rest of us at tables that radiated out from the raised platform. There were place cards, and a seating chart; Charlie Halleck of Indiana[255] took me in, and I found Nelson Rockefeller on my other side, so I was well attended and had excellent table conversation. The Hallecks had had dinner the night before in Rome, and it was interesting to have him say that he really had to alter his ideas and his voting in the last decade because things had changed so fast, and that no one could have told him ten years ago that he'd be supporting Foreign Aid… He and Nelson had a discussion across me as to whether we were being unnecessarily panicked by the Russian technological advance.[256]

We were standing by our chairs when the guests filed in. The cheerful buzz suddenly stopped and it was still as death and just as solemn. The Queen came right along three feet in front of me, and she is lovely. Poor hearty Halleck couldn't stand the excessive silence, which is what we were all feeling, so he started a good clapping, and instantly everyone joined in applause and the ice was broken and she knew in *our* language that we Americans liked her.

Dick Nixon made a delightful speech about three things we had in common: our legal system, our legislative system, and our language; all represented by the room we were in, for it had served as the Senate, the Supreme Court, and famous earlier orators had spoken there – although, he added, they say English hasn't been spoken in America for some time. But that was about to be remedied by one who would speak English language more beautifully than anyone else – and he toasted the Queen. After applause she rose and replied graciously and briefly, then she toasted Ike. We sat fifteen minutes and drank coffee and visited, till the Royal table guests withdrew.

The Queen walked slowly, smiled and bowed graciously as she went out to the car. Traffic routes were jammed, and I had to get home and change to something dressier – and get to the British Embassy for the reception given by the Commonwealth Ambassadors. We stood in line an hour before we wound our way into the building. It was fascinating to watch people arriving. The dresses were stunning, the dressiest afternoon affair I've ever been at. Even the men were beautiful: military dress uniforms with decorations, many of the Commonwealth Countries men carrying swords, many

---

254   Elizabeth II, Queen of England, and Prince Philip were visiting the U.S.

255   Charlie Halleck was a Republican congressman from 1935 to 1968 and former House majority leader for eight years.

256   Sputnik 1, the first artificial satellite to orbit the Earth, was launched by the Soviet Union on October 4, 1957.

of our diplomats with striped trousers and cutaways, and even some pearl grey vests, spats, gloves, and toppers. Two sons of the Pakistani Ambassador had gorgeous dress-white turbans, wrapped so one end trailed down below their waists and the other end perked stiffly up like a sail on a ship. The men from Ghana had their brilliant reds and yellows wrap-around skirts to the ankles, not to mention the Scotts in their kilties…

Now to get down to the humdrum facts of life, like raising *my* United Givers Fund quota: I've kept busy at the details, with only a third of our $954,000 pledged at the second luncheon… We had Helen Hayes[257] there, and she graciously told us how proud she was to claim Washington as her birthplace when she saw how hard we women were working in this community responsibility – nice of her, wasn't it? And believe it or not, Pearl Mesta[258] came, and crowned our Quota Queen of the week with a lovely John Frederick hat, contributed by John Frederick himself. There were 550 women present, and they will come for this kind of program, and that's what we want, for when they come for the lunch, they bring in their reports and collections.

I had set up a "roving reporter," getting one-minute human interest stories (previously prepared) from workers on the floor. One of the ladies brought down the house when she stood, set her adorable three-year-old son on the table and said she couldn't go soliciting without him so he went with her every time, and he would not go without his dogs so he took them – and here he was holding two cute wiggling toy terriers and a larger dog in the basket beside him, all alive – and then the cat unexpectedly followed them and wouldn't go back – and here a beautiful cat jumped out of the basket on the table. So here was the menagerie she solicited with – but she had made over 200% of her quota! The press had a heyday with *that* story.

Miriam, Helen Hayes, and Mrs. Frederick B. "Pillow" Lee at
the United Givers Fund luncheon

257   Helen Hayes was considered the first lady of American theatre and in 1986 received the Presidential Medal of Freedom.
258   Pearl (aka Perle) Mesta was a well-known Washington socialite and hostess.

U.S. Mission to the United Nations in New York City   *Thursday, November 21, 1957*

Dear Folks –

Here I am working in Walter's office (at no pay!) and learning a lot fast. State Department has discovered that Press loves to talk to Walter, and they are besieged with requests for interviews. It's strange to be under their jurisdiction and to have to clear every request for his time with one department or another: Press, Radio, Protocol (for *all* engagements). Walter has been used to being his own boss and it is a new life to have to report every time he turns round. Then to see the kind of staff and equipment and outlay they have to run their operations, with organization and personnel ad infinitum, requisitions and reports and blanks to fill, is a revelation. I'm all the more amazed now at the volume and variety of work he turns out in his Congressional office with a limited staff and none of these side helps (or hindrances?).

Every evening there is one or more events: receptions, meetings, speeches. Went to one given by the new Malayan delegation. Someone inadvertently introduced me to Mr. Zarubin. Walter usually doesn't bother to speak to the Russian delegates, or else just nods if spoken to by them. Fortunately, I quickly managed to have both hands full so didn't have to shake hands! From there we went to a reception at the Carnegie Peace Foundation building, given by the Associations for the United Nations. He went back to the office to dictate long and late, and I went to a meeting of the New York City Holyoke Alumnae club, both without any further dinner…

On this Russian relationship, I fully expect some cloak-and-dagger stuff against Walter. In a Committee session the other day Mr. Sobelov, a Russian delegate, was haranguing and reviling against the USA in a speech and Walter interrupted on a point-of-order to suggest to the Chairman that the speaker was not on the subject. He wasn't, either, technically, for they were discussing a part of the Korea program that applies only to South Korea, and Sobelov was scolding about alleged difficulties in North Korea. But the Chairman unfortunately is a Czech, tho' one of the milder ones; still, he could not see himself calling down the Russian delegate.

Walter continued to be embarrassing (he told me he was sick and tired of listening to the same record of lies and incriminations in polite and respectful silence, and besides, some of the State Department advisors were secretly egging him on to battle – the big sissies!) and finally Czech asked the Russian Delegate to speak to the subject. Russian didn't change one bit from his prepared script, and when Walter interrupted again he turned on him and made slurring remarks about the dictatorship of the United States trying to control everything. Walter replied that he wasn't an expert in dictatorships, but he did know something about the democratic processes and he would like to call for a vote of the committee as to whether the speaker was in order or not. The vote was taken with more than fifty members voting he was out of order, a few satellites voting loyally that he was not. Sobelov had to quit and did so fiery mad. We do have our fun.

Another day when Mr. Menon[259] got more than usually insulting in a speech in committee, attacking personally one of the other delegates, the Chairman, a member of one of the smaller countries, ruled that Mr. Menon's speech was terminated. Better such verbal insults than violent physical ones, I guess.

---

259   Ambassador Menon was the Indian Ambassador to the United Nations, 1952-1961.

As for domestic duties: had two free hours between jobs today, so went across to our Hotel, dumped into the bathtub all the soiled sleepwear and underwear, male and female, added soap flakes and hot water, removed my shoes, got in, and tramped around on the stuff up and down the tub singing happily, "He is trampling out the vintage where the grapes of wrath are stored."[260] This served several purposes, besides washing the clothes. It exercised my voice and my power of balance in a slippery tub. It got my nylons clean as I still had them on. And when I wearied, I sat on the edge of the tub and read *Auntie Mame* while swishing with my feet the laundry back and forth, up and down. The rinsing was accomplished in a similar thorough manner, after the tragedy of losing one nylon down the drain, which pulls the water out with the power and roar of Niagara. Now our bedroom is filled with hangers of drying sox and underwear, and the heat is turned up high. Don't let anyone tell you we don't work for our living at the United Nations!

---

260 From "The Battle Hymn of the Republic."

11
Campaigns and Community
1958 – 1962

With her daughters out of the home and her parents deceased, Miriam gave herself fully to volunteer commitments, including serving as trustee of Mount Holyoke College and President of the Washington Area YWCA. These honors came with travel obligations and necessitated hours of work. She dutifully accompanied Walter, whose stature was enhanced when he gave the keynote address at the 1960 Republican National Convention to a crowd that leapt to their feet when he concluded. But her distaste for notoriety and conflict continued.

Official trips with Walter to Puerto Rico and Canada and Asian countries brought stimulation and new understandings to her curious mind. Despite Walter's role as a statesman in Washington and the broader world, he faced increasingly strenuous campaigns and eventually redistricting in Minnesota after the 1960 census. Walter's decision to "run" in the newly defined district had been conflicted, and Miriam had reservations.

She spent more time with her grandchildren in Minneapolis that fall – and both Carolyn and Ellie came and worked intensely for the campaign. But it was not to be, and Walter was defeated in his eleventh campaign with new boundaries (although winning in his old district). Miriam was not sorry to leave the public arena. Unfortunately, no letters exist covering the final campaign or the aftermath.

Her responsibilities in the YWCA would escalate and require sensitivity. Her attention also had been turning toward her adult children, and she made it a priority to visit her daughters whenever possible. Carolyn worked in Boston, New York, and Cape Cod, and Ellie completed college in Providence and moved to New York City and got a job with American Airlines. I worked for three years in Ann Arbor, Michigan while my husband studied law. During that time we had our first child, a son. After graduation and relocation to Minneapolis, our first daughter was born.

❧

Washington, D.C.   *Wednesday, February 19, 1958*

Dear Gals –

There are deep drifts of snow out front. I've enjoyed staying in and working on house decorating projects. Have straightened out both attic and cellar storerooms. In the overhaul, came onto the wardrobes of Sarah Betsy and Roseanne.[261] I was astounded at the extensive wardrobes they had and at the enormous amount of sewing it all involved, and wondered where I ever got the time for all that plus the more demanding housekeeping when you were small.

Washington, D.C.   *Sunday, March 2, 1958*

Hi Family:

This week we have our regular three-day sessions evaluating our YW work and planning for next year. Then Wednesday I am going to take twenty-five students from the Hannah Harrison School[262] on a sightseeing session of the Supreme Court, Library of Congress, and Capitol and finish up with sandwiches and coffee in Walter's office while I answer questions. Wonder what the official guide's salary is?

Had a fun day last week, when I was one of the official hostesses at the Eric Johnson Nationwide Conference on Mutual Security. They had many more acceptances than they expected for this one-day conference, at which Harry Truman addressed the lunch and Ike the dinner, with Nixon chairing excellently in the afternoon a question-and-answer session. So they asked a bunch of forty of us "outstanding" women and gave us a good briefing and assigned duties to help with registration, answering questions, carrying messages, keeping people buttered up who were mad that they couldn't have a front table in the unassigned meal seating.

As they told us, the guests were as distinguished as the head table, and everyone deserved special treatment, and we were to give it to them, and did. I pinned Harry Commager's identifying nametag on for him; bumped into Danny Kaye when he was talking with Myrna Loy and Ralph Bunche; got a photographer for some people who wanted their picture taken with Adlai Stevenson; gave my identifying badge to a friend from Boston who wanted to hear Truman speak, so she was Mrs. Walter Judd for the session. It was an excellent day's meeting.

Another new experience last week: went to the funeral of our great Matriarch, Julia West Hamilton, ninety-one-year-old famous leader of negroes, herself the daughter of slaves, twenty-eight years President of the negro YW here,[263] President of the Board of deacons of her Methodist church, and instigator of practically all advances for negroes hereabouts. It took nearly two hours, was addressed by Dr. Mordacai Johnson, President of Howard University. Ten of us from YW had to march in the funeral procession behind members of her family and negro YW Board and sorority sisters and church circle members and members of the Eastern Star… She was a beloved leader and a wonderful person, and if they were Catholics they would surely have made her a saint…

---

261   The large dolls Miriam had made Carolyn and Eleanor fourteen years earlier.
262   Hannah Harrison School was the residential vocational training program run by the YWCA.
263   This branch of the YW was known as the Phyllis Wheatley branch.

They have asked me to be a member of our Washington Delegation to the Triennial National YWCA convention in St. Louis. I went to the last one in New York City. Dad cheered me by the news that he would be out at men's dinners six nights during that week, to which I'm not invited, so why should I stay home? The National Board of the YW has brought home its fifteen Staff members who work abroad, and is having them in Washington for briefings by Chris Herter...James Reston before they go to convention. They wanted to have a tea for these gals when they could meet the wives of the Ambassadors to USA from the countries in which they work. So I'm giving the tea. I have handwritten longish notes of invitation to Pat Nixon and sixteen wives of Ambassadors. We expect a tea of 35-40. This is the first time that we've ever invited any official Embassy people to our home. I'm polishing silver, cleaning out cobwebs, readying up the joint like mad.

The Congressional Elections Committee hasn't decided whether a recount in the Minnesota First District Election is called for. All look for them to say the Republican Quie was properly elected. He and his wife are due in town by 10 p.m. and are coming to stay here.[264]

Washington, D.C., at Walter's office   *Saturday, March 22, 1958*

Dear Family –

Down at the office this afternoon where I have devised a tabulating form for use in checking the replies Walter gets back from the 100,000-plus questionnaires he sent to everyone in the phone book in our district, on their opinions on public matters…

The Convention at St. Louis was a wonderful experience. Nearly 3,000 there and they kept us busy. We heard excellent speakers. Many of the sessions took up reports of studies we'd been doing in the last triennium, and recommendations were voted up or down. On public affairs there was lively discussion on a resolution to ban atomic or nuclear weapons testing, but it was voted down, because it was a scientific problem on which authorities differed and we didn't have enough information to be intelligent.

Another resolution was that we make a more "vigorous" effort to get integration in schools, housing, transportation, restaurants, etc. Someone from Mississippi said that "vigorous" sounded so aggressive and belligerent that if they had to pledge to that, all YWCAs would be run out of the State. The word "effective" was finally adopted as a substitute, many thinking it was a stronger word anyhow. Many felt that if this would help our southern sisters who had to struggle firsthand with the problem we should do it. But a few became exceedingly bitter over it, stating that we were pussyfooting, and had withdrawn from our original strong stand, weakened our Christian purpose, etc. Another instance of how we can fail to communicate in these controversial areas where emotion plays so large a part.

There was a huge dinner, with me at a head table of forty, wearing the orchid Dad sent for our anniversary. Paul Hoffman[265] gave the address, mentioned Dad's work at the UN as part of positive steps toward peace; 3,000 blue balloons were released from the high ceiling with lights out and spots

---

264   Al Quie was elected in a special election after the death of his predecessor. The Quies became good friends.
265   Paul Hoffman was the former assistant in the CIA.

playing, and the bouncing looked like huge champagne bubbles. A cute skit when someone in space clothes arrived in a spaceship from the YMCA – the Young Moons Christian Association, where she was on the Board of Moonishment, hoped our Y-Teens would come visit their Crescent Adolescents, etc. Quite a dramatic evening.

Washington, D.C.   *Sunday, May 18, 1958*

Dear Family –

This running back & forth to Minneapolis has gotten me so I hardly know where my toothbrush is. We'll be flying out there for State Medical Society meetings on the 23rd with Walter speaking; on the 24th our Republican Convention at which Walter also speaks; on the 25th, the opening of the World Health Organization Tenth Annual Meeting, first one ever held outside Geneva, Switzerland, to which Walter is an official delegate of the House of Representatives.

Doings out there a week ago for the Minnesota centennial were tremendous, amusing, highly political. I went out by train, because ears & sinuses were still bothering. Actually our STATEHOOD day was last Sunday, and they had half of the football stadium full of folks, and the Minneapolis Symphony. Royalty & official guests were introduced and several brought greetings in their own languages. They included Princess Astrid of Norway; Prince Bertil of Sweden; Foreign Ministers, Prime Ministers, and Ambassadors from many of the Central European countries, some of the Far East ones, and all of the Scandinavian ones.

The Governor gave greetings, which got off into politics…an entirely outa place exhortation for that sorta gathering. All the way thru the Democrats acted as if they had built and maintained the State singlehanded, with no notice of the fact that eighty of the last 100 years have had Republican Administrations. For instance, the Governor & State officials went to the airport to meet the distinguished visitors at various times and with proper ceremony, but when the Dulleses flew in on Sunday noon, directly from Copenhagen, the Thyes and Judds were there to meet them, with the inevitable newsmen. It was a disgrace, and too bad that such obvious partisanship crept into a centennial celebration.

General Norstad, Commander of the Allied Powers in Europe, and a Minneapolis product, flew in from Paris with his wife and spoke at the big banquet, was Marshall of the big four-hour parade at the State Fair Grounds. Judy Garland, also born in Minnesota, was there, being quite temperamental and quite pregnant. She sang at the Sunday afternoon affair, scared to death, trembling like a leaf at the mike just six feet in front of us, making a mistake in her first lyrics and having to stop the orchestra and start all over, turning towards Norstads & Dulleses (and Judds) who were seated directly behind her and gasping "It's so damn big – I never was so scared," asking for a drink – it *was* terribly hot – and Walter rushed off platform and came back with a paper cup for her and she asked suspiciously, "What is this?" And when he said, "I think it's orange juice," she sipped it suspiciously. When Dulles got up to speak he started by saying, "I think I must apologize for not having been born in Minnesota," which I thought was cute. It was a great program, the Apollo club singing the official centennial song.

After the big banquet of Saturday night, with nearly a thousand present, they cleared out tables, had a grand march of royalty, international and official guests, with a huge birthday cake being cut right at midnight and champagne toasts to the next hundred years. Dad cheerfully took me into the grand march and as we came down the center in fours, we drew the Pillsburys, and as we came down in eights, I linked arms with Chuck Mayo. Eight was all the room they had abreast so they called for everyone to waltz with his partner and there was Dad in the middle of the room of distinguished and official guests, with all the others lining the sides several deep and watching the procedures. I grabbed him and he waltzed, knowing it would be conspicuous to walk me off the floor, but he alternated laughing at his own predicament and being terrified that someone might cut in to exchange partners and he'd have to dance with the Lady in Waiting to Princess Astrid, or the Governor's wife. Gotta give him credit, he did all right, though he managed to push me towards the sidelines fairly quickly and get himself (and me!) out of danger.

Washington, D.C.   *Tuesday, July 1, 1958*

Dear Family –

The *Career Workshops* program, put on by the YW, and of which I was chairman this year, selected ninety youngsters from the high schools who spent two weeks in five workshops such as social service, foreign service, engineering, etc. We had twenty-one in the medical & biological sciences, whom I helped drive and stayed with them a good bit of the time. A day at the cancer research institute of the National Institutes of Health, where they got in the labs and had scientists demonstrate tissue transplants, genetics of the cancerous mice. They had six of the Ph.D. research people eat with our kids and answer their questions. Next day at the Bethesda Naval Hospital they demonstrated their radio isotopes lab and explained its usages for diagnosis as well as treatment, and their huge atomic reactor and the way it functions for cancer treatments. Next day at Walter Reed Research we had a demonstration of the blood pump used in the "dry heart operations"… It was exciting.

La Fortaleza (The Fortress), Puerto Rico   *Tuesday, July 29, 1958*

Hi, Folks –

Such a wonderful three days we had there. The place itself, equivalent of our White House, is a fabulous old Spanish edifice over 400 years old, used as a fortress only a couple of decades till the Spanish built the Moro Castle Fortress in a more strategic location commanding the mouth of the harbor. The view out to sea is breathtaking, and we had breakfast each morning on one of the verandahs where we could watch a gunboat, a tanker, or fishing boats sail slowly in front of us.

Official visitors from Congress were to help celebrate this sixth anniversary on July 25 of the Commonwealth. We arrived at the enormous airport of San Juan, most beautiful I've seen, at the sleepy hour of 3 a.m. We were up for 8:30 breakfast where we met the other visitors, and our genial host and hostess, Governor Munoz and his wife. First event was the Commonwealth Day parade. The floats showed work of various departments of the government: like 175,000 adults having been taught to read & write in the last five years; like the traveling bookmobiles with places on the rear for a lecturer; like extension work in Agriculture and in-home economics; etc. The other sight of importance were thousands of school children in organizations like Boy & Girl Scouts, 4H Clubs, Junior Red Cross etc.; but largest numbers in a Junior Fireman Auxiliary, where they rode on fire wagons, sang, or shouted in rhythm, made faces, and acted like boys & girls anywhere. This was a popular movement to keep pre-delinquents off the street and give them civic training. It was interesting to see constructive and creative national and local ideas, whereas our parades specialize in scantily-dressed baton-twirlers and waving smile-frozen beauty queens.

That evening there was a formal dinner for about fifty officials & visitors. Afterwards the Governor and his wife and we visitors from the States, formed a receiving line in the courtyard and shook hands with about 1,200 guests, all possible combinations of racial couples, all kinds of names, even some Judds, and all the ladies dressy and high style. We wandered round the extensive gardens, leaned over the parapet and watched the ocean and the moon, listened to orchestra or to a singing group, visited with various ones of the community…

Saturday we visited the International Center, an activities spot for those from other countries who are brought by USA under Technical Development Program to see what can be done in a country by Planning Council, Slum Clearance & Housing Development, Rural Extension work. We had been assigned as personal escorts a couple who took us everywhere in a government car, showed us sights, shops, on a tour thru the famous Morro Castle, etc. Sunday they drove us thru the countryside an hour and a half, south from the coastal plain where the sugar cane grows, into hilly ground where they raise tobacco and coffee, up 2,000 feet to the summer home of the Governor where he and his wife had a wonderful lunch ready. It was cool there; conversation in this small group of a dozen was most stimulating. Mrs. Munoz is a fascinating, able, energetic person, has taught school, raised three girls, gives speeches, tries to stimulate women to improve their condition, is full of laughter. It was a fascinating and delightfully different three days. We left before seven Sunday night, were home around 3 a.m.

Three a.m. seems to be getting to be a habit for arriving places. Week before when we flew to Minneapolis, with the Nixons, we got there almost that late. We left the MATS airport[266] about 9 after a late session of the Senate. Both Senators Thye & Humphrey were aboard with us. Pat & Dick sat by themselves, then asked us to come back and visit. Pat & Myrtle Thye and I talked about campaigning, and her children and how she manages when she has to be away so much, and clothes – good feminine talk, while the men talked politics. Arrived at the Minneapolis airport at one a.m. (two by D.C. time), we were amazed to see vast hordes of people waiting to welcome Nixons, as well as the police band, waiting since 10 p.m., his scheduled arrival time. By the time we got to the hotel there were more hordes to welcome him, roses for Pat, who is always gracious, and to our rooms down the hall from the Nixons and to bed by 3 a.m.

Our weather for the Aquatennial Centennial Day was perfect. Half a million people lined the streets to watch the parade, led by Dick & Pat. He told us later he had been in many parades, but this was the friendliest and warmest and appreciative of practically any. Walter & I watched from the reviewing stand, then returned to the Hotel where Dick & Pat were meeting quietly with a small group of influential Republicans, and where he again answered questions clearly & logically & intelligently. By six p.m. we were at a dinner given for the State legislators & wives, and he went on

266   The Military Air Transport Service.

to yet one more group before we all met at the airport around nine to board his Air Force plane for the return. We loved our day with them, saw lots of friends and constituents, had a good flight home and were back again by – you guessed it – three a.m.

Next was Madame Chiang's visit. The Madame herself looks hardly a day older than when I met her first in Peking in 1934. We went to three formal 8 p.m. dinners. The first at the Chinese Embassy drew the Dulleses, Speaker Rayburn, twenty-six altogether. The Speaker toasted the honored guest and her husband, the Chinese Ambassador replied with a toast to our President, and that left Secretary Dulles on his feet to make a few remarks. He said that he knew we would all like to hear from Madame Chiang. She did make a good talk.

Later people were interested to see the large painting she had done and presented to the Ambassador, and which hung in the entry-reception room. She has taken up painting these last three years, has studied the Chinese style with the contrasting heavy & light brush strokes, and has done lovely things in the style of the old masters. Thirty-two of these have been reproduced in black-and-white and beautifully bound in a large book with an introduction by Chiang Kai-shek himself, and she presented us with a copy inscribed to us. She has studies of the bamboo, which are feathery and graceful, some of the lotus or pine or winter plum. I love best her Chinese landscapes. The Chinese make profound & fundamental assertions about philosophy and the nature of man and the universe by a few brush strokes.

Madame Chiang (right) presenting a pin to Miriam

Next night was a small dinner, sixteen, at Admiral Burke's residence inside the Naval Observatory grounds. They had a Navy string group playing, oriental servants and wonderful food. Admiral Felt took me in to dinner – he is leaving immediately to take over in Hawaii from Admiral Stump as Commander of the Pacific. Fortunately, these dinners break up fairly early – everyone there is working early & late on important matters. In fact, we had to be interrupted once with an important dispatch brought in for Admirals Burke & Felt to O.K. Next night Secretary Brucker entertained over fifty at the Officers Club at Fort McNair. The Madame made another good speech. She is an amazing person. Everyone is pressing for the adjournment of Congress now – "Look Homeward, Angel" is the Congressmen's theme song to their wives.

Washington, D.C. at Walter's office   *Monday, September 1, 1958*

Dear Gertrude & Myrtle:

Walter was appointed to the Atoms for Peace Conference in Geneva, representing the House.

Minneapolis, Minnesota, at Walter's office   *Sunday, October 5, 1958*

Dear Family:

Working at the office on a quiet Sunday afternoon, trying to get caught up. Would be nice to be watching the World Series game, but we took our recreation yesterday at the first home football game and saw Pittsburgh defeat Minnesota in the last two minutes– an excellent game.

This week I went to Chicago for a two-day workshop of eighteen metropolitan YW's on improving the administrative process with the changing and complex problems in big cities.

When Walter was in Geneva he ran into a science editor of our Minneapolis papers, Cohn. Chatting informally about atoms, fallout, physical dangers, Walter automatically mentioned his facial cancers and x-ray burns. Cohn was intrigued, asked intelligent questions, then wrote up an article for our papers with the headline, "JUDD TELLS OF HIS LIFE WITH CANCER – Has Personal Interest in Radiation." The article was essentially correct in detail, but it focused attention on his personal matters, quoting Mayo Clinic doctors who had worked on his face. Some of our supporters were scared that the election was lost, as "no one will vote for a person with cancer," although the first paragraphs said plainly he is in no more danger than he has been ever since he was eighteen.[267] The others thought that it would help his election because everyone would be glad to vote for one who has struggled so long with cancer. But Walter prefers to win on issues, not on personal sympathy. There's been a bit of comment and some mail… That's the part of this game I love: Thinking up how to answer his letters in ways that will suit him, not offend the writer, and not sound like Hubert Humphrey.

Minneapolis, Minnesota   *Sunday, October 19, 1958*

Dear Family:

Thursday Walter flew to New York to speak that evening at the big kickoff dinner of United Jewish Philanthropies. After he left I got word that Ellie had a large tumor in her left breast, was in Baker Memorial Hospital of Mass. General, where Carolyn had the operation scheduled for 8 a.m. Saturday, but needed parental permission. I spent a busy day trying to find Walter – the first time he

---

267   Walter was treated for acne with the then-new radiation technology and his face was badly burned, resulting in permanent scar tissue.

ever went away, I think, that he did not leave word what hotel he would be in, or where speaking, as he had planned to fly back immediately after his speech. Called *New York Times*, called Jewish friends in Minneapolis to see if they knew where the New York City event was to be held, finally found myself sitting next to Minneapolis Mayor at the head table of a dinner I went to that evening to represent Walter, and asked him how he found "missing persons" and he put his police network on the ticker to see what he could find in New York.

Meanwhile Walter got found by no one, as he was in Great Neck, Long Island and not on Manhattan. He blissfully took his plane to Minneapolis, taxied out on the runway and after some delay they said they would have to transfer to another plane. During this wait, he called El at college to say, "Hello," found out from her roommate that she was in the hospital in Boston, got to talk to El tho' the hospital was not going to put the call thru because it was late, and was up in Boston shortly, with Car and her boyfriend meeting him at the airport. Car had called Mary Lou to say that she would not be stopping in Ann Arbor the next night on her way to Minneapolis, and Mary Lou then called me to say that Walter was found and was in Boston.

Next morning, Walter saw El and the surgeon, found that this was a hard tumor, different and difficult and uncertain. Walter wanted her to come to Mayo, but El was determined this was going to be non-malignant and over easy, so she could be back at college this week for the important things she is involved in. Walter was pleased with everything he learned about the surgeon. So they went ahead, while I went on attending Walter's meetings and interpreting his absence the best I could. I made no speeches for him but did get introduced to give a word of greeting. The tumor popped out easily and a frozen section showed no malignancy. We were vastly relieved. She insisted I not come to stay with her, as Carolyn planned to stay on a few days.

Walter left Boston at noon Saturday and got back here by 5 p.m. in time for a huge Republican carnival in the armory, which pepped up over 5,000 people with bands, speeches, free rides for the kids, fancy booths for candidates where we gave away shopping bags with big red & blue JUDD stickers on them… We're both weary today, but still pitching.[268]

Washington, D.C. at Walter's office   *Wednesday, November 12, 1958*

Dear Folks:

Came down to be present at the unveiling in the Capitol rotunda of the second statue of a famous Minnesotan in the Statuary Hall. This is a beautiful bronze of Maria Sanford, educator and professor at University of Minnesota. She is only the second woman to be put in this Hall of Fame of the States, the other being Emma Willard.[269] President Merrill of the University of Minnesota gave the address and was moving. Governor Freeman presented the statue for the State, and Senator Thye received it for Congress. A group of Minnesota young folks performed the "Legend of Paul Bunyan." Many officials down from Minnesota. It was a most impressive occasion.

---

268   Walter won the election in November with 59,739 votes or 57 percent. Joe Robbie, the DFL candidate, had 44,433 votes or 43 percent.

269   Emma Willard was an educator in Massachusetts in the 19th Century.

My weekend at Holyoke was interesting and fun.[270] We had a reception at the faculty center with heads of departments – and a dinner with the President, and I am an honorary member of the Faculty Club. I am keen about the contacts and the people and the interests they represent.

Washington, D.C.   *Thursday, December 4, 1958*

Dear Gals –

Saturday morning I'm taking the Staff at Hannah Harrison School to a color Japanese film of a Chinese classic, *Legend of the White Serpent*, then bringing them home for lunch. Had Miss Cook and Gretchen[271] here for dinner Wednesday before we went to see the Archibald McLeish play *J.B.*, which was magnificent. Now I want to read it, for there is much that is intriguing and complicated that you can't get on the first hearing.

Washington, D.C.   *Sunday, December 7, 1958*

Hi Gals –

Gateway Nursery School is celebrating its 25th Anniversary. I don't know how vivid your memories of the Nursery School are or your feeling about its influence on you. But I will be eternally grateful that they were there when I got home from China with 2 & 2/3 children, with the concern of not hearing from Walter in China, living in the grandparents' house, with the strangeness and readjustments necessary in the lives of little gals. Ethel[272] was a godsend, and she understood and helped Mary Lou particularly. Guess I don't remember specifically those persons or events that influenced or guided me when I was four and five, either. I was thinking of this especially because of visiting the McClure girls this week.[273] Probably when Holly grows up she'll never remember getting out of bed at night and tiptoeing to peer over the banister at Bep & Jim and me talking in the living room and asking with a troubled frown why all of Baby Jesus' angels (in the crèche) have brown hair. Little blondie that she is, she was likely lying in bed worrying that she could never grow up to be an angel for Baby Jesus.

Washington, D.C.   *Sunday, January 18, 1959*

Hi, Gals and Pals:

Most noteworthy fact is enormous numbers of letters and newspaper clippings continuing to come in regarding Walter's Mikoyan stand.[274] Thursday night this week Steve Allison had Dad on his late night show that broadcasts weekly from the downtown Peking Restaurant. I went with Dad about 11, sat at a table with Chinese tea till Dad got called to the mike. Then Steve asked him one question about Mikoyan and he was off to the races. When he finally paused for breath minutes later he got a huge hand from the drinkers and diners present, and Steve shook his head and said "I never got to ask him all the questions I had jotted down." I said, "Never mind, I've been trying twenty-seven years to get a word in edgewise too," which got a laugh over the radio.

---

270 Miriam had been elected an Alumnae Trustee of Mount Holyoke College in May 1958.
271 Mabel Cook was Executive Director of the Washington YWCA; Gretchen Feiker was on the staff.
272 Ethel Bader was the director of the Gateway Nursery School in Montclair, New Jersey.
273 Betty Lou (née Barber) and Jim McClure's five daughters.
274 Mikoyan was Russia's First Deputy Premier, Khrushchev's cohort, unofficially visiting the U.S.

Washington, D.C.   *Sunday, April 5, 1959*

Dear Family:

Walter and I went to the 8 p.m. formal dinner given by Chris Herter[275] for the NATO foreign ministers and dignitaries in town celebrating the tenth anniversary of NATO. About 125 people in that Pan American building ballroom gorgeously decorated. Walter and I were the only people from Congress. The Air Force Band in their scarlet coats lent color as well as gaiety to the scene, and during the meal the "wandering strings" walked around the guests at that U-shape table playing. Foreign Affairs has its romantic moments!

Minneapolis on Easter Monday was lovely, not too cool. The Republican dinner had 1,300 at it, and they made $100,000 on the $100-plate affair, leaving the state party only $50,000 in debt from the last campaign. I sat next to Secretary of Defense McElroy. He made a fine speech, followed by a good Armed Forces movie that tells about our achievements in missiles, defense, etc. Walter had given a ten-minute tribute to Ike, reading from letters Ike wrote him from SHAPE[276] before he came home to run for President. The State Republican Committee had a peppy skit showing our districts on a huge map, introducing those in charge, pledging increased votes for "Victory in Sixty" and performing with enthusiasm and vigor for a change. It was heartwarming.

The visit with Mary Lou in Ann Arbor was wonderful. I went to help get Mary Lou to a surprise baby shower that Ann Barber was giving for her.[277] We had difficulty getting Mary Lou to go over to Ann's. Granted it was pouring cats and dogs, and she felt we could go the next day. I remained stubborn till Mary Lou gave in, feeling that I was becoming set in my ways and inflexible! Well, it was a beautiful party, with Ann having made Petit Fours, and tiny creams puffs. Mary Lou was overwhelmed when she found what she was into, and delighted with the baby things she got.

Washington, D.C.   *Sunday, April 26, 1959*

Hi Family:

Last two weeks D.C. had the National Republican Women's convention, the DAR convention, and the International Chamber of Commerce convention. Three black-tie dinners in ten days. I had to reconstruct one spring evening dress, as well as a few hems on daytime dresses and re-doing some hats. I am buying no clothes.

Went to a function opening the office of American Friends of the Middle East. One night Walter spoke at the Mosque (in the downstairs lecture room) on the anniversary of the death of Pakistan's great poet & philosopher Iqbal; we met many Muslims & Middle East friends.

Gotta work on a speech to make to the Delaware Holyoke alumnae at Wilmington next Monday on the work of the Trustees; the "honor" also necessitates hard work.

---

275   Chris Herter was then the U.S. Secretary of State.
276   SHAPE was the Supreme Headquarters Allied Powers of Europe, the central command of NATO's military forces.
277   John Barber and wife Ann lived in Ann Arbor where John and Mary Lou's husband were both studying law at the University of Michigan.

Washington, D.C.   *Monday, June 29, 1959*

Dear Folks:

The Canada trip was as much fun as the Puerto Rico one a year ago. I could get to enjoy these official trips with Walter, given a chance!! Walter is on a small committee of our Congress & Canadian Parliament members, to discuss bothersome matters between our two countries. They meet twice a year, had their first sessions in D.C. last January, and their "return engagement" around the celebrations of the opening of the seaway St. Lawrence. I think their idea is not to get into the press. I did hear him say that we don't need Canada's uranium since discovering our own supply, yet have a contract for years ahead to buy theirs, and they have built up good-sized cities at the uranium spots and can't suddenly abandon them. What to do?

This "inter-parliamentary" group, plus wives, went to Montreal by Navy planes ahead of official Washington. Were met with the red carpet treatment and escorted into town. Stayed at the dignified old Windsor Hotel. There the men had two long afternoon sessions while the ladies played. Wives of the Canadian members of the group entertained us. We had a fancy ladies' luncheon, and that evening their Secretary of State, or Secretary of External Affairs as they call him, gave a formal buffet dinner for 100 of us. I'd forgotten how French Montreal was. Walking along the shops and streets you hear as much French as English. Everywhere all the welcoming signs for the Queen were printed in both languages – and every tiniest shop had a Queen's picture or a jeweled crown.

The dedication ceremonies on Friday went off like clockwork. Everyone went out on chartered buses, officials and public alike, and there was no traffic jam. It was a beautiful day, hot but breezy. We got more burned than we realized we could. Bleachers were set up in a huge green mall alongside the lock; flags of Britain, Canada, and U.S. were flying on tall standards; each side of the roofed, royal stand were bands, the Canadian playing the Star Spangled Banner, our Navy Band playing "God Save the Queen."

Loud speakers kept us advised when Ike and party landed at the airport and were greeted by the Queen, when they got into the long line of black Cadillacs. Finally, the line of shiny cars appeared, drove slowly down a road lined with thousands of cheering citizens, and the ever-present Canadian Mounties whose scarlet coats give a spectacular touch to any occasion. The Queen raises her right hand slowly to acknowledge the cheers. I'm sure some enterprising scientist must have measured stress factors and fatigue and decided how high her arm should move up, and how often. Do you suppose she counts to thirty between moves? She looked lovely in the brilliant aqua-colored loose-hanging coat; even the most distant little child could pick her out of the crowd and say he had seen the Queen. Her voice when she read her speech was lower pitched than it used to be, and stronger. Voice lessons? Everyone said her French accent was perfect, which no one could say for Ike, much as they admired his spunk in saying one French sentence.

After the speech-making and book-presenting and thanking, they reloaded the cars and drove down the river edge a few hundred yards to where the yacht was parked. Each guest was piped aboard, which is another custom I can't understand because the sound is so frail and sickly and strange. I'd rather have Ike's twenty-one-gun salute, loud and booming. Then the yacht started up the canal, coming toward the bleachers where we were seated, and the Queen and Ike so close to people on the banks, because the canal was about wide enough for the yacht to get thru… The fireworks releasing small parachutes that broke out U.S. and Canadian flags…truly a sight.

That evening the Prime Minister of Canada had a buffet supper, formal, for 3,000 guests, tho' Ike and Mamie and the Queen and Philip were not there. We had fun, met a bunch of Minnesotans there, as our Duluth is the end of the Seaway, and it is to have its dedication July 11 with Fred Seaton[278] doing the honors, Walter accompanying.

Ann Arbor, Michigan   *Friday, July 24, 1959*

Dearest –

I hate to think of you coming home to an empty house, but I do feel needed here.[279] Mary Lou was weary and anxious, but is beginning to see daylight altho' she is still concerned about spit-up & feeding. I've kept busy doing wash & iron, fixing special foods to tempt Mary Lou's appetite, cleaning, doing baby wash from each spit-up. I think it helps Mary Lou to have me around to discuss "Shall I let him sleep or get him up & feed him?" "He spit up, shall I try to give him more?" "Is he more comfy on his tummy or side?" Greatest satisfaction of all is feeling that tiny thing on my shoulder! But I miss you: it will be wonderful to get home.

Paris, France[280]   *Sunday, August 23, 1959*

Dear Family –

Such fun we had yesterday – thanks to Harriet Curry.[281] She picked us up in her grey Volkswagen. The countryside was lovely to drive thru to the impressive war memorial to Americans killed in World War I, placed in a commanding position looking down the valley of the Marne, quiet idyllic farm countryside where it is impossible to visualize the heavy tank and artillery fights of those awful war days. You certainly get a feeling about how much suffering we in U.S. were spared by not having our country fought over. Arrived at Reims, we went to the old schoolhouse, which was used as Army headquarters during World War II and where the German surrender was signed on May 7, 1945. From there to the Reims Cathedral. Drove home thru a glorious sunset, reflected in the Marne & the Seine.

Friday El & I had a tour thru the new UNESCO buildings. I was impressed at the way all countries had had a part in putting this building together and yet not making it look scrappy. We ate lunch looking out on the Eiffel Tower. Today we went to Notre Dame for the 11:15 a.m. service commemorating the liberation of Paris, August 25, 1944. A colorful event: officers & dignitaries of SHAPE, France's military and civil leaders, dressy clergy, lovely music, taps played, flowers & wreaths for those killed – again brought home the importance of war's *end* to those in the midst of the fighting and suffering.

---

278   Fred Seaton was the Secretary of the Interior.
279   Miriam was helping with her first grandchild, Kevin Capenter, born on July 13, 1959.
280   Miram and Ellie took a three-week trip to England, France, and Spain after Ellie's Pembroke College graduation.
281   Harriet had grown up next door to the family in D.C. and was serving at the American Embassy in Paris.

Madrid, Spain   *Thursday, August 27, 1959*

Dearest –

We found your letter and clippings when we got to the hotel at 6:30, as well as birthday cards, which El won't let me open until tomorrow.

At Irun, on the French-Spanish border, we were met by Francesca (Ambassador John Lodge's wife) and their driver. She whisked us through all barriers and took us home with her. She was friendly and genuine, and we loved the half-hour drive to San Sebastian. About 10 we got to the small rented house where John uses one room on ground floor for his office – and obviously feels it pretty inadequate in comparison with other countries, which have impressive summer embassies there. He was cordial, spoke in highest and glowing terms of you, and complimented El on her beauty – so that she *knew* he was insincere (but I know he has good judgment!). We dined with John and Francesca, everything nice, but simple, enjoyed the conversation.

Madrid, Spain   *Friday, August 28, 1959*

Dearest –

Such a wonderful birthday this has been, with a feeling that my family is closer than the miles we measure distance by. As we were having breakfast in our sitting room, up came a messenger with your cute birthday cable, making you seem as near as yesterday. When we went out, Mary Lou's letter had come with your note on the envelope. How wonderful to have the snapshots of my grandchild – not to mention of my husband, who seems to have the baby spellbound!

Cambridge, Massachusetts   *Monday, November 9, 1959*

Dearest –

I'm staying a coupla days with Car after my Holyoke meetings. It was comforting to be with one of the family when Mary Lou phoned to say Betsy McClure had died of leukemia.[282] Mary Lou was quite broken up, had been with Ann Barber when the phone call came. It was a shock to everyone, except Jim & Bep who have known a year and a half and told *no* one. I can't get over what great strength & courage they have had all this time to let life go on as normally and happily as possible for all. There *can* be so much drama & maudlinity when it is known a child has a terminal illness… Trustee meetings were strenuous & controversial but stimulating too. Won't write in detail as you may not be getting my mail. I need you specially today.

Washington, D.C.   *Sunday, November 15, 1959*

Dearest –

It's a nice Sunday, and I'm wondering where you're spending it. The YW Food Fair on Friday was a huge success, over 5,000 there at the Mayflower. I worked till my feet ached and my back ached worse. Had work to do tonight on Hannah Harrison Committee luncheon for tomorrow… I'm

---

282   Betsy McClure was almost seven – the oldest daughter of Betty Lou and Jim McClure.

announcing a study committee to help us evaluate the needs of women in 1960, employment trends, etc., to recommend changes.

Washington, D.C.   *Sunday, December 6, 1959*

Hi, Gals –

Dad finally got to this hemisphere Wednesday. The story of his riding to Kabul with Ike's Naval Aide who was trying out Ike's route, is pretty confused in my mind. Thursday he took 6 p.m. plane for Minneapolis so you can see I've not had time for much news…

Today at church I asked Dr. Vincent if he would baptize Kevin at the 11 a.m. service on the 27th, and he said he would be delighted. Besides being our interim preacher till the end of Jan., he was minister of the church in Upper Montclair that helped with our missionary support in Fenchow, and Mary Lou went to Sunday school there and sang at Christmas time in the "angel choir" when she was four. I think it will be wonderful to have someone with this connection with our family.

The Dutch Embassy sent me 100 tulip bulbs with a cordial note from the Ambassador. I gave some to Betty Curry,[283] planted the rest in various beds in front yard on our warm beautiful Friday. Also raked all the leaves, cleaned up the place. Wow, my aching back!

Washington, D.C. at Dad's office   *Friday night, January 8, 1960*

Hi, Gals –

How good to have all home, and still I see evidence of your visit on every side. Partly that's because I haven't got the Christmas things put away. Dad watched football on New Year's, so I took down Christmas ornaments, with him doing the lights; then I sorted Christmas cards for sending the pictures to my missionary friends. I wait till I have a miserable cold to wind the good pieces of ribbon and iron out the saved pieces of tissue paper.

Today I went to a 10 a.m. coffee of the Republican Congressional Wives, where we discuss our problems of campaigning and entertaining constituents and the like. Pat Nixon nudged her way into the group of three I was talking in, got talking about her gals liking Friends School. She said Tricia is in eighth grade and they now let the girls wear lipstick to the six evening parties at the school during the year. One of the Judds must have pioneered that, for I remember you nearly getting put out of the school for sneaking into the girls' room during the dance and lipsticking up.

Watching Ike give his State of the Union message before Congress yesterday gave me as much thrill as if I'd never seen it before. I sure don't get blasé. Most of our pals tho't it was one of his best – whether he felt it was his last year and he could let loose and say what he pleased, or whether he's matured and grown, who can say. Great guy, this Ike.

---

283   Betty Curry and family lived next door and was a beloved friend to Miriam.

Washington, D.C.   *Thursday, January 21, 1960*

Hi Family –

This has been society week with us. Last two nights we've dined at official dinners with Prime Minister Kishi of Japan. Dad was at the White House for the official signing of the defense treaty Tuesday afternoon. The Japanese gave a dinner for sixty in the State Room of the Mayflower, complete with gold dishes and gilt-edged, Japan-seal-embossed menus in French, and starting with gorgeous fresh strawberries in Cointreau. I learned from my Japanese dinner partner (thru the attractive State Department interpreter who sat between/behind us, complete in dinner jacket, but getting no food, alas – eight of them at the dinner scattered round near the distinguished Japanese) that Japan grows amazing strawberries, planting them in the chinks of a wall for protection and to get the warmth from the stone, covering each individual berry with plastic bags to protect them from blight or bug, and eventually harvesting enormous, juicy flavorful fruit – practically like growing an individual melon!

Last night's dinner was given by the Herters at the Anderson House on Massachusetts Avenue. Lots of Defense Department people there… The table had fifteen flower arrangements…each built on a piece of driftwood, with dozens of the largest white or purple orchids set onto the driftwood… It was breathtaking. After dinner when having coffee in the beautiful paneled drawing room with art treasures all around us, they brought the orchids in on huge trays and gave them to everyone – I got only five – ever seen men in formal dress with orchid boutonnieres? I have. Quite an occasion! My turquoise Chinese brocade dress was finished for last night's party, and a number of people asked me where I had it made up. You know my pat answer to that: I have an old lady that has sewed for our family a long time, but she won't take on any new people, and she's slow!

Washington, D.C.   *Sunday, May 8, 1960*

Hi, Folks –

I've had two opportunities to dance recently, and I wonder why I love it so much and yet don't miss it when Dad doesn't dance. One evening was when the Canadian Parliamentary delegation was here. A couple of their members asked me to dance – something about maintaining the good-neighbor policy, no doubt – but I did enjoy it. The other time was when the Horans gave a dinner for some of our close gang[284], on the occasion of Betty Johnson being here on a visit. She has had a grim time, for since LeRoy was defeated he has had a serious hardening of the arteries. She has him in a hospital near her in Sacramento, and goes three times a week and takes him home for dinner or to drive in the afternoon. Everyone tried to give her a good time. With us that night was our good friend Laura Mack, whose Congressman husband from Washington State died on the floor of Congress a month ago, and who cried going out in the car, telling me how terribly unfinished all the details of their life were… The limited number of men did nobly dancing with all of us, and what fun it was…

Another event that brought me joy was the evening I went alone to the Library of Congress to hear Robert Frost. He had expected to be talking to Congressmen and their wives, but for the third time

---

284   Many of these people were first elected in 1942 to the seventy-eighth Congress and had become close colleagues and friends.

in the eighteen years we've been here, the House invoked "Calendar Wednesday," a technical device to call up bills committees won't report out, and in the ensuing bitterness Members used stalling devices, till they were in session till nearly ten. I wish the Congressmen could have listened to his wisdom and his humanity and good sense. He puts things in balance and perspective for me – and we could stand a little (or a lot!) of this in our public life at the moment. Just one quote: "How often we're occupied with *upkeep*, when we should be busy with *uplift*."

Washington, D.C.   *Wednesday, June 29, 1960*

Dear Folks:

A whole bunch of pressure-y situations seem to have arrived at once and wear me down. Include my work with Hannah Harrison School, United Givers' Fund, and Westmoreland Church Education Board. Each has a difficult situation that you've watched growing over two years, and suddenly they all come to a head and require policy discussions and conferences and decisions. I've spent literally hours on each one, and fortunately begin to see some order coming out of chaos. The Givers' Fund, for example, has been operating under an impossible situation that came about when they organized five years ago, and made concessions to certain agencies to get them to come along on the United Drive. This meant some agencies were getting favored treatment in the allocation of funds, and it naturally made the rest of the agencies mad.

I've been protesting the system these last three years I've sat on the Admissions and Allocations Committee, feebly the first year as I was learning the ropes and was overawed by some of the men on the committee. But this year I got up my nerve and spoke out, and voted no, and found I had support for my ideas, and after talking to everyone who would listen, we got thru a plan to have every agency admitted and allocated on the same basis. The whole thing can still be scuttled in the Executive Committee of the UGF – and I find that lots of men work in terms of a "private understanding" worked out "over steak and coffee" instead of in terms of committee understanding worked out in the open. I think men are more hesitant to vote no, when it involves someone they know or work with, even if the merits of the case are obvious, than are women. Well, we'll see what comes.

Another set of pressures are the hundreds of people who have written, wired, phoned, or wanted to talk to Walter about the Keynote speech. Night before the announcement was made I was home alone and newspapers phoned all evening to try to get me to confirm that he was to be chosen, so they could get it into early editions, or on the late news, in the case of radio and TV. They hound you to death. Fortunately, he hadn't been home for dinner that night, so I could honestly say I knew nothing. Then Walter had to call them back when he came in, and satisfy them that no decision had yet been made, as it hadn't, only to have someone start calling us at 6:30 the next morning. The powers and pressures of news agencies, under the slogan of "freedom of the press," frighten me…

The YWCA had bought out the National Theater for the second night of *My Fair Lady*. I had dinner for eight ahead. Since I got my silver polished up, and my hand on making fancy dishes again, I'm having ladies to lunch two days to get some obligations off my conscience.

Washington, D.C.   *Thursday, August 18, 1960*

Dear Family:

We have had four blissful days in a Garden of Eden spot on the Skyline Drive… Walter had about 2,000 communications about the speech, [285] and I think they have all been answered, largely by original letters done on the robot-typewriter and with personal P.S.s added, but many dictated originally. The demands to speak have been enormous. He has given a coupla October weeks to the National Committee for national campaigning…

As for the Convention, mostly I stayed in our suite daytimes and answered the phone, the door, read the mail and the wires, and tried to keep things sorted and important messages passed on. Fortunate that we had El to help Monday & Tuesday, and my nephew Jim McClure all week till he left Friday. They were marvelous! One person could never have handled phones & messages, and gone down to the drugstore for sandwiches and coffee for Walter while he worked, or for us who were too busy opening mail to stop for food.

Part of the flood of letters came because Walter was head of the Minnesota delegation and there was a drive in the State to draft Rocky,[286] and this elicited an anti-Rocky drive, or a draft Goldwater drive, or almost anything else, and there were thousands of letters for Walter coming in bundles. We had to get them opened and sorted, for a few were personal messages or requests mixed in with the "please vote for —" stuff, and we worked solid all day till it was time to go out to the Amphitheater by six p.m., where we would snag a hot dog and a milk shake at one of the counters.

Walter was hurrying between hotels and Headquarters and Minnesota Delegation caucuses and several speeches he had to make. I went with him when he spoke to one luncheon group, and when he talked to the "Nationalities Group," mostly representatives of the captive peoples of Central Europe. But I cut all the rest of the special women's breakfast, luncheons, receptions, etc., till the PAT FOR FIRST LADY breakfast the morning after Dick was nominated.

Thursday night Dick & Cabot gave a small buffet reception for about 100 in their hotel that was fun – mostly governors, senators, bigwigs, and the ubiquitous press. We left there about midnight and went on to where the California delegation were giving what they called a Victory Champagne Party. Every once in a while some MC would stop activities to bring IMPORTANT PEOPLE up on the platform. Walter got an enormous ovation when he was introduced, and we literally couldn't move two feet without people interrupting his progress to grasp his hand. Someone said it took half an hour on Monday night after the Speech, for him to get from the front door of our hotel where the car left us out, to the elevator. I left him to struggle with the crowds and well-wishes and went on up to change; but Carolyn stayed right at his elbow. She didn't want to miss one ounce of glory, and loved every second.

---

285   Walter gave the keynote address at the Republican National Convention in Chicago on July 25, 1960. At the convention, Nixon was the nominee for President; John Cabot Lodge was the nominee for Vice President.

286   Governor Nelson Rockefeller of New York was known as Rocky.

*Miriam (right) with daughters Carolyn (center) and Ellie (left) at
Walter's keynote address*

Minneapolis, Minnesota   *Thursday, September 22, 1960*

Dear Folks:

The Nixon visit here was exciting. Crowds jamming the airfield and all the streets on their
caravan route downtown. Right on the minute the chartered United plane landed, with two others
carrying newsmen following it. I had a huge armful of red roses to present to Pat, gift of the
campaign committee here, which I finally did get into her arms. Then Walter led them back to
where the reception line of about fifty dignitaries was waiting to be introduced. Dick paused to say
something personal to each person, and thus Pat got ahead and no one was taking her down the
line. So I made an end run around the mass of photographers and caught her and finished taking
her down the line. Then she stopped to talk to some high school cheerleaders who had a song for
her, and some cute little tykes who had homemade signs. And each of these got an autographed
card and a ballpoint pen, which the two staff men with Nixons kept hauling out of pockets and
handing Pat. Quite an organization.

They took the Nixons and Walter and me up onto a rickety landing platform from which Dick could
be seen by all the crowds, and he made a wonderful short talk, not missing a trick about our people,
our candidates, our weather, etc. The cavalcade took us downtown where Nixon stopped to cut
the ribbon and officially open the Nixon headquarters, with swarms of people and traffic blocked
off. Thence to Leamington Hotel for a press conference, and Pat and the ladies took off for the
University where they had 7,500 people to meet her, and she was gracious and calm and poised and
unhurried shaking all those hands. She was tired, but still lovely.

After supper at our suite in the Curtis, Norm and Mary Lou joined us, and we four rode in the official
car for Dad (with his name on the outside) in the cavalcade over to Macalester College Field House
in St. Paul, with cheering people on the street, and an enormous crowd to hear Nixon, both jammed
into the Field House, and overflowing to gym and outside bleachers. Nixon went to both these places

to greet the overflow folks after he finished speaking, even tho' his speech had been loud-speakered to them. He made a good speech, tho' you could see that he was tired. From there out to the airport where Mary Lou & Norm got to meet Pat and Dick.

Now a bit about our trip to the West Coast last week. Denver had a fine money-raising luncheon, where I got a lovely orchid. At Colorado Springs there was a good dinner for candidates. Drove through the Air Force Academy grounds, aching acres of space and gorgeous buildings at the foot of mountain ranges, but why does government have to do things so extravagantly?

Took my first jet ride from Denver to LA. On the field there was a helicopter to fly Walter to his noon talk in Long Beach while I drove home with Gert and Myrt. Jim was home early and he took us the nearly two-hour drive to Santa Anna to the Balboa Beach Club where we met Walter for the evening rally. Here I got white butterfly orchid spray corsage. Next a.m. drove to San Bernardino to a county Republican lunch. Here I got red-white-and-blue carnation corsage.

From here flew by special plane (four seater) down to San Diego where there was a huge rally at the famous Coronado Hotel that night. We loved the gorgeous room and the view from our windows out to sea and to the bay and would have so loved to stay there. But again: meet people, shake many hands, smile, say thank-you, a quick supper, a good speech by Walter, and we're off for a 10:30 plane and all-night trip back to Minneapolis in order to greet Nixons on Saturday afternoon. Much too fast, too wearying, but fun and worth doing and helpful, we hope.

Now the usual coffee parties, committee meetings, working in Dad's office trying to keep people mollified who can't get to him, getting Dad to his engagements on time and times he's away enjoying Kevin and his parents to the utmost. [287]

Washington, D.C.   *Saturday, April 15, 1961*

Dear Folks:

This is the first time I've been home for a weekend alone in nine weeks; one weekend El was home with me, which was fun, but the others I've been off gadding. I sat at my desk and the typewriter practically all day typing the last bits of the income tax.

Yesterday morning, Walter and I attended an Inter-American Day affair at the Pan American Building to try to cement (or create!) better relations with our Latin neighbors, at which the President spoke. Cuba's chair was conspicuously empty! Only members of the Foreign Affairs & Foreign Relations Committees had been invited, and I was astounded that Smathers was the *only* Senator present, and Walter the only Republican. When Jacqueline Kennedy came in, she sat in the front row a few seats to our left. She is a beautiful person to look at. When Jack finished his brief and well-written talk she winked at him. This is the closest I've been to her, but wait till next Tuesday when Members of Congress are invited to the White House for a formal reception.

---

287   That November, Walter won with 86,223 votes or 61 percent. Joe Mitchell, the DFL candidate, received 55,377 votes or 39 percent. In the presidential election, John F. Kennedy defeated Richard Nixon.

Our trip to Minneapolis was a satisfaction to me, for I quite approve of the way my grandson is being raised. I can hardly wait for June and my REAL EXCUSE to go.[288]

Washington, D.C.   *Monday, April 24, 1961*

Hi Gals!

We've had the annual Shuckspedition from MHC to D.C.[289] and this year it was in high gear because of the New Frontier.[290] It was good to have girls again in the house – been much too long. Their schedule had not a House Member on it (Status is only in the Senate!) and not a Republican. Several of their Democratic-scheduled Top Boys never showed up or sent underlings to talk to the gang. But we gave our friends a little Glamour. We went to the 10-12 p.m. White House Reception and they could see us in full battle-array, and could have the engraved invitations and the car-park instructions with the mistake in grammar, and one of them sat up to hear all the gore on our return – made us homesick for our own gals! The event was nice: I liked the absence of a receiving line.

We could wander on the first floor and visit with friends and look at the gowns and dance in the East room or sachet into the State Dining Room for the excellent buffet, or pick up champagne punch at any of several stations. The Kennedys wandered, danced with each other and the Lyndons,[291] and shook hands with anyone who presented themselves in front of them. Talking to Senator Mike Mansfield, I said my Holyoke friends had been delighted to talk with him, it meant so much, etc.; went on to say he'd been a poli-sci professor so he could likely understand; and he said Yes, and how differently he'd teach it now, after having had experience in "practical politics," which is entirely different from "classroom"![292]

Went to a fancy luncheon given by the famous Mary Roebling, outstanding woman financier, for "66 of the leading women of today," honor guest Ivy Baker Priest, the new U.S. Treasurer. The entertainment was an astrologer who told our horoscopes by birthdays. Ridiculous.

Washington, D.C.   *Sunday, July 16, 1961*

Dear Folks:

This has been Pakistani Old Home Week in D.C. Never have I seen the government put themselves out so lavishly to honor any visiting head of state, whether because Jackie & the New Frontier want to show they can, or because they feel we haven't given Pakistan the aid or support they want and this kind of show is a sop to them, I wouldn't know. That's in the political department, not in the social life. And don't think we haven't heard the criticism and sniping at the Mount Vernon dinner. Naturally folks will criticize anything new or different. This was a beautifully planned & executed

---

288   Cindy Carpenter was born May 30, 1961.
289   Professor Shuck of Mount Holyoke College brought political science students to Washington, D.C. every year and several stayed with the Judds.
290   The term "New Frontier" was used at the Democratic National Convention by John F. Kennedy in his presidential nomination acceptance speech.
291   Vice President Lyndon Johnson and his wife Lady Bird Johnson.
292   Democrat Mike Mansfield was respected as the longest-serving Senate Majority leader and longest-serving U.S. Ambassador to Japan.

affair, gay, happy, and meaningful. The food was eminently more simple than other State dinners I've been to: no soup or fruit entre to start off, no salad course. The great enjoyment came from the careful planning, the setting, the kind of entertainment.

Our engraved invitations included a printed note asking us to be at the pier at 6:10, so Walter took his dinner clothes to the office and dressed there, and I left home in the requested "short evening dress" at 5 p.m. to drive down, pick him up, and on to the docks where the four ships were berthed: *The HoneyFitz, The Sequoia* (official entertaining yacht), a yacht owned by JFK, and a PT boat, which was the largest and fastest of the four. Everywhere Navy personnel snapping to attention, directing where to drive with clicking of heels and of arms, someone to take our car and park it, leaving us with a call number for our return, handing out envelopes with our table assignments numbered, etc. We were on the PT boat with Lady Bird as our hostess (Lyndon Johnson, Jackie, and JFK each on one of the boats) and it was gay on the small, open deck with a scarlet-coated Marine playing pop music on a small organ, and folks circulating most of the 1¼ hour trip and watching the shores slip by. A Japanese boy brought out a suit box of gaily colored scarves as soon as we were afloat, for the ladies to tie their hair on with, and there were dressy sweaters provided, too, for those who hadn't brought sufficient wraps for the windy river. Protocol sure has to think of everything!

Ours was the first boat to land, and tho' they had cars to drive the guests up the hill to the house, a bunch of twelve or sixteen of us strolled up the brick walks, enjoying the balmy evening, the dressy guards at attention every five feet, the view, the lowering red sun in a crimson sky. Eventually, all 138 guests had arrived at the house – tho' I've heard various figures as to the number of guests; the gold dinner plates that belong to the White House have complete services for 138 people, so I'm going to stick to that number.

Then we were summoned from our strolling in the green slopes, or from our conversational groups, mint juleps in hand, to watch on the land side of the house, the drill put on by the Colonial Fyfe and Drum Corps in their Continental Uniforms. The hordes of press, who had been at the docks when we left Washington, had motored quickly to Mount Vernon and had to be shunted off to one side of the green to allow the drill. When the green-coated colonial hunters fired their muskets in unison with a real bang and smoke, everyone laughed, for they were facing right into the bunch of press. One press guy took his white handkerchief and signaled surrender! It was historical to watch our revolutionary soldiers drill against a sky with the sun sinking, and a jet making smoke scratches on the blue backdrop.

We strolled thru the house to the front, and to the garden pavilion off to the left of the house, where the fifteen tables were set up. I found myself seated between Dean Rusk and General Maxwell Taylor,[293] while Walter was at a table with Jackie and Ayoub Kahn, President of Pakistan. He and Ayoub are good friends from way back, so they talked across Jackie and, as Walter says, got across good ideas in the process to Jackie – where they may just stop, if she doesn't talk things over with Jack! The Air Force strolling violins played during the meal, and the dusk and dark slowly

---

293   Dean Rusk was Secretary of State and Maxwell Taylor was to become Chairman of the Joint Chiefs of Staff.

descended as we watched the river and the green hills and trees darken. All the lighting was by candle, both on the tables, and on two enormous wheels sitting partway up the two tent poles, wound with green smilax and with a candle in a glass shade on each spoke.

Dean Rusk & I talked about the wedding next day of his son to a Latin American girl in Buenos Aires, which neither of his parents could attend, tho' Mrs. Rusk hopes to go down for the religious ceremony. Interestingly, Mrs. General LeMay with whom I talked on the boat, was marrying her only child, a daughter, four days later, and had to leave all the festivities and dinners and visiting guests three nights in a row for the Pakistan affairs, but seemed relaxed about it. Mr. Rusk & I also talked about the inaccuracy & unreliability of the press. He was furious because he had talked to the Press Club at lunch and in the question period someone asked him if he thought Communist China would be recognized, or admitted to the UN this fall, and said he thought this very *un*likely, and the *Washington Post* reported his saying "very likely." I saw a day later that he had made them correct it, but the damage is done. While I'm discussing press, a couple more comments. Next day at the lunch for ladies at the Pakistan Embassy, I sat between Betty Fulbright and Mrs. Angier Biddle Duke, wife of the Chief of Protocol. First Betty said to me that Bill was getting wild at the terrible inaccuracy of the press (including all TV and radio media) while they continue to focus attention on a "*free* press."

Then Mrs. Duke got talking about the article in the *Ladies' Home Journal*, current issue. They told her American women were interested in the way officials live and they wanted to take pictures of her, her home, her clothes, her way of life. They came; they brought their own tables, lamps, knick-knacks for setting and background. They brought dresses for her made by Dior or someone who could get his name into the paper, and would not let her wear her own clothes. They wanted someone to do her coiffeur different from the way she naturally wears her hair. They tried to insist on gobs of facial makeup, eye emphasis, etc., that made her not herself. Their excuse was that these things photograph better than the things she had. She fought every step of the way with them, saying if people wanted to know about *her*, they better see *her* furniture, *her* clothes, *her* hair, *her* face – and she's a stunning young French gal – but she lost 'most every time.

So what America is seeing & reading about Mrs. Duke is something the *Ladies' Home Journal* created, not the person herself, and they know no better than to believe it. Several others at the table said this was standard procedure, and they had declined to submit to requests from women's magazines. This is why I don't waste time reading newspapers or listening to news. If they're only half-right, half the time, and you don't know which half, where are you?

Back to the romantic Mount Vernon dinner: we strolled across the lawn to where the platform & shell had been set up for the National Symphony, and chairs facing it and the river. The tall, graceful trees behind the orchestra were all spotlighted from the ground, and waved gently in the breeze, and the concert-with-coffee-and-champagne was delightful: Mozart, Berlioz, Gershwin's "American in Paris." Then it was time to return to the dock, and as we strolled toward the waiting cars, JFK found Walter in the dark, and said I want you and your wife on my yacht going back. So we were aboard the only yacht that had a combo and dancing on deck – and those men didn't stop playing once on the whole hour-and-a-half trip!

Sandwiches, nuts, hors d'oeuvres & drinks were passed, some danced, others leaned on the rails and conversed, or sang, or waved to craft in the river. Walter talked to JFK quite a while…and talked lots with Ayoub, and when Jackie was tired dancing she sat on a low coffee table and beckoned Walter to come sit beside her so she could hear more of the kind of conversation he was putting out at dinner, or so she could charm him, or you say why? She did ask him "Where have you been all my life?" And told me, "Your husband is simply fascinating!" Think I should worry? She looked beautiful in white, a long dress, saying no one had told her to wear a short one.

It was 1:30 when we landed in the District, and our cars were driven up by aides and delivered to us, and everyone agreed that it had been a charming, relaxed, thoughtfully arranged, and appreciated evening. We wished that all the official men, Cabinet, Military, Monetary etc., who had to sit thru negotiations and discussions next day, might have gotten more sleep – but President Ayoub didn't evidently suffer from the late night, for everyone said he made a magnificent talk before the joint session of Congress, leaving his notes aside and talking straight-forwardly and getting much applause, because of his direct hard-hittingness if not because they always agreed with him.

I didn't attend, but did go afterwards to a luncheon the Pakistani Ambassador's wife gave for President Ayoub's daughter who was his official hostess on this trip. I had sat with her on the yacht and she is an attractive and intelligent girl. She is married, has three small children whom she left with her mother, who is old-fashioned Mohammedan and would not come with the President. She told me she hoped to get a minute to go shopping to get presents to take to the children: the little boy wanted a cowboy suit and guns, and the little girl wanted small high-heeled and pointed-tip shoes she could play "dress-up" in. At this I remembered that the married daughter of the Japanese Premier who accompanied him to this country a few weeks ago told me *her* son wanted a cowboy suit and guns as a gift from USA. Our westerns sure are giving us a stereotype round the world. Begum Aurangzeb (the President's daughter) described the huge doll dressed in a jeweled sari they brought for Caroline Kennedy.

Washington, D.C.   *Monday, July 31, 1961*

Dear Folks:

Today arrived Chen, the Vice President of China.[294] This noon the President gave a luncheon for him at the White House. Protocol doesn't let JFK give a State Dinner for Chen, because Chen is not a head of State, so this was in its place, and all the elite were there, and many of our China friends. Jackie is away, so Mrs. Johnson was the official hostess. They served cocktails in the green room before lunch – and I believe this was never done under the last administration.

Halfway thru the lunch Walter and two other Representatives left hurriedly when they got word from the Capitol that the voting had started on the authorization of the emergency draft measure. When JFK was nearly thru his short speech of welcome to Vice President Chen, he apologized for the three men having to leave, explained the circumstances, then added that Vice President Chen had told him

---

294   Official of the Republic of China (on Taiwan), not the *People's* Republic of China.

that Walter lived in a Province in China that kept a tight hold on the money bags (referring to Shansi where many of the bankers of old China came from). Cute, eh?

I'm teaching two weeks in a daily vacation Bible school for underprivileged children, twenty youngsters ages nine to twelve, as well as directing music for the whole group of 60, and loving it. And Saturday while Walter was gone, I had ten students from Hannah Harrison School for a buffet dinner, which I did all myself so I'm keeping busy and forgetting the heat.

Washington, D.C.   *Monday, August 28, 1961*

Dear Folks:

This has been a happy birthday, thanks to all of you. El was home over the weekend. Walter took us to the ball game, his second one in eight days, and it was fun. Saturday night Walter was speaking in New Jersey, so El and I went to the amphitheater and enjoyed seeing *Carousel*. The music in that is so beautiful, and it was a starry night.

Walter has speeches in Minneapolis over the weekend, and then will return to D.C. for the finish of Congress, but I will stay three weeks, give Mary Lou & Norm a chance at a slight vacation while I take care of the grandchildren. I am flattered they would trust me. Hope I don't drop anything!!!

Washington, D.C.   *Thursday, October 12, 1961*

Dear Family:

When Walter gets back home a week from today, he will have been gone twenty-four days. He has three days to clear up the accumulation at the office and he's off Oct. 23 for Korea, flying commercial and joining the rest of us on the MATS plane in Tokyo five days later.[295]

I've had a little success in making myself go out evenings to things Walter & I were both invited to, but I find it hard going alone. One night I climbed into evening clothes and took a taxi for the buffet supper given by movie officials preceding the World Premiere of the movie, *Bridge to the Sun*. I had been fascinated when I read the book years ago at the life of the American girl who married a young Japanese diplomat here before Pearl Harbor, and the time they had adjusting to each other's culture & customs, especially during the War. The movie was interesting – but I wouldn't have liked to be Gwen Terasaki,[296] nor her daughter and watch Hollywood's idea of how she and her husband made love, exchanged cultural ideas, fought, lived. After I got by the first icy plunge of walking into that Press Club ballroom alone, acquaintances started coming up to ask for Walter and took me under their wing, sat with me – taking me home.

On Double Ten (10/10), China's National Day, I went to lunch honoring the Chinese Ambassador & his wife, who had been presented by the Postmaster General our new commemorative four- & five-cent U.S. stamps, with pictures of Sun Yat-sen and George Washington, Fathers of their countries.

---

295   Walter would catch up with Miriam and the Southeast Asia subcommittee of the Foreign Affairs Committee in South Korea.

296   Gwen Terasaki's autobiography *Bridge to the Sun* was the basis for the movie.

This is the 50th birthday of Republic of China. And by gum when they were calling on Important People to make a few remarks, they unexpectedly announced me. I got a laugh by saying that I was *not* the speaker of the family, and any ability I might have had, had atrophied from disuse. But I did extend WHJ's (and my) greetings.

Have done extra YW work in anticipation of my absence. Have helped several Tuesday evenings with their regular Penthouse Lounge for foreign young people to drop in, meet friends, have coffee & cake. Mostly these are not students but employed people, lots in embassy clerical jobs, domestics in embassy families. I play piano for group singing, help with language difficulties…talk to the lonely ones, play gin rummy, whatever is needed. About fifty come and it means much to them. Also, led a "Look in the Mirror" personality and attitudes study & discussion with Hannah Harrison students, which took careful preparation but was evidently useful.

Honolulu, Hawaii   *Wednesday, October 25, 1961*

Hi, All –

The four men sans wives on the trip are taking care of me till we meet Walter. They call me their Den Mother. These first days are the longest hops we have. Today to Honolulu, 10½. The most interesting thing has been Pearl Harbor. We were taken to the Navy Yacht and sat in chairs on a windy deck while a gob gave us a moving account of Pearl Harbor day, as we cruised the harbor. We saw which mountain gaps the waves and kinds of attack came thru, told of the action at the supply base, battleship row, the submarine base, the dry docks, the carriers. We saw the submerged Arizona with the 1,102 men who went down still inside, memorialized by a bronze plaque and by a memorial platform the Navy is building over her – the U.S. flag flying above, raised and lowered each day with the official ceremony, taps at sunset – lest we forget. We were really on the water in the midst of the horror of December 7, and it left a lump in your throat.

Hong Kong   *Tuesday, November 7, 1961*

Hi –

There is no time and energy to write details. I'll omit Japan, except to say (1) we got to hotel in Tokyo between 2 and 3 a.m. Sunday; (2) Walter met us but has a cold and real aches; (3) aside from an all-day trip to sacred temples of Nikko on Monday for us ladies, with Embassy wives – tremendous! – nothing else too important. At both Taiwan and Hong Kong we've been welcomed with banners, decorations, flags and lanterns and streamers everywhere, fireworks, cheering crowds. Actually, in Taiwan these were for Chiang Kai-shek's 75th birthday celebration, and in Hong Kong for the arrival of Princess Alexandra, who landed a few hours after we did – but we appropriated them to our trip.

What was *really* meant for us – that is for Walter! – was a student brass band from the middle school of our Congregational Church, formerly in Peking, now functioning on Formosa,[297] and playing at a great rate (if slightly sour) while the girls' contingent lined up, also in uniform, and presented me a

---

297   Formosa was the current name for what is now known as Taiwan.

huge bouquet of red roses. Please call me Jackie Kennedy! This was slightly embarrassing, for the rest of our Congressional Delegation had to stand by and watch Walter get the kudos, and the three Democrats outrank us. Soon I had three flower bouquets, the others brought by former students and Fenchow friends, and such a handshaking and jabbering in Mandarin, and picture-taking in front of the banner – Welcome the Honorable Walter Judd. From that moment to this has been a steady procession of Chinese friends, phone calls, dinner invitations.

Saigon, Vietnam   *Saturday, November 11, 1961*

I'm going to revise my plans for letter writing. With Jim's death,[298] our Judd family has other things on their minds than to read a travelogue. There is never going to be time to write in detail. I will keep my diary record for future reference, and finish up this letter sketchily.

The highlight in Taiwan was our day's trip to Kemoy.[299] An Embassy wife went along with me, and the wife of the Chinese General Li who was taking us in his military plane, about eighteen in all. I loved it that in the pocket of our Mae West-sorta vest that we had to wear while flying low (to avoid radar) over water, there was a shark repellent tablet that would dissolve in 3½ hours, it said. After that you join the Jonah society, I guess.

We landed in Kemoy and went by jeeps to various parts of the island. I can't describe the energy, determination, high morale, stiff discipline that was everywhere felt in this outpost of the free world. One fascinating bit was where we went to the Psychological Warfare Center, got bits of captured Communist propaganda leaflets – you should see the caricatures of Dulles and Kennedy and Eisenhower! – and where we loosed balloons carrying our USA propaganda leaflets, which winds would waft to the mainland in forty-five minutes. Walter signed his leaflets! Proudest moment was when the Chinese Commanding General pinned on me the small gold and green button given only to those who have visited Kemoy and thus become a part of the family that defends and understands not just China, but freedom for the world. No one can buy this. It is priceless.

A fascinating afternoon visiting village improvement projects and dinner at the Chiang Kai-sheks were two more excitements in Taiwan. The last morning Nurse Chao came to breakfast with us – the nurse who helped with the delivery of Carolyn in Fenchow.

Hong Kong was six days instead of three because Manila was cancelled, I'm sorry to say. I'm afraid some of our group overemphasized the shopping and nite club element. One morning Embassy men were taking us to see work with refugee resettlement, housing projects, community centers, feeding stations that use our U.S.A. surplus wheat, cornmeal, oil – an intriguing morning – two Congressmen and wives showed up – the two Republicans. Republicans work – Democrats talk!

Took a trip to the Communist border; junk trip to the sampan populations who raise pigs and children, cook, give birth and die all aboard those small craft; watching the fabulous fireworks put on for Princess Alexandra; a magnificent sermon by a young Britisher at the Union church; big,

---

298   Jim was Walter's brother. Walter missed a week of the trip to return to the U.S. for Jim's funeral.

299   Kemoy, also known as Quemoy, was an island eight miles off the China coast that was under Taiwan's control for years.

high-ceilinged room with excellent Chinese servants at the Peninsula Hotel; the last day the airplane carrier Ticonderoga coming majestically up the harbor and anchoring right outside our bedroom window, practically. My Chinese language seemed to come back as I heard it around me, I used it a lot, talked to a class of boys in an orphanage in Chinese – we got homesick for China, with the familiar people, sights, sounds, smells. It's wonderful.

Vietnam has got me confused and frustrated. Is it no-Chinese language, no-French language that leaves me helpless? Is it that women here don't seem to be doing things in social welfare and public life, except for a few at the top? Of course, they are fighting a war; they have been under a strict colonial system so long; things do change slowly, there are signs. Today we went to a large government hospital that has an excellent nurses' training school. But it is the only one. Has over 200 students, and the need is enormous. Yesterday I saw two orphanages, one run by thirteen sisters (for 600 children) one run by a Vietnamese lady, and they were incredibly awful – flies, open drains, dirty cloths for diapers, cases with matchstick arms and legs, all with scalp disease or boils, and at feeding time coolie women going up and down the rows of cribs with one bowl of soft cooked rice, one spoon, shoveling it in each mouth in turn. Is social welfare only a luxury that more developed countries can indulge in? The American Women's Association with several hundred members, works as volunteers in institutions, blind, tuberculosis, leprosariums, schools, plus raising money for desperate needs. But their own ministry of health, the UN Government, is slow to accept offers of aid, which are looked on with suspicion as having a political tie-up. It's an eye opener.

Our Embassy people here are wonderful – as everywhere – but the Ambassador seems specially super… I'm feeling fine in this strenuous routine, tho' many of our group have had upsets. Tomorrow a.m. off to Bangkok early.

Delhi, India   *Saturday, November 18, 1961*

Dear Family –

Walter got back right on schedule from his trip to the U.S. but was exhausted and continues to have

a deep, heavy cough. We did make it to Delhi, but are having to be put up in private homes of Embassy officials, which is difficult both ways. We landed in India from East Pakistan yesterday, which was November 17, to continue a bit of India Barber-Clarke history: My grandfather Andrew Clarke landed here November 17 in 1856 (or '57?) with British troops and fought in the Lucknow Mutiny. (He was extremely young when he joined the Army.) Then my parents landed in India on November 17 in 1899 after their end-August marriage, coming for their twelve years of work in Calcutta. Coincidence?

Industrial Fair in Delhi, India;
silicone exhibit in American Pavilion

In Dacca, East Pakistan we were out in "hinterland"

city – growing and building but still more Indian than modern, poor hotel, etc. Lots of Americans there in ICA doing agricultural work, mostly on contracts Dacca University has with Colorado and Texas A&M. A co-ed Peace Corps group of twenty-four had recently arrived, were getting their six-week orientation, three weeks in classes at Dacca University and three weeks living in outlying villages with a family. They'd had six weeks Bengali language study in Putney, Vermont, plus other orientation, and one we met reported, "Nothing in our U.S. orientation prepared us at all for Dacca!"

We went to visit the struggling American School for children of all these two-year term workers. Up thru sixth grade they have regular teachers, recruited from wives of Americans living there and changing frequently. About sixty thru sixth grade; and the twenty-five in high school are doing California correspondence course study, with eighteen-week units and a supervising mother to keep them using the reference library, moving along, getting help… I so wanted to stay and teach there!

Washington, D.C.   *Sunday, December 31, 1961*

Dear Myrtle –

We tried to phone you when all the kids were here over Christmas, but got a report of busy circuits. I loved every minute of the confusion. I had earlier made out tentative menus for each day and had cooked up cakes, cookies, pies, and desserts ahead, but they certainly went fast. I get practically no chance to cook with Walter gone so much, so this was a treat. One evening we talked about our trip and showed photos. Sunday we all sat in a row in church, first time together since two years ago when Kevin was baptized. By Tuesday noon everyone was gone but Carolyn who left that night. It was a good Christmas – but we all missed Jim.

Washington, D.C.   *Sunday, June 24, 1962*

Dear Myrtle & Gertrude –

Well, where were we? Last time I wrote, I mean? Life goes on too fast and too full for me and I go chasing after it like a man trying to catch a train that's already left the station. Then I sit down for a bit and sew or read or do nothing and try to remember what, if anything has been accomplished.

We did go to Minneapolis for Memorial Day, Cindy's first birthday, to celebrate; and for Walter to make his TV announcement that he would run next fall. I'm glad it's settled – I suppose it's right, but I can assure you I hate every breathing minute of his being a candidate.

From Minneapolis we went to Holyoke where I had Trustee meetings, where Walter attended the events of Alumnae day and commencement. Other Board members bring their wives or husbands each time, so I'm glad I got Walter there *once*. I have one more year and will be Vice Chairman.

We've had Ike and Mamie in town for the big fundraising dinner of 3,000 people. He was in excellent form… Next morning, our Republican Congressional Wives Club had a garden breakfast with them, with a chance to visit informally.

Walter had to go to White Sulphur Springs, Virginia to speak, so he took me to that Greenbrier

Hotel. We had twenty-four hours to relax, roam the gardens, read aloud, have our one-day summer vacation. We read aloud a book about Dr. Benjamin Rush, Philadelphia signer of the Declaration of Independence, and so unorthodox in his medical treatments of yellow fever that the newspapers castigated him (and for his political views too) till he brought a lawsuit and there was a famous trial hinging on Freedom of the Press. It was interesting how others had struggled for the public good, and to read how much more violently vituperative the press used to be than now – anyhow, we had a good weekend.

Minneapolis, Minnesota   *Saturday, July 21, 1962*

Myrtle & Gertrude –

It's been Aquatennial week & Walter and I had to ride in the opening parade, attended several affairs for Minnesota Mayors, editors, and tonight the ball to crown the new Queen of the Lakes. Kevin adored the parade with the bands, clowns, horses, floats, costumes, display – but it's a bit old to me after all these years! However, it is a wonderful way for a candidate to be seen, and to show

Miriam and grandson Kevin Carpenter at Aquatennial Parade

community interest and civic pride so I go along with the game. I went with Walter when he filed for Congress last Tuesday, and our pictures got into the evening TV news, important in this city where the Cowles newspapers remain struck by the unions after fourteen weeks!

Walter's campaign office opened earlier than formerly and in a magnificent downtown location. The gears are starting to grind and money is beginning to come in. They call it this year "The All-City Judd Committee," trying to bring in the added-on north side that is so strongly Democrat.[300] Mary Lou and some of her friends have been helping with the door-to-door survey in those new wards, came back with reports of two Republicans in forty-four doorbells rung – and even where there are more Republicans than that in an area, they decline to put up lawn signs for Judd as they are scared for their jobs, for the ruthlessness of the Democrats, to have anyone know they are Republicans. There are some Democrats who say (when asked) they will vote for Judd – but many who have never heard the name – lots of work to be done![301]

---

300   After the 1960 census, Minnesota was redistricted and two largely DFL wards were added to the Fifth district (Walter's district).
301   Walter lost the election that November, with 80,865 votes or 48 percent. Donald Fraser, DFL, won with 87,002 votes or 52 percent. Walter did carry his former district.

12
YWCA Leadership
1963 - 1971

Life after Congress was certainly different for Miriam. There were fewer letters and more domestic details, reports on the daughters and visits with grandchildren, most of which are omitted here. With the daughters "launched" (Ellie married on June 5, 1963, and Carolyn on November 6, 1971), Miriam eagerly embraced providing support as a grandmother, pitching in during pregnancies, ill health, and vacations, allowing us to recuperate, rest, and renew. More grandchildren arrived: Kathryn Judd Carpenter on March 4, 1964; Ellie's four Quinn children, Patrick Walter on March 10, 1964, James Edward on September 20, 1966, Mary Josephine on March 28, 1968, and John Paul on July 2, 1969.

As a private person, Miriam must have been relieved to be out of the public eye and the obligations that came with the political position. The combative nature of politics was never her style. She still had strong energy, creativity, and dedication but at age fifty-eight was thankful to have fewer demands on her schedule. Visions of time and activities with Walter, no doubt, danced in her head. She had more time for correspondence and friendship with women she knew in her volunteer work. They delighted in attending theater and music performances and discussing ideas, books, and aesthetic opportunities. People enjoyed her warmth, graciousness, and thoughtfulness.

But even as Walter's responsibilities and obligations slowly began to diminish, he continued to engage in public affairs for another twenty-five years. His expertise in many areas, from government to foreign relations to medicine and missions, made him useful to worldwide humanitarian endeavors as well as to national organizations. He chaired the Judicial Council of the American Medical Association (AMA), was a contributing editor to the *Readers's Digest*, lectured and spoke on world affairs, ethics, citizenship, and provided leadership to various civic groups.

In 1964, Minnesota Republicans selected a majority of delegates committed to him for the National Convention, where he was nominated for President as a Favorite Son. He reluctantly acquiesced in that effort, with Miriam notably disagreeing. This political tactic was an attempt to offer a moderate alternative to conservative candidate Barry Goldwater, who ultimately became the Republican nominee. Walter did his best to campaign for Republican candidates, as well as to speak out on policy issues important to him.

Miriam continued her work with the YWCA during the strident civil rights era. In Washington, she played an instrumental role in the integration of the five Washington-area YWCAs – a landmark action in its day. That accomplishment required courage and persistence under fire. She sometimes referred to herself as a pacifist, with her strengths in negotiation and compromise, seeking conciliation. These skills were sorely tested as she served as the first President of the newly formed Metropolitan Area YWCA.

As she made history she also graciously attended historical, social, and political events with Walter, and was active in church positions. They traveled for AMA meetings, Young President's Organization (YPO) gatherings, Walter's teaching at University summer programs at Boulder, Colorado, to see siblings, and for pleasure, with trips to South America, England, Scandinavia, Russia and a boat cruise around Greece.

Washington, D.C.   *Saturday, February 2, 1963*

Dear Gertrude –

The big DO Saturday night in Minneapolis was some affair. They sold over 3,300 $100 tickets. The money raised went to the Republican Party, but the whole thing was advertised as "in honor of Walter H. Judd." Dr. Lawrence Gould, just retired as President of Carleton College, gave an excellent twenty-minute tribute to Walter – witty, not boringly chronological but dealing with of his accomplishments, not fulsome or embarrassingly overdone, but with real feeling. Walter gave a response, which turned out to be about a half-hour speech, but it was good and people listened eagerly. It was something to sit at the head table and look out over 2,800 plus diners. They gave Walter a color TV. And they gave me a gorgeous Steuben glass compote with a cover. I've never owned a bit of Steuben and have always loved it. I made a response in accepting it, telling of the "water jug" fund in the Omaha church when Walter first went to China and seem to have wowed the audience.[302] They gave Walter a solid Steuben glass elephant, which is a beauty, and which I find excellent to build a centerpiece around for the dining room, when I'm entertaining. It was a thoroughly nice occasion and we have many good friends there.

The grandchildren are a lively pair and a great joy. Mary Lou doesn't have much patience with them, and I hope she develops some soon, for she'll have better kids if she doesn't snap at them. Their great intellectual curiosity delights me – you can get them interested in anything. I don't know anyone in the world who's as glad to see me as they are, so we get on famously.

---

302   A young child of the First Congregational Church Sunday school who was saving pennies in the 1930s for the missionary Walter Judd Fund, thought it was the Water Jug Fund.

Had twenty of our Congressional Club ladies here for lunch this week, and tomorrow will have former members of Walter's staff (ten of us altogether) for Sunday supper. They want to see his new office in the lower-level recreation room. It is cozy, comfortable, and convenient.

Washington, D.C.   *Friday, March 22, 1963*

Dear All-the-Family –

It's been nice to have Walter in town this past week, tho' he's left now. We went to the Arena Stage to see *All The Way Home*, the Pulitzer Prize play, and were moved by it. Another night we went to the Cleveland Park Church (where we have started going again on Sundays) to hear the negro choir and Minister from Lincoln Temple Church. We have decided to build a porch off our sitting room. It will be twelve by fourteen and have both jalousies and screens and a 1000-watt wall heater we can use in the winter if we want. You can see that my spring will be enlivened with making small daily decisions, like how many plugs and whether to get an air-conditioning unit.

Now to try to keep everyone up with all the travel plans of this peripatetic family:

- *March 31* – I go to Baltimore to speak at a pre-freshmen tea about Holyoke. Dad speaks at the Marion Cricket club near Philadelphia where I will join him for a dinner someone is giving for us, including Betty Lou & Jim McClure.
- *April 16* – We expect Mary Lou here with Kevin & Cindy. Walter doesn't leave till next day…
- *April 17* – Expect El & Paul will fly to Los Angeles for a couple of days, then land here.
- *April 20* – Mary Lou will have driven to New York for Pat's wedding,[303] and to see Carolyn up there before returning here to see El and Paul on
- *April 21* – before they have had to return to New York and their jobs by 2 p.m. on
- *April 22* – Expect the Carpenters will stay and visit until Walter returns noon of
- *April 23* – It's beautifully planned and I can hardly wait for it all to come off.

Walter and I are going to Charlottesville, Virginia three days over Easter as he is weary.

Washington, D.C.   *Friday, June 28, 1963*

Harriet Dear –

We leave tomorrow morning to drive to the Mayo Clinic where Walter will be operated on for a growth on his larynx. He has continued hoarse since a cold and throat infection bothered him weeks ago. He went to have a doctor check him, who found two tiny growths, likely to be cancerous, or pre-cancerous. If they feel that they had better take the vocal cords to prevent reoccurrence or because it has spread, that will be done. Is it possible that the Lord is trying to shut Walter's mouth, and turn him to writing or some other medium of serving? I should have thought he could make use of Walter's voice for a while longer – and perhaps he still will.[304]

---

303   Pat was a college classmate of Mary Lou's.
304   No cancer was found to their great relief.

Washington, D.C.   *Sunday, September 15, 1963*

Dear Elizabeth and Clarke –

One night when Walter was away, at 4:20 a.m., a rolling car crashed into our parked Chevie out front, did about $150 worth of damage and demolished the other car. I got the police promptly, scared to go outside lest a drunk, or delinquents, be uncontrollable… The owners, who live a couple of blocks up Ordway on a completely level place where they had parked it with the brakes on, are sure kids must have pushed and steered it, for other cars were parked along the curb, which it wouldn't have avoided if it were rolling by itself. I have to appear in court for a hearing, and if they prove theft their insurance is invalid for their loss and our damage.

Helen Smith was here the night of THE MARCH.[305] Walter, who was participating, ran into her in the midst of the 210,000 other people down at the Memorial. That was a most impressive and well-managed occasion, even if I can't see that it accomplished much immediately. Tomorrow would be Dad's birthday, bless him.

En route from Seoul to Tokyo   *Wednesday, November 20, 1963*

Hi, Mary Lou –

These two days in South Korea have been grand – weather lovely. Embassy people met us at airport, provided a car, personal attention, including mailing home the gifts Koreans gave us. Today was super special: Up at 6, breakfast in room, off at 7 a.m. in military car to drive to demilitarized zone. Fabulous drive thru the countryside with all it tells of the industriousness, strength, vigor of the people: Everywhere evidences of the military exercises just concluding: U.S. boys finishing re-stringing communications wire; tanks, & motor equipment returning to bases; repair units, camouflage units, chemical warfare units all active along the way. Were taken into the rooms where the negotiating teams meet, with its line right down the middle of the table dividing North & South Korea; saw the Czech & Swedish members of the Neutral Commission coming to meet; climbed into a sandbagged gun emplacement on the brown hills, guarding the road; passed six feet from Communist guards & saw others watching us thru field glasses from their checkpoint – had an overpowering sense of this war that still isn't over.

Grand Hotel, Taipei, Taiwan   *Saturday, November 23, 1963*

Dear Family –

An official "tea-reception" was cancelled because of the President's death.[306] We are to leave in an hour for dinner with Generalissimo and Madame Chiang. This is *not* an "official" function, had *not* been announced with our extremely full "official schedule" we found prepared for us on arrival (unbeknownst to us!). So the dinner has not had to be cancelled, ruled the American Ambassador here, whom we called when the news of the assassination reached us. Dad had a good talk with him earlier at his office and was well impressed by him.

---

305   The March on Washington for Jobs and Freedom was led by Martin Luther King, Jr. The March culminated with the "I Have a Dream" speech at the Lincoln Memorial on August 28, 1963.

306   The world and the Judds were shocked by the assassination of President John F. Kennedy on November 22, 1963.

No use going into the thoughts & speculations that immediately rush into one's mind about how our country's and the world's situation is changed by this turn of events. Newsmen have been after Dad for comment on future political & election possibilities & he's declined comment – only that we're shocked & grieved. We've cabled Mrs. Kennedy and President Johnson. Don't know if Dad feels the same, but I'm a little glad we're this far away when it happened. By the time we get back, official mourning will be over, Congress should be over, Johnson should not have made any significant changes – so we'll take it from there. All flags are ordered at half-mast here for three days, all U.S. flags for thirty days.

Our own schedule has been like nothing human. Evidently the feeling is that Dad's long and out-spoken friendship with China may have had some part in his defeat last year, & they want to let us know they appreciate it. We have the presidential suite at this gorgeous *new* wing of the hotel, in our living room never less than five huge baskets of flowers sent by well-wishers – fruit baskets – parquet floors with mirror-polish; jade-green satin brocade upholstered furniture; balconies with view of the city, the mountains beyond through ceiling-to-floor glass wall with gold brocade drapes. Calling cards with messages are stacked in dozens; gifts, books, pamphlets keep arriving. How to deal with it, get it back to USA is our problem. Phone rings constantly. Foreign Minister told me he had innumerable "applications" to entertain us. I'm sorry I forgot to bring my diamond tiara. But it is touching and genuine, to hear people express their gratitude to Dad.

Yesterday I was taken (separately from Dad's schedule) to visit Madame Chiang's war orphanage with the most adorable children, a veterans' hospital built and equipped like the Mayo Clinic, and the Women's Social Welfare Center, where 100 donated Singer sewing machines are manned daily by volunteer Chinese wives from different branches of the government & military making underwear for soldiers, hospital needs, children's clothing for orphanages – what a buzz! Each spot had the red carpet out for me, I was given jasmine tea (kidneys are floating), was introduced by *The Head* in flowery flattering phrases as the wife of That Man, was given low bows, standing ovations, corsages pinned on. I'm sure glad I know me!!

Our overnight trip to south of island was *lovely*. We'd planned to go by train, see much of village life, crops, conditions, as we ride through the county. Oh no! We were sent by private plane. Wish I could give a description of Naval Exercise. We were the honor guests on small, highest pavilion built on the rocky coast – together with President & Madam Chiang, our top Navy advisor, MAG officer, Marine General & their wives; & Chinese top Admiral and Marine man. Our Marine General said U.S. Marines could do no better. (Did you know Madame Chiang is a General of U.S. Marines? She's also four-star commander-in-chief of Chinese Air Force.) It was the most thrilling & exciting thing I've ever seen.

Peninsula Hotel, Kowloon, Hong Kong   *Thursday, November 28, 1963*

Hi Family Mine –

Today we're going to a hospital-in-construction that two young energetic able American doctors are getting going. Their salaries are paid by a U.S. mission board and they have been working in a small clinic, but no money handy for the necessary facility. One of them came to see Dad in D.C. & he put them next to some givers and he has raised more than half the cost of the hospital, is still there collecting, leaving wife & six kids here. The one who takes us around today has seven kids here! After that to the Thanksgiving service at the Union American church where we'll meet a good cross-section of the American community.

Majestic Hotel, Saigon, Vietnam   *Thursday, December 5, 1963*

Hi Family –

Dad has gone to see Big Minh.[307] This place has little *objective* signs of any disturbance. They've worked twenty-four-hour shifts to repair Palace, which gleams with new whiteness; want people to forget the old regime & fighting. Some pockmarked walls, broken windows, charred or smoke-stained plaster still to be seen. *Everyone* here divided on extent old & new regime were good or bad but all hate Mrs. Nhu & husband passionately.[308] School kids are in revolt against their professors who were employed under Diem. New regime says it must be lenient till things settle down.

Hotel Rama, Bangkok, Thailand   *Thursday, December 12, 1963*

Hi Family –

Here we are as far away as we can be from y'wal; in distance, halfway round the world; in time, exactly twelve hours; in climate, hot; in the shops, signs up saying Merry Christmas, but little evidence of "Christmas shopping" as we know it. Perhaps this is why I got an acute attack of homesickness. In two weeks we'll be back and able to talk to you all.

In Manila, Singapore, Kuala Lumpur, and here, Chinese friends or officials were at each airport to meet us. This is loyal and touching from the Chinese – they adore Dad. But I didn't realize the natives of each country are not too happy with their large Chinese community, and there are real tensions & jealousies. The Philippines passed a law excluding Chinese – so thousands are there illegally, smuggled in. In Vietnam they made the Chinese choose to become Vietnamese citizens or

return home, which they did. In Kuala Lumpur at the beautiful new (seven years) University we visited, run by Government, native Malayans have government-paid tuition & housing, Chinese have to pay high fees, tho' 41% of the total population is Chinese, 37% Malayan. Perhaps this is because Chinese are *so* industrious & skillful, "out work & under eat" the natives, that they are in competition with local labor and earn their way to good positions as shop owners & business people, causing jealousy. Anyway they continue to entertain us everywhere. In Singapore at dinner at the U.S. Ambassador's

307   "Big Minh" was an army General who had led the coup in which Vietnam's President Diem was assassinated. He led the country for a few months.
308   Mrs. Nhu was the de facto First Lady of Vietnam. She was a highly unpopular figure, and sometimes called "the Dragon Lady." Her husband was the brother and chief advisor to Diem.

(just us four – no official entertaining American officials because of JFK mourning, which suits us fine) he told us when he was in Korea as Ambassador & Doug Dillon[309] came to visit, Koreans brought enormous gifts in casket-like boxes, & Dillon told him to get rid of the damn things, & he told Dillon he didn't care what he did with them after they were outa the country, but they *had* to go with him – or Korea loses face! What a system.

Off we go to stay with the Chester Bowles in Delhi, much to Dad's disgust![310] He wants to keep his appointment with Nehru without Chester's chaperonage!

Washington, D.C.   *Tuesday, May 5, 1964*

Classmates –

Isn't spring gorgeous! Our dogwood are falling after three weeks, and our azalea and bridal wreath are in bloom. I have a bouquet of lilies-of-the-valley from our garden, fragrant & delicate. I can't work in the garden to weed, but I have all this beauty anyway.

I was in Cleveland for the YWCA National Convention, a thrilling occasion for the 22 of us who went from our national Capitol YW, and Mrs. Johnson[311] giving a grand talk, telling specifically of our building here where both her girls learned to swim (and Luci still comes twice a week with her secret service agent sitting in the swim director's office since men aren't supposed to be allowed on that floor!) We had excellent speakers and discussions, and took responsible action, no matter what you may have read in the newspapers. We did *not* take the "Christian out of the Y" or remove the religious emphasis – another example of the poor reporting of discussion on how to make our work *more* meaningful and Christian in these revolutionary times.

Don't anyone ask me what the political situation is in Minnesota. All I could tell you is that it is a mess. I have never approved of what Walter did (or didn't do) about the Favorite Son business, and I don't like all the dirt his name got dragged into during his absence, which he still has to take responsibility for, so we don't talk about it. He does want me to go out there for the state convention June 13 at which time it will be determined whether he is to be a delegate to the San Francisco Republican Convention, and whether he will withdraw his name as Favorite Son (depending on the strength of elected delegates). I'll hate it, but I'll go.

Washington, D.C.   *Thursday, August 13, 1964*

Dear Harriet, Betty, & Helen:

Just to catch up on the particular events that have taken my attention: two trips of ten days each to San Francisco: the first for the AMA[312] Convention, on whose Judicial Council Walter sits, plus a

---

309   Douglas Dillon was the U.S. Secretary of the Treasury.

310   Chester Bowles was the U.S. Ambassador to India.

311   Lady Bird Johnson was the First Lady.

312   AMA is the American Medical Association.

visit to his aging sisters in Los Angeles; the other for you-know-what![313] In between these, a week staying with the three little Carpenters in Minneapolis while their parents took a trip to New York. And a week's trip to New England to see Carolyn and old friends. Now back in Washington to catch up, I've had to face the heartbreaking word of the resignation of our wonderful new (just one year) director of Hannah Harrison School…

The other bit that has been taking my time is the writing of a speech for the fall membership meeting of our Area YW. I needed to get it done, so that the rest of the program could be built around it. I am appalled to find the aging process seems to show itself in a lack of ability to discipline myself to write when I should. I *wanted* to do this, but there were times when – not weariness, really – but some lack of energy prevented me, when I couldn't make my mind respond and write down what comes next, or think out logically what it should be. I got terribly annoyed in the process. I don't mind my body having creaks and groans at sixty, but why should my mind?

Part of what I was writing about was trying to make crystal clear exactly what did happen at Cleveland about the historic "basis of membership." There has been confusion in many quarters. The statement of purpose was not changed. Membership is open to all women & girls twelve or over, and voting membership to all seventeen or over, and there is no longer any electoral membership, or a requirement to sign the purpose to belong. But the most significant provision safeguards the integrity and nature of the YW as a Christian movement. It is the absolute requirement, more explicit than ever before, that the Boards of directors, standing committees, voting delegates to convention, and staff must accept individual responsibility for furthering the Purpose in the life of the Association and must be held responsible for making possible the growth of members toward understanding the Purpose and sharing in its realization.

It's hard to describe how strong the above was as an expression of what people at the Convention were feeling and saying. People were caring about how Christian principles could be applied in these solemn times, and yearning to make our Associations more Christian, not less. *How* we can do this, when we function as a social agency in this mixed-up Capitol community, is what I was trying to challenge our members to think through.

The Republican Convention was something else! It was fun to have Mary Lou and Norm there. Mary Lou and I were a team at producing meals from our kitchenette at any hour, or snacks for a caucusing group or whoever happened to be conferencing with Walter. We couldn't eat in restaurants – a continuous jam, irregular hours, and always someone who wanted to shake Walter's hand or ask advice. It was fun, too, to have Eleanor and Paul there at the time Walter was nominated for President. It was important these last months that he try to keep our Minnesota Republicans from starting a civil war, badly splitting the party between conservatives and liberals. It was a difficult time, full of misunderstandings, beratings, accusations. But it was a useful function his "favorite son" movement served, and if more states had been willing to do something similar we would have had an "open" convention with a discussion of issues and a real choice. It was successful in our state.

---

313   Miriam was referring to the Republican National Convention, which nominated Barry Goldwater for President. Walter was nominated as Minnesota's Favorite Son.

Washington, D.C.   *Saturday, October 24, 1964*

Dear Betty, Harriet, Helen –

The thing you were writing about, Betty, the expanding power and bigness of government, Walter has discussed in a speech which the *Reader's Digest* has reprinted in their November issue. Needless to say, Walter and I are not happy about the choices put before the voters, and in a time of such national and international crisis, when there ought to be most thoughtful and courageous leadership and statesmanship.

The YW is going great guns, with challenges and problems in the enlarged responsibility. We had an excellent luncheon with Esther Peterson giving the talk.[314] She is splendid, and she says vividly that it was working with industrial girls in the YW while she was teaching in Boston, and learning about child labor firsthand, and about strikes as her class of industrial girls chattered about them, that turned her to work with Labor – and here she is one of the highest positioned women in our country. We also honored Mrs. Pat Harris, a member of our Board and the negro gal who gave one of the seconding speeches for Lyndon Johnson. She teaches law at Howard and is a great person, an ex-YW staffer in Chicago. But what a range of members we have to satisfy, from sophisticated, bright energetic new young mothers in the new Branch, to rather stodgy and fundamentalist negro group, not the bright negro leaders by and large. It's fun.

Washington, D.C.   *Saturday, March 20, 1965*

Hi, Family –

This year, the end of our first year as a metropolitan YW, our Annual Luncheon will be April 27. Before that, each of the five branches is having their annual spring lunches and I have to go to all of them. It is important to keep the "family" YW interest at the Branch level, and they have to give their annual reports and elect their Branch Boards too. Yesterday I went to the Phyllis Wheatley Branch luncheon. They, the former all-negro branch, are always the dressiest, for they have achieved status by taking their lunch to the Statler Hotel. They had an excellent speaker and meeting. Last Wednesday I had to go out and speak at our newest Fairfax Branch, in the Virginia County that is the fastest growing in the USA.

Another YW activity that filled our schedule: there are fifty YW women leaders from thirty-five countries of the world in USA for a four months' training period. The end of their first month's briefing brought them to D.C. to see our Capitol, and our YW had to do the entertaining. We had a big coffee with Foreign Service wives invited, because they may sometime be stationed in these countries and be interested to work in their national YWs. I had to preside at this, and I wish you could have heard the black-as-ink Mrs. McGrath from Nigeria who spoke for the training group. She is a graduate of London School of Economics, and she really challenged women of the world. One afternoon the group and their American staff helpers were received at the White House by Mrs. Johnson, and they had included my name and Miss Cook's, so we went. The group got the A+ treatment, being taken by the guards to see rooms I had never been in before, including the ground-floor library, which was set up for a tea that Lynda was to preside over later that afternoon. It was the

---

314   Esther Peterson was the Assistant for Consumer Affairs for President Lyndon Johnson.

first time I'd gotten to look at the changes Jackie had made, which Lady Bird has left undisturbed. While we were milling around on the lower floor, Luci came running in with her arms loaded with school books, socks, and saddle shoes, just like one of my girls – except for the secret service man hurrying to keep up with her.[315]

Upstairs, Mrs. Laurence Rockefeller, Vice Presdent of the World's YW stood to receive with Mrs. Johnson and to introduce the foreign women; there was a uniformed aide and when he stopped me to ask my name and state so he could say it to Lady Bird, she looked over and said to the aide, "Oh, don't bother, we know each other, don't we. How are you, Mrs. Judd?" Well, I don't believe I've spoken to her in ten years, so I have to say she is good at her briefings. They had a huge battery of USIA[316] news people and photographers to get clips for their broadcasts abroad, a special concession of Mrs. Johnson's, for photographers are usually not allowed at receptions. While we were circulating with our tea cups in our hands and delicious sandwiches & cakes on our plates, she asked Mrs. Rockefeller to tell about this training seminar, which she did, and then the President of the National YW of Kenya, and a former member of their Parliament spoke for the group to Mrs. Johnson, and did an excellent job. So the YW had a lot of publicity in our papers this week, not always easy to get.

Washington, D.C.   *Wednesday, March 31, 1965*

Dear Family:

About our plans for the next two weeks with the Young President's Organization. We leave Saturday for Puerto Rico where we will be at the San Juan Hotel. There will be 500 YPOers & wives, an alert, intelligent cross section of Americans in business.

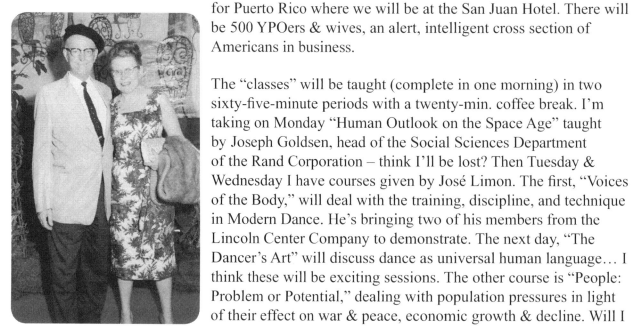

Walter and Miriam in Puerto Rico

The "classes" will be taught (complete in one morning) in two sixty-five-minute periods with a twenty-min. coffee break. I'm taking on Monday "Human Outlook on the Space Age" taught by Joseph Goldsen, head of the Social Sciences Department of the Rand Corporation – think I'll be lost? Then Tuesday & Wednesday I have courses given by José Limon. The first, "Voices of the Body," will deal with the training, discipline, and technique in Modern Dance. He's bringing two of his members from the Lincoln Center Company to demonstrate. The next day, "The Dancer's Art" will discuss dance as universal human language… I think these will be exciting sessions. The other course is "People: Problem or Potential," dealing with population pressures in light of their effect on war & peace, economic growth & decline. Will I know a lot when I get through.

315   Lynda and Luci were Lyndon and Lady Bird Johnson's daughters.

316   USIA was the United States Information Agency.

Walter teaches two courses, one on the "Explosive Far East," the other on "You & Your Government," what's happened to the traditional concept of the nature & purpose of government as it's evolved, and where the individual is in the democratic process. Afternoons there are informal discussion groups so you can talk with persons whose classes you don't attend. Saturday, the 10th, we start on the GREAT ISSUES SAILING SEMINAR, with about seventy members of the YPO, and for the two resource people, Walter, and Dr. Alden, president of Ohio State.

Washington, D.C.   *Monday, May 31, 1965*

Dear Family:

Tomorrow I drive up to Holyoke for meetings, then come back to El's at Edgewater, New Jersey, where she and I are going to take care of the four grandchildren while Mary Lou is leading the Alumnae Day festivities at Holyoke, and then going for a couple of days with three of her college friends and husbands to a cottage near Atlantic City. Then the Carpenters are going to drive down to visit us for ten days, and I've been getting ready.

Puerto Rico and the Virgin Islands – was a fabulous time. Walter was off to Europe after we returned. I had a few days in New York with El and Car, and a week in Minneapolis at Carpenters. I landed there right in the midst of their hurricane[317] and we had a tough time getting home. There was plenty of damage. Meanwhile, crisis situations here in the YW and church devolved on me.

Washington, D.C.   *Monday, June 28, 1965*

Dear Friends All: Holyoke classmates –

Does life become more tense, pressury, full of strategic and deep-down questionings and concerns as we grow older? Was it so for our parents? Is something special in the tenor of the times stirring into a giant mixing bowl former patterns, standards, values, morals till all is a scrambled-eggs mess, and we have nothing firm to stand on?

I am plunged into a real crisis with the Phyllis Wheatley YW Branch sending a sudden legal document terminating its relationship with the YW of the National Capitol Area, and all of us saying why? Why? What gave rise to this? And feeling completely numb, unprepared, heartsick.

We thought we were working well with the negro branch, bending over backwards to give them extra attention, consideration. Perhaps because of this we were not completely honest with them. This community has not too much respect for their leadership. The forward-looking energetic negroes have bypassed them, but they had a good membership of the more simple, church-centered negroes. Their personnel practices, salaries, programs, procedures on submitting reports to National Board or Health & Welfare Council, etc. were all substandard, but we were trying to protect them and bring them along slowly to raise standards as we established practices for the whole area. In April they questioned seriously our annual Planning & Priorities report in two sections that applied to them, and we went through a thorough and long-drawn procedure of meeting with them and ironing the misunderstandings out and accepting their re-statement of the questioned parts.

---

317   Miriam called it a hurricane, but it was a tornado.

Then out of the blue a three-page legal document that is bitter beyond belief, ignorant, with unsubstantiated charges and unexplained references that make not the first bit of sense, received on June 15 and stating that as of June 15 all relationship with us is terminated. No matter what is back of it, if we ever find out, it will be interpreted everywhere as a *racial* matter, and as a tremendous step backward in this whole struggle for integration, and in the Nation's Capitol that is so carefully watched, and with a group that was being held up by National Board as a model to about twenty places in the country that are working with mergers or consolidation.

We are finding that the negro community is split over this action; there are many fine negro women of long association with the YW who deplore this withdrawal, and who question if a small number of misunderstanding (or misled?) Board members can speak for a large group; that a few leaders, including their President, are deliberately falsifying reports and misinterpreting relationships, and that many do not have the first idea of what they have done. The Health & Welfare Council has ruled that they may receive no community funds, and they cannot go on without this support.

Oh, it is such a blow to find that a group of women in the YWCA cannot work together within our Christian purpose and work out differences. If *we* can't, how can this whole race issue in the world ever be resolved? How do we make sure we are actually hearing what each other is saying? How do we distinguish between appearance and reality? How do we all learn to help them preserve what is fine and creative and unique in their culture without the necessity of destroying another's culture? What a lot of learnings there are ahead in this whole area.

A book that is helpful: *The Silent Language* by Edward T. Hall. His thesis is that *culture* is the language of people that we should learn *before* their spoken language, and that the varying national traditions, taboos, environments, habits, and customs profoundly affect character, personality, relationships. I struggle with the day-to-day question: What do we do now?

Washington, D.C.   *Sunday, August 1, 1965*

Harriet dear –

Your letter was so heartening, and touched me deeply. To know that your prayer group was lifting up our Phyllis Wheatley problem was such a support. What has become clear is that a small group, four or five clever, shrewd, scheming women on their Board, including their President, know exactly what they are doing and have misled most of the rest. The fact that they happen also to be negroes only complicates the picture, for they can count on a sentimental element in the community who will say, "Give them anything they want – they have been so deprived so long – we have to bear a burden of guilt – we don't want a major blowup."

Many fine negroes are begging us to stand firm against the destructive group, as the constructive negroes seek to discredit and oust this leadership. It has gone beyond being simply a YWCA problem now. They *have* gone to the community with their grievances: they have set loose a factually dishonest editorial in the widely circulated Afro-American newspaper; they have talked to Congressman Adam Clayton Powell to urge him to attend their Board meeting and support their "cause" (he declined); they have furnished dishonest material to the negro ministers and urged that they preach on it in their pulpits; they got into the office of their negro YW executive when she was in hospital and tampered with records, xeroxed many, got at private personal files, erased signatures on documents and "lost" some.

Although they joined the Area YWCA on the same basis as every other branch, including *equal* representation of each branch on all committees (branch memberships varied as much as 2,000 to 45,000), now they have decided they want complete autonomy and maintenance of their negro culture and ways of doing things without accountability, while having the advantages of financing, staff help, and prestige that comes as a part of the large Area YW. They are not serving the community needs of today. Their membership has declined in the last few years from 6,000 to 1,200 – but they falsify official records so this is not evident to the supporting public.

Actually, the few leaders of the revolt are not YW trained or background women; they have been brought in the last few months, at most two years, have ousted most of the responsible regulars through devious devices of their nominating committee, they do not have a basic understanding of the YW purpose or way of work, and don't want to. It is heartbreaking to the negroes who have worked for years in YW and were cooperative and pleased to see it moving ahead so well.

Dorothy Height, head of the National Association of Negro Women, an outstanding leader known the country over, a staff member of National Board, had a grant to work on civil rights in YWCAs, and our percentage of integrated YWs has risen from 15% to 65%. She has been working with the group here and is highly disturbed. She says never has she seen Hitler at work, never before has she been treated with such personal rudeness, that nothing in her last two years experience has been as dreadful as our situation. You can see what kind of forces we are up against. How can we ever come to understanding with those who do not want understanding?

Walter and I did take ten days to drive out to the Mayo Clinic where we had thorough check-ups. They find us in excellent condition. They did remove some of the too-fast-growing cancers on Walter's face, and did a skin graft. Thank science (and dollars) for the air conditioning in our new car! We could drive in comfort in hottest days, no fear of infection from dust blowing in.

Washington, D.C.   *Tuesday, September 14, 1965*

Dear Betty, Harriet, and Helen:

You haven't been hearing from me because our darling eighteen-months red-head Katie has spinal meningitis, and I've been out in Minneapolis helping in the crisis. Fortunately, it was a non-infectious type, so the other children were not involved. She was in the hospital two weeks, at first with special nurses; Mary Lou went twice a day to be with her, feed her meals, and try to restore her faith in human nature, destroyed because nurses and doctors were constantly giving her needles and tests and procedures of every kind, which she couldn't understand! She is home now, the pus count lowered, a bit wobbly. They will test her sight and hearing later, and hope there will be no permanent slowing in her learning processes.

I flew from Minneapolis to New York to meet with National YW leaders on our Phyllis Wheatley problem. No, they had not condescended to sit down with us and talk. But they had made some impossible requests from our Health & Welfare Council for special funds for support and special status, which brought HWC strongly into the picture, and this has been helpful. HWC appointed a special committee to deal with the problems and "hear" the grievances, chaired by a wonderful negro woman who is respected by everyone and having excellent community leaders on it. The result has been to educate the Phyllis Wheatley Board members as to what their three leaders were trying to do and the methods being used, and when it came out what actions their President had taken without any Board discussions or vote, their indignation was great.

Last night for the first time since June 14 when we received the legal document severing their relationship, we sat down as an Area YW Board with the Phyllis Wheatley Branch Board, called together by this special HWC Committee, and with their lawyer and ours, and two National Board staff, a group of nearly sixty. And with the wonderful individual conferences that had gone before in this "long, hot summer," and with the prayers and thoughts of so many, we were able to set in motion and vote the machinery for getting together again, with some of the misunderstanding ironed out. Their negro lawyer is a man of prominence and respect in the community, and he admitted he had been misled. Their President didn't quite admit that she had made a bad mistake, but there are still two of her cohorts who showed their viciousness and who I am afraid will continue to undermine and tear down. But so much was revealed in front of many responsible persons, that they surely can't go back to the hidden evil that has been eating away for three months.

It was a wonderful meeting, and I'm sure God can use the difficult, yes, even bitter experiences of these last weeks to bring us closer together. The war is not won. There will have to be increased patience and slow workings-out and long hours, but we have established a basis of communication and an agreement about trying to work together. I have to give greatest credit to this HWC lay committee of six men and women, all busy and employed, who have literally given hours and hours to work with this, contacting scores of people, making a real effort to understand the way of work of the YWCA, and with an executive who is Jewish!

Now I must dress for another busy day – resignations among teachers and our church school superintendent over the summer, and a brand-new religious education director to work with; much YWCA work that can now go ahead after a summer of marking time; and some Holyoke responsibilities that will take me to college in mid-October. I am representing the College in the Smithsonian celebrations that begin tomorrow with scholars gathered from all over the world for symposia, and beginning with a huge academic procession on the mall and dinner and reception afterwards in the colorful circus tents they have erected on the mall.

Washington, D.C.   *Tuesday, January 11, 1966*

Hi, Mary Lou –

Dad began to express deep concern over his condition. I listened to him talk and worry, read aloud while he rested on the couch, and when we finally got him convinced to go and get checked up, he got into the most awful flurry about his will and his accounts and income tax return, as though it was his last week on earth. Well, you talked to him and know the results of his Mayo trip. I am relieved that he went, and if he will slow down, it can be the best thing that ever happened to him. But that's a large *if*, for he has longstanding commitments he feels he has to fulfill, and later on he will get feeling so good that he'll go on racing his motor, I'm afraid. We'll see – or in the timeless Judd phrase: TIME WILL TELL.

Washington, D.C.   *Monday, June 20, 1966*

Dearest Betty, Harriet, and Helen:

Our Phyllis Wheatley Branch declined the opportunity of housing this wonderful program that has been offered us under the Poverty Program. Mainly they wanted to negotiate the plans, the personnel and the funds directly with the O.E.O.[318] and not have the Area YWCA involved at all, and this O.E.O. was unable to do because of their policy.

But the project itself the Area Y has voted to do, housing it in our downtown residence at K Street, and we are enthusiastically enmeshed in plans. Westinghouse has become the "prime contractor" with the YW & YM working with them. They are drawing on their Laboratory of Behavioral Sciences in Albuquerque for both personnel – and for know-how and new techniques. The Westinghouse people are wonderful to work with. They will do the "educational" or "class" or discussion work with our girls and the groups housed at the YM, and supervise the counselors and guidance people and job placement people. They will work closely with us as we house and feed the girls, provide for their recreation, supervise the spending of their clothes allowance so they learn good buying and what sorts of things to wear in offices when they're employed and how to deal with the public and answer telephones. They will learn to budget on food buying for they will have a weekly food allowance and if they eat it all the first day, they will go hungry till the next week; they will have swimming in our pool and other exercise and health instruction.

Their "internships" in government agencies will give a chance to get over fear of a job, and to discuss the questions that come up about both the work and the relationships. They will be placed in jobs whenever Westinghouse decides an individual is ready, and her place will be taken by another girl, so some may be ready in six weeks and some not for six months, but it will be at their own pace. We hope to serve 200 in the course of the year, but there will be only forty-four living with us at any given time…less than half Caucasians, the rest Negroes, Mexicans, Indians, Puerto Ricans. I know our regular YW work will benefit from this new venture.

Walter and I are back from a ten-day trip west: first to Oklahoma to a Board meeting of World Neighbors. It was fascinating to hear the projects that have opened up in many parts of the world

---

318   The Poverty Program was administered by the Office of Economic Opportunity.

and how they work to make them self-supporting. They can do wonderful things because they have a minimum of organization and aren't tied down by any church Boards' hierarchy…

We went on to San Bernardino to a conference of Campus Crusade for Christ, and that was a different experience! What I missed was any challenge to growth, to discussion as to how we can put these Christian teachings to work in our complex and tired world. Horizons were narrow – their eyes seemed to be turned inward on themselves and to whether they had been led to Christ in the approved manner. Walter, the only "outsider," was giving them the challenge to go into today's world to work at redeeming it. Any number of students came to talk with him about *doing* something with what they *believed*. I hope some of them left with an enlarged vision.

Washington, D.C.   *Tuesday, November 15, 1966*

Dear, Neglected, Girls —[319]

What a lot we are learning through our big experiment with O.E.O. and government funds. We have a fascinating negro director for the project, a YW employee who has been with the State Department in Germany. But oh, the girls that the Job Corps Centers sent us, supposed to be their most promising! It is hard to believe in this day of "compulsory education" that many could be at first to third grade level when they reach 18-20. Westinghouse insists that a tangible incentive is essential to keep them from getting discouraged; so the boys are allowed into the corridors to smoke between classes if they have passed so many grades; the girls get a raise in allowance. You can't build on satisfaction and pride in achievement in these realms, for it just isn't there. In order to teach punctuality, which will be essential in their future jobs and which has never been a part of their life, Westinghouse makes clear that fifteen minutes of accumulated lateness at class or job is cause for dismissal from the project – fifteen minutes in a three- or four-month training period is drastic, but they maintain absolutely essential to inculcate ideas of time in people.

One boy turns out to be a mathematical genius, has gone soaring from grade to grade in mathematical concepts while his grammar and reading remain at first grade level. His supervisors said to the math teacher: Please don't start on calculus till you've taught him to use a deodorant! They devour adolescent etiquette books and child's history books, are being readied for a bus trip to Williamsburg to learn about the beginnings of our country, have to be in their rooms at eleven week nights, will be dismissed for possession or use of alcohol, have YW counselors living on their residence floors, can hardly get over the luxury of single rooms with a basin in each, access to TV lounge, wash-and-drying machines, city transportation. They are having magnificent training – and if we reach 200 in one year at enormous expense per person, how can the taxpayers not go bankrupt, with the hundreds of thousands we need to reach. I know these government funds are being well spent; I wish I felt as sure about other Poverty Projects.

Now a word about the YW Statement of Purpose. The Commission set up to study this at the Cleveland Convention 2½ years ago, has come up with a suggested statement, which will be taken to the triennial convention in Boston next April for discussion and vote. Like any compromise statement, it satisfies no group fully. But the commission has worked hard to hear all points of view,

319   Mount Holyoke College classmates.

to study the needs of our day in our pluralistic society, to use contemporary expressions. There will undoubtedly be a move at Boston to strike out any reference to Christian, for a strong contingent questions if the Y can be Christian and still open to *all* women, but I do not think they will prevail.

People will probably try to "edit" the statement, which is one's first impulse, for it is certainly clumsy or unwieldly, doesn't "swing," would be hard to memorize. Our committee is trying to study what it says for content, for meaning, before we go to each of our branches in January for a 1½ hour discussion with the branch boards, before our convention delegation is selected. I want the growing YW to be true to our Christian heritage, but contemporary enough to meet today's challenges.

Washington, D.C.   *Thursday, February 9, 1967*

Dear, dear H. –

Your letter – how achingly unexpected – and what a window into the explosion of questioning, heartbreaks, and heart-searchings, of deepest bitterness and hurts and recriminations and yearnings and hope and bafflement that you have been living with. How grateful I am that you wrote it, so that I can hold you close in these impossibly difficult days and hours.

What can I say? Anything sounds trite, superficial in the face of such fundamental uprooting of your past thirty-five years. Yet in your letter I find seeds of healing: your generous understanding of the human needs of those other two, and of how your own preoccupation and challenges had kept you from sensing them earlier. There *is* love there, with both of you, only it has got a bit confused or mixed through lack of communication (the hardest thing in the world) and lack of nourishment, and it *will* grow again if you both are patient and feed it and want it. *I am sure…*

And the jealousy! I *know* how it can eat searingly at everything within you, and cloud all your outlook and judgment. It is not subject to reason. Or frontal attacks on it. But it can be pushed out – slowly, perhaps – by the re-growth of love, understanding, forgiveness, consideration. I know because it has happened to me.

I am *not* wise. I felt bewildered and lost for both of you when your letter came. So I sat down with a book, to have a dialogue with the author about you, my best way to meditation and prayer. This time it was Frederick Buechner's *The Magnificent Defeat*. How understandingly Buechner talked to me in his chapter "The Breaking of Silence," p.126. May I lift bits here to send you, to soothe and encourage and give strength to your aching heart, as it did to mine?

"Prayer is…the breaking of silence. It is the need to be known and the need to know. Prayer is the sound made by our deepest aloneness. I am thinking not just of formal prayers that a religious person might say in church or in bed at night, but of the kind of vestigial, broken fragments of prayer that people use without thinking of them as prayers: something terrible happens and you might say, 'God help us' or 'Jesus Christ' – the poor crippled prayers that are hidden in the minor blasphemies of people for whom in every sense God is dead except that they still have to speak to him if only through clenched teeth. Prayer is a man's impulse to open up his life at its deepest level. People pray because they cannot help it…

"You do not have to persuade him to heal. You do not have to ask him to change his mind and be merciful instead of indifferent. You ask God to use your prayer as a channel through which the healing power of his love can flow into whatever body or soul you pray for, your own or that of another. The channel of your prayer is apt to be clogged with all kinds of doubt, not only about God but about yourself, and clogged also with disuse – and at the same time the love that you feel for the person you are praying for or for yourself is clogged with ambiguity. And yet, I believe that little by little, as you persist in prayer, the power begins to trickle through anyway. The healing begins. Perhaps first it is the healing of yourself, and then gradually, through your prayer, it becomes the healing of others.

"In honesty you have to admit…that prayer is not for the wise, not for the prudent, not for the sophisticated. Instead it is for those who recognize that in face of their deepest needs, all their wisdom is quite helpless. It is for those who are willing to persist in doing something that is both childish and crucial."[320]

My wisdom is quite helpless, H. dear. But I send you both my surrounding love and faith, and my persisting prayer.

Washington, D.C.   *Tuesday, July 4, 1967*

Dear Gals –

When *two* of you write me and ask, When are we going to hear about the Boston Convention action on the new YW Statement of Purpose? Then I know I've got to put my lethargy aside. (Don't any of you find the aging process brings you *days* of not wanting to do anything but sit on a cool porch and read? I need clues as to how to make myself do the things I know I ought to do and want to do, but can't seem to find the push for.)

I have been deeply impressed with the *way* the YW handled this whole three-year study, from the Convention in Cleveland where the Commission was authorized with Lilace Barnes as chairman. This group of thirty women, widely representative in age, geography, theology, faith, did an excellent study of the YW as a Christian Movement in Today's World, and made available their questions and study materials and group discussion guides to all YWCAs.

The Commission had over thirty "Consultations" with groups of YW leaders all over the country at the end of the first year; and at the end of the second, took the Purpose Study as the major agenda item to the four Conferences in the Regions. So persons everywhere had a chance to be heard before a "Position Paper" was drawn up by the Commission. From this paper they evolved a suggested new Statement of Purpose which was sent to all YWs six months before Convention for study & discussion. It was this Statement of Purpose which was acted on at Boston, and finally adopted:

> "The Young Women's Christian Association of the United States of America, a movement rooted in the Christian faith as known in Jesus, and nourished by the resources of that faith, seeks to respond to the barrier-breaking love of God in this day. The Association draws together

---

320   Selections from Frederick Beuchner's *The Magnificent Defeat,* Harper Collins. New York, pp 126, 128, 130.

into responsible membership women and girls of diverse experiences and faiths, that their lives may be open to new understanding and deeper relationships and that together they may join in the struggle for peace and justice, freedom and dignity for all people."

Not words of deathless prose. Not easy to memorize, to say aloud together. Nor perfect, not complete. But truly it grows as you live with and work with it…

At Convention that darling Lilace Barnes opened up the question of our underlying purpose with such tenderness and grace and love, when she urged on us all "an intensity of listening with understanding so that we might hear what *isn't* said, hear what is felt, what is behind words not spoken." She was cute when she said many had come to Boston quite sure of our own ideas, of how the purpose ought to read. Since we were that sure, it ought to free ourselves to something new, so that from the pieces all of us bring we might evolve a more perfect instrument. She pointed out that words are imperfect communicators – "they are often barriers, not bridges." I loved her expression "Recognizing we differ, determined to listen, resolved to trust."

It seemed to me a stroke of genius to divide the Convention into seventy luncheon-discussion groups of twenty-five to thirty-five each, where *everyone* had a chance to be heard on this subject. People too timid to talk before the huge convention, people with a deep conviction that what their YW had studied and agreed back home needed to be said out loud before someone, people with minority points of view, people repeating in different words what had already been said by countless others, young or new ones still groping in their understanding of what the YW could or should be – all kinds and conditions spoke out in these informal groups, which were carefully chaired by YW leaders – I was recorder in one where everyone felt relaxed and able to speak out. The next day when the discussion came to the convention floor, much of the fire had been spent…

A wonderful chairman we had for this discussion in Beth Marti, for there were amendments offered and defeated, and amendments amended and re-amended. She kept a clear parliamentary judgment, but was at all times permissive and not by a tone of her voice or a slump of her body did she suggest impatience or weariness; was fair in calling alternately on delegates speaking pro and con, not allowing delegates or delegations to repeat at the microphones if others were waiting, was dignified but not tense – relaxed us…

"Barrier-breaking" bothered many, yet it was the word that spoke to the students, challenged them for the world they need to work in, seemed to say more to them than our more theological "reconciling." And since we were aiming, for the first time in history, to have *one* purpose for both Student and Community YWs, and the students were less revolutionary and violent than they were three years ago at Cleveland, I felt we should go along with them. After all, this Purpose is for the future, not the past, for the students and the young ones, not for us has-beens.

Gradually it became clear from the speeches on the floor (limited to three minutes) that to delay for three more years of study, or to delay to try to find "the statement perfect," was but side-stepping the inevitable; there was urgency in the condition of our world and we needed to be involved with dealing with the problems, not more time spent discussing purpose. "Words are but the shadows of action." How can we be hurt by changing? This statement doesn't *limit* our responsible involvement, it challenges it. It allows greater freedom, but imposes greater responsibility. It is a call to *action*. So it was passed by a large majority. The discussion and study stirred up has been good for us, brought a new kind of thinking and new depths to many, given us a vision of what may be as we put it into action, united at last with the Student YW. *What a day!*

Washington, D.C.   *Tuesday, September 19, 1967*

Dear Gals –

Dad left here yesterday and will be gone twenty-two days. He phoned Bill Bundy[321] about going to Vietnam and was given permission. I got back from London[322] to a busy time here: Clarke & Elizabeth came in next day. Went sightseeing all one day: Bureau of Engraving to see how the stamps and bills are made; the FBI, which I'd never seen, which was fascinating. They had large pictures of the ten most wanted men posted on the wall, and across one of them printed in red that that man had been captured Sept. 8 by information furnished by a tour member on Sept. 4 who had recognized a former employee of his parents!…

I forgot to write that in London we went down to Tunbridge Wells to see cousin Tom Clarke. Tom's father and my Grandmother Matilda Clarke were born in Beragh, Northern Ireland.[323] He drove us to the Judd School in Tunbridge, founded in the fifteen hundreds by Sir Andrew Judde, an ancestor of Dad's, and still going strong as an excellent public school for boys. Dad was tickled to get a glimpse of where his ancestors held forth.

Washington, D.C.   *Friday night, September 22, 1967*

Dearest –

I don't even know if this can reach you still in Taipei, but I hope so. Partly because it's going to seem funny not being able to talk with you on your birthday. But more especially 'cause I have to tell you how *much* what you said on the phone to me this afternoon meant. You were wonderful to think it, and to say it, and you were right; I didn't need you to tell me, because I knew it. How many thousands of ways your actions over the years have proved that you loved and thought about and provided for me. I've felt like singing out to the people at the church supper tonight, I am loved, and cherished, and appreciated by the most wonderful, most discriminating, most human man in the world. I *do* get lonely when I am here by myself, but to hear you say you *need* me, need me to come home to, depend on me, will help me through the separations. And if you need to hear that I am grateful forever for you, too – come back and I'll whisper it in your ear some night in the dark.

Washington, D.C.   *Sunday, July 28, 1968*

Dearest Betty, Harriet, Helen –

Imagine getting back two days ago and finding letters from all three of you. What a beautiful time

---

321   Bill Bundy was Assistant Secretary of State for East Asian and Pacific Affairs.

322   Walter had meetings in England and Miriam traveled with him.

323   Matilda Clarke and Tom's father were siblings.

we had in Minneapolis: the glorious weather, the pool full of fish-children much of the day and the delightful patio area, with all our dinners out of doors under the white birch clump, the large yard – it couldn't have been a better vacation spot.

June days in San Francisco were lovely, with sightseeing and visiting and installing new AMA President. Then to Boulder eight days, where Walter had seven lectures in a summer course at the University, and where we had time to drive up to Estes Park and on for an overnight at gorgeous Grand Lake, and a full day trip to Colorado Springs and Royal Gorge.

Walter and Miriam at a Presidential reception after Walter received the
American Medical Association Distinguished Service Award

A week at home to catch up on YW and Church matters – and then were off for five days at Grand Bahama Island, a conference of "Family Doctors." The weather, surroundings, activities, and companions there were utterly delightful – doctors had brought their wives & children, and my faith in human nature was restored. Best of all, three outstanding *women* doctors were on the program for lectures… I went to these sessions and was so proud, for these gals were knockouts – women competing in a man's field have to be better than the men usually. One was Mary McCauley, psychologist from Gainesville who drew on her clinical experience with college youth, and their parents, in helping the "family doctor" see his responsibility as "sex educator," "listener and counselor" – what a wise, practical, & intelligent lecturer.

I evidently needed this kind of shot in the arm. Our year in Washington had been grim, anxiety-filled, riots & conflicts & rumors & Resurrection City & decisions about where and how best to help. I was utterly weighed down. I find, for example, in Minneapolis where Mary Lou had a group of girls who were working on programs for the underprivileged and broadening their own attitudes about the races, that they have an entirely different emphasis as I listened to eight of them talk at a patio luncheon, than we have had to have in a city were 65% are negroes. They have done some fine things, got programs going, taken sensitivity training and been in T-groups, but they are largely solving "academic" problems, not the "reality" of daily contacts. Our YW Staff who worked with Resurrection City children, for instance, got stoned by some of those they were trying to help, because they were white. We still have a lot of problem-solving to do with our emotions and inner attitudes when it comes to living with people of extremely diverse attitudes and backgrounds and cultures.

One spot this became a personal question: In June, Mary Lou brought a seventeen-year-old gal with her from Minneapolis to help with the children while she was east three weeks. Kathy has worked for Mary Lou two summers and is a fine girl. While Mary Lou was up in Boston and I had the kids alone, I let Kathy go one day to sightsee in the Smithsonian and Mellon Art Gallery, since this was her first trip outside Minnesota, and I chased kids. When I picked her up in the afternoon she had met a nice guard at Smithsonian, had talked to him a long time, he wanted to take her out and he was negro. She said frankly her own parents would not permit it, and she supposed I wouldn't because, being of the Older Generation I was surely prejudiced against the negro (that hurt). But here we were in Washington in the summer of '68, racial tensions sky high, I responsible for her, not knowing one thing about this Al Smith, wondering why a twenty-six-year-old negro Washington resident would want to go out with a seventeen-year-old gal.

We compromised. I let her have him on the porch where they visited all evening till midnight, drinking cokes from the icebox. She talked to him an hour on the phone next day, but after that left town and didn't see him again, tho' they were corresponding and hoping to get together during his vacation. After that she voluntarily put a stop to the correspondence. Her parents found out when she got home, and there was a terrible fight with name-calling and face-slapping and she left home and went to Mary Lou's "to live, because she could never go home again." This developed into a problem of counseling about family communication and understandings, and Mary Lou & Norm handled it well, getting their minister and someone trained in counseling to give continuing help with the family. Kathy is back at home till college in the fall. Oh, how complicated it is when racial tensions involve also the generation gap and differences in vocabulary and attitudes.

John Dewey years ago described tendencies of youth. He said they hugged ideals to themselves as if only they possessed them; that they sought to destroy what disappointed them; that juveniles had a tendency to assume power to achieve their ideals.

We are planning an exciting "Family Reunion" September 20 to 26 at Mary Lou's in Minneapolis. Walter will be seventy on September 25, and there is nothing anyone can "give" him as a gift; but to have his family all around him would make him happiest of all…

Washington, D.C.   *Friday, January 3, 1969*

Hi, Gals:

Dad has gone to the opening of Congress, to see what fireworks there may be. He seems to have a renewed interest in political events, now that the Republicans are coming in, and also a feeling of hurt (he hasn't said so in so many words), that the Nixon people have not called for any counseling in regard to Foreign Policy, or personnel. He has talked and made his own recommendations, but I do think he feels bypassed by the top.

Washington, D.C.   *Tuesday, July 29, 1969*

Dear Girls:

The touching service for Aunt Elizabeth at the Mount Hebron Cemetery in Montclair last Saturday, was a cool, grey day, and we gathered around the plot in that lovely quiet place. They had opened a small square for Elizabeth's urn. Clarke spoke first, very quietly. I spoke about Elizabeth being my "sister" before she became my sister-in-law, about our shared adolescence, which is always an impressionable time. I appreciated that she had been a real daughter to my parents; when they were in Florida and I was in Washington, she had been a close comfort, and help to them. I would always be grateful for this. The Barbers and McClures sang in parts "Breathe on Me, Breath of God." Betty Lou spoke of remembering her mother's lovely voice as she sang beside her in church. John had a prayer poem that he had sent his mother once. Then Clarke asked Dad to close with a prayer, which he did, and it was over.

Somehow this was more meaningful to me, and satisfying, than that more formal, impersonal service in Florida. The immediacy of death then was keeping us all not daring to let down or express our feelings, keeping steady on the surface because we couldn't quite say how we felt inside. Now time had passed for us to know what memories we wanted to keep from her lovely life, and there was a beautiful, quiet honesty about our appreciation of her.

Aboard ship near Mount Parnassas, Greece   *Saturday, August 16, 1969*

Dear Family All –

We are getting to the Greek Cruise end – It's been great – I love everything about the shipboard. But hiking over spread-out ruins of a town or palace, dirt paths or uneven cobbles, and doing it day after day, has not been the best thing for my back, and I have had extra pain and weariness. Today buses took us up Mount Parnassas, 2,000 feet above the sea, to Delphi where the oracle was consulted by early Greeks. From the top we looked down on the largest olive growth in Greece – what a martini!! We've read no newspapers, heard no news, thought of nothing more recent than 331 B.C. It's good for Dad. His mind's completely off his work at home and engrossed with the fascinating Greek civilization.

Washington, D.C.   *Sunday, April 26, 1970*

Hi, Gals —[324]

Got back from Houston Sunday. The YW Convention came off better than many of us had feared. The preliminary caucuses or assemblies of Blacks, Students, Young Adults, and Y-Teens had been worried about by some as a divisive element. But they drew off the squawking of the dissenters and

---

324   In this case, "Gals" were her Mount Holyoke classmates.

disaffected, allowed leadership to evolve in each of these smaller groups and ironed out some of the differences and difficulties before they got brought to the Convention.

Many of us "over thirty-five-year-olds" had been making a conscious effort to hear what other groups were saying and provide some of what they wanted, in their own idiom. We opened the Convention with Maxine Weldon. She is a negro singer from LA who brought her group of "SOUL PLUS TWO" on piano, drums, guitar. Aside from a gorgeous voice, and the most beautifully mobile face, she was sensitive to the purpose and aims of our convention and the diverse elements present, chose her songs to fit situations – and had delegates eating out of her hands, clapping, snapping, humming, joining spontaneously but in response to her. It was an inspired and unexpected "opening" for convention, and started us off united…

About the worship services, the first was not good – too long and preachy and full of words. Second one was done by blacks and was full of denunciation and pity for their long oppression, and loud rock and gospel music done well by a Houston high school group. It was more of a performance than of worship. So when ours came the third morning, with its emphasis on silence, it couldn't have been better timed, for contrast, and many people thanked us for this…

Our assigned theme was diversity within the YWCA. The voices of diversity were twelve members of our Washington delegation at a mike at the back of the huge auditorium, speaking their words fairly promptly one after another. The variety of tones and quality and accents of the voices was good – several negro, one Chinese American. Elizabeth Ann and I were at two reading desks with microphones on the stage, where I introduced the worship service, and she read THE HEARER RESPONDS, which she had written. The Litany I had written, and I led that. The *entering into the silence* Elizabeth Ann explained as similar to entering a great cathedral where all our diversities could be caught up together (over 2,600 at the convention) and where we could listen and hear and speak – and she asked us to write, or draw, our protest or petition or psalm or prayer on the pages provided, in silence. It was wonderful watching the thoughtful quiet for the next five or six minutes – some writing, some reading the printed selections at the back of our program, some sitting quietly. For *breaking the silence* we had a wonderful negro girl with guitar at the mike start softly singing "He's got the whole word in his hands" and by the second or third verse, getting progressively louder, many of the delegates had joined in.

For the Benediction we had, again at the back-of-the-room mike, four international YW visitors to the convention, one each from Asia, Africa, Europe, and South America. Each prayed briefly in her own language, starting with the President of the YW from Taiwan in beautiful tonal Mandarin. (No one announced who these were nor what language or country.) The second was the head of the YW in Columbia from Bogota. She prayed in Spanish to the Virgin Mary, for we had many Roman Catholics present. Third was a graduate student from Sierra Leone, and last, the President of our World YW who is Greek.

After these we entered again into the silence, with the Lord's Prayer done by a deaf and dumb girl on the stage. You could almost follow her hand signals, ending with the perfect circles she traced in the air for "forever and ever," and then her bowed head and clasped hands for AMEN. Then our girl with guitar led us in the glorious AMEN that we had sung the first night with Maxine Weldon, which starts soft, gets loud and fades away. Somehow you got a feeling that an atmosphere of worship had been created in which each one could and did participate in her own way…

On the business of the convention, the young did not follow well the structure or rules or plan of the convention, and kept flooding us with resolutions on good subjects that should have been sent in months before to get into our workbooks and pre-convention discussion. We took up as much as we could, and referred all remaining ones to the National Board for action. Someone wanted more classes in YWs on how to be good wives and mothers, to strengthen the home & family, and she got roundly booed and her resolution voted down by militant student *Freedom for Women* advocates, who feel "good wives & mothers" is exactly the image they are seeking to erase. I could just see the headlines in the news: "YW Against Motherhood!"

It intrigued me that the resolution to legalize marijuana was roundly defeated by the young who spoke several times on the difficult problems they have to deal with and please don't make easy access to marijuana another hurdle for them. "Work toward the admission of Red China to the UN" passed, tho' some of the Chinese there tried to amend it. I voted against it…

We voted to make "the elimination of racial injustice wherever it exists" our main imperative for the next triennium, as many of our other concerns like poverty, hunger, crime, drugs, etc., are related to it. Some of the young were impatient, the college students seemed humorless to me, but all in all the spirit was good and so was the overall effect. I enjoyed it…

Dad was home most of the time I was in Houston and he didn't like it. Now he's to be gone more. I'm going to College for 45th reunion. We are planning a trip to Scandinavia and Russia.

When I was in Houston Dad went to a White House State dinner for Prime Minister of Denmark. Tuesday he went to a stag White House dinner for Chiang Ching Kuo,[325] which he enjoyed. Sat next to J. Edgar Hoover and was amazed at some of the things he said. Dad and Brooks Hays[326] have gotten up a Former Members of Congress group, starting with invitation to all they could reach, having the group vote to organize, to keep good addresses, use those that can be used for speaking to various groups and particularly in colleges 'round the country, keep information going to them. They're working on possible Congress chartering, a seal, outside funding. Many members have responded enthusiastically.

Washington, D.C.   *Monday, September 14, 1970*

Dear Family:

Yesterday was a lovely day for Dad & me. We drove to the White House for the first Sunday Worship Service of the season, to which "Former Members of Congress, Inc." and wives had been invited. Dad and Brooks Hays are bipartisan, co-chairmen…in on the planning. The President asked that Dad give the "message" and Brooks do the scripture and prayer. An aide took (the Hayses and

---

325   Chaing Ching-kuo was son of Chaing Kai-shek. He eventually became President of the Republic of China.

326   Brooks Hays was a retired Democratic Congressman from Arkansas and a close friend of Walter's.

us) to the family sitting room. We were served coffee and Nixons and Julie and David Eisenhower came in and we visited while the men checked details for the service.

Just before 11:30 we were escorted downstairs and ushered into seats in the East room. I found myself sitting between Julie and Pat Nixon, with their husbands on either side of their ladies. Dad and Brooks sat beside the lectern facing the audience, of whom there were 250, every seat taken. Dad spoke not more than fifteen minutes, about Moses' experience as helpful to those of us who are trying to build a nation in these days. He ran thru the Ten Commandments with a sentence or two for each, but he was inspired, I felt, and did an excellent job. Afterwards we and the Hayses met friends in the Blue Room, while the Nixon family received in the State dining room, and everyone was served orange juice, coffee, and fancy coffee cake. At the end we went into the State dining room where the Nixons and Eisenhowers were lingering talking to friends a full hour after the close of the service, and they were most cordial and friendly.

Washington, D.C.   *Monday, December 7, 1970*

Helen, dear –

I went to Minneapolis the end of September. Mary Lou landed in the hospital with peritonitis of unknown cause, and Norm's stepfather died and he had to go New Hampshire to help his mother. So I was running the children and that big house for nearly two weeks. Mary Lou's friends were most helpful, but I was tired when I got back.

In a week I was off on my New York-New England trip of twelve days, with the car – Holyoke College, friends, and family. Next jaunt was five days driving in Pennsylvania, with twenty-four hours visit to Betty Lou and family and on to Williamsport to do my first "Association Review" of the YW there. This was strenuous but rewarding. This Review process once in each triennium brings a team of national staff and a board volunteer to each association after they have done a self-evaluation, to give an outside and perhaps more objective appraisal and help them think how to meet their problems and move and grow. We met all sorts of people – staff, Board, Review Committee, individual chairmen, community leaders, etc. It seemed to me this was exactly what National should be about, helping local Associations know how to serve their communities better and assessing what resources they need from National. I'll be asked to do others. I loved it. Then Walter came, returning from Chicago, and he drove home with me on a glorious autumn day.

My most recent jaunt was six days in Boston after Thanksgiving with Walter attending AMA meetings and me seeing friends and museums and having a delightful time. And the day before Thanksgiving I went up to Philadelphia for the funeral service for John St. John. It was a time of reminiscence for me, for our association goes way back to our parents all being in college together. I was the only one there from our high school days in Montclair. I kept thinking how much was built into our lives by our parents in that old gang, and wondering if our children would have any such foundation to meet their peculiar needs.

13

Reflections

1972 – 1991

Miriam and Walter gradually slowed down in "retirement"; the few letters were to old friends and to the daughters, sometimes from abroad. Miriam had two hip replacements, eight years apart. She volunteered weekly for "Meals on Wheels," read weekly for a blind woman, and worked faithfully at the YW and to support the church. She enjoyed outings with friends, neighbors, and fellow volunteers. Many Augusts found them at family reunions at the YMCA Conference Center at Silver Bay, New York. They traveled to Africa, England, New Zealand, and repeatedly to Taiwan, with each daughter accompanying them on a trip there. A week-long tour of Ireland was enjoyed in June 1981 by Miriam and Walter with the Carpenter family (minus Katie who was in France with her high school French class).

Miriam's domestic arts skills continued to enrich the lives of her friends and family. Her love of cooking provided inspiration for daughters as she shared recipes and ideas. Most grandchildren still treasure knit sweaters she churned out — as well as shawls, bed throws, needlepoint quilts, pillows and piano bench covers. Sewing provided hours of delight and lovely clothing for her and all of us.

At long last, Miriam's private writings returned as she moved into a period of greater personal reflection. When Walter's increased presence and intensity became a struggle for her, Miriam drew on her faith to find the "quiet silences." In looking back at their lives together, she pondered their differing styles, preference, and conflicts. Did her hesitancy or reluctance to speak out for her own needs limit Walter's true understanding of her disappointments? Or was his strong voice always overwhelming? Or did she keep her opinions to herself in order to "maintain the peace" in the household? She seemed more forceful in supporting desires of their daughters. Her yearnings continued as well as her loyalty and love for Walter.

A lifetime highlight was the bestowing on Walter of the Presidential Medal of Freedom at the White House by President Ronald Reagan. Other celebrations were in honor of their fiftieth wedding anniversary (including a Caribbean boat trip with Mary Lou and her daughters) and Walter's ninetieth birthday.

They lived independently in the family home into their old age. Indeed, Walter was still hand-mowing the vacant lot next door the year he turned ninety in 1988. That summer, they did sell the house and moved to the nearby Collington Episcopal Life Care Community in Maryland. There they participated in activities while continuing some outside involvements. And they began the process of disassembling the remarkable volume of letters, documents, speeches, official photos, and other materials they had compiled over a lifetime together – and enjoyed unearthing memories in the process.

∼

Minneapolis, Minnesota   *Tuesday, March 21, 1972*

H., dear –

Mary Lou and Norm are skiing in Aspen for a week, and I am doing the routine of homework & hockey, ballet and Brownies, clarinet practice and paper route and music lessons, church & cooking and allowances & rubbers and combing lovely red hair & bedtimes. Do the young realize that these are the best years of their lives, I wonder?

The Africa trip was fascinatingly interesting, but I haven't been able to write about it. Perhaps the size of the country, the numbers and diversity of the people, the complexity of the problems, overwhelmed me. Perhaps the seeming unconcern about any of the people or problems on the part of our twenty-four teammates, their only interest seeming to be the wild animals. Perhaps mine was an emotional reaction produced by the death of one of our teammates. We were at Murchison Falls up in the interior of Uganda. After our farewell dinner party, while we were watching beautiful native dancing on the patio with wild elephants and rhinos grazing not thirty feet beyond, our friend had a massive coronary attack. No doctors, no medicines, no hospitals anywhere near. Walter did what he could to ease his last few hours and to care for the body afterwards, and next day to make arrangements by phone with our Embassy in Kampala. It cast a pall over us, and made me realize so vividly how quickly our experience on this earth can end. Are we ever ready?

We got back just as Nixon was going to China, and that whole "extravaganza," was difficult to live through with Walter who was almost wild about it, who argued and corrected and answered back every commentator on radio or TV, every newspaper account. He cannot see one good thing coming out of it all, only disaster, and his anguish and hopelessness are hard to live with.

Minneapolis, Minnesota   *Tuesday, March 21, 1972*

Hi, El Dear –

How good of you to bring your brood and pick me up in New York and do the chauffeuring to the airport. I thought you looked pretty and well – tho' I know how well you dissemble – the pain, the discouragement and depression and hopelessness.

I thought about you on my plane ride to Minneapolis. I suffer for you and want to help. You need physical healing, it is true;[327] but you need mental and spiritual healing also, to make you a whole person, to help you deal with your complex relationships and numerous family needs. I yearn over you. Then I think of all the human resources yearning to help and not knowing how, but being motivated by LOVE. How much more then is the Divine Resource yearning to break through to you with help and support and wise answers and courage. Your Judd family can give so little, and so falteringly. But I am sure there is help available, starting with the overall knowledge and judgment that is beyond our poor abilities.

Most of the time we can't say – or write – these things. I hope you don't think we aren't concerned. Only you have the task of dealing with the specific daily-ness of the problems. We have to be generalized in our care, and love and concern. Tell us where and how we can help.

Taipei Hilton, Taipei, Taiwan   *Sunday, October 7, 1973*

Hi, USA Gang –

On 9:30 p.m. arrival at airport complete with various welcoming officials, we were whisked to the pressroom for a brief picture-taking and question answering – and thus avoided our personal friends who were waiting for us where ordinary folk exit. We were handed a two-page official schedule which left few free minutes for our own desires – but also furnished us a car & driver, and a twenty-nine-year-old Chinese escort to care for our needs. We expect to make changes in their plans to include our own friends. Dad has had a furious chest cold & cough. Let's hope it clears up before the Tuesday evening speech.

A most interesting experience this morning grew from our acquaintance with the Liaos in D.C. We got a cable yesterday saying his father-in-law, General Wu, had died here and would we represent the D.C. Liao family by paying respects today at the funeral home. We drove to the temple-like place all painted red & gaudily decorated. Outside the building were twenty or more huge tributes to this well-known general.

In the large barn-like room a shrine was set opposite the door, with a larger-than-life-size picture of the deceased, large candles burning, a place for a lifesaver-sized white-paper flower wreath. We were escorted to 12-15 ft. in front of the shrine, handed the round paper wreath to hold, stood straight while some official spoke a few words, then told officially & loud to bow: "Once, twice, thrice" (all in Chinese), which we did slowly & with dignity. Then the wreath was taken from us and hung in front of the picture, immediately taken off again and handed to the next group who took our place. Each time a person or group stood to bow thrice to the deceased's picture, the two lines of close family and mourners on the floor on their knees went forward thrice and touched their foreheads to the floor in concert with the official loud count. Then we went on to an anteroom where the elderly & frail widow and friends helped her up from the floor to receive our word from her daughter in USA. Actually it was a dignified and warm and supportive way of showing respect to one gone on, a Confucian ceremony, tho' they would likely have a Christian burial also. I was impressed.

Went to church today at the chapel where Generalissimo & Madame Chiang always worship, tho'

---

327   Ellie had been diagnosed with rheumatoid arthritis in 1971 at age 33.

they weren't there as she's in New York City. Took communion on this Worldwide Communion Sunday, and felt close to you all, as we sang familiar tunes with Chinese words. Everyone is feasting Dad, & I'm uncomfortably fat. Tomorrow I see YW work & new building.

Washington, D.C.   *Thursday, September 25, 1975*

Dear Heart –

You don't need anything I can give you for your birthday – except perhaps my deepest love and appreciation for all you have meant to me in support and patience and guidance and caring these last weeks through my Mount Holyoke[328] and Mayo Clinic[329] ordeals! These you have in unbounded measure. You are remarkable – unbelievable – for seventy-seven or any other age. Keep up your enthusiasms and interests – and enjoy the nine *National Geographic* lectures this fall which I have ordered for ~~you~~ – us! With all my love – Miriam

– Private Writing –

Silver Bay, New York   Friday, August 20, 1976

Things I like about my spouse:
1. *He lets me know he loves me.*
2. *He supports me in, and appreciates my activities.*
3. *His enthusiasm is contagious and creative.*
4. *He is widely respected and admired and sought after.*
5. *He makes an interesting life for us – travel, friends, events.*
6. *He provides superbly for me economically.*

I have accepted the responsibility of a wife – How do I satisfy my obligations to Walter simultaneously with my own inner needs? What does he need from me? Am I looking for a partner in real human dialogue? Discuss ideas, grow intellectually? But Walter is not this person – he imposes ideas, does not help one to reach their own personal convictions. Walter is too busy, too dictatorial (method), not interested in my interests.

Washington, D.C.   *September, 1977*

Dear Harriet and Betty:

Our Silver Bay weeks were absolutely delightful, and twenty-eight family members there. And such interesting families who have been coming for years, with all activity geared to family events.

We had twenty-four hours with Ellie in Hartford, Connecticut, on our way home, and it was a joyous time. She had that week finally sold her New Jersey house.[330] The children were looking forward to starting school there. And El had gotten relief and rest during the six weeks the children were with their father in Texas, but she has a lot to combat for his attitudes and values and lifestyle are disruptive to what she is trying to establish. We bought the family a piano, and this should give them another activity when their mother is away.

---

328   Miriam was awarded the Medal of Honor by the Mount Holyoke College Alumnae Association in May.
329   Miriam had her first hip replacement in August.
330   Ellie was divorced and moved to Hartford, Connecticut, for her full-time job at American Airlines.

About the Europe trip. Nearly 400 "Continuing Congregationalists" went to the week's meetings of the International Congregational Fellowship in London, where we were joined by about 200 British. Separatists, we were called in the 16th century when we broke away from the Church of England, some going to Leyden in Holland for fourteen years to "worship as they chose" and then proceeding by the Mayflower to America, so their children could be brought up speaking English, not Dutch. The ICF[331] was formed three years ago by members who wanted to continue their autonomous church structure, after Congregationalists merged with other denominations to form the United Church of Christ. (I belong to this latter; have finished two years as moderator of our church here. But Walter remained a Continuing Congregationalist.)

Miriam and granddaughter Cindy Carpenter at Silver Bay

– *Private Writing* –

1978

I am sure God is reaching out to me (working in my life); else why this dissatisfaction at having run down (goofed off) in my daily quiet time, this restless desire to improve & enlarge my relationships? I get frustrated at not knowing how to act, how to choose, which way to go – so I quit! I need to learn how to understand better and respond to God's leading of me.

Sunday December 31, 1978

In the name of the Father (who loves me unconditionally) and of the Son (whom he sent to show me The Way) and of the Holy Spirit (who is always available as my comforter & guide):

I started the year with enthusiasm & conviction & joy. What happened?
1. *Extra travels away abroad interfered with my daily quiet time.*
2. *I started finding excuses: too cold mornings, too little sleep, etc.*
3. *I began reading about, rather than experiencing, or reading from the Bible.*

What do I need to deal with now?
1. *Learn how to "pray with scripture." Where does "devotional reading" come in?*
2. *Learn to love & forgive myself even as I try to love God more perfectly.*
3. *Learn to deal with my moods: stubbornness, anger, self-pity.*
4. *Love Walter better, learn how to be more supportive of his needs (not just physical).*
5. *Deal more realistically with my needs to share, to risk, to deepen my confidence.*

---

331   ICF was the International Congregational Fellowship.

Washington, D.C.   *Sunday, February 25, 1979*

Hi, Gals!

Seems everything has gone off schedule with unprecedented snowstorms. I haven't done Meals on Wheels for three weeks. I haven't been to my YW volunteer job in three weeks; our wash machine broke, too expensive to repair and they can't deliver the new one till the drive is cleared of snow; we ran out of heating oil and were cold, but not nearly as bad as others (except Dad's fussing was bad!); being shut-in, we were getting neglected correspondence of Dad's reeled off – and did accomplish plenty – when his Dictaphone went silent; no trash removed for a week…

But it hasn't been all bad. The first day of that deep, fluffy, beautiful snow, when gatherings were called off, people got out and had a ball, built snowmen, had snow fights, skied cross-country on Connecticut Avenue, spoke to every stranger that had the guts to get out, helped people dig out. One columnist wrote something I liked: Washington had been uptight from weather, farmers and their trucks, foreign policy problems, etc., etc., like a cross and tired and complaining child, so God put us to bed for an afternoon winter's nap.

I've had more time for reading, and study these days. One thing that struck me: In the story of Jesus healing the paralytic at the pool of Bethesda, it said the man had been sick thirty-eight years. Jesus asked "Would you *like* to get well?" But the man seemed to be enjoying a "poor me" complex: "I don't have a friend to help me into the pool. In the competition I can't make it. But I am patient, I am persevering. I come every day. In adversity I always wear a broad smile and am warmed by the thought that others see my plight and know me to be long-suffering."

I went on to realize that it sounded a little like the "Poor Mother, she tries so hard" stuff you girls used to say to me. Did I enjoy being a martyr and suffering patiently through all the guff you girls gave me, when you were in high school? Was I happy with the sense of guilt I heaped on you all that El was talking about once? A little late to go back now! But there's still the future. Don't *let* me be an ECM.[332] Don't offer me any easy kind of comfort – "sloppy agape." Don't let me sit idly by "thirty-eight years." Ask me if I want to be healed, and make me do something about it.

I did enjoy greatly the Mount Holyoke Mary Lyon dinner even if I did go without Dad, and on buses, taxis, and subways because of the snow. There were nearly 250 there, and lots of younger alums and husbands.[333]

—Private Writing—

Fall, 1979

I have a fear of saying something to Walter that I might regret, should he die suddenly. So I don't say what I'm thinking. But it festers inside. He says "I am wrong. El is wrong. The State Department is wrong. President Carter is wrong." If we would all do it the way he says, everything would be O.K.

---

332   Her daughters used to taunt her by calling her an ECM – an early Christian martyr.

333   The dinner was in Washington, D.C. to honor the founder of Mount Holyoke College, Mary Lyon.

But he is confused and tired and discouraged & depressed and full of mistakes. I keep trying so hard to be patient, supportive, loving – but it is so difficult. He won't listen, he wants to argue, to win.

I am sure Walter loves me absolutely. And since we were sure, I was sure that this marriage was the will of God for both of us, then it still is. I can't conceive of God changing his mind. But I can conceive of God wanting it to be a better marriage, more satisfying to each. How? I have been at fault in not finding ways to communicate. Would W. be surprised if he knew the way I feel? Would he be able to change? Would he want to? Is it fair to expect changes in attitudes or actions of one eighty-one-years-old? Is it kind to upset his declining years, which should be happy and relaxed in mind as the reward of the good and active life he has lived, by suggesting mistakes or lacks in his earlier years which he can't now change? Then how can I change, or what attitudes can I adopt, to make our relationship more bearable, more satisfactory, more loving?

Why do I feel I have to correct him? Why am I embarrassed about his constant "testifying?" Must I achieve a superiority over him? Is it possible that God made him for others, to be a great stimulus, energizer, convictor, creative force, opener-up, initiator, inspirator, leader – often with only one single contact with persons so that contact had to be convincing, concentrated, demanding, dynamic – and I who have daily contact with his intense personality find it too much? When Mother heard I was going to marry him she said, "Oh Miriam, he's so intense." Now that he is home more hours and my faculties are declining, is he too intense for me? But God put us together, has loved us in our love. Surely he will show me how I can live with his intensity. Then I must be ready, used, to listen to the Inner Voice. This demands practice.

Why need I puzzle with all these unanswered questions? They are for God to take care of. If I am wholly committed to Christ and follow daily in holy obedience the Inner Voice, all will be well.

When I try to cope myself, it gets too complicated. I get mad at ML. I get mad at El. I get mad at Car. I get mad at W. I disagree with each one but can't tell them. I have not developed the art of communication. And they have answers that are at cross-purposes with one anothers'. I want to support each one, but can't. No wonder I get confused listening to all these external voices. I am not hearing or obeying, the Inner Voice.

At Silver Bay and at Lewisburg this was cumulative – too many conflicting voices, no time for the Inner Voice. "He who waiteth upon the Lord shall renew his strength." Can I imagine a place inside of me that is my Center? It is full of light, it is the dwelling place of the Holy Spirit, it is where I go to find my collectedness, to compose myself. It is where I retreat to when cares, confusions, wearinesses, disaffections, unrest, assail me. It will lighten my darkness, still my unrest, stop my judgmentalness. It is always there waiting for me to come in, the center of power, my proper being. It knows no distraction. It is the other level at which I live... To find this Center, to live more and more in its brightness, takes practice. Help me, God, in this practice. Help me with my commitment to Holy Obedience.

*Mary Lou and Miriam at
1980 Mount Holyoke College Alumnae reunion*

—*Private Writing*—

Friday, October 10, 1980

I have always esteemed highly the art of listening. Walter's great gift is in speaking, articulately with conviction, lecturing. Either of these, carried to excess, cause difficulties. I have worried at Walter's not listening. How about my not speaking? It was too hard, it was a debate, I always lost.

In the family we could talk ideas not feelings. Because the girls found it difficult to speak to him, I became the go-between, interpreter. Did this keep them from developing their own relationship with him? Or his with them? In those early times he was too busy to "hear" them, be with them. I resented this. Now he has more time, wants to be with them more, "hear" them. Is it too late? Do I resent this? Do I still feel the need to be the interpreter? Can they at this late date tell him what they feel? Can he listen? They are adults now. And he is seen as old. To what extent am I responsible for the way they see him? Or is this important?

—*Private Writing*—

Friday, October 24, 1980

"Ask and you shall receive; seek and you shall find; knock and it shall be open to you." – Mt. 7:7 And so I ask, for Walter and for me, both wisdom and strength, in facing the knowledge that "his book" is published.[334] When we find out, Walter is in Oklahoma, I am here alone. Alone? Never! But I am where I can find some help, some answers in the stillness and awareness

---

334 A Colorado professor had published a book with excerpts of Walter's speeches, without his knowledge or permission. He was dismayed and took legal action.

He provides. My recent tendencies have been to escape the confusions, disaffections, diatribes – to run away physically. Now I see I can better escape to the Center of my Being, where God waits to still my unrest, stop my judgmentalness, restore me to collectedness. Help me to remember, to practice daily my commitment.

Washington, D.C.   *October, 1981*

Dear Friends:

The thing that was a great joy and lift to us both was when President Reagan conferred his Presidential Medal of Freedom on Walter at a White House luncheon and Ceremony and all our daughters (with Norm) came to be present for the occasion.[335] It was the first time we had all been together at home here since 1961, and what a joy it was. When Walter said on their leaving "it's been just like old times," Mary Lou quickly replied, "No, it's been better, because we've grown up and enjoy talking with each other more and are more understanding." That was great!

The White House occasion was beautifully arranged: Six medals were presented, including a posthumous one for Ella Grasso.[336] Each recipient was allowed to invite six people (other than spouse).[337] Cabinet members and top aides were present, so there were about eighty at the luncheon in the East Room. There was a citation read by the President for each: Walter's read: "Legislator, physician, missionary, and orator, Walter Judd has served his nation and mankind with unfailing courage and distinction – as a youthful medical missionary in China, as a highly respected Member of Congress for two decades, and as a lifelong foe of tyranny and friend of freedom both at home and abroad. The skills of a healer, the eloquence of a great communicator, and his firm grasp of domestic and international affairs have made Walter Judd an articulate spokesman for all those who cherish liberty and a model for all Americans who aspire to serve mankind as physicians, spiritual leaders, and statesmen."

The Judd Family in front of the White House

---

335   The ceremony was on October 9, 1981.

336   Ella Grasso was the first woman elected to be governor in her own right (not succeeding a spouse). She was the Governor of Connecticut 1975-1980 and also a Mount Holyoke College alumna.

337   The current Minnesota Governor Al Quie and his wife Gretchen filled Walter's quota.

Miriam and Walter with President and Mrs. Reagan during
Presidential Medal of Freedom Ceremony

Washington, D.C.   *Tuesday, March 16, 1982*

Dear Family:

We're still living in the glow of our fiftieth Anniversary celebrating. Got started Thursday the 11th when five longtime friends had a dinner for us at the Cosmos Club. They had got Xeroxes of the *New York Times* for March 13, 1932, not just the front page, where the Lindberg kidnapping had headlines, but the sports pages, advertisement showing prices at that time, pages of women's styles, etc. It was a great way to reminisce, and a great way for the Quinn children to learn unbelievable history as they looked at them later. A really warm, close, evening.

Friday Quinns got here around nine, having driven almost without stopping from Connecticut. Then there was lots of chatter, ice cream & cake, and finally, bed. Saturday the Quinns prepared a "wedding dinner" for us, complete with decorations and candles, appetizer, pork roast, home-baked wedding cake and beautifully wrapped packages. We talked about the time in 1949 that Judd girls made a "wedding celebration" for my parents' fiftieth, with El writing words for the girls to sing, special place cards and all sharing and caring.

After dinner, the Quinn children were dropped off at a movie (*Chariots of Fire* – good!) while El & Walter and I went to the Kennedy Center for the performance of the Minnesota Symphony, with Neville Mariner.[338] Afterwards, a lovely buffet-reception in the atrium for the orchestra and Minnesota people, and we were glad to greet the John Pillsburys, Warren Bergers, McKinnons, both Senators & wives and numerous friends. When we got home we had more ice cream & cake and got caught up on the missed phone calls. Cindy had reached us in the afternoon with her greetings and the wonderful news of her being selected for a Hall President for her senior year. We had missed Kevin who had twice talked with Mary Jo,[339] but he faithfully persisted, and we had a good talk with him Sunday, as also with Mary Lou. Carolyn called about midnight Saturday while we were still celebrating, so you were all a part of our loving and doing. Sunday morning for the after-church coffee, we had a decorated sheet-cake for all our friends. Since weddings are one of the sacraments and belong in the church, we wanted our celebration to be there, with gratitude for our fifty years together.

Washington, D.C.   *Tuesday, December 1, 1987*

Hi, Katie dear —[340]

You've been on my mind a lot recently – tho' I don't know how you'd know it. You were thoughtful to send messages – You don't know how it helps and encourages. I'm fine!![341]

Writing "December" on this letter tells me how near the end you are of this two-year activity (ordeal?) that has caused you pain and questioning.[342] I'm proud of the way you've stuck to what

you started, even when you couldn't make it fit your immediate thinking. I feel sure you'll feel glad you did, eventually – which doesn't help much in your decision for "what after May." Keep on ploughing away. Things will come clear, I'm convinced, at the "right time." Hear you're going skiing – fun! Enjoy it all to the limit – you deserve it! Love ya – Gram

Miriam with granddaughter Katie Carpenter

---

338   From 1903-1968, it was known as the Minneapolis Symphony. Then it was renamed the Minnesota Orchestra.

339   Ellie's only daughter.

340   Katie and Cindy both lived with the Judds in Washington, D.C., while working at summer internships in 1986.

341   Miriam had her second hip replacement.

342   After college Katie was in a New York City bank training program.

March 13, 1991

Dear Walter:

The Greek woman Marpessa, given her choice between the God Apollo, and Idas, a mortal, chooses Idas. On our wedding anniversary, I *choose* the mortal, Walter, and borrow Marpessa's words, to dedicate all my love to Walter.[343]

> "… But if I live with Idas, then we two
> On the low earth shall prosper hand in hand
> In odors of the open field, and live
> In peaceful noises of the farm, and watch
> The pastoral fields burned by the setting sun.
> And he shall give me passionate children, not
> Some radiant god that will despise me quite,
> But clambering limbs and little hearts that err.
> And I shall sleep beside him in the night
> Secure; or at some festival we two
> Will wander through the lighted city streets;
> And in the crowd I'll take his arm and feel
> Him closer for the press. So shall we live.
> And though the first sweet sting of love be past,
> The sweet that almost venom is, though youth,
> With tender and extravagant delight,
> The first and secret kiss by twilight hedge,
> The insane farewell repeated o'er and o'er,
> Pass off; there shall succeed a faithful peace –
> Beautiful friendship tried by sun and wind
> Durable from the daily dust of life,
> And though with sadder, still with kinder eyes,
> We shall behold all frailties, we shall haste
> To pardon, and with mellowing minds to bless.
> Then though we must grow old, we shall grow old
> Together, and he shall not greatly miss
> My bloom faded, and waning light of eyes,
> Too deeply gazed in ever to seem dim;
> Nor shall we murmur at, nor much regret
> The years that gentle bend us to the ground,
> And gradually incline our face; that we
> Leisurely stooping, and with each slow step,
> May curiously inspect our lasting home.
> But we shall sit with luminous holy smiles,
> Endeared by many griefs, by many a jest,

---

343   For their 59th wedding anniversary, Miriam gave Walter a card. She typed the following in the middle pages. Six months later she had a stroke.

And custom sweet of living side by side;
And full of memories not unkindly glance
Upon each other. Last, we shall descend
Into the natural ground – not without tears –
One must go first, ah god! One must go first;
After so long one blow for both were good;
Still like old friends, glad to have met, and leave
Behind a wholesome memory on the earth.[344]

*Outside their final home; Miriam is
eighty-five years old and Walter is ninety-one.*

344   An excerpt from *Marpessa* by Stephen Phillips. Pp. 36-43 Dodd, Mead and Company, Inc. N.Y. 1922

Epilogue

Following a stroke in 1991, Miriam moved into the Assisted Care facility at Collington. For the last few years of her life, she could no longer write, so her letters ceased. Eighteen months later, Walter was transferred to Collington's skilled nursing floor after a failed attempt to end his own life. Being a physician, combined with his practical nature, he had figured out a way to prevent being a burden to his family as his lifelong facial cancer spread. But a nurse found him, and he was revived at the hospital. Never fully recovering, he died nine months later, February 13, 1994 at the age of ninety-five. Miriam lingered a few months on her own; she died on June 23, 1994, just shy of her ninetieth birthday.

So when I had found myself standing in the late afternoon sun in my mother's room, the unsent letter to her long-ago fiancé in hand, I wondered: Did my mother lead the life she wanted and was suited for?

I could no longer ask her; I could only surmise. I do know my mother had a rewarding life in so many respects – the many places she'd lived, her continuing hunger for learning, the whirl of the Capitol, and the fascinating people she had known. She befriended many, and witnessed historic events. In early life in India and in her life with my father in China, she had traveled and lived in places so exotic they existed for most people only in their imaginations. Mother experienced it, and then brought it back to America with her.

The Judd Fellows Program at the University of Minnesota each year awards scholarships for Master's level and professional school students to intern or do research abroad – something I know my parents would be pleased about and grateful for, as they strongly believed that exposure to other cultures is essential for a broad education.

Miriam was witness to unfolding world events and made her mark at a time when such paths were open to few women. Truly, she lived life as a palm in a desert, as Mount Holyoke College graduates were admonished to do. When her desert was her emotional life with my father, she drew on her strong faith in God and her deep love for him. She said once that she had no regrets about marrying Walter, even though she only got a small percentage of his time and energy focused on and with her. When that meeting point occurred, it was well worth it – enough to compensate for her frequent aloneness and his never-ending preoccupation with his concerns and "commitments."

She also let us know that it had been enough in a poem she wrote at age eighty-four and read aloud at a public ninetieth birthday celebration for Walter in September, 1988. Although the first two lines are attributed to Sara Teasdale's "The Beloved," from *Dark of the Moon*, the rest are Miriam's own words, something it took me years to discover.

To Walter at Ninety
It is enough of honor for one lifetime
To have known you better than the rest have known;
The shadows and the brightness of your voice,
The searching mind, the stubborn will like stone;
The passionate words grown out of strong conviction and love of God;
Your bearing the whole world's pain;
Protest, nor conflict, nor no man fearing;
No sense of time, or self; no thoughts of gain.
Quick laughter, and strict honor, dogged persistence.
Deep pride in family, friends; fierce love of life.
These among others will I hold forever within my heart,
your always grateful wife.

Miriam remained intensely private to the end of her life. Those of us closest to her – including Dad – knew little of her struggles and suffering. Yet by leaving such a rich vein of letters as well as private writings, we can at last know the more complete woman, Miriam Barber Judd – celebrating her complexity, marveling at her accomplishments, understanding her spiritual foundation and resources. It is a privilege to give *Miriam's Words* an opportunity to ring out.

Miriam and Walter's family at Miriam's funeral

Acknowledgments

The process of bringing this book to life has been amazing, not unlike the evolution of a garden. The seeds came from Miriam's writings – unknowingly taking root in my head. As a complete neophyte in such hard toil, I relied on resources from countless communities in my world – supplemented by professional expertise – and extensive handholding by friends. The book is the outcome of this organic growth, possible under the banner of nature, both human and divine.

Using gardeners' language, here are some of the ways I have been nurtured and cultivated by numerous teachers and mentors. They have shared experiences, wisdom, and hopefulness with me. Without them, *Miriam's Words* would have remained dormant.

It takes foresight and inspiration to envision a garden where none exists. Two "Marys" started me on this pathway. Mary Music Lindberg, a creative and devoted high school friend, was always a fan of Miriam, often reminding me of her exceptional energy, sensitivity, and literary vigor. Then ten years ago, my spiritual director, Jesuit Fred Maples, introduced me to his brilliant sister, author and historian Mary Maples Dunn, who quickly saw the potential in the writings Miriam left. She reviewed much of the original work and tutored me in structure and decision-making. These two women are my muses.

The writings and I spent twenty-four weeks over several years in residence at Saint John's University's "Collegeville Institute for Ecumenical and Cultural Research" in central Minnesota. Founder Father Kilian McDonnell, Director Dr. Don Ottenhoff, and their cohorts were guides there, along with Rev. Gary Reierson, then Board Chair. Other "homes" were generously shared by Joyce and Dick McFarland on the North Shore of Lake Superior – and by the late Betsey Marlowe in the woods of northern Wisconsin – places where beauty and solitude enhanced my labors to read and select. A fruitful week was spent at Saint Benedict's Monastery Studium space in St. Joseph, MN.

Libraries and academics brought "fertilizer" to my latent seeds. Ryan Mattke, head of the University of Minnesota Bochert Map Library, assisted with geography, and Mark Lindberg, Director of the University Cartography Lab, produced the map of Miriam's locations in China. Dean Meredith McQuaid and staff at the University's "Global Programs and Strategy Alliance" have been enthusiasts and hosts of the publication launch event, coordinated by Diane Young. At Saint John's University, Professor Annette Atkins offered encouragement, and Professor Richard Bohr's gentle wisdom and expertise made possible the China historical background page. Other advisors include Al Eisele, editor of *The Hill*, Mitch Pearlstein of the Center of the American Experiment, writers Beth Schucker, Susan Eilertsen, Jill Breckenridge, Margaret Brentano, and Scott Edelstein, as well as Dr. Donald Lindberg, Director of the National Library of Medicine and his associate, Dr. George Thoma. Thanks also to historian Douglas Smith for the quotation from Richard Holmes.

Germination was stimulated by the sun and warmth offered by Mount Holyoke College classmates Bonnie, Debbie, Dee, Gay, Jane, Joyce, Lois, MC, Pat, Tee, Win, and Wink, who read portions of the materials. Minnesota friends (Lynn and Carol, Mary, Bryce, Judy, Jane, Gloria, Nancy, Ann, Marion, Marcia, and others) were always there for me. The Plymouth Church community, First Friday groups, two book clubs, and First Nighters were optimistic on my behalf when my spirits lagged in the face of the vagaries of the publishing universe. My sisters and cousin John Barber offered helpful memories when my own recollections were hazy, as did writer-daughter, Cindy Carpenter.

Seeds cannot sprout without rain. I cherish the soft showers brought by spiritual directors and therapists Ann Meissner and Jan Swanson. Mary Lilja, founder of Lilja LifeStories and her then associate Kadee Crottier, provided the bulk of the editorial work, helping to identify the strong stories amidst multitudinous details. When weeding was necessary, Technical Reinforcements' two computer whizzes, James Allard and Adrian Preston, brought crisis assistance and prevented withering of the tender plants!

The Minnesota Historical Society and several national libraries assisted with photography permissions, as did Sandy Date of the *Minneapolis Star Tribune*. Sherfy Jones assisted with this effort. Business and accounting advice was provided by Brian Knutson.

A special thank you goes to Martha Head for her support and encouragement. Her mother, Virginia Myers, and Doug Head, who later was her husband, were the Chairpersons of Walter's last campaign and outstanding associates over the many years.

The first sampling was done by the eight readers who tasted the finished product and offered their perspective in the blurbs – Dr. Mary Bednarowski, Dr. Richard Bohr, Mary Maples Dunn, Al Eisle, Dr. Donald Lindberg, Lynn Pasquerella, Governor Al Quie, and Lori Sturdevant. My astonishment and gratitude for their generosity of time, talent, and spirit knows no end.

The final harvest has been completed by two professionals. Writer Patti Frazee patiently brought her superb editing, publishing, and technical expertise to the formatting, photo placement, and cover design. Linda White planned and executed the publicity and marketing. I met both of them through their classes at the Loft Literary Center in Minneapolis, directed by friend Jocelyn Hale – a place of support and encouragement for literary gardeners.

To all these givers and gardeners and many others unnamed, I express my deepest appreciation and thanksgiving. I trust you know how indispensable and valued your unique gifts have been. May all your seasons be blessed.

Photo Credits

Every reasonable effort has been made to contact copyright holders of material reproduced here. If there are errors or omissions, corrections or additions will be made in subsequent printings.

Most photos are from the Judd/Carpenter family files, with exceptions noted below:

Page 40: 1930s map of China, prepared by the Cartography Lab, University of Minnesota, Minneapolis, MN

Chapter 7

Page 155: Photo by Lee Brothers, Minneapolis, MN

Page 161: Courtesy of Marcia Giske, Minneapolis, MN

Page 179: Used with permission of the *Minneapolis Star Tribune*, Minneapolis, MN

Chapter 9

Page 213: Photo by Seth H. Muse, used with permission of Joyner Library, East Carolina University, Greenville, NC

Chapter 10

Page 256: Photo by Don Berg Photography, Minneapolis, MN

Page 264: Reni Photos, Courtesy of Reni Newsphoto Service

Chapter 11

Page 269: Photo by Hessler, Washington, D.C.

Page 275: Photo by Wu Chang Yee, Taiwan

Page 287: Used with permission of the *Minneapolis Star Tribune*, Minneapolis, MN

Page 296: Courtesy of United States Information Service – Washington, D.C.

Chapter 13

Page 334: Courtesy of Ronald Reagan Libraries, Simi Valley, CA

Index

Abbreviations MJ and WJ stand for Miriam Barber Judd and Walter Judd, respectively. A page number followed by "n" and a number, indicates the page number and footnote number (e.g. 31n42 means that the reference will be found on page 31 in footnote 42).

About the Editor

Mary Lou Judd Carpenter was born in Rochester, MN but lived in China until she was almost four. After several years in Montclair, NJ and Minneapolis, MN, her father, Dr. Walter H. Judd, was elected to Congress and the family moved to Washington, D.C., where she grew up. After graduation from Mount Holyoke College in 1955, Mary Lou worked in New York City and at the University of Michigan. Since 1960 she has lived in Minneapolis where she has participated extensively in volunteer efforts on behalf of human rights, social welfare, and church, school, and community well-being. She has three children and seven grandchildren.